Scandinavian Blue

Scandinavian Blue

*The Erotic Cinema
of Sweden and Denmark
in the 1960s and 1970s*

JACK STEVENSON

McFarland & Company, Inc., Publishers
Jefferson, North Carolina, and London

LIBRARY OF CONGRESS CATALOGUING-IN-PUBLICATION DATA

Stevenson, Jack, 1955–
Scandinavian blue : the erotic cinema of Sweden and Denmark in the 1960s and 1970s / Jack Stevenson.
p.   cm.

Includes bibliographical references and index.

ISBN 978-0-7864-4488-5
softcover : 50# alkaline paper ∞

1. Erotic films — Sweden — History and criticism.
2. Erotic films — Denmark — History and criticism.
I. Title.
PN1995.9.S45S74   2010   791.43'65380948 — dc22   2009039615

British Library cataloguing data are available

©2010 Jack Stevenson. All rights reserved

No part of this book may be reproduced or transmitted in any form or by any means, electronic or mechanical, including photocopying or recording, or by any information storage and retrieval system, without permission in writing from the publisher.

On the cover: (top) Sisse Reingaard in the 1969 film *Stine and the Boys*; (bottom) Essy Persson in the 1965 film *I, a Woman*
Front cover from a design by Dr Manta (www.mantagraphics.com)

Manufactured in the United States of America

McFarland & Company, Inc., Publishers
Box 611, Jefferson, North Carolina 28640
www.mcfarlandpub.com

Table of Contents

Acknowledgments viii
Photo Credits ix
Preface 1
Introduction 3

One. To 1966: Birth of a Mythology   7

One Summer of Happiness 8
Summer with Monika. 12
The Duel. 26
Weekend 28
Crazy Paradise. 37
The Silence 39
Street Without End 41
Nymphomania; Call-Girls; "Heroes" 46
I, a Woman 59
Soya's 17 68
Venom (a.k.a. Gift) 71
Loving Couples and Night Games 82

Two. 1967–1970: Censorship's Last Stand   85

I, a Nobleman 85
I Am Curious (Yellow) 88
Inga 98
Sweden: Heaven or Hell? 101
Danish Blue 103
Without a Stitch 107
Heaven and Hell 118
Sensuela 124
First Prize Irene 128
The Language of Love 130

Relations — The Love Story from Denmark 137
Christa 140
The Daughter 141
Quiet Days in Clichy 147
Censorship in Denmark — A New Approach 154
Bedside Manner 157

Three. 1971 and Beyond:
Total Freedom in Fact and Fiction   163

The Swinging Stewardesses 171
Freedom to Love 172
Why? 174
24 Hours with Ilse 177
Facts: Copenhagen Sex-Report 182
Bordello 189
Sexy Girls of Denmark 193
Adventure in Denmark 194
The Sinful Dwarf 199
Young Playthings 208
They Call Her One-Eye 210
Confessions of a Danish Cover Girl 213
Danish Pastries 215

Four. The Passing of an Era   220

Appendices   233

I. Jens Jørgen Thorsen: The Jesus Chronicles 233
II. Ole Ege, the Gentleman Pornographer 247
III. The Wet Dream Film Festival 255
IV. The Players 258
V. English and Original Titles 273

Notes   279
Bibliography   285
Index   287

To Anna Biller, saint, genius, visionary and
all around wonder woman of the sexual revolution (movie)

Acknowledgments

There are too many people to thank individually here, not least the hundreds of Danes who over the course of my 17 years as a resident of their country have contributed to my understanding of it.

Those who merit specific mention include first and foremost my Danish wife, Martine. As the editor of the film magazine *Kosmorama* she was well placed to help clarify some of the fine points about the local film culture, and her insights in a more general sense helped me to get a grip on the peculiarities of the Danish language and social condition.

Thanks are also owed to Mads Jensen, Lauri Lehtinen, Ole Stranddorf, Jim Morton, Dennis Nyback, Scott Moffett, David Naylor, Barbara Gentikow, Is Hoogland, David Landolf, Erik Scriver, Nicolas Barbano, Antti Suonio, Bertrand Grimault, Morten Lindberg, Carl Nørrested, Hans Peter Rosenmeier, Bart van der Put, Nikolaj Pors, and Jørgen Gjerstrup for various contributions, and to the Danish photographer Jørgen Angel (www.angel.dk).

I am particularly indebted to Dr Manta (www.mantagraphics.com) for the cover design, and to Nils Markvardsen and Kristoffer Gansing, two experts in the field whose assistance was absolutely essential. Nils, who publishes Denmark's most committed independent film magazine, *eXtase*, helped me track down many hard to find films and provided a wealth of insights, as did Kristoffer, whose invaluable contributions focused largely but not exclusively on the relevant aspects of Swedish cinema.

Photo Credits

The Danish Film Institute
The Swedish Film Institute
Nordisk film studios
Bent Christensen Film Production
Palladium
Hermes Film
Pingvin Film
Novaris Film
Henning Karmark, Knud Leif Thomsen & Bo Christensen
Axel Film
Athena
Scandinavian Booking Agency
Les Films de la Boétie (Amour)
Laterna Film
Con Amore Film
Scandica Film

ASA Filmstudie, Movie Art of Europe, Edda Film (Røde Kappe)
Jørgen Angel
Merry Film
Zentropa
Scorpio Production
Jens Jørgen Thorsen, Superfilm
Nordisk Tonefilm
Svensk Filmindustri (SF)
Sandrews
Cannon Films
Contact Film
Swedish Film Production (SFP)
Panorama
Edward Small
Les Films du Carrosse
Shaw Brothers
Preben Niemeyer

"If sexual morality crumbles, everything crumbles with it. It is clear that the disintegration of sexual morality has always heralded the disintegration of a culture."
— Knud Leif Thomsen, 1964

"The devilish truth is that all censorship comes at the expense of art, encouraging laziness and paving the way for works that are devoid of talent."
— Poul Henningsen, 1965

Birte Tove (right) and friend yawn their way through a typical Danish night out in *Between the Sheets.*

Preface

As the reader will readily perceive, I have drawn extensively from the accounts of the day in writing this book. My goal is not just to catalog and review the movies as autonomous works but to present them within the context of the period and to make this era come alive. To do this it was necessary to call forth the voices and the spirit of the times.

This is clearly an overlooked chapter of film history. No Danish or Swedish writer — these being the two countries of principal concern — has yet delved into it in a substantial way. For their part Scandinavian scholars generally dismiss the idea that the '60s and '70s produced any kind of cohesive movement worthy of study. They shrug it off as an embarrassment, not least because in the hallowed halls of academia exploitation cinema, of which "sex films" are by definition a part, is rarely deemed worthy of interest or investigation. There is a certain class prejudice at play, and understandably so as this period produced some outrageously rude, artless and even blasphemous works that can still today set sensitive souls back on their heels. And as for the Danes, it also constitutes in large measure the down time between the active periods of their two acclaimed masters, Carl Th. Dreyer and Lars von Trier. The great Swedish director Ingmar Bergman did play a central role in the early stages of this era, but this book is not in the main about him. This is not so much the story of immortal directors creating timeless masterpieces as it is a tale of rogues, renegades, opportunists and fantasists who seized the moment.

Things were different then. Cinemas attracted a broader audience, and movies sought to a greater degree to exploit or investigate the public fascinations of the day. As foreign cultures started to buy into the mythology of Scandinavian sexual freedom, Danish companies began to shoot more co-productions with foreign partners who knew they could sell tickets to their own audiences with this stuff. It was a fair trade. They could make and play films that were in many cases impossible to shoot on home soil because no lab would process the film, no paper would write about it and no theatre would play it, and Danish companies got to release movies into vastly larger markets. More purely capitalistic motives were also at play in film production which was less state-funded than today, giving more slack to "rogue-independents" to make and play their pictures. The lure of potentially huge profits and the intense curiosity about Scandinavian sexuality attracted all types of filmmakers, from those who just wanted to make a killing to those who would go on to explore the subject with honesty and insight. This infused Danish/Swedish cinema with money, energy and momentum and created a singularly exportable film culture that caught the spirit of the times. At the crest of this wave films from Denmark and Sweden travelled the world and sold tickets in numbers never approached before or since.

It is therefore by no means just a Scandinavian story I am about to tell, as these movies provoked controversy, became hits and influenced the course of censorship in many countries.

This book will discuss the immense impact these films had in places like Italy, France, Germany and the UK, and particularly America. Nobody bought into the myth of total sexual freedom more readily than the Americans.

While this is a book about film history, the issues that these movies raised and the discussions they set in motion about the dynamics of personal freedom and the commercial exploitation of human sexuality are universal and ongoing. They have never been (and never will be) fully resolved.

Technical Note: The subheadings in parts one through three are mostly movie titles which are arranged in chronological order. They are intended only as a loose guide: Many other films and related phenomena enter the discussion and the reader will derive most benefit by reading this book as it was written rather than selectively seeking information on specific films. This is one interconnected narrative — not an encyclopaedia, video guide or collection of free-standing essays — and should be approached as such.

That said, certain aspects of the story require a separate and more sustained focus. The careers of filmmakers Jens Jørgen Thorsen and Ole Ege receive special attention in appendices I and II, respectively, while Appendix III takes a closer look at the Wet Dream Film Festival, a groundbreaking event in the history of erotic cinema. Appendix IV, "The Players," offers updated information on key figures mentioned in the text. Appendix V lists the original titles of foreign films that are referred to in the text by their English-language titles.

Introduction

The place: Copenhagen, Denmark. The year: 1971. In this city, in this year, all that was revolutionary about Scandinavian sexuality and the peculiar brand of open-mindedness that made it possible reached its furthest stage of evolution.

But aside from a street (Istedgade) full of tacky and lurid window displays, where exactly was this revolution taking place? In bedrooms? In minds? In some indefinable space in the collective consciousness? What exactly was it all about? Few foreign reporters were willing or able to delve into the story in all its complexity, and the picture they ended up painting of Denmark was frequently one that Danes themselves did not recognize. There was a strange disconnect.

"What the foreign journalists can't forgive us for is our unconcealed lack of depravity. They find the porno clubs, etc., but outside on the street everything is normal; children go to school, hospitals function, the buses run. This, apparently, is what galls them the most."

So declared Danish author Klaus Rifbjerg in 1971 about these most unusual times and the refusal of his countrymen to play the roles that scandal-mongering foreign journalists had assigned them. No, Denmark wasn't just one big open-air bordello after all. The apparent moral anarchy co-existed alongside a typically Danish addiction to the humble pleasures and routines of everyday life, and Danes seemed extraordinarily at ease with the radical proposition that what other people did was their own business. Sent off to get the dope on all this sex revolution stuff, foreign journalists were now forced to decipher a somewhat more complicated story about a society grappling in the flesh with concepts of personal freedom and public morality that in most countries were not even being debated on a theoretical plane.

But a revolution was in fact occurring, and like all revolutions it was characterized by rampant self-righteousness as well as endless naiveté. Lofty theoretics and humanistic homilies collided with crass opportunism and fortunes made overnight to create a very schizophrenic moment in time. And yet while many aspects of this social and sexual uprising had parallels in other western societies, what was happening in Denmark was unique. This was not just another youth-culture rebellion but something infinitely more ambitious and rooted deep in the Danish mentality, something that in a handful of years had transformed a small and in many ways isolated country on the fringes of Europe into a radical social experiment in free speech and free love. Denmark had entered the future first — not least in a legislative sense: In 1967 Danes had abolished censorship of the written word, and in 1969 they repealed all image censorship, freeing films and giving legal sanction to pornographic picture magazines. Now all was permitted. Total freedom could only be a good thing — right?

On the contrary, to many it was a frightful prospect. With the abolition of censorship the country had become, according to alarmists, the transmitter of a dangerous virus called pornography, and the situation was loudly condemned by everyone from the Pope to Billy Graham to the queen of England.

If to some this revolution seemed like nothing less than the complete moral collapse of an entire society, to progressive thinkers, writers and filmmakers Denmark was a beacon of enlightenment and a sanctuary of free thinking, and they moved there to study, celebrate and document *it*. Others just came hoping to have sex or to leer about. But if the bawdy goods were often tailored for the tourist trade, participation in the pleasures to be had in Copenhagen at the dawn of the '70s involved more than simple buy-and-sell; it involved a kind of a pact requiring that you shed your hang-ups along with your clothes. This revolution took the battle for sexual and spiritual liberation into — literally — the streets, the goal being to shatter barricades in minds as well as on the pavements, to throw light on all of society's dark and hidden spaces.

During the peak years of Liberated Denmark, from 1968 to 1972, the cobbled thoroughfares of Copenhagen exuded a kind of frontier mentality as old school sexologists in herringbone tweeds mixed on the streets with gaping tourists, gaggles of curious housewives from the provinces and long-haired hipster businessmen who dealt in the new coin of the realm — hard-core pornography — for fun, liberation and profit. All of them came to taste the forbidden fruit available nowhere else: sex, open and public.

There were vast profits to be made, there was knowledge to be gained, and there were absolutely far-out and once in a lifetime experiences to be had — or so one had to believe. And while today's digital and Internet technologies have turned sex into a private home-use experience, this was group therapy on a grand scale. Until they were shuttered by police, the live sex clubs barred no position or perversity. But even academics were getting into the act, organizing bold debates and symposiums like the one held at the Copenhagen University student union in 1970 where over 700 students paid to observe various sexual acts. The bleachers were packed with so many curious observers jostling to get a peek that at one point a plank in the stands shattered. The next year a similar exhibition, featuring one lesbian and two heterosexual couples, was arranged for the students. This time spectators sat on the floor.

And then there were the movies.

Cinema played a key role in the story of Liberated Denmark. The movies set things in motion, and the court cases and scandals they inspired added the allure of the sensational and the forbidden. The movies made the sexual revolution bigger than life. They provoked the debates. They explored this new world, explained it, distorted it and in various instances *were* it, as producers sought confrontation with the courts in order to challenge censorship rulings. It was via the movies that the wider public was able to share in these exciting experiences they were hearing so much about, experiences that were otherwise of a very private nature. Movies gave light and form to the myth of Liberated Denmark and exported it around the globe, spreading the news of this enlightened land where apparently all things were possible.

It was an experiment in living that demanded no small amount of daring; no one had ever been here before and nobody knew where it would all lead. As Phyllis and Eberhard Kronhausen, psychologists and filmmakers, warned, "There are personal and social risks — grave risks even — if one opts for this kind of total freedom."[1]

Like Socialism's New Man, this total freedom was supposed to produce a new human being, the Liberated Individual who would be the hope of the future: sane, healthy and functional, cured of all sexual complexes, inhibitions and self-hatred. Virtually unnoticeable, these new humans now moved about in the crowds on the streets, the professional sex performers employed in the films and particularly the live shows. Men and women, according to the dogma, at ease with themselves and taking advantage of the radical new freedoms on both a personal and professional level. They, the happy and well-adjusted inhabitants of this brave new world, were liberated *and* making a living while also engaged in a kind of political act, flouting taboos that had enslaved previous generations in ignorance, repression and guilt. Making the private public.

A noble experiment had been set in motion, and there was no turning back.

Two Words...

These two Danish words are key to understanding the changes that took place in '60s Scandinavia, and since they cannot be easily translated into English they will be explained here and used in their original form throughout the text.

Frisind can be defined as "liberalism, libertarianism, broad-mindedness." The literal translation is "free mind: *fri* = free, *sind* = mind. As a concept in Danish culture it goes back to the 1800s and influenced various historical trends, yet its usage in the '60s took on an increasingly partisan application. The term became a badge of all-is-permitted hippie excess but was also vague enough to be later embraced by dissenting movements on the left, such as feminism, which questioned whether a free mind necessarily meant free love. The concept remains something of a riddle. If the new generation was really in possession of *frisind* then one would not need to bind oneself to any cause of movement and true individualism would be possible.

Frigjorthed is translated by the Gyldendal Danish-English dictionary as "emancipation ... free and independent consciousness and behavior in relation to conventional norms, for example sexuality and sexual politics." In a clunky literal translation the word means "made free-ness" or the state of being made free. It is all about becoming progressive and enlightened in a more active and transformative way. The term is more specifically bound to sexual consciousness and more connected to the 1960s and 1970s than *frisind*— more trendy, so to say — and it quickly became the password to a new identity for the "liberated" set.

Part One

To 1966: Birth of a Mythology

While revolutionary developments were taking place in Denmark that would transform it into the most liberal society in the West, Sweden had actually pioneered this tradition of open-mindedness and had been producing movies with groundbreaking erotic scenes and themes at least a decade before its smaller western neighbor had started to thaw — going back to 1951, when Arne Mattsson unleashed *One Summer of Happiness* on an unsuspecting world. The film became a big hit, not least in the States.

In the immediate postwar period it had been the French and Italian directors who had captured the imaginations of Anglo-Saxon male viewers with the fiery realism of their films and the bewitching beauty of their female stars. And many young American males, in particular, had some experience with these countries, having been stationed in them during the Second World War and having been exposed to their more progressive sexual attitudes. Things were just not the same back in the good old U.S. of A.

Allied troops never occupied any of the Scandinavian countries, and lonely GIs never occupied the beds of admiring local lasses. There were no preconceptions about what Nordic women were like other than that they were blonde. Scandinavian sexuality was not as much of a recognizable brand, so to speak, in the late '40s.

Not that they didn't have a history. There was Garbo of course, and both Sweden and Denmark had produced an outstanding body of silent film work that had often explored erotic themes with candor, not least the erotic melodramas pioneered by the Danes. But for a variety of reasons the international popularity of Scandinavian cinema had been in decline since the early '30s. Producers and directors there responded by turning inward and fashioning product almost exclusively for domestic consumption, giving birth to an endless cycle of lightweight comedies known as "pilsnerfilm," or beer flicks, in Sweden — and predictable folksy dramas populated with stars almost completely unknown outside their respective countries.

By the dawn of the '50s this was where things stood: Scandinavian cinema in a global context was clearly marginalized. Carl Dreyer was a lonely genius who was not at all representative of what was happening in Danish film, and while Ingmar Bergman had been making challenging fare since the '40s, he was still relatively unknown outside Sweden. His compatriot, the extremely productive Arne Mattsson, who had thus far achieved some recognition for a string of thrillers and light comedies, was even less known, but in one stroke that was all about to change.

One Summer of Happiness

In Sweden, as in many countries, the postwar period brought anxiety. The country was in the process of changing from a rural culture to an urban one and many agricultural and small-trades occupations were no longer needed. A way of life was disappearing. In response people began to long for certainty and a return to more traditional values, and this was reflected in a specific type of film that became very popular. These films were set in the countryside and usually involved a young couple who had fled the pressures and conformity of the city for a simpler life in nature. *One Summer of Happiness* (*She Danced One Summer* is the literal translation of the Swedish title) was in many ways the epitome of this type of film.

The story line was simple enough. We meet Göran, a strapping 19-year-old Stockholm lad who's shipped off to his uncle's farm to spend the summer holiday. He is none too thrilled about it until he meets a young 17-year-old pretty called Kerstin, played by Ulla Jacobsson. He falls for country life — and for her. They enjoy walks in nature and join local youth activities, including a theater group. When the summer ends he must return to the city to begin classes at a technical school, and so he does, but the attraction of the new life he has found out in the bosom of nature proves too strong and he throws away city and school to go back.

In the meantime Kerstin's devoutly religious parents, deeply troubled by her romance with Göran, have sent her away from the village in an attempt to end the relationship. Still the lovers manage to reunite. Continuing their involvement with the local theater group, they end up performing the lead parts in an old traditional play, *The People of Värmland (Värmlänningarna)*. It's a success, and all is well with the world. They have each other and life in the country is good. (Göran Strindberg's evocative photography depicts the pastoral landscapes and the spirit of the light summer nights in enchanting fashion.)

But tragedy strikes. After the performance they depart on Göran's motorbike, riding double, and are hit by a car. Kerstin dies. Her funeral constitutes the opening scenes of the film, the story being told in flashback.

Kerstin's death can easily be read as a metaphor for the loss of traditional values and the loss of innocence, but she was not too innocent to go for a nude swim with Göran in a moon-speckled lake and then (it is implied) to make love with him on the beach. During the funeral he runs down to the shore of that very lake and stares out into the rushes, conjuring up that earlier, happier moment. He can hear Kerstin's voice beseeching him from beyond the grave never to forget her. She has passed away but the happiness of this time and place must live on, the movie seems to say, for all Swedes.

In an American movie her actions would have cast Kerstin as a classic fallen woman who courted her own violent end and deserved it, but in a Swedish context where the state of nudity is not synonymous with sin and where she was in any case over the age of consent (15), she was innocence personified in life *and* death. Nonetheless it was she who paid the ultimate price, not Göran. Whether this was just a convenient plot device or a traditional moral solution remains an open question, but it was in any case a clear departure from American-style exploitation films where unlucky female characters so often met similar fates. This was a quality piece of film art that was awarded the top prize at the Berlin Film Festival (1952) and praised by critics around the world, including the reviewer of *The Times* of London who called it "disturbing and beautiful."

Folke Sundquist and Ulla Jacobsson as Göran and Kerstin in *One Summer of Happiness*.

The iconic landscapes of the film are portrayed as a kind of vessel or manifestation of the national soul. Most countries have some kind of similarly idealized approach to nature[1] but it's germane to note that in Denmark things were a bit different. Because it is a much smaller country, the concept of escaping into nature is less plausible, and for many decades there has been little in Denmark that could be called true wilderness. One

A classic Swedish midsummer's night in *One Summer of Happiness*.

can still find solitude on one of the hundreds of tiny semi-forgotten islands, but this can evoke perhaps a feeling of confinement rather than freedom. Sweden, on the other hand, is a sparsely populated country of low mountains and forests dotted with innumerable freshwater lakes, and Swedes, particularly in the immediate postwar period, subscribed to the idea of nature as a spiritual entity. This almost religious adoration of their natural surroundings was reflected in films like *One Summer of Happiness*. Further, the film depicts a kind of lake culture (nonexistent in Denmark) that made possible an entire subgenre of "summer lake films."

But a lake always looks even more interesting when there are young, attractive *naked* people swimming in it. That was the scene in the film that clearly drew the most attention and helped to make it an explosive success in Sweden, where it still ranks as the country's biggest selling domestically-produced picture.

In foreign markets it was also a major breakthrough hit, to some degree because its message of a return to traditional values struck a universal chord, but mostly because the brief nude scenes — when left intact by censors — showed more skin than was available in local product. It ended up playing in over 80 countries, some of those behind the iron curtain. (In East Germany it was hailed as potent anti-religious propaganda.)

Released in America in 1954, it ran into trouble with the authorities in Alabama, Massachusetts and elsewhere, solely due to scenes that showed a boy of 19 and a girl of 17 swimming and embracing in the nude.

Its biggest successes were in the southern regions — Italy, Spain, Brazil, and so on —

where it virtually launched the concept of "Scandinavian sin" and came to personify Sweden in the popular imagination as a country of endless erotic possibility. Along with Alf Sjöberg's *Miss Julie*, which was co-winner of the Golden Palm at Cannes in 1951, it put Sweden back on the international film map. (Sjöberg's 1944 film *Torment*, with a script by Ingmar Bergman, told the tale of a schoolboy and his sadistic teacher who both have a relationship with a promiscuous young shop clerk, well played by young Mai Zetterling. That film was notable for its depiction of loose sexual morals but didn't have anywhere near the impact of *One Summer of Happiness*.)

At this point to call it "Scandinavian sin" was a bit of a stretch since at this point only Swedish films qualified. Denmark was as yet producing almost nothing of international significance, and Norway, a more religious country with an altogether different and more conservative mindset, would become more famous for banning erotic films than producing them. Iceland and Finland never really factored into the collective mythology.

Nevertheless, for all intents and purposes Sweden *was* Scandinavia in the popular conception, though things happening elsewhere in these northern climes occasionally attracted the world's attention. Most notable perhaps was the pioneering sex-change operation that took place in Copenhagen's city hospital in 1952, the same hospital later made famous by Lars von Trier's *The Kingdom*. Here, under the glare of surgical lighting, George William Jørgensen Jr. was turned into Christine Jørgensen as headlines quickly trumpeted the news around the world. It indicated that a more liberal view of sexuality dominated "over there" and spawned a series of movie spin-offs, among them *The Christine Jorgensen Story* and Ed Wood's *I Changed My Sex*. (Meanwhile, also in 1952—a fateful year for the city's reputation—Danny Kaye hammered his way through *Hans Christian Andersen* and created a Disneyfied portrait of the city that still holds sway with tourists and continues to irk the natives.) Years later another famous movie character would do her sex-change shopping in Copenhagen: Myra Breckenridge.

Danish poster art for *The Christine Jørgensen Story* (a.k.a. *Jorgensen*) inspired by the famous 1952 sex-change operation.

The Christine Jørgensen affair was in any case an isolated event and most folks in Iowa City still couldn't find Denmark on a map. Sweden remained the most prominent and representative Nordic country and possessed the most intriguing allure.

It was no surprise then that the next groundbreaking erotic movie also came from Sweden, from the hand of the country's most celebrated *auteur*—Ingmar Bergman.

Summer with Monika

The phenomenal success of *One Summer of Happiness* could not have been lost on Bergman, who had himself made a "summer film" that same year—*Summer Interlude* (as it was titled in the UK). His next picture, *Summer with Monika*, had uncanny similarities of theme and setting with Mattsson's film. It also depicted Swedish nature in an idyllic light and did much to advance the notion that Swedes were an open-minded and uninhibited lot. And the fact that it was shot for a pittance, largely outdoors, with a tiny cast and crew and—most importantly—nudity, virtually guaranteed that this tale of young love in the wilds would be a money spinner.

But that's not why he made it. He made it because of the teenage temptress he saw one night in a Swedish crime drama called *Defiance*, a saucy lass named Harriet Andersson for whom he fell head over heels. She radiated a combustible mixture of innocence

Monika (Harriet Andersson) gives her father the evil eye in a scene from *Summer with Monika*.

and toughness that captivated Bergman, and together with writing partner Per Anders Fogelström he scripted the story of a sassy, headstrong and sexually aggressive girl who would come to reflect the moral ambiguity of the times. She had to be hot — and she was. "There's never been a girl in Swedish films who radiated more uninhibited erotic charm than Harriet," he would say.

She was to play the rebellious Monika, an unhappy teen who lives in a cramped ghetto flat with her noisy siblings, passive mother and alcoholic father. By day she works at a vegetable market where it is strongly hinted that she's had sexual relations with her male co-workers who make her the butt of dirty jokes. Moviegoing offers her a form of escape and she dreams of finding a boyfriend in the mold of one of these glamorous leading men. When she meets the awkward but not unpleasant looking Harry at a cheap cafe she decides that he is that movie star in the rough and initiates contact by getting him to light her cigarette. He too has a troubled home life; his mother is deceased and his relationship with his father is dysfunctional and distant. And he too works a boring day job, in a glass and porcelain shop where his co-workers pass the long hours by making sport of him. That night the two of them go see a movie called *Summer and Love*.

When Monika runs away from home, Harry offers her a place to stay in his father's boat and they spend that night together there. The next day Harry arrives late for work and is fired. At Monika's suggestion they commandeer the boat and motor out among the rocky shoals of Stockholm's archipelago where they find an uninhabited island to camp on.

Here they live in the boat, which is pulled up to the shore, and build campfires on the beach over which they boil coffee and cook up for supper what odds and ends they have managed to forage. They spend their days exploring, sunbathing, swimming in the clear waters and making love. Just as in *One Summer of Happiness* the difference between the urban and countryside environments is starkly drawn. Bergman depicts the city (Stockholm) as menacing, brooding and claustrophobic while the island represents freedom and hope. It is not always comfortable but they are their own masters with no bosses or parents to answer to, and this new life brings out different qualities in them. Monika is happy, for once, and Harry is no longer just a wage-slave at the bottom of the totem pole. When they encounter Monika's previous boyfriend, Lelle, at a dance club they sail over to one night, and he later shows up uninvited on their island, a newly confident Harry sends him packing.

Perhaps Harry and Monika are even in love, in a way, but when Monika announces that she's pregnant everything changes. Meals of berries and mushrooms no longer suffice. One day they decide to search for food on a nearby inhabited island, and Monika comes across a farmhouse and sneaks into it. She is collared and brought inside while the police are called. The family is just about to dine on a roast, and there it sits, steaming on the table. Left alone for a second, she snatches it and flees, savagely ripping at it with her teeth and fingers, stumbling in flight through the marshy wilds. They clearly cannot survive like this. Harry was no help and she snarls at him for his lack of courage.

The next day in defeat they take the boat back to the city where all their old problems await. Their dark mood colors their surroundings, and the island and the open water are no longer depicted in such idyllic fashion.

Back in Stockholm the adults around them scurry to make everything proper and above-board. They are married in time for the birth of the baby, and Harry's aunt installs them in a flat and procures some furniture. Harry is found a proper job and enrolled in night school which shall supply him with an engineering degree. He devotes himself to his studies and the child while Monika grows bored and resentful. This was not the life of adventure she expected, and having a crying baby around all day is such a drag.

Returning home from a business trip one day, Harry finds her in bed with old flame Lelle. The marriage is clearly over and soon they go their separate ways.

Monika has left Harry not only with the junk furniture but also with the kid, and in turn she gets her freedom. She is hardly ready to be tamed, and in one of the closing scenes is getting familiar with another fellow she's picked up in the beat cafe. In a famous scene she turns and stares directly into the camera (in contravention of the unwritten rule that an actor should never do this) with an expression of stony indifference. She doesn't give a damn what anybody including the audience thinks.

Back on the street, out in front of their old flat, Harry's aunt barters with a junk dealer over their stacked up furniture. Harry is lost in somber contemplation, his youthful illusions shattered, but despite this setback he appears headed for a respectable life. It's the kind of life a girl like Monika could never abide, but he will always have the memories of his summer with her, and he flashes back to scenes of the lively and defiant lass capering nude over a rocky outcropping on their island paradise. (For a female character in the early '50s this was revolutionary behavior.)

Today critics regard *Summer with Monika* as an important film in the Bergman canon, but few count it among his most significant works. Yet he would never make a film that had greater impact on popular culture.

Bergman's enduring achievement was not the film as a whole but rather the character of Monika, a bold new female figure. However unhappy her choices might make her, and however immature and insecure she might be, she was in charge of her own sexuality and refused to be cowed by the chattering classes. Where she was headed God only knew, but at least she didn't have to die in the end for her "sins" as did the squeaky clean Kerstin in *One Summer of Happiness*.

A tough gal, "a slut in the making," as Peter John Dyer wrote in the periodical *Films and Filming*, a teenage temptress who was "all animal, sensual, uninhibited, lazy, promiscuous, highly strung, chain-smoking, all lips and baby fat and dark straggly hair."

She was a singular creation and achieved a lot: she turned Harriet Andersson into Sweden's first erotic star of the modern (postwar) period, won Bergman his first major breakthrough outside the country and contributed immensely to the mythology of a sexually liberated Scandinavia which *One Summer of Happiness* had set in motion.

Was there a grain of truth to the myth at this early stage? Were all Swedish people so liberated or was it just two filmmakers slipping some mischief past a lackadaisical state censorship committee? (Not so lackadaisical really since they did, over Bergman's heated objections, insist on substantial cuts, permitting nude shots of Andersson only from behind and at a distance.) If all Swedes were so open-minded and nonchalant about sex, why had both films been such big hits there? They seemed to be lured in just as easily as any other audience by the sexy exploitation-style ad campaigns that accompanied both pictures. No doubt they were attracted by the stories but the sex and nudity were clearly the major selling points. If true liberation breeds indifference, in 1952 they were not yet indifferent.

That both films actually delivered conservative old-fashioned messages — even today

Harriet Andersson poses in a suggestive exploitation-style publicity still for *Summer with Monika*.

Summer with Monika can be read as a potent cautionary against premarital sex — didn't seem to bother American audiences already glutted on staid Production Code product. They were used to ignoring messages, and were in any case served up a print so chopped to bits that the message was indiscernible.

That butchery was the handiwork of the legendary exploitation duo of Kroger Babb and David F. Friedman who had purchased the American rights from a fellow named Gaston Hakim in 1955. More interested in Harriet Andersson's naked romp on the rocks of the lagoon than in sad endings or somber realism, they cut the film down from 97 minutes to 65, dubbing it into "American English" and laid a jazzy Les Baxter soundtrack over Erik Nordgren's "sonorous semi-symphonic score," as Friedman characterized it. They retitled it *Monika, the Story of a Bad Girl* and spiced up the promotional copy with taglines like "The devil controls her by radar!" (Americans also being fascinated by radar at that time) and "a picture for wide screens and broad minds." (Cinemascope and other wide-screen formats were also very much on people's minds.)

They played it for years on the "cow-pasture circuit" (rural drive-in theaters) and raked in a small fortune. As Friedman wistfully recalled in his autobiography *A Youth in Babylon*, the hotted-up poster art featured "the back of a lithe lass running naked toward a serene tree-shrouded lake, her silky long hair streaming, her pert, rosy, rounded buttocks the focal point of the artist's rendition."

Of course no lake figured into the film but that geographical glitch was one of their lesser sins. These provincial Americans couldn't see that it was the character of Monika as a whole that was provocative, and not just her naked backside, and it was this character in its essence that was vandalized by their ham-fisted re-editing job.

She was all there in the uncut, subtitled version that Janus Films released a year later to art-house theaters, but fewer Americans would see that version. (As it turned out, Babb's contract with Hakim hadn't been 100 percent above board and they were forced to pay additional monies to the producer, Svensk Film Industri, to keep rolling with their version. Thus two radically different versions of the film played in America for years to two radically different audiences.)

More Swedish films with erotic themes were released in the profitable wake of *One Summer of Happiness* and *Summer with Monika*. *Unmarried Mothers*, produced in 1953 and released in the U.S. on the exploitation circuit in 1955, was one. As David Shipman notes in his book *Caught in the Act*, there had been a long tradition in Scandinavian cinema for "tales of deserted unmarried mothers."

Literally translated, the film's Swedish title was the somewhat less exploitive *Unmarried Fathers Sought*, which is indicative of how such films were sold to their respective publics. What might be an adult melodrama in Europe was pitched as a sordid tale of sin and degradation on the American market, given the pulp treatment, so to say. The American title, a mere two words, speaks volumes. "Unmarried mothers"— plain enough! It had to be all about sex, shame, guilt, regret, loose morals, a slide into the gutter and what have you. Script lines on the American trailer spelled it out for those somehow in danger of missing the point: "These are unmarried mothers! ... The step-by-step, kiss-by-kiss account of unmarried mothers and their unwanted children! ... It will shock you! The unvarnished truth about unmarried mothers revealed for the first time. It will startle you! A truer than life story film of girls in trouble...." By such means a rather tame

Two lads ogle a still of Harriet Andersson from *Summer with Monika* in François Truffaut's *The 400 Blows*.

Swedish B-movie set in a home for unmarried mothers became pornography, or as close to it as permitted in the sleazier main street theaters and drive-ins where it tended to play in America.

The burgeoning myth of a sexually liberated Sweden meant haystacks of money to be counted by theater owners, but it fed suspicions among conservative Americans that the country was an immoral cesspool. Unmarried mothers indeed. Sweden was, to a far greater degree than Denmark, deeply suspect.

These suspicions were as good as confirmed by one Joe David Brown in an April 25, 1955, *Time Magazine* article headlined "Sin and Sweden." Here Brown describes a Sweden "where sociology has become a religion in itself, and birth control, abortion and promiscuity ... are recognized as inalienable rights." The church, in his view, was little more than a department of the government prone to shocking passivity in the face of a looming moral crisis. "Whatever the cause," he continued, "sexual moral standards in Sweden today are jolting to an outsider." Unmarried mothers in Sweden were "practically viewed as heroines." According to his figures illegitimate births were skyrocketing while the overall birth rate was shrinking to levels that could even endanger the country's national security.

"The sex education given in public schools would make even the most modern broad-minded American parent blanch," he claimed. He quoted a Swedish Roman Catholic priest who called the Swedish people "incapable of imagining a world where there are not unwed mothers, where abortions and birth control are not necessary. They say, 'Since these things exist, then let us do something constructive about them.' They don't believe it is possible to change human nature. They attack the problem as a sociological and medical one."

"But what will this lead to?" Brown asked the priest. "After all, sexual morality is basic to Western ethics."

Brown claimed to have found a partial answer to his question in a Stockholm newspaper column entitled "Swedish Youth Speaks." Here a 19-year-old wrote in to confess, "I have no real morals. And I would never marry a girl because I made her pregnant. Why should I give up my liberty for the sake of a child?"

The previously mentioned movies constituted exhibit A in the case against the country and served to further blacken its reputation in the eyes of the deeply religious. The following year another (unidentified) American writer described the country as "a polished nightmare, sterile and empty and without a face."[2]

Perhaps this kind of thinking was to be expected at the height of the Cold War when socialism and all its variants were being roundly vilified. To ardent anti–Communists Sweden was a special challenge; here was a country that had embraced many socialist concepts and was actually doing well. While Eastern Bloc countries were forced to repress their own populations by military means, Swedes seemed to believe in at least some form of socialism. They seemed to believe, as the dim view had it, that the government should control their lives. Additionally their pacifist tradition which had resulted in neutrality during World War II and Vietnam and had kept them out of NATO was cause for deep concern in right-wing circles. (Denmark, by contrast, joined NATO in 1949 and was, and is, more receptive to towing an American foreign policy line, though it is just as inclined to socialist remedies in the domestic sphere.)

But was the "Swedish experiment" succeeding or failing? Some thought the latter, and Sweden's high suicide rate was often touted as proof. President Eisenhower himself, in a 1960 speech, claimed that the country's socialist style welfare policies had led to sin, nudity, drunkenness and suicide. No matter that the suicide rate was high all over Scandinavia, and that it certainly owed more to the lack of sunlight than to socialism.

This suicidal, morally degenerate people continued to produce erotic films, and stars, at a pretty good clip. When the voluptuous Swedish diva Anita Ekberg strode the streets of Rome in connection with her participation in *La Dolce Vita* in 1958, the pope himself proclaimed her a "danger to traffic." That same year the 1954 picture *Time of Desire* was released in the U.S. and promptly banned in Chicago. *The Horse Trader's Daughters*, as the Swedish title is literally translated, was the tale of two sisters who live a carefree country life, exploring the woods and riding their horses. This close (sexual) relationship is shattered when the younger sister falls in love with a man who has come to town on business and the older sister is left disconsolate.

The film is full of pastoral interludes and seeks to leave the impression that people are freer and happier in the country, while the theme of lesbian incest provides grist for director Egil Holmsen's dramatic mill. In a remarkable twist the story is resolved without either of the sisters' going "straight," going mad or committing suicide, fates usually reserved for gay characters at the time.

Time of Desire has recently received some play on the gay and lesbian festival circuit, but upon its American release in the late '50s there was no openly gay audience and instead it was pitched as kinky exotica to curious heterosexuals in the same manner that most Swedish films were pitched — luridly. As its trailer script proclaimed, "Such things do happen.... A time of desire, a time when the veil of innocence is gently lifted revealing a young girl's haunting initiation into the tender mysteries of a strange love ... call it passion, love ... or sin. With girls so young what strange dreams may come alive at the touch of a forbidden love?"

On a parallel but quite separate track from the naturalist films were what could be called the youth problem pictures, movies about juvenile delinquents and crime or gangster films in which teens figured and which usually took place in urban settings. These were popular in the mid– to late–'50s and reflected a trend emanating primarily from America, though in Sweden the sex and nudity were often more on display. Swedish films like *The Vicious Breed* (1954), *Girls Without Rooms* (1956) and *Britta—the Artist's Model* (1956)—were part of this pattern. And there were the somewhat later "Raggare" films: *Blackjackets* (1959), *Swedish Punks* (1962) and *Just Once More* (1962) that depicted gangs of Swedish greasers who drove hot cars, got in rumbles and listened to rock music. While Denmark and Norway really had no counterpart to the Raggare films, the American movie *Rock Around the Clock* had played in all three countries in 1957 and caused riots. In Copenhagen young motorbike riders laid siege to the Bristol cinema, while in Oslo leather-clad teens swarmed out of the Centrum Theater after the show to overturn cars and smash windows. The same scenes were repeated in Sweden. The juvenile delinquent plague, born of the virus of rock 'n' roll, had come to Scandinavia, and movies like this one and *The Blackboard Jungle* had brought it. The problems depicted in these movies stemmed from lousy home lives and hanging out with the proverbial wrong crowd, and the characters preferred drag strips and dance joints to the fields and meadows of the countryside. And for once the films' original titles were just as sensational as the American tags.

Britta—the Artist's Model was by contrast something more akin to the morality tales of the '30s. Here Nina, a fast-living young gal, gets pregnant and ends up at the door of a quack doctor who performs an illegal abortion, resulting in sterility. She later changes her ways when she meets a nice decent chap called Hans. They get married and he wants to start a family, but she is torn with guilt about her past life and sees only one way out: suicide. She pens a despairing goodbye letter and disappears. He discovers the note and sets out to find her, deeply distraught.

So far so standard, and so melodramatic. Moralistic films like this had been in vogue in almost every western country since the '30s, and in the best tradition of exploitation they often tried to slip in a little nudity — as did this film, in scenes that were completely exploitative and extraneous to the plot. The American title was also misleading: Nina was not an artist's model but a nurse, which to Stateside crowds in the '50s was shorthand for slut. (Actually both were shorthand for slut.)

Blonde in Bondage (1957), about an American journalist named Larry who comes to Stockholm to write an article about Swedish morality, is another film of note in this context although it was no youth picture, being more closely a part of the nightclub and gangster genre. Larry is knocked out by all the Swedish blondes and becomes involved with one of them, a drug-addicted nightclub singer. One thing leads to another and he discovers that the villainous strip club baron Max is dealing dope.

The American title again oversold the goods; there was no bondage, and the strippers never shed all. Yet its premise, that a different kind of morality was at play in Sweden, is worthy of note. It also played on the assumption that Stockholm nightlife was one wild ride.

None of the above films was a particularly big hit abroad, and to most foreign viewers Swedish cinema meant Bergman. With his well received *Smiles of a Summer Night* (1955), a comparatively up-tempo, joyous and accessible romantic comedy in which Harriet Andersson again starred, he could now lay claim to being Scandinavia's most important director. This film had nothing that shysters like Babb and Friedman could exploit, and exhibition in America was confined to the art-house circuit, as was his 1960 picture *The Virgin Spring*, which, however, would prove more controversial.

Unlike *Summer with Monika*, *The Virgin Spring* was no modern film, based as it was on a fourteenth century ballad of violence and revenge, but its particularly startling 90-second rape sequence attracted outcry and got it banned in Texas (in 1962) and elsewhere in America. The scene was "the most uncompromising thing of its kind on film," noted a critic at the time.

This was certainly no erotic film. The rape sequence (and death of the woman) could in no way be considered titillating in the manner of a Russ Meyer movie, for example, where sex and violence were part and parcel. It did, however, push the limits of what was permitted in cinema at the time and proved controversial in Europe as well. Alton Cook of *The New York World Telegram* characterized the rape scene as "explicit enough to shock sophisticated European audiences, perhaps leaving local censors too dumbfounded to cut it."

Critics were conflicted. "Audiences will likely leave the theater torn and shattered by an unpleasant experience," wrote *Variety*, while adding that it was also "an extremely powerful film." And although Bergman himself would later dismiss it as "an aberration ... touristic, a lousy imitation of Kurosawa," it won widespread praise and awards, among them the Oscar for best foreign film of 1960.

Much more digestible for general audiences was Lars-Magnus Lindgren's *Love Mates* from the following year. Filmed in gorgeous color, it featured beautiful scenes of the Stockholm coastal area and introduced audiences to the next Swedish sex star-in-waiting, Christina Schollin. Here she plays a perky blonde beauty who catches the eye of Jan, a lowly bank janitor who intends to work his way up to the top of the banking business (and does). Lindgren tries to pass off Schollin as a classic sex bomb, but she's really more of a girl-next-door type and none the less appealing for it.

He was attempting to make a modern erotic comedy that had trace elements of Tati and was charged with the irreverence and nonsensical poetry of the French New Wave. This was mostly conveyed in the casual layabout bed scenes and the quirky editing. In other ways the film was determinedly traditional: another summer adventure with the obligatory nude bathing scene. While the story line of Jan's hunt for success and material gain was a popular theme of the day, it was hardly the kind of thing that advocates of the New Wave could be expected to applaud. Nor was it particularly realistic in any sense.

But, as Danish critics noted, it was still far ahead of what was happening in Denmark. "Swedes are in the lead in Scandinavia," wrote *Aktuelt* in their review. "They are simply much better at conveying this type of thing than we are." Other writers agreed. "Swedish films get straight to the point. Whereas Danish films are contented with decent, proper tête-à-têtes, Swedish films shed both inhibitions and clothes. While Danish films stay comfortably within the limits, Swedish films cross the line and then some, and in this film they allow the young couple to violate the sixth commandment in front of open curtains."[3]

Other critics were starting to lose patience with all the shots of sunsets, waves and wind-blown wheat fields that had become almost obligatory in Swedish films. These summer flings and all this naturalism were becoming somewhat clichéd. And there *always* seemed to be a nude bathing scene.

Most thought it a sweet little comedy, but the reviewer for Denmark's weekly Catholic paper detected something more ominous at play. "This is no lecture on sexual liberation delivered by true believers because here it is taken for granted, as a matter of course, and it is precisely because of this the film is dangerous. There is in this film, just as there is in *Never on Sunday*, an atmosphere of purity which seems enchanting. These films don't seem immoral because they are faithful to their own home-made morality which is woven into the pleasant fabric of the film. [But] they are immoral and reflect a decadence of the times. When they are made with talent and charm, that only serves to make them all the more so."

Decadent or not, *Love Mates* caught the spirit of the moment and became a huge hit in Sweden. Today it ranks as # 4 on the all-time Swedish hit list after *The Jungle Book*, *The Sound of Music* and *One Summer of Happiness*. It would go on to become a perennial favorite, frequently replayed on TV down through the years.

Arne Mattsson belatedly followed up the success of *One Summer of Happiness* with one of his quirkiest numbers, a bizarre tale of frustrated love entitled *The Doll* (1962). Enter one lonely security guard who toils away on the night shift at a department store, all the while developing a crush on one of the store's female mannequins. One night he steals it and brings it back home. And one day ... she comes alive. Said mannequin was played by the attractive Gio Petré who had previously appeared in serious films, such as Bergman's *Wild Strawberries*, but who was now about to become much better known for her roles in sexploitation movies.

Up to this point Swedish films clearly had the edge. They had market share, they had buzz, they had Bergman. And they had a head start on open-mindedness, Sweden being the first country in the world, in 1957, to introduce mandatory sex education in public schools and having the lowest age limit —15 — for entrance to adult oriented films, to name just a couple of qualifications.

It wasn't that Danes were particularly prudish. Nudity had been shown in Danish films before. As far back as 1934 actress Karin Nellemose had bathed in the nude in *Life on the Hegn Farm*, although it was not until the 1955 Cold War thriller *Delusion* that unclothed people were seen for more than fleeting glimpses. Yet these remained isolated scenes scattered in movies that never laid claim to a liberated mentality in a wider sense. Swedish movies showed nudity in a way that seemed to promote a life philosophy, however casually conveyed, and they were thus far much bigger hits abroad.

Danish films could break taboos. In 1957 26-year-old debut director Palle Kjærulff-Schmidt depicted homosexuals in *Sin Alley*. This was the tale of a 17-year-old lad from the provinces who comes to Copenhagen to seek a trade but is unable to secure an apprenticeship. Instead he is drawn into a life of crime, compelled to act as bait for a couple of street toughs who waylay, beat and rob homosexuals. Although modern in its social-realist style and groundbreaking simply because gays were made visible on the screen, it was no bold exposé of the discrimination and prejudice homosexuals faced. Rather it is the young students who cannot get apprenticeships that are portrayed as the victims. Nonetheless it was crowned the best Danish film of the year with a Bodil award.

It was not until 1959 with *A Stranger Knocks* that a Danish film dared something on a par with the Swedish competition. Like many dramas of the period, it dealt with the German Occupation of 1940–1945, but the sexual element was prominent. On a stormy windswept night a stranger seeks shelter in an isolated cottage near the sea where a woman lives alone. Ignorant of the fact that he was a Nazi collaborator during the war and is on the run, she allows him to stay. She is lonely and welcomes his company and eventually his lovemaking. In the course of their sexual relationship she learns something even more terrible about him.

During a love scene the woman reaches climax. It was the first such scene in a Danish film and one that caused problems with censors in various foreign territories.

In the U.S. New York banned the film outright in 1964 and Maryland in 1965. The picture had appreciable impact on screen censorship in America and was even spotlighted by Amos Vogel in his landmark study from 1974, *Film as a Subversive Art*. "The entire plot pivots on an act of intercourse," writes Vogel. "The complete absence of nudity and total relevance of the scene to the plot posed an impossible problem for the American censors, and led, upon appeals against its prohibition, to the abolition by the Supreme Court of the entire system of American *State* censorship in 1967. This development contributed significantly to the later era of sexual permissiveness in the American cinema" (emphasis added).

Even Danish censors felt compelled to snip 15 seconds from it. Danes, however, did not look kindly on such butchery, however minor it might seem to be, and there were protests. A similar outcry arose over another film a couple of years later, *One Among Many*, a youth film that nonetheless was banned for viewers under 16. "People Went Away Furious — Over Film Censorship," ran the headline in a local paper.

The ratings tiff over *One Among Many* pointed up a number of things about Danish culture. Youth films, for which there was a proud tradition in Scandinavian cinema, were to be taken seriously and not disrespected. Adolescents had rights too. It also reflected the libertarian strain in the Danish character that reflexively bridled at any hint of paternalism or interference by the state in matters moral or artistic.

In America and Britain, for example, the attitude toward film censorship was very different. By the late '50s it was firmly established in those two countries, not just the mechanisms but the mentality. There was a general feeling among people that there was a need for censorship: youth needed to be protected, ratings codes were necessary and "indecent films" had to be regulated. Particularly in the States, political and religious bodies played a central role in sorting out moral issues, and this relationship had been institutionalized in the system going back to the early '30s when the Catholic church had forced Hollywood to regulate itself with the mechanism known as the Production Code. The church in Denmark also had a voice; there was a Catholic paper specifically tasked to review films and there were (and are) a number of Christian papers. But no religious denomination ever felt compelled or sufficiently empowered to issue ultimatums to the industry itself, and the public would never have countenanced such meddling.

There were other skirmishes with the authorities. When *West Side Story* was restricted in Denmark in the early '60s to 16-and-over, it caused a furor. Even at this early stage censorship was being questioned in its essence, in all its forms. In part this was spurred on by a highly publicized trial initiated by the Danish surrealist Wilhelm Freddie, who was seeking to get back works that the police had deemed obscene and confiscated years earlier.[4] Although the Freddie trial did not bear directly on film censorship, it brought the same issues to the surface and stirred the debate in a major way.

Among those agitating for the end of film censorship altogether was the politician Helge Larsen. After all, what was there to hide from children? Back in 1948 Sten Hegeler had authored the frank sexual education book *How, Mom? (Hvordan, Mor?)* for children of kindergarten age and it had become a standard text. And if films did need to be regulated, surely there had to be a better way than ratings codes, not to mention the cutting out of footage, an act of vandalism perpetrated in secret.

The controversies surrounding the release of *A Stranger Knocks* and *One Among Many* were merely surface ripples that indicated something deeper at play in society. As evidence, suddenly in 1962 liberated characters started appearing in Danish movies. This was the year that filmmakers started to wrestle with and exploit the concept of *frigjorthed*.*

As was so often the case, the filmmakers owed a debt of gratitude to the novelists and publishers who had already fought many of the important battles. Back in the mid-'50s a handful of these novelists and publishers had chosen a more open-minded path, prominent among them one Hans Reitzel who in 1955 had published Jean Genet's *The Thief's Journal* (1948). He was the first to translate the works of his friend Henry Miller into a Nordic language, starting with *Tropic of Capricorn* and then in 1956 *Sexus*, and later others. *The Perfumed Garden of the Shaykh Nefwazi* was another erotic classic he published. He took a lot of heat for this; he was personally attacked from all directions and was made the target of threats and abuse of the kind that no filmmaker would ever have to endure. Headlines were scathing: "A scandalous new book from the cesspool of erotica" ... "The mud puddle of perversity; Sexus" ... "A case of literary cancer."[5] Although never charged in a court of law, he received many anonymous threats by mail and telephone. One angry citizen sent him rotten meat wrapped in gold candy paper.

In 1958 another "scandal novel" was published in Denmark, Agnar Mykle's *The Song of the Red Ruby (Sangen om den Røde Rubin)*. It had been banned upon publication in Mykle's native Norway in 1956 and caused a furor in many other countries, but after a highly publicized trial in his homeland the ban was overturned, the publicity having been a windfall for sales. In Denmark it was printed by Schønbergske publishing house. This tale of the sexual escapades of Ask Burlefot (Mykle's alter ego) during his student days in '30s Oslo would, like so many of the period's other controversial novels, later be made into a film.

A year later a reprinting of John Cleland's 200-year-old novel *Fanny Hill* was seized from Danish bookstores on court order. It was charged with "presenting such an offensive depiction of sexual congress that it must be considered obscene," marking the start of a case that would wind on for years.

Publishers like Reitzel, Schønbergske and Morten A. Korch, who had released Hegeler's *How, Mom?* back in 1948, were pioneers who blazed a path for a more challeng-

---

*See the Introduction for an explanation of this term.

ing and honest kind of literature, but they were at this point still catering to a very limited public.

In 1961 two Danish books, *The ABZ's of Love* and *I, a Woman*, changed everything. They crossed over to a mainstream book-buying public and sold in unheard of numbers. And they gave immense impetus to the nascent mythology of a Liberated Denmark.

The ABZ's of Love was authored by Sten Hegeler and his German-born wife, Inga Stähr Pedersen, whom he met in the '50s while she was studying psychology. By day she went to class and he attended to his duties as head psychologist at the Harlang and Torsvig Company. By night they researched and wrote *The ABZ's of Love*. It was published that year by the Chr. Erichsen's book company with Eiler Krag providing illustrations. Although Alfred Kinsey's books[6] on sexual behavior were all available by now, this went further, giving definitions of sexual terms and illustrating a myriad of sexual positions and techniques in an objective and straightforward fashion that shocked many. A blank piece of paper and an envelope bearing the authors' address was tucked in the flap of each copy so that readers could respond with feedback.

"Naturally we have no perfect recipe for human happiness," wrote the couple in the book's foreword. "We know as yet all too little about the dynamics of relationships.... We have tried to be straightforward and open-hearted. That will possibly shock and appall some. Our goal has been to write a book which can provide some help. Help

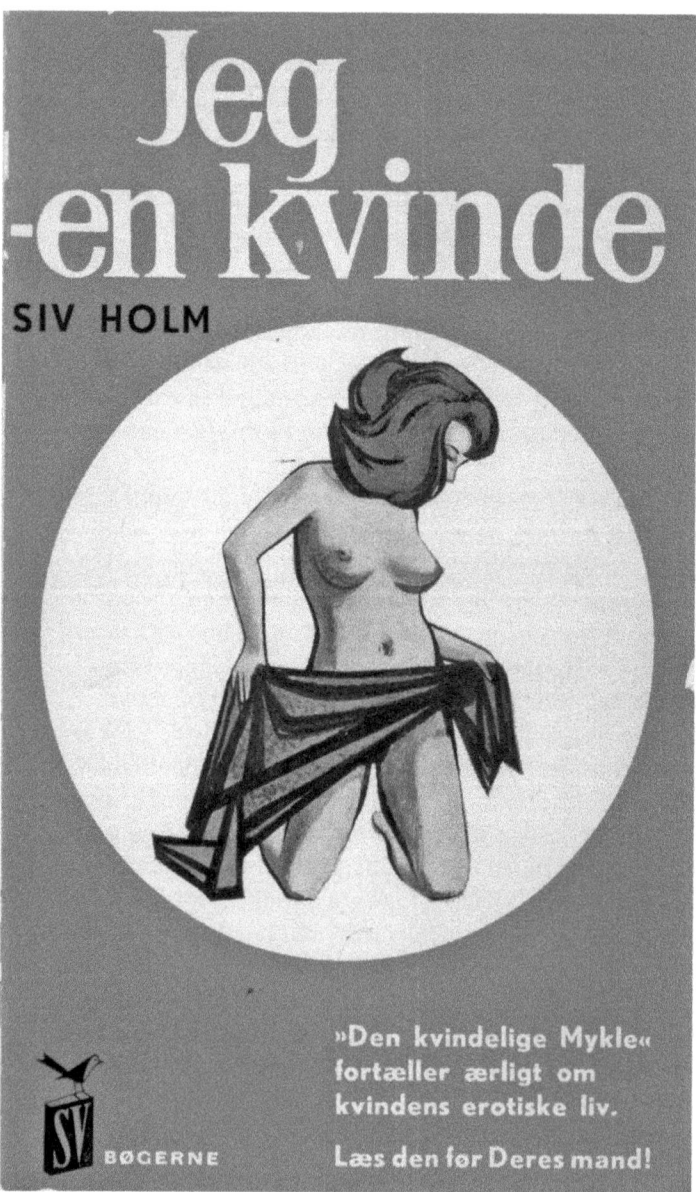

The cover of *I, a Woman* — the book.

for the young and the younger who are in a relationship or are about to enter into one. A relationship that is hopefully beneficial to both partners and lasts as long as possible."

Good intentions couldn't blunt the widespread outrage upon its publication, and it was immediately reported to the authorities as pornography.

Over the course of the next eight years it was published in 15 more countries, in Scandinavia with pictures intact, elsewhere with the illustrations deleted. In Denmark alone it sold over 60,000 copies. Similar books, such as the Danish translation of Masters and Johnson's *Human Sexual Relations*, followed in its wake. If they were not the founders of Danish sexual liberation, Inga and Sten Hegeler were without doubt its newest celebrities.

The other significant book, the autobiographical *I, a Woman*, was published by an anonymous young lady going under the pseudonym of Siv Holm. It caused an instant sensation, rife as it was with episodes of rape, masturbation, exhibitionism, etc. And this erotic adventure was written by a woman, no less. The Danish cultural intelligentsia dismissed it as a work of nil literary value, and had to look on in shock as it eventually sold more copies than the works of esteemed authors like Johannes V. Jensen and Martin Andersen Nexø. It was a huge success for the maverick publisher Stig Vendelkær who promoted it with an aggressive American style ad campaign. "Read it before your husband does" was the phrase he had the whole country repeating.

Nineteen sixty-two was the year things began to change in Danish cinema, the year a new kind of character began to appear in movies. All of the above had played a part; the Swedish films had been influential as had the books and people's ingrained resistance

An illustration (by Eiler Krag) from the 1962 Danish edition of *The ABZ's of Love* that was deleted in almost every other version.

to censorship. Despite their provincial veneer Danes really were somehow indefinably different, and they were ready to embrace this new age. And now filmmakers were starting to populate their stories with "emancipated" characters.

But did these characters represent real people? Nobody really knew.

The Duel

*"All those who fight for the right to have something
to believe in have my absolute sympathy."*
— Knud Leif Thomsen, 1962

The first substantial reaction to this new spirit of emancipation, this *frigjorthed*, now at large in Danish society was a movie called *The Duel*, and it was a negative reaction. It was nevertheless an auspicious debut by the 37-year-old director Knud Leif Thomsen, a man who held fierce opinions and who would become the most controversial figure of '60s Danish cinema.

Originally educated as a painter, Thomsen later enrolled in Copenhagen's music conservatory as a pianist, only to eventually realize he would never reach the top levels. At one point while traveling in France he contracted tuberculosis and was bedridden for 10 months. Recuperating back in Denmark and unable to work for the next two years, he threw himself into painting and honed his writing skills. In 1952 he found work at Nordisk Film Studios. There he learned the trade and began to direct short films, commercials and documentaries.

Ten years later Nordisk gave him total creative freedom to make his first feature film. He wrote the script based on his own idea, directed it and had a hand in every other aspect of production — very much, as the press would point out, in the *auteur* style of the French New Wave directors.

His story centered on Frits, a young medical student who works in a striptease club to help pay his way through college. He has a casual help-yourself relationship to the girls, but all that changes when he falls in love with one of the dancers, Marlene, and gets serious. Marlene also works as an assistant to an older film director named John with whom she's also had an affair, largely with a view to getting herself a career in the movies. Frits is crushed when he finds out.

John is making a movie that contains a dramatic scene involving a duel. On the set Frits overhears him comment that since Darwin proved that man evolved from apes, duels are obsolete because animals have no honor to defend. Idealistic young Frits is offended both emotionally and intellectually, and in his anger he challenges the cynical older man to a duel. "But," noted a reviewer at the time, who was loath to divulge the ending, "it is himself he ends up dueling with — and he loses."

The film is a classic three-way romantic drama and also a deeper rumination on the difficulties of life in the modern world. The character of John represents a new 'liberated' figure who sees sex as nothing more than a physical act.

The Duel opened on February 1, 1962, and caused an immediate stir. "With *The Duel*," breathlessly declared the tabloid *B.T.*, "Danish film has recaptured its honor," something that had, according to their scribe, been in short supply since Dreyer's *The*

Frits Helmuth plays the young student in Knud Leif Thomsen's *The Duel* from 1962.

Word in 1955. *Politiken* agreed: "*The Duel* is the most meaningful Danish film since *The Word*."

Thomsen was suddenly a director to be reckoned with. There was an expectation, *B.T.* continued, that he would figure as an agent of change in Danish film art and that the long drought was over. "An artistic nerve has been hit at a point in time when motion pictures had very little motion — or life — left in them."

If, in retrospect, these two writers were perhaps excessive in their praise, their reviews clearly indicate how desperately people were waiting for something new to happen and how different the film was from anything else at the time. It came as a jolt. Other critics were just as enthusiastic if somewhat more qualified, the general consensus being that this was no masterpiece (too polemic, too constructed) but perhaps something even more valuable; a film that finally believed in something and took a moral position. Others were repelled by the positions Thomsen was taking.

As for the tag of *auteur* and comparisons to the New Wave directors, they didn't hold. While Thomsen claimed to admire Godard and Antonioni, the traditional style of his filmmaking had little in common with the spontaneity and realism they favored, and what he was trying to say couldn't have been more at odds with what they believed in. They embraced the giddy spirit of youth and the new tide of liberality sweeping the West while he saw something much more ominous in it.

No, the New Wave had not yet reached Denmark. But it soon would — in October of that very same year, with a film called *Weekend*.

Weekend

Like *The Duel, Weekend* was the result of a producer giving his filmmaker total creative freedom, in this case the producer being Bent Christensen. He had earned a lot of money the year before with *Harry and the Butler*, a classic folk-comedy, and now he was giving a big chunk of it to Palle Kjærulff-Schmidt and an outspoken young Turk of the New Left called Klaus Rifbjerg to make something quite the opposite—what was in essence an experimental film.

The project started to attract attention that summer of 1962 as shooting got underway at a beach house near the seaside village of Rørvig. It boded to be one of the most daring Danish films ever, and it was already known that a couple of major stars had declined to participate, fearing that the film might damage their careers. It was to be a raw, revealing, "now" slice of Danish life that would prompt countless loose comparisons to the French New Wave and to the director Michelangelo Antonioni in particular. All the better, then, that they were using mostly non-actors, commented Rifbjerg to the press that July, "real people" for a real life film. Although he reckoned that the lack of major stars might hurt at the box office, these stars always came burdened with associations from their last big films and viewers were never able to completely disassociate. New faces would bring a freshness to the story.

The plot was almost plotless. Three couples and a footloose bachelor, Lars, all in their thirties, spend a weekend together in a summer house by the sea. The house belongs to Knud and Bente and they've brought the kids along, tended by a curvaceous young blonde nanny called Birthe (played by Lotte Tarp). They lie in the sun, they go to the beach, they gather around the table for traditional black-bread lunches well lubricated with beer and schnapps. Inhibitions fade. They converse in aimless fits and starts. They seek diversion, connection, fulfillment, all without much success. The couples all have marital problems.

An unplanned afternoon visit by an elderly couple, friends of friends who happen by, transpires in an air of unspoken tension. The superficial niceties fall flat and the atmosphere is soon completely poisoned by Lars' sadistic sarcasm which brings the lunch to an awkward close. That night, at loose ends, they all pile into the car and motor over to a seaside club for some dancing and more drinking, but the men-folk end up in a fight and they're all ejected. Outside in the high-summer night they go their own ways—with each other's spouses.

The next morning they wake up hung-over and sprawled about the cottage. Even these impulsive dalliances have failed to bring anybody much enjoyment. Things get worse when the most troubled member of the bunch, the school teacher, Kjeld, apparently attempts suicide by curling up in the fetal position on the road, only to have a milk truck driver get out, stare at him, and then drive carefully around. Later he attempts to rape Birthe on the beach while an upset child flails at him to stop. In the end the group gathers around him in a kind of despondent huddle as Ilse utters the final line, "It's just too much to bear."

And that's the end. Just a big slab of silence—a shock for audiences expecting the usual neatly resolved happy ending.

Here was a kind of lost generation that the filmmakers, themselves in their thirties, were a part of. Children during the Occupation, they'd been raised amid the fear and

"Upper-class beatniks" Bente Dessau and Jesper Jensen loosen up in *Weekend*.

paranoia of the Cold War in a tiny little country brushing against the Iron Curtain and sure to suffer the worst possible fate if the A-bombs ever started to fall. It was also an only-child generation with its share of spoiled personalities. They were the first generation to enjoy the material blessings of an economically revitalized Denmark and the first to experience the initial glimmerings of this new morality, and yet their personal lives were a mess. The film touched on a number of issues that would soon be the stuff of pop psychology: The men were grappling with mid-life crises long before the term had been coined, and the lunch time visit by the elderly couple was an example of the generation gap. Relationships were dysfunctional. If they were sexually liberated, they still seemed to be caught up in all the old traps, and although they considered themselves intelligent and educated they didn't appear to have a clue.

And Rifbjerg wasn't giving them any. "Unlike most films, I don't attempt to solve a problem. My intention is just to give the viewer something to work further with — in their own way." To call *Weekend* an existential film, he noted, was not totally off. Kjærulff-Schmidt himself had staged a production of *Waiting for Godot* back in 1956, and now the way they were shooting it—on location with available light for the most part, and lots of improvisation — was ideal for conveying a tone of bleak realism. (Comparisons would later be drawn to Dogme95.[7] While not a Dogme film in the strictest sense, it is one of Lars von Trier's favorites and would figure as a major inspiration for *The Idiots*, particularly in its use of ensemble acting.) What little staged atmosphere there was came in the form of the soundtrack music, moody jazz scored by two of Denmark's top musicians, Erik Moseholm and Bent Axen.

Advance hype on the film was substantial and its October 29 opening was eagerly awaited. This would be the first modern Danish film, a debunking of all the conventions enshrined in the folk-comedy.[8] And while sex was promised, the film would not tease, titillate or pander, would not be prurient. It would be "sensationally unsensational" as one scribe put it.

Sensationally unsensational maybe, but the tag lines were tempting enough: "A weekend of loving, dancing and drinking." It sure enough sounded like a good time, but viewers expecting such were quickly put straight. Many found it to be a crashing bore, and their disappointment was echoed in a fair number of reviews in which writers took the opportunity to slam the picture as amateurish, uninspired and not particularly engaging. "Not a nice experience," sniffed the tabloid *B.T.*

Key promotion for the film tried to set the focus on the characters. They represented a demographic that had never appeared in any significant way in a Danish film before. "Is it like that? Are *they* like that?" But the characters were exactly the problem for *Berlingske* reviewer Mogens Lind, who dismissed them as "upper-class Beatniks." *Aktuelt*'s reviewer wasn't buying it either. "Neither the people as individuals nor their behavior is in the remotest way interesting. Rarely have I been so intensely bored." "A wasted 'Weekend'" headed another review.

And yet at least as many writers were unabashedly positive about the film, praising its realism and refusal to resort to conventions. What others saw as faults they saw as strengths. Some complained about the occasional long silences, while others found these the most revealing parts of the movie. It was a film that dared to leave things unsaid. And when people did talk it was often drowned out in the background noise and general chatter ... but doesn't that happen in real life? Don't people interrupt, talk at the same time, etc.? Offensive to many was the dialogue itself, peppered as it was with slang and vulgarities, and yet advocates of the picture found this nearly revolutionary — to go to the movies and hear people talk the way they do in real life.

Many simply couldn't suffer the fact that "nothing happened." But some could. As Jens Kruuse of the newspaper *Jyllands Posten* put it, "A film where 'nothing happens' is vital and good." Finally even the film's advocates had to admit that the violent scenes — the punch-up at the nightclub and the rape attempt — were awkwardly and stiffly executed, almost ridiculous, comic. But here again, these kinds of people weren't used to violence. They were educated folk who *discussed* things. That was part of their problem; they couldn't even successfully connect with other people through violence.

A masterpiece? Few would go that far, but once again maybe it was something *more* useful: a wake-up call. A third school of thought was sympathetic to its aims but disappointed that a film so boldly conceived had not managed to be really artistically innovative or groundbreaking.

One thing was certain: never had a film provoked so much debate in Denmark. In classrooms, in the op-ed sections of newspapers, in theater lobbies and in cafes discussion flourished for weeks and months afterwards. Regardless of whether it was a good or bad film, it had brought a number of issues into sharp focus and made a generation aware of itself.

The sexual content figured as a major selling point but there was, in fact, hardly any. While wife-swapping and attempted rape occurred, nudity was almost nonexistent and intercourse was never directly depicted, only implied off-screen in the vaguest sense. Clad in their swimsuits, the women were sexy enough but not particularly because they were trying to be. It was no typical sex film but to many it was surely indecent enough. An oft-published still of the rape attempt that pictured Lotte Tarp's breasts exposed and her face hidden in a swirl of blonde hair was yet another scrap of damning evidence.

The film was seen by some as a kind of status report on Denmark's spiritual condition and the debate it sparked as a kind of group therapy. The pastor Claus Bang, speaking at a forum in the country's second largest city, Århus, had his own take: "In my profession I've learned that you don't get very far giving advice when the patient asks for help in solving their personal conflicts. The only thing you can do to help them is to tell them how you view their situation in general so they can see things with some distance and then decide what to do. I think that is what the film has tried

Lotte Tarp, the (almost) silent star of *Weekend*.

to do, to give this kind of status report. To objectively and dispassionately give a life-like depiction of reality."⁹

Weekend had received a 16-and-older rating but many parents were still nervous. When the film was shown to students in the 15 to 17 year age group in the town of Slagelse (as a last minute substitute when the car carrying the original film skidded into a ditch) all hell broke loose.

In March of 1963 the film opened in Sweden, and in April in Norway. In both countries it was praised to the skies. That spring it also triumphed over 24 other films to win the Bodil award, marking it as the best Danish picture of 1962. Yet the prestigious Cannes Film Festival, which had introduced the world to the French New Wave in 1958 and where boldly unconventional films were usually welcome, rejected it.

Undeterred, its distribution company, Constantin Film, arranged a special screening just before the start of the festival at the Studio Publicis theater on the Champs-Elysées. Here the French film establishment could view a subtitled print and make up their own minds about the movie. French censors, however, banned the screening at the last moment: they found the dialogue too strong, and word was that they objected to the fact that children had been present in the movie to witness all the (off-screen) debauchery. (Despite considerable contributions by the French to modern erotic cinema in the '50s, Bardot et al., France was still a Catholic country. As far back as 1926 when Benjamin Christensen's Paris premiere of *Häxan* was picketed by 8,000 Catholic women who objected to its nudity and profanity, Scandinavian films had proved too hot to handle and would continue to do so.) *Weekend* eventually opened in France in January of 1965 to passionately mixed reviews, e.g., "The people in the film are no more interesting than the larva one steps on in the road" (*Les Nouvelles Litteraires*), and "Birgit Brüel's wonderful face confirms that Scandinavia will always be Greta Garbo's homeland" (*Candide*).

The Danish producers could at least console themselves with the fact that the film had been selected by the Berlin Film Festival, but events there also took an unexpected turn when in mid–May festival officials informed them that it had been dropped, supposedly because it was also playing around the same time in Warsaw as part of a "Danish film week." That shouldn't have mattered since the Warsaw screening was not part of a competitive award-giving festival, nurturing suspicions that perhaps Berlin also considered it too controversial. But even though it didn't screen there it was *the* hot topic of conversation when the festival finally rolled around at the end of June.

Herr Kaul, editor of the German magazine *Der Kurier*, was particularly enthused about the film and arranged a special screening for it on June 25 in hopes of getting foreign critics to demand its re-inclusion. There was even some talk of its receiving a special Golden Bear award.

"It's a scandal," he declared after the show, "that a film which in a few years will be among the world's great and unforgettable classics has been rejected by the festival committee. For the first time we have a Danish film which really stands as a rebuttal to all the sensationalist sex-and-nudity pictures people expect when they talk about Scandinavian cinema. Those few in the audience who expected that today left in disappointment. Those who remained got to see an artwork that will take its place among the best."¹⁰

The screening earned *Weekend* some very good reviews but the festival stood firm; the film stayed out. When it finally opened commercially in Germany in a dubbed version at the start of 1965, it was warmly received. Declared the magazine *Film Kritik*, "After many years of indifferent and superficial comedies comes a film—*Weekend*—that has meaning outside Denmark."

British critics had been much less kind, greeting the film's London opening at the foreign-language La Continentale Cinema in October of 1963 with scorn. *The Sunday Times* claimed that the film's Scandinavian characters, who drink and dance in various states of undress in the summer night, who wife-swap and soul-search ad infinitum, were becoming clichés. The film's intention, reckoned *The Times*, was probably to show that without love sexual liberation is empty and that total freedom is boring. Yet in their opinion it only managed to demonstrate how eight unintelligent and unattractive people who come together end up boring each other and everyone else who is unfortunate enough to be witness.

The reference to sexual liberation by *The Times*' unaccredited scribe is revealing. While some Danish writers had referred in passing to the characters as being liberated, British and American reviewers largely saw the film as a treatise on sexual liberation, capital S.

From a Danish perspective the film was not mainly about sexual liberation. While the characters are aware that they are supposed to be "the liberated ones," sexually and otherwise, their wife-swapping leads only to more awkwardness, guilt and confusion and just shows how emotionally dysfunctional most of them are. It's clear that there is a gulf between the kind of people they are and the kind of people they think they are, or think they should be, and this is the point. But in general critics from the English-speaking countries had little patience for such nuances and could rarely get beyond the sexual element, or lack thereof, to see the film for what it was: a slice of modern Danish life in all its uncertainty and pointlessness. To focus on only one aspect was to miss the point. This film was the sum of its parts or it was nothing. The secondary characters and the general surroundings, as the filmmakers themselves would point out, were just as important as the main characters. It had to be taken as a whole.

Weekend was sold to foreign markets on a much larger scale than any previous Danish film. (Up until about 1967 most Danish films didn't even have export titles.) Viewers around the world now got a chance to become familiar in some small way with the land of the Little Mermaid, but most Danes living abroad who saw it as an opportunity to reconnect with the old country left theaters appalled.

The reaction of Danish expat Ise Keller, who lived in Zürich, found its way back to Denmark in the form of a letter to the editor.[11] Keller criticized the film for giving outsiders the impression that Denmark was a country where

> small-minded people consume great quantities of beer and schnapps, where inebriated men plow around in their cars ... where gatherings around the table are characterized by either monk-like silence or an orgy of caddishness and maliciousness. A country where young blonde servant girls prepare food, wash dishes, clean up after ten people and tend the children 24 hours a day without protest ... where school teachers go amok on the beach or in nightclubs to a degree that puts even leather-jacketed hoodlums to shame. Where housewives and mothers—not servant girls—willingly unbutton their blouses for every man, where such a film as this has been acclaimed the year's best, and where even in religious circles it has been praised as a "unique document of the times."

As *Weekend* opened in more and more foreign countries, a rift was clearly developing between the film intelligentsia who praised it as a bold and uncompromising piece of film art and average Danes—at home and abroad—who were disgusted by its depiction of their country and culture.

In November of 1963 the film struck ground in America, selected as Denmark's official contribution to the San Francisco Film Festival. This prompted yet more letters of protest. "It's a tragedy if Denmark doesn't have any other movie to present than this depiction of its own moral and spiritual bankruptcy," wrote Elmard Larsen.[12] "Who selects these films for international festivals? What tiny clique (of film milieu insiders), ever promoting each other, have we allowed to take control of our spiritual lives? It can hardly be the aim of the Foreign Ministry that we participate in these festivals in a way that discredits our country and attracts a specific type of tourist, namely those who come to Denmark because they've gotten the impression that the country is one vast bordello."

Most of the leading San Francisco critics thought otherwise. Stanley Eichelbaum praised the direction, placing it on a par with the films of Antonioni and calling it an unusually distinguished work. It was "pure and honest filmmaking," declared *The San Francisco Chronicle*, which went on to single out Bente Dessau's performance for praise.

Reaction at the sold-out festival screening was decidedly more mixed, no doubt because the advance hype had promised "sensational outspokenness," usually code for the kind of sex and nudity that the film lacked. Others were shocked. "We have two married daughters living in San Francisco," wrote a Danish woman in *B.T.*,[13] "who attended

Mentally disturbed? Seven "average Danes" enjoy a wet lunch in a scene from *Weekend*.

the festival screening of *Weekend* at which the Danish Council held a talk. They were shamed by all the dirty expressions used in the film ... and by the fact that such a film reinforces the perception that Scandinavian girls are easy to get under the sheets. I think we have films in Denmark that could make a better impression."

The festival still succeeded in giving the film a big push and a couple of weeks later Constantin could report with satisfaction that both *Weekend* and another Danish movie, *Street Without End*, had been sold to America. The American distributor had paid a lot for *Weekend*, twice as much as any other Danish film had ever received from a Stateside buyer, and now it was being prepped to open on the art-house circuit there. By the end of the year it had also been sold to Norway, Sweden, Finland, Holland, Germany, Austria, Israel, Canada, Australia and New Zealand, with others standing in line, and *Street Without End* had been picked up in just about as many territories.

Pundits proclaimed another golden age of Danish cinema to be officially underway. Now it was not just Swedish films that would be seen and debated by an international public. As *B.T.* triumphantly summed up in a December 27 end-of-the-year report, "The times are past when one adhered to the wisdom that only a Danish public could possibly be interested in a Danish film."

On April 22, 1964, *Weekend* began its U.S. run in New York, opening at both the Trans Lux and the Globe Theater, which had been modernized for the occasion. It got the full treatment: viewers were required to don formal attire, and those involved with the film were introduced beforehand in front of the stage, just like at a festival. A select group of Danish-Americans attended the Trans Lux premiere and afterwards were ferried over to the Rockefeller Center's Rainbow Room for a late dinner. Most agreed that the film hardly conveyed a favorable picture of Denmark but that to do so was not the intention.

To help launch the film the American promoters had chosen to bring Lotte Tarp over to New York. Even though Birthe, her character in the film, hardly uttered a single line it was reasoned that the well-endowed blonde conformed more to American perceptions of a Scandinavian sex kitten than the brunettes Birgit Brüel and Bente Dessau, as attractive as they undeniably were. (According to one enthusiastic American film mogul the untrained Dessau could have been an international star if she'd come out in the right picture. She did three more films in Sweden between 1965 and 1968 before returning to Denmark to resume her career as a psychiatric nurse — a profession she could have put to good use in *Weekend*.) For two weeks Tarp was wined, dined and photographed, mingling with the likes of Richard Burton and Elizabeth Taylor as the Danish press wired back stories of her whirl through the Big Apple.

When considered purely as a sex film, *Weekend* was found badly wanting, but it was by this measure that much of the American press now judged it, including *Newsweek*: "Danish wife-swapping is a subject of interesting possibilities, but somehow none of the seven participants in *Weekend* seems to have a very good time, which is a shame.... This unhappy over-sextet fumbles its way through an orgy so dismal as to be boring, which is the lowest common denominator of art movies. *Weekend* was named the best Danish film of last year — as sorry an indictment of Danish cinema as one could imagine."

Wanda Hale of *The Daily News* found it a tawdry depiction of Danish middle-class morality that included "small orgies, big orgies and medium-sized orgies." Scandinavians could give sex a bad name if they kept this up, added *The World Telegram*. For many

Americans the film was guilty of the worst crime: not making sex dirty, but making it boring.

Esteemed New York critics Bosley Crowther and Judith Crist piled on with outright dismissals. *Time* (May 1) offered criticism a shade more thoughtful: "The camera records what the characters do but offers few insights into the individuals or the society that produced them." Lonely praise was voiced by *The New York Post*, which called it a thoughtful and revealing portrait of love, passion and Scandinavian weekend morality. "The filmmakers," noted the paper, "have not been satisfied just to create sensation but have alluded to an emotional depth behind the people's behavior and implied criticism without turning it into a sermon."

But sex was still the big issue for most reviewers, many of whom seemed to have psyched themselves into seeing things that weren't there. (What orgies?) It almost qualified as a case of mass hypnosis. SEX-SMORGASBORD! screamed the headline of the *Los Angeles Times* review on occasion of the film's May 7 opening in that key city. Publicity out west had billed the picture as one that had been prohibited and condemned but could not be ignored. True enough, but unavoidably that conjured up the allure of forbidden sexuality, which made for unrealistic expectations.

The Danish tabloid *E.B.* had its Hollywood correspondent Sven Rye on the street after the show to canvass reaction. He had trouble finding anyone who had a good word to say about it but managed to turn up more appalled Danish expats. "If that's the Denmark of today," moaned one such elderly woman, a Los Angeles resident for 35 years, "then I'm in no hurry to go home for a visit. I've dreamed about taking a trip back to 'the old country,' but after seeing this film I've completely lost the desire!" A Danish-American travel agent voiced alarm that the film could single-handedly lay waste to efforts by the Danish government to burnish the country's image. "It gives a totally erroneous picture of Denmark and Danes. Efforts have been made to explain how friendly and charming Danes are and then this film portrays them as a bunch of deadly dull, mentally disturbed and frightfully ill-bred people that normal folks wouldn't want to get anywhere near."

The film was wreaking havoc with the good impression many had of Denmark, even as far away as Argentina. There two carloads of Danes had driven 90 km from Casallares to see a Danish film and experience the Danish language. "That was a shock for all of us!" related Mr. Frode Jørgensen, one of the participants. "...Never before have we been so ashamed to be Danish!"[14]

Back in America the film won the ultimate stamp of disapproval: the condemnation of the Legion of Decency. Without missing a beat the American distributor, David Barling of Cinema-Video International, transformed the attack into more publicity for the picture, taking out an ad in the trade publication *Box Office* and challenging theater owners to play the film and let the public decide.

Weekend played in some theaters for many weeks, but from all indications this was certainly more due to the hotted-up ad campaign than good word of mouth, and eventually it tanked. The American public didn't take to having its screen sex served with a side of existentialism. Only Bergman could get away with that. They wanted things to happen — a lot of things.

In light of this a jazzed up Americanized version was later prepared and re-launched in seven U.S. cities in December of 1966. According to Wray Davis of Capital Pictures, it would soon have a Hollywood re-premiere and after that a wider roll-out in 17 prints. New scenes had been shot with American actors as stand-ins, pictured from behind or at a distance, and the dialogue was dubbed in American English. Some scenes were shuffled around and a new ending was shot, but according to Davis the action and the basic tone remained intact.[15] There is no indication of how this version fared.

Crazy Paradise

Weekend was a declaration of war against the folk-comedy which still ruled at the Danish box office. Exhibit A: *Crazy Paradise*, the third key Danish film of 1962.

This satirical yarn was set on a mythical island that decides to declare its independence from Denmark. The island's economy is based on the locally produced eggs that restore potency, a sub-plot that gave occasion for all sorts of erotic foolery. At the helm was one Gabriel Axel, a debonair fellow who cut a dashing figure and would go on to direct some of the more important films in the erotic genre.

He was half French so he must have known something about love, right? He had spent much of his childhood in France, later returning to Denmark to attend the Royal Danish Theater School of Acting during the war years. As an actor he would submit a number of memorable performances. He played an hysterical film director in the 1954 picture *Jan Goes to the Movies* and was thoroughly convincingly as a creepy Gestapo collaborator in *There Comes a Day* from 1955. That same year he directed his first film, *Always Trouble*, a gritty portrait of the daily travails of a working-class family from Copenhagen's tough Nørrebro neighborhood. Although it was a comedy he neither sentimentalized nor moralized about the lot of these folks, and in this way he broke from the standard formulas that dominated Danish postwar cinema. Inspired by the unpolished style of neo-realism and particularly the works of Vittorio de Sica, Axel sought to recreate the authentic atmosphere of the neighborhood and the family's cramped, squalid flat which was frequently rocked by the passing of an elevated train. The film was considered an accurate depiction of working class conditions and critics praised Axel's feel for the milieu. He knew how to direct.

But *Crazy Paradise* was a very different kind of a film and reviewers were not enthused. They called the political sub-plot unwieldy and misplaced. Still, audiences got a kick out of the basic story and the generous supply of beautiful, accommodating and often naked gals. Starring two of the country's most popular actors, Ove Sprogøe and Dirch Passer, the film was well received at home and became a hit in other European countries, particularly Sweden and Germany.

It was no debate film, no scandal film. It did not impress the critical establishment and no one considered it a part of this so-called New Wave, and yet because of the nudity and the relaxed way it was woven into an often serious story it had managed something new. It underscored a difference between America, where nudity was considered criminal or shameful, and Denmark or Sweden, where nudity could figure in a commercial feature film without the entire population having to take a stand on it.[16]

The casting of two stars of the stature of Sprogøe and Passer in such a film also said something about the nature of the Danish film industry. In America this would have been something akin to Jack Lemon and Walter Matthau appearing in a soft-core porn film,

Paul Hagen bravely confronts a nude Ghita Nørby in *Crazy Paradise*.

albeit a well-produced one, in 1962. It would have been inconceivable and their agents simply wouldn't have permitted it. In Denmark actors have always had much more freedom. (The fact that Lars von Trier got so many top Danish actors to star in his oddball ghost story *The Kingdom* in 1994 shows that that freedom continues.) But it was also out of necessity that actors now began to accept unconventional roles and to appear in non-performing parts (not engaging in actual sex) in erotic films. In a small film milieu like Denmark few could afford to be too choosy, and as we will see many so-called legitimate actors, directors and crew would participate in some fashion in sex films when they were the happening thing and then go on to something else later.

By contrast the situation was very different in America's highly niche-driven film industry where throughout most of the '60s movies with any overt erotic content or nudity were stigmatized and banished to the "exploitation" circuit. This consisted mainly of tacky urban grind-house cinemas and drive-in theaters, the latter playing a major role in specialty exhibition in America, particularly in the '50s when they nourished the emergence of a number of B-movie sub-genres and gave people like Roger Corman a chance to establish themselves.

The American film industry was based on a strictly enforced class system, so to speak, in which everyone knew their place. Danish cinema was much more fluid and at this point in the early '60s there was very little segmentation in production and exhibition. Films were not forced to be so niche-specific. Theaters had their own profiles, of course, but generally speaking low-budget movies opened in the same venues as the prestigious first-run productions, and mainstream films could also incorporate exploitation elements of sex and nudity. Danish directors did not face the same class prejudice as their American and British counterparts, even if the Danish critics themselves were often insufferably class-conscious. In any case this unusually flexible system gave birth to some interesting hybrids.

Crazy Paradise was just such a hybrid and initiated the folk/*sex*-comedy genre. That it was not in any way a "porn film" would have been impossible to explain to the Americans who could never abide the revolutionary assumption being advanced by the Danes that sex and pornography weren't necessarily synonymous. (The terms hard-core and soft-core porno were American inventions and implied that *any* degree of nakedness constituted pornography.) Yet while this film was as innocent as could be, it would lead to harder stuff, serving as the precursor to a genre that Danish film historian Carl Nørrested would later dub "family porno."

A scant three years before, in 1959, Russ Meyer had released *The Immoral Mr. Teas* in America. That film contained nudity as harmless and chaste as nudity could be, and yet Meyer had to fight tooth and claw to get it played on the fringe art-house circuit — and pay vast amounts of his own money to defend himself against lawsuits from all possible directions.

Now over in Denmark it was soft-core fun for the whole family.

The Silence

Fun was not the word one would use to describe Ingmar Bergman's 1963 film *The Silence*.

"Almost like death," as a *New York Times* reviewer put it, was perhaps more to the point. Judith Crist called it "a symphony of despair." This atmospheric tale of two feuding sisters, Anna and Ester, who have embarked on a mystical journey together was Bergman at his bleakest.

It begins in a train traveling through some unidentified European country that is seemingly on the brink of war. Anna's son, Johan, is also along and much of the subsequent action is seen through his point of view. Ester is ill, and as her condition worsens they are obliged to disembark and seek lodging in an old hotel. She stays ensconced in her room while Anna takes a walk. It's a strange city they've ended up in, with the inhabitants speaking some kind of incomprehensible gibberish. She visits a tavern, then a theater where a troupe of dwarves is giving a bizarre performance. She turns her head away only to spot a couple making love further down the row of seats and is shocked — and sexually aroused. She hurries outside to find herself on crowded streets populated only by men. She returns to the tavern to catch the attention of the waiter who had previously flirted with her, and they soon become lovers.

Back at the hotel Ester sips a bit of brandy, smokes, reads and does some translating work, which is her profession. At loose ends, she lies back on her bed and masturbates.

Anna returns and hurriedly takes a bath. Ester is suspicious and examines her clothes for traces of sexual activity. Things get tense. Anna resents her paternalistic manner and goads her by describing her tryst with the waiter which she claims took place in a church.

Anna then leaves, only to encounter the same waiter in the hallway. They hurry to the nearest empty room to make love, and yet this encounter seems to leave Anna disenchanted and unfulfilled. The fact that they speak different languages and can't understand each other seems rather a blessing.

Anna realizes Ester is spying on her through the door and she initiates a new bout of sex with her silent partner to spite her. Ester comes into the room. Anna accuses her of hollowness and hypocrisy, of preaching that life must have meaning while spending her time in empty pursuits, of talking about love but radiating only hate ... and yet Anna is clearly the more troubled of the two, and her unresolved feelings and resentments are destroying her. Ester departs.

Anna weeps, kneeling on the mattress, gripping the bed's iron posts like prison bars while the waiter slowly takes her from behind in a sexual act that seems coldly mechanical. She is the latest version of the liberated woman but her sexual freedom brings her no joy.

The next day Anna and Johan depart, leaving Ester in the hotel room in the care of the elderly porter who has been assisting her. Pain-wracked and despairing, she dies after a last spasm of loneliness and regret and some extremely coarse X-rated dialogue. This is anything but a peaceful and dignified passing.

Young Johan (Jörgen Lindström — center/right facing away from camera) finds sanctuary in a hotel room occupied by dwarves in *The Silence*.

Anna has long yearned to be free of her sister's meddling but this brings her no satisfaction. In the closing scene on the train she opens the window to allow the drops of rain to moisten her face, as if to cleanse her, but her expression is one of abject terror.

This was truly the feel-bad hit of the year. According to contemporary reports many of those who had shown up primarily to see some sex left theaters shocked and bewildered and too numbed to respond to the occasional moments of subtle low-key humor that Bergman had also included.

"The film has disturbed some viewers enough to impel them to walk out in the middle of screenings," reported the *New York Times'* Swedish correspondent Werner Wiskari. "Others have muttered angrily throughout much of the picture. But in general it has frozen audiences, and embarrassed smiles have been a widespread reaction as the lights went up."

In Norway censors demanded that the scene of female masturbation and two scenes of intercourse be deleted. In America the version released by Janus Films was cut by ten minutes but still managed to become the most-seen Bergman film to that point, and reinforced the perception that Scandinavians were a doom-haunted folk given to existential bouts of soul-searching.

Over in Denmark the big talk of 1963 was also a very bleak film. Bleak was "in."

Street Without End

Split opinions aside, *Weekend* had shaken the ground under Danish cinema. It had shown average Danes that moviegoing could be an interactive mental pursuit and not just an act of passive consumption, that everyone could join the debate — that there *was* a debate. It had importance far beyond mere box office numbers, and the new thinking that it engendered made possible the next big sensation, 1963's *Street Without End*, a grim depiction of big city prostitution.

At the time of its filming, clichés abounded in films about the world's oldest profession. *The Christine Keeler Story* was then in production in Copenhagen, albeit with foreign money and mostly foreign personnel. It was based on the scandal that had just brought down the British Defense Minister, Dennis Profumo, after his affair with the young prostitute Christine Keeler had been revealed. But the last thing director Robert Spafford wanted to do was portray prostitution in realistic terms.

In 1962 Danish viewers had had the opportunity to see yet another film on the subject, *Rikki and the Men*. Here a gay divorcee tries her hand as a high-class call-girl in order to spite her two boyfriends who've refused to help her out of a financial bind. The film is conventional in the extreme. Prostitution is used as little more than a titillating plot device, and Rikki comes to regret her choices and in the end is saved by a noble male protector waiting in the wings. And yet the character of Rikki is interesting because she is meant to represent a sexually liberated woman who rejects the old morality — the first of her kind to appear in a Danish movie. Yet the film makes no attempt to understand the dynamics behind this new way of thinking and in every other way is thoroughly old-fashioned.

Street Without End would be a scalding rebuttal to such nonsense. It was directed by the 28-year-old Mogens Vemmer, who, since earning a teaching degree in 1956, had been employed by DR-TV, Denmark's public broadcasting channel (and until 1986 the country's only TV station). There he had been grinding out documentary news featurettes for the highly regarded *Focus* program. But it was grunt work; of the 380 half-hour shows he had made in seven years, he only really liked about ten of them.

One of the programs that left a lasting impression on him was *Letters from Copenhagen*, where he interviewed young people from the provinces who were struggling to make it in the big city. That opened his eyes to the harsh realities some girls faced, and he decided to make a film about prostitution. The film medium would allow him to explore the subject in more depth, and he was in any case eager to take a break from the factory-like pace of television production.

Together with Kirsten, his young wife of 19, he plunged into the project. An unnamed associate who worked with the down-and-out, and who would himself play a part in the film, introduced Vemmer to a number of prostitutes. Over countless coffees Vemmer and his associate gained their confidence and explained that they wanted to make a movie based on their real life experiences. Through doubting anyone would be interested, the girls agreed to talk.

Vemmer started taping these conversations and they formed the basis for the film's various situations. They ended up with 25 hours of tape from six or seven different women. From that they chose three main characters to focus on. One was Sunny, a young prostitute from the seedy Vesterbro neighborhood. She becomes a kind of main character whose story weaves throughout the film. Then there was Lene, a victim of abuse from a broken home. She works for a classier clientele she meets at private parties in the well-heeled suburbs. Finally the viewer becomes acquainted with Dorthe. She is what is known as an "American girl," a term applied to Danish women who had a thing for American GIs who came up from their bases in Germany. With every American guy she meets, she deludes herself into believing he will marry her and take her back to the States. She is not yet a prostitute per sé but is not far away from becoming one.

Although they were usually on the set giving advice, none of the girls, except Sunny, who played herself, appeared in the film. Vemmer instead largely cast the picture with non-actors who resembled the girls or who were also from the streets and were credible in their roles. He did not feel himself capable of directing professional actors and in any case that would have ruined the whole vibe of the film. So instead he aimed for a kind of improvisational role-play based on the transcripts and lots of discussion. Without a shooting script or any written dialogue, the whole thing hinged on the participants' simply immersing themselves in their roles. The language was coarse and full of slang and vulgarities. There were no tests, no rehearsals.

They used a small three-man shooting crew: Vemmer and a sound-man and a lightman he had worked together with on TV productions. Armed with the latest lightweight sound-sync gear, they filmed over 20 days and nights in February. The sound and picture were recorded at the same time and nothing was laid on post-sync except the jazz score. That was composed by a musician before a single frame of film had been shot. He just listened to the tapes and riffed on the mood.

No soundstages or sets were used. Everything was shot on location: on the mean streets of Vesterbro, on notorious Istedgade, in the prostitutes' flats, in dive bars and cafes, in the seedy courtyards and cul-de-sacs and down dark side-streets. Light-sensitive film stock allowed them to shoot with available light in many situations. It resulted in a visual style that captured the feel of Vesterbro's rain-slick, neon-lit landscape to perfection.

Shooting in the authentic locales wasn't easy. Some of the restaurant scenes had to be filmed with hidden microphones and cameras. "That can of course be infuriating," noted Vemmer, "when people who had no idea they were going to be in a movie suddenly see themselves up on the screen, but those scenes could not be filmed in any other way and they were absolutely necessary. When shooting took place in indoor locales with the establishment's local clientele on the premises it often had to happen quickly since it was not infrequent that someone would get angry when we refused to buy more rounds or otherwise grease palms."[17]

During the filming, Godard's *My Life to Live* opened in Copenhagen. It was also a story about a prostitute told in documentary fashion, but was infused with the Frenchman's trademark artistry and was as different from *Street Without End* as could be. Vemmer purposely avoided it. After shooting wrapped he sat down with his editor and worked the 9.5 hours of rough footage down to a finished film of 86 minutes in time for the June 24 premiere. A film edited and released in a mere four months!

It came as a shock to critics and public alike. Here was a movie about prostitution shorn of the usual clichés, a movie that didn't glamorize or titillate or condemn or moralize, that didn't have a happy or hopeful ending. It drew no conclusions and offered no answers, and that threw some for a loop. Others appreciated this withering blast of reality.

Critical reaction was unanimously positive although no one was willing to predict how such an unorthodox film would do with the public. Would they want to see it? It almost didn't matter.

Street Without End was submitted as proof that a new wave was gathering strength in Danish cinema. Last year there was *Weekend*, and also Henning Carlsen's *A World of Strangers*, a film about racial divisiveness. It had been shot in South Africa — secretly, due to the fact it was based on a Nadine Gordimer novel that had recently been banned there. And now *Street Without End*.

"Something is happening in Danish film," declared Herbert Steinthal in *Politiken*. "New forces are stirring. While the big established film companies blindly produce folk-comedies, harmless farces and idyllic family films — and when they get really daring a 'Rikki romance' on prostitution in an artificial silent-movie style — the young filmmakers deal seriously with racial questions, the need for contact and the erotic difficulties of adults."

It appeared that going to the movies to think and feel and be confronted by something was coming back in style. There was a new spirit of social consciousness abroad and it was even reflected in some of the critical feedback. "To live life without hope on the street without end," wrote a scribe for *Aktuelt* on August 6, "seems to be the fate of these girls. Now that life is captured on film stock. Whether one likes it or not doesn't really matter. That's also a part of life and neither you nor I can deny that we both bear a responsibility for the fact that it has come to this, that we have a responsibility for every single little fate on this dismal 'street without end.'"

The acting, or rather the non-acting, was also a revelation for many. Ib Monty, an influential critic who would become director of the national film museum, saw *Street Without End* as further indication that Denmark's second golden age was underway. "This film makes it clear how necessary it is to remove Danish actors from films for a moment. In the long run, of course, we cannot do without them, but it would certainly be revi-

Sunny Nielsen in a scene from *Street Without End*.

talizing for Danish cinema if for a while we could dispense with professional actors who would have, for example, ruined this movie.... A film like this can force Danish actors to better comprehend how to present people. And it is people that the modern Danish film deals with."[18]

In its mixture of direct interview-style reportage and casual "arranged" realism, with its hard edits, its cross-cut narrative form and the use of so many close-ups, *Street Without End* seemed more a creature of TV than film. That didn't sit well with some who felt this style was unsuited for use in a feature film and failed to hold interest, but on the other hand it was being judged as sociology, not art or entertainment. In any case Vemmer had brought something essential over from the medium of television: he had shown that TV had a role to play in energizing cinema. Young TV directors had been doing that for years in other countries, but now eyes were being opened in Denmark. And it was not the dark, intriguing corners of Paris or London or New York that were being probed, but Copenhagen, right there in provincial little Denmark.

Predictably, *Street Without End* was being likened to cinéma vérité — though Vemmer denied he even knew what that meant, claiming that he'd been too busy with TV work in recent years to go to the movies. Another critic thought its impressionistic style was more akin to Cassavetes' *Shadows*.

The public did show up, and a film that was not primarily made to turn a profit or further careers became a certified hit. True, for some viewers, it was too much. Vemmer recalled that after one screening in Copenhagen a viewer came out onto the street and vomited, and that in Svendborg people streamed out of the theater in the middle of the show, furious. Elsewhere, however, it played to packed houses night after night and won the Bodil for best Danish film of 1963.

By the time it was ready to travel it had the aura of controversy about it. "Danish Shock-Film Comes to Sweden" blared a headline in a Swedish paper — this from the country that had just given the world *The Silence*. The film was sold to numerous foreign territories and along with *Weekend* it represented the modern breakthrough of Danish cinema to an international public. These two films were serious, important and weighty and were well received on the festival circuit, even if other Danish films were more popular with the home audience.

Vemmer had no plans to make another movie. "You can only make a film like this once, and I only made it because I was so extremely interested in the topic. It has to be like that every time. And I like to involve myself with subjects that everybody assumes they already thoroughly know but that turn out to be completely different than they thought, and to present them differently from the way they are usually served up. People assumed they already knew everything about prostitution and that irritated me."[19]

While the prostitutes whose stories he drew upon eventually disappeared back into the anonymity of the streets, they continued to visit him at home for some period of time after the film came out and to sit around and confide their problems to Kirsten. Though much younger than most of them, she had come to represent the kind of life to which they claimed to aspire, a life which most likely would remain forever beyond their reach.

The year 1963 ended with a scandal that rocked Denmark. It had nothing directly to do with movies but everything to do with the new spirit of sexual openness.

Tall, waifish, classically blonde and with large somber eyes capable of fixing opponents with a dead serious stare, 21-year-old Ulla Dahlerup had grown up in a home steeped in free-minded Grundtvigianism.[20] An attractive young lady, she could have chosen to scandalize the public in some provocative erotic film but instead she picked a much more disturbing way to confront her fellow countrymen. The pen was her weapon of choice and she unsheathed it in a youth magazine called *Eksponent* which students could purchase for a single crown. There in the December issue she proposed that school doctors instruct students about birth control and supply girls with diaphragms if they so desired and were unable to go to their parents for advice and support.

She was talking about girls 14 to 15 years of age, telling Danes what they didn't want to know, that sex was happening anyway. The message was upsetting, but the messenger, a liberated young woman speaking her mind even on sexual matters, was still more disturbing to some. School doctors were against the proposal, and wise men from every walk of the professional world came up with reasons why it wasn't a good idea. A few sided with Dahlerup, but in any case they were all oldies and this was about youth.

The issue exploded in the media and soon debate was raging over the looming specter of adolescent teenage girls demanding the right to sex. Dahlerup was the first true media celebrity of Liberated Denmark and was soon touring packed auditoriums to present her case. She came armed with statistics: 17,000 illegal abortions performed annually in Denmark, 25 percent of all girls between 15 and 19 unmarried mothers, and so on.

Thirty youth organizations backed her, signing on to a resolution that demanded sex-education be made obligatory in schools and that access to birth control be provided without cost. But she was opposed by many. Pastor Asger Højlund collected 87,121 signatures demanding that instruction about birth control in schools be prohibited, and he delivered the petition to the culture minister. Nicknamed "Pessar-Ulla" (Diaphragm-Ulla) by detractors, the woman who had started the fuss found herself the target of ridicule and taunts: "Did you remember to put yours in today?" people shouted after her.

Youth in Denmark had been furthered empowered, and the debate Ulla Dahlerup sparked that December made a hush-hush subject suddenly audible. Yet the subsequent backlash also illustrated how much of a gulf still lay between this new open-mindedness presented in the movies and the norms to which average Danes still subscribed. Liberated Denmark was still a tenuous concept.

Nymphomania; Call-Girls; "Heroes"

> *"That was a horrible movie — we have no need for that kind of thing in my country."*
> —Jevsej Avrusin, a young Russian taking part in a Communist youth convention in Copenhagen in 1964, after seeing *Copenhagen Call-Girls.*

Street Without End proved to be an anomaly and the next year it was back to the same old clichés about prostitution with *Copenhagen Call-Girls,* a film that used the theme simply as an excuse to show nudity in all possible situations.

This was the brainchild of 30-year-old Poul Nyrup. A jack of all trades, he had knocked about at various jobs before becoming a sound technician and signing on at Saga Studios where he worked on numerous productions, including *Reptilicus.*[21] He later also worked as a technician for Radio Mercur, a pirate station based on a ship cruising in international waters. Since 1958 it had been the Trojan horse bringing rock 'n' roll music into Danish homes. It was at Radio Mercur that Nyrup hatched plans to become a filmmaker and found his actors, giving most of the parts to his fellow shipmates — who in 1963 suddenly found themselves unemployed after the boat was beached by the authorities. Now Nyrup and his little cast had plenty of time to make movies. It was also a great way to launch pop careers and meet women, which might have been the main idea from the start. They published casting calls, and hundreds of would-be starlets from the provinces showed up to strip down. It was a mob scene.

Nyrup's first movie, made that same year, was called *Mellem Venner,* which literally translates into "Between Friends." For the export market a far more daring title had been chosen: *Days of Sin and Nights of Nymphomania,* a tag that his amateur cast of would-be pop singers, aspiring actresses and pals from the radio station had a hard time living up to.

That film figured as the first installment of what was to be a hard-boiled gangster trilogy. The plot centered on Kim, a convicted rapist who has just been released from prison only to fall back in with his old gang and begin plotting new crimes. In its own tawdry way the film was an attempt to blow life back into the myth of the sexy Scandinavian female, which thus far had been mostly a Swedish invention, and to make a no-holds-barred exploitation film in the style of recent American movies.

Preben Nicolaisen (in back) looks on as Eric Chris enjoys some female companionship.

Unable to deliver craft, Nyrup went for the throat. "Nobody can say," he commented to the press, "that nothing happens in my movie; there are tons of parties, break-ins, kidnappings, rape, striptease, people getting run down by cars, police raids...." The possibility that the film might be banned in Denmark didn't unduly concern him as he reckoned he could sell the picture abroad. Accordingly he had a "soft version" prepared for Scandinavian countries, including his own, and a harder version that his foreign distributor David Goldstein would schlep in Southern Europe and in South America where they had hopes of making a big score. In America (where it was distributed by Radley Metzger, about whom more will shortly be said), it bombed. In Denmark it was wildly hyped as "the most powerful Danish film yet," "a behind-the-scenes look at orgies, girls, nightlife and criminality."

The women in all these films were compliant fantasy figures who would strip (semi)naked and offer sex to any man in any situation. This was a sailor's paradise, no doubt the product of all those lonely nights out at sea on the radio ship. But all that sweet dreaming aside, what *Days of Sin* actually delivered — leering, lushing and party gals in pantyhose doing the twist while curiously impassive drunks look on — was somewhat less spectacular and no doubt left audiences feeling short-changed. In 1963, though, even the barest insinuation of an orgy was pretty potent stuff and Denmark had never seen the like of this film before. And while it was pure crime-doesn't-pay formula, its grade-Z production values did give it a certain rawness and immediacy that was notable, and the dialogue was extremely coarse. Predictably trashed by Danish critics, it nonetheless drew

Karen Birgit Petersen (reclining) and Karine Smidt in a scene from *Copenhagen Call-Girls*.

well and was a successful export item, reportedly grossing cost several times over. This was no doubt thanks to the steady parade of gals in sexy underwear (which they shed only in brief glimpses).

Smarting from the bad press *Days of Sin* attracted, Nyrup vowed that his 1964 follow-up, *Copenhagen Call-Girls*, would be that much better. (He apparently had a sense of irony, though, and when a character in *Copenhagen Call-Girls* stumbles upon an add in the paper for *Days of Sin* he remarks that such a movie couldn't possibly be worth a crap.) This one was set in a secluded bordello run by a colorful little gang of toughs. They lure in horny men off the street with promises of wild parties full of hot gals, the whole set-up reportedly inspired by a story Nyrup had read in the press.

The film's villain is a shady pusher who sells one of the girls dope. She can't cope with the hectic night-life and collapses in the middle of a party. Carted off to the hospital, she's examined by a doctor who is himself a regular guest at the bordello. He refuses to become implicated in a narcotics investigation and calls the cops. They raid the place. Slut! (End.) Thus the real evil in the story is drugs, not prostitution which is treated in a more positive light. Very positive, in fact. At one point brutal bordello boss Erik Chris gives an impassioned defense for the legalization of pornography, apparently so that there will be more of it, and, if logic follows, more naked women.

Copenhagen Call-Girls was also fiercely low-budget, filmed in producer Leif Jedig's villa and cast mostly with the same non-actors Nyrup had used in the previous picture,

The less than glamorous occupation of getting naked in *Days of Sin...* (actress unidentified).

many with a yen for exhibitionism and some with an apparent need for pseudonyms. The female lead, for example, was Elinor Infred — real name, Inga Frederiksen. A former beauty queen from the provincial village of Nakskov, she'd moved to Copenhagen and landed some bit parts on TV shows like *The Problem Girl*, and had been a stand-in for Yvonne Buckingham who played the lead in the aforementioned *The Christine Keeler Story* which was shot locally.

In what little press the film got, reviewers slaughtered it. Nyrup was "totally helpless and almost touchingly ignorant" as a director, the film was "rickety, careless and chaotically assembled"—in short a "badly made, scruffy film." Almost worse than its technical shortcomings was the feeling among many that it was simply sleazy. And it was—with a vengeance. While critics were busy accusing an art film like *Weekend* of pandering just because it showed a glimpse or two of bare breast, here was full-bore pandering without apologies.

Censors blocked its release in Sweden even though Nyrup had supplied Corona, the Swedish distributor, with the soft version. Authorities there were more concerned with the presence of narcotics in the plot and the implicitly pro-prostitution stance than the nudity, but couldn't be bothered to nit-pick about a film they deemed utterly substandard. Corona objected in a written statement, conceding that the film was no masterpiece but maintaining that it had value as a semi-documentary exposé of everyday life and the moral attitudes at play.

Sven Norlin, a member of the Swedish censor board, thought otherwise: "The film is frightfully badly made and has numerous episodes that hinge on boozing, narcotics and such like. All considered it's a completely unsavory film. There isn't a hint of artistic ambition to be found." As for its claim of being a semi-documentary exposé, there was something to that. All three of the films Nyrup would make did possess a kind of documentary quality, largely due to their amateur production values, the use of non-actors and lots of location shooting.

Sweden, like Denmark, was liberated but couldn't help gagging on this one. They could tolerate controversial movie themes if the movies were "art" and (preferably) made by a master director like Ingmar Bergman or Jan Troell, but in general Sweden was more of a control-oriented society where things had to be kept to a certain standard. That mentality carried over to film censorship, and a certain class prejudice was brought to bear on movies Swedes considered worthless—movies like *Copenhagen Call-Girls*. Danes, on the other hand, chafed a bit more at the notion that standards of decency should be set and enforced by the authorities. This smacked of paternalism. A number of Danish films would be banned in Sweden, but the reverse almost never occurred (although films from other countries did on rare occasion get slapped with a total ban in Denmark, among them Jean Genet's *Un Chant d'Amour*, Roger Corman's *Wild Angels* and Russ Meyer's *Lorna*). Most if not all films were releasable in Denmark. The Danish critics could howl but increasingly movies were pretty much free to stand or fall on their own. In that sense the Danes were more like the "merchants of Europe," the Dutch, in that they believed there should be freedom to conduct business. (Copenhagen does after all mean Merchant's Harbor.)

Even after it faded from screens, *Copenhagen Call-Girls* continued to harvest publicity. Nyrup was shameless about product placement and had taken money from a sewing-machine company in return for promises that their factory would be pictured in the film. When said pictures didn't materialize the company sued. Updates on the lawsuit kept the film in the public eye much longer than it deserved, in the estimation of many, and gave scribes occasion to jibe that the gals in the movie hardly seemed like the type to stay home and sew.

Critics had sentenced the film to the lowest rung of hell, but a funny thing happened on the way; it came back. It experienced a revival of sorts, on video, embraced approximately thirty years later by American B-movie aficionados. Reviewers at the time

Sylvia (Karen Birgit Petersen) with customer (Finn Andersen) in *Copenhagen Call-Girls*. The characters existed but not the scene.

had been unable to appreciate Nyrup's films for what they were, pure-blown exploitation, a genre better understood, if not necessarily more respected, in America. The titles, the exaggerated ad campaigns, the daring stills of scenes that existed nowhere in the film, the treatment, tone and subject matter — all of it exploitation in a nutshell. (Trace elements of exploitation can be found in earlier Danish films but only in superficial form. The 1951 picture *Young Girls Disappear in Copenhagen*, for example, was certainly hyped with an exploitation style ad campaign but was really just a tepid melodrama. Nyrup's films, on the other hand, went for the jugular.) Reviewers also failed to appreciate all the great pop music in the film, supplied by the likes of the Weedons and Otto Brandenburg, the latter a mechanic's apprentice who went on to become the Danish Elvis/Sinatra/Tommy Steele all rolled into one.

Most prominent, though, were the Sharks, a power-pop band that had chosen that name after seeing *West Side Story*. Fronted by a new gal sensation called Anette, they perform with great energy at the debauched parties in the film where grotty geezers glom the gals. After scoring a breakthrough hit in 1960 with "Shakin' the Battle Hymn" they went on to set the Copenhagen club scene ablaze. They also appeared in the short music film *Hit House*, which featured several of the bands that were regulars at the club of same name. Søren Strømberg, the group's leader who handled vocals and bass, would also go on to become a porn star, so to speak, and one of liberated Denmark's most star-crossed personalities. This was his screen debut.

Copenhagen Call-Girls ended up receiving the blessings of Denmark's cult movie connoisseur Jakob Stegelmann when he praised the film in his column in 1999. "Upon its release *Copenhagen Call-Girls* was judged rude and primitive by an oblivious group of (Danish) critics. Today we can see how this masterpiece shines. The raw dialogue, the vile over-indulging 'johns,' the beautiful Copenhagen streets and the bars of Nyhavn. Americans have long embraced the film as one of the best examples of the genre. When will we in Denmark give it the acclaim it deserves?" (In April of 2005, actually, when Copenhagen's Night Film Festival staged a Poul Nyrup tribute.)

The final installment of Nyrup's gangster trilogy, and his last film altogether, was *City Street "Heroes"* from 1965. This was more of a classic juvenile delinquent picture than a boozy gangster film, and was no doubt influenced by the Raggar films from Sweden.

Here the sadistic Devil John leads his gang on a spree of break-ins and robberies. Back at the hang-out they drink booze, sleep in the same bed and for kicks force an old goof of a neighbor to get drunk and dance with their chicks. Ever thirsting after a bigger score, Devil John hits upon the scheme of making porno films. They steal equipment and force their molls to participate, resulting in some amount of ridiculously innocent semi-clad posing (this was still the early '60s, after all). The women eventually object and a couple of likely lasses are rounded up off the street and brought back to fill in. The gang prepares the set while Devil John leaves with one to have sex in the bushes. When he gets back he discovers that the other woman accidentally overheard talk about a murder they had committed (they had killed an old man while shaking him down for cash, then placed his body on train tracks to make it look like suicide). He confronts her, gets violent, slugs her around — she's half naked by now — and ends up strangling her as his eyes bulge with the kind of demented glee that only a true ham actor can summon.

This ploddingly paced film is, like all of Nyrup's pictures, goosed along with slabs of low-tech instrumental garage rock and surf-pop music and scenes of juvenile delinquent excess that occasionally exude an endearing grade-Z *joie de vivre*— like the memorable episode at a club where a teen band called The Jolly Boys plays while the gang does the twist. (The Jolly Boys? Nyrup's ability to get name rock acts was clearly in decline.) That leads to a rumble with another group of hoods, one of whom pulls a knife, the glint of the blade illuminating Devil John's psychotic visage and sending him into a fit of particular nastiness. Erik Chris is again memorable here as the teen cutthroat Devil John, submitting one of the most unhinged performances in the annals of Danish B-cin-

Where are they now? The Jolly Boys perform in *City Street "Heroes."*

ema. That his gang buddies are anything but menacing only adds to the film's naive charm.

Despite laying claim to social relevance, *City Street "Heroes"* was still far too amateurish to ever be appreciated by the critics. Nyrup was Denmark's answer to renegade directors like Ray Dennis Steckler, Herschell Gordon Lewis and Ed Wood who were making the same kind of ultra low-budget films in America and trading in the same kind of willful sleaze. These directors were also being scorned and dismissed but they found refuge on the exploitation circuit, which, as noted, consisted largely of drive-in theaters. Denmark only had one real drive-in theater and there was no place to hide from the critics' rain of poisoned arrows. Worse than their arrows, though, was their silence when they chose to ignore a film altogether — which is pretty much what they did with *City Street "Heroes."* That Nyrup had cobbled together a clutch of hoary stereotypes in his final film was something they never even bothered to criticize. It was all just too much; a youth gang starts up a pornography ring but when the psychotic leader can't keep from beating and strangling one of the girls (something that also happened in *Days of Sin*), things unravel fast and the body count rises. Criminality breeds pornography, or vice-versa: this seems to be the message, if there can be any talk of a message. It's a whopping exploitation fantasy, a throwback to the most primitive stereotypes of the '50s, and what it lacks in energy and execution it makes up for with ultra-salacious intent and punk attitude. Teen youth culture is depicted as depraved, debauched and just plain evil. Rape! Murder! Plunder! Brawls! Sex! screams the trailer for a film that tried its damnedest to be every adult's worst rock 'n' roll nightmare.

Above: The glint of a switch-blade sends "Devil John" (Erik Chris) into a murderous rage in *City Street "Heroes."*

Left: Line-art for *City Street "Heroes."* Blurb in the center reads, "The most powerful Danish film about wayward youth in the big city."

    Another low-budget wonder, *The Sweet Life of Majorca*, which was written, directed and released just before *City Street "Heroes"* by Nyrup's erstwhile associate Leif Jedig, is sometimes mentioned in connection with this trilogy although it lacks Nyrup's over-the-top approach. Silver-haired, in his seventies and at the time of this writing the proprietor of a Copenhagen video shop, Jedig admits with little prompting that the film was shot in Majorca because that's where the cast and crew wanted to go.

    The two met in the early 1960s at Jedig's camera shop, Platan Foto, where he sold 8mm striptease shorts that he shot in his spare time. He did huge business, selling 1,600 films the first week alone. The proceeds from this allowed him to expand his business and undoubtedly convinced Nyrup, who frequently came by to chat, that there was gold in striptease. Fool's gold in Jedig's case, at least in regard to one risqué little number called *Bibbi Dances the Twist* that proved his undoing. It featured a young cutie who discards clothing while dusting a TV. The TV was turned on and suddenly the face of John

Danstrup, Denmark's most prominent foreign correspondent, appeared. A tabloid got their hands on the film and printed a still with the caption: "Danstrup watches striptease" — and the TV station sued him.[22]

That same year Knud Leif Thomsen was back on his soapbox with *School for Suicide*. This was an attack on various aspects of the Danish welfare state that he abhorred, a series of skits and episodes served up in a broadly satirical, almost cartoonish style. His targets were numerous this time, and though his aim was shaky he was on a mission and firing from both barrels. This guaranteed that at least a few targets would be hit.

Jørgen Ryg was center-stage, reprising his customary role as the befuddled "average" Dane who mucks about troubled and despairing. In the middle of a suicide attempt his attention is caught by a newspaper ad promoting a suicide school that will teach people how to do it right. He joins and makes the acquaintance of Doctor X who represents the quintessential welfare bureaucrat providing state-financed solutions for every problem, however absurd, allowing clients to escape responsibility for their own lives.

Thomsen heaps scorn on just about everything from governmental interference to pre-packaged mass culture to the hollowness of the church and the meaninglessness of political demonstrations. He slams modern art ("I hate the concept of modern art and even the concept of 'modernism'"), along with loveless sex ("If sexual morality crumbles, everything crumbles with it. It is clear that the disintegration of sexual morality has always heralded the disintegration of a culture").[23]

Sex is easy but love almost impossible in a scene from *School for Suicide*. The book's title: "Sex in a Hundred Different Ways."

He was particularly alarmed by the swelling tide of teen pop culture. He had already attacked the twist craze in his film *The Duel*. Now in *School for Suicide* he pictured people doing the dance cross-cut with a piano concerto. "Modern dance in its most far-out forms," he would state, "is not an expression of happiness, it's an expression of quite the opposite — an urge to sedate oneself, an urge to forget. It is an escape into unconsciousness, into soulless-ness. It is a step back toward the hole in the ground."

Exhibit A: The Beatles. A film about the group had opened for *School for Suicide*. Thomsen approved. It illustrated his point. "I think it's appalling, not what the Beatles are doing on stage but the crowd's wildly disproportionate response to it. It is as if the crowd *must* hurl themselves out into madness. What we see here is not happiness, not a moment of honest enthusiasm.... They make this their false God."[24]

The broadly satirical style of the film stood in contrast to the seriousness of his message. It was a farce but not a joke, suggested a writer. Thomsen agreed: "It's a very serious warning against fatal developments which, if allowed to continue, will make life valueless — in any case for me ... though for others it might be the ideal existence."[25]

Critics were not as enthusiastic about *School for Suicide* as they had been about *The Duel*. Great that a director had such fierce opinions, but too bad they were *those* opinions.

Where did all these antagonisms come from? Born and raised in the middle-class Copenhagen suburb of Ballerup, Thomsen always took pains to point out he wasn't from the city, city life being some kind of perverted existence in his opinion. But this was hardly the kind of background that would nourish the rabid conservatism that critics saw in his films. He was no gnarled fisherman, no farmer from a lonely windswept village in west Jutland, not one of those types who normally considered Copenhagen the realm of evil. Nor did he even consider himself conservative. From his scattered comments it seems that what he most objected to about Liberated Denmark was the almost fascistic way that its advocates demanded everyone else agree with them and embrace these new values.

But what were these values all about in a purely sexual sense? Were these new freedoms bringing any joy to people's lives? The evidence one could glean in theaters painted a mixed picture.

As generally depicted in lighter fare, Scandinavians, or at least Scandinavian women, seemed to be a happy-go-lucky bunch. The 1958 Swiss study of nudism in Europe, *Lust for the Sun*, which opened in New York in 1961, prominently features two uninhibited Swedish gals, Anna and Ingrid, who go for a nude romp on the German island of Sylt with two fellows who have given them a lift. In this same film, apparently re-edited and re-released in 1963 as *Around the World with Nothing On*, we meet the radiant Gretchen Bjorling, the Danish nudist beauty queen who holds court at Camp Solbakken (Sun Hill), the country's nudist center. In foreign made exploitation films like this Scandinavian girls were presented as innocent, gentle, sensuous and fun loving.

On the other hand sexuality in Bergman's films and in the work of other Swedish directors was often depicted as a dark force. These films were, for the most part, deeply serious affairs with tragic endings that confirmed the stereotype of Scandinavians as a dour and angst-ridden people. If Hollywood was addicted to happy endings, Swedes seemed to abhor them.

As Danish authors Ove Brusendorff and Poul Malmkjær wrote in 1965 in their groundbreaking study *Erotik I filmen: Den nøgne bølge (Erotica in Film: The Naked Wave)*[26]:

What Scandinavian cinema lacks is an alternative to Bergman's portrayal of sexuality, an alternative to a (purely) intellectual understanding of erotic physics, this guilt-ridden and repressed sexuality rendered in dark shades. We need more films that present sex as a jubilation, as fun, liberating, inspiring and healthy, films that send the message that sex is not a burden but can be a value in and of itself, that sex without eternal love and faithfulness can be a nice way to pass the time.

Others agreed; the (Finnish-born) Swedish director Jörn Donner had addressed this issue after the release of his 1963 film, *A Sunday in September*, a tragedy about love lost. He was tired, he declared, of this tendency in Scandinavian cinema to convey only the failings of eroticism. His next movie, *To Love*, from 1964 was an attempt to show the positive side of sex. Here a woman loses her husband in a car accident but goes on to find love in the arms of a younger man with whom she experiences an ideal erotic relationship. Their physical enthusiasm for each other is obvious and sex is depicted as life-affirming and fun. For the first time in her life the woman feels confidence and value as an erotic being, and this helps to keep the couple grounded when the mundane realities of life once again intrude.

Lars-Magnus Lindgren's *Dear John*, also released in 1964, was a similar attempt to portray the positive if not entirely painless side of sexuality. In this follow-up to *Love Mates* Lindgren again cast Christina Schollin, who this time played a young divorcee toiling in a harbor town cafe. There she meets a sailor called John, and they spend the rest of that weekend together in her beach house that she shares with her four-year-old daughter, enjoying each other and eventually falling in love. Their short time together is filled with laughter and tenderness and the mundane joys of everyday life. With casual references to things like contraception and penis size, the dialogue had a frankness unheard of at the time.

Yet John must return to his ship and they part without knowing when or if they will meet again. Brief, halting exchanges on the phone represent the end (or the beginning) of their relationship. But regardless of whether they will see each other again, their time together has been a positive experience.

It was an ambiguous ending. As Lindgren stated in program notes, what he tried to convey was the unpredictability of human nature and the inexplicable ways that people react when they come in contact with reality. The film was a hit domestically and abroad.

Another Swedish director on the rise was Vilgot Sjöman. The son of a construction worker, he had been a student of Bergman's since the '40s and had directed his first feature, *The Swedish Mistress*, in 1962. This was an erotic drama that depicted the relationship between a young girl and a married middle-class man. In 1963 the Swedish film industry received a shot of adrenaline when The Film Reform Agreement was enacted for the purpose of promoting so-called quality films. Sjöman, along with future star directors like Bo Widerberg, Kjell Grede and Jan Troell, was a beneficiary of this initiative.

He made his next film, *491*, in 1964. This drama about Sweden's vaunted youth care system was based on a controversial novel by Lars Görling which dealt with an idealistic social worker who is allowed to share his home with six young juvenile delinquents as a kind of an experiment. Yet the boys constantly exploit him and take advantage of his leniency, at one point bringing home a teenage girl, Steva, whom they pimp out when they need money. Two of the lads are themselves abused, homosexually, by the inspector to whom they must report on a daily basis. Things go from bad to worse, and after they force Steva to perform perverse sexual acts with a German shepherd the youngest boy commits suicide and the experiment comes to a tragic end. The title, *491*, is an allusion to the Gospel According to Saint Matthew:

> Then came Peter to him, and said, Lord, how oft shall my brother sin against me, and I forgive him? Till seven times? Jesus saith unto him, I say not unto thee, Until seven times: but Until seventy times seven. [Matthew 18: 21–22, King James Version].

Thus the 491st sin (490 + 1) would be the final and unforgivable one.

In casting the film Sjöman conducted numerous interviews with teens from drama schools, youth clubs, bars and girl's homes, and finally chose Lena Nyman to play Steva. Nyman already had acting experience and beyond-her-years attitude (her parents were divorced). She was on the chubby side, not a classically sexy type, and yet she was nice looking and uniquely photogenic. He was intrigued; "Wasn't there something experienced about her — despite her plumpness? There were shadows under her eyes — I imagined she looked worn and haggard. Perhaps she had been a mod-girl? Perhaps she knew more about the world of *491* than I suspected?"[27]

Even though Sjöman had bowed to studio pressure to cover his actors in skin-colored gauze tights during the sex scenes, the film was banned outright by Swedish censors. This decision shocked many and sparked heated debate in the press. The studio

A social experiment; Lena Nyman and "friends" in the film *491*.

appealed the ban to the government but opinions there were also divided and it was eventually ruled that the film could only be released with cuts.

This was Sweden's first big sex film scandal of the '60s, and it quickly became more than just a debate about screen censorship as activists from both the right and the left used it to trumpet their broader positions on sexual morality and freedom of expression. For their part the Swedish Pentecostal movement used the controversy to depict themselves as defenders of good old-fashioned morality and parlayed the visibility and momentum they gained from the issue to form a new political party, the Christian Democrats, who remain an entrenched part of Swedish politics to this day. A group of 140 physicians more or less agreed with them, arguing for stronger censorship and publishing a report that criticized the "over-sexualization of society."[28] Yet the film also led to calls to re-examine film censorship and a committee was empanelled to come up with a new approach. Their conclusion: completely abolish all censorship for adults in four and a half years.

In Denmark the film was also released with cuts. In Norway it was banned outright and wouldn't open until 1968. It was denied entry into the United States, put on trial there and found obscene, despite the testimony of numerous expert witnesses who spoke on the film's behalf. The decision was later reversed by the U.S. Court of Appeals and it was allowed to open in 1966, distributed by Janus Films.

Lars Görling would go on to write and direct his own film, *Guilt*, in 1965. It bores deep into the psychology of a young couple who hit and kill an unknown stranger while motoring the picturesque country roads of Sweden in an old Volvo. They are plunged into a state of confusion as they try to deal with the situation, and the story soon comes to bear more on their relationship than on the car accident. The few sequences with sex and nudity stole the spotlight and the film only just managed to win the approval of the censorship board.

I, a Woman

"This film preaches a fraudulent message about life. It is a lie and a deception,
a false prophecy that leaves misfortune and sorrow in its wake. That is
far worse than stealing cars or smuggling liquor."
- Bishop Haldor Hald writing about *I, a Woman*.

By 1965 the pattern was clear enough to Danish film producers: a beloved Danish folk-comedy that did major box office in Denmark might go nowhere outside the country — *Harry and the Butler* a prime example — but any film with nudity or sexual content was almost sure to play big in foreign markets and make real money. The time was ripe for Danish films to travel, like Swedish films had — but only if they could be promoted as sex films.

Enter Peer Guldbrandsen, Denmark's fearless rogue producer and self-made movie man, a stubborn fellow who had always been driven to challenge authority and to do so in flamboyant ways. In 1935 he had staged a play that poked fun at the Nazis, and he went on to further ridicule them in theater pieces he and his troupe performed in back country inns and public houses during the Occupation. In 1942 the Germans put an end to his frivolity and outlawed his performances.

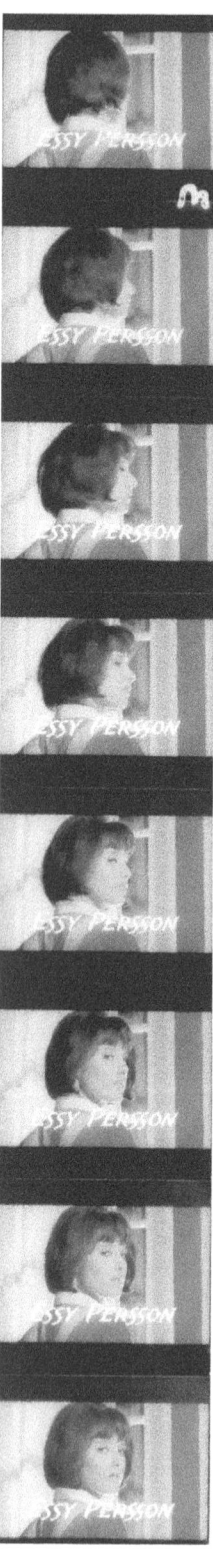

He sought refuge in Sweden where he threw himself into writing. He published a bunch of books and continued to write upon his return to Denmark, but was unable to make a living at it so he turned to filmmaking, directing his first movie in 1954. In 1958 he purchased an old farm and converted it into a film studio, equipping it with Scandinavia's largest soundstage and opening it as Novaris Studio in 1960. Soon he was pumping out seven to eight films a year, all without a crown of support from the Film Fund.[29] In early 1965 he bought the rights to *I, a Woman* from publisher Stig Vendelkær in a deal that also made Vendelkær a co-producer. Guldbrandsen himself would pen the script.

A film based on a racy book seemed natural enough as naughty books were currently getting lots of free publicity. At that very point in time the novel *Fanny Hill* was attracting huge press as it worked its way through the Danish court system. Officially banned in 1958, it had been reprinted in Denmark in 1964 by Thaning and Appel who did a careful test run of just 60 copies. Now, in 1965, *Fanny Hill* was about to be found not guilty by the country's highest court. This ruling would help bring about a change in the penal code and set "indecent literature" free.

I, a Woman, infinitely more topical, was directed and photographed by a Swede, Mac Ahlberg, who had been the cinematographer on *The Cats*, Henning Carlsen's Swedish film of the previous year. (Based on a play about 15 women and a man who kill time gabbing in a laundromat, that film is peripherally germane to this study due to its treatment of lesbianism and the fact that its cast included up-and-coming sex kitten Gio Petré.) Now Guldbrandsen and Ahlberg began to search Denmark and Sweden for the sexiest and most beautiful actress of all. There were countless such women to be had — this was after all Scandinavia — but what they really needed was a girl willing to cast her inhibitions to the wind. A hip new modern girl. A new face.

Soon enough they found her, or rather Ahlberg found her: a long-legged 22-year-old named Essy Persson who already had acting experience and was performing in a play at Stockholm's City Theater. Oddly enough she was a brunette, not a blonde, but she had other attributes which included, as one Danish scribe put it, "big eyes, a naughty mouth and a nice figure." She wasn't exactly voluptuous but was supremely fit and her sensuous and teasing smile was unforgettable. She had acted in plays by Dario Fo and Jean Genet, among others, but aside from a single commercial this Danish-Swedish co-production would be her debut in the film medium.

But she had to be convinced first. She was sent a copy of the book but thought it so repulsive she threw it away and vowed she'd never do it in a million years. Ahlberg persisted, promising that they'd only

Essy Persson introduced to audiences in the trailer to *I, a Woman*.

take the basic story and transform it into something else. She was young and could be gotten to, and finally agreed.

Meanwhile, Guldbrandsen needed convincing to accept Persson, and this was harder. "She has no ass!" he thundered the moment he laid eyes on her, and quickly ordered a fake ass constructed of some kind of cushioning. Persson refused it. Guldbrandsen also claimed she had no bust. Persson thought he was nuts. She was *Ahlberg*'s choice for the role and he had to fight for it, and there was plenty of shouting. In the end she was signed.

The movie was reasonably faithful to the book. The main character, Siv (a common woman's name in Denmark), has been raised in a strict, religious home. She and her parents and her boyfriend are all members of a puritanical Christian sect. When her boyfriend insists on waiting until after their wedding to make love to her, she allows herself to be seduced by a patient in the small-town hospital where she works as a nurse. He is married and has two children but becomes so obsessed with her that he offers to divorce his wife and marry her. But she is not about to be owned by anyone and leaves him to take a job in a hospital in Copenhagen. There she meets a lonely young sailor in a cafe and they begin a relationship, and he too gets serious and wants to marry her; however, she refuses to live in abstinence while he is out at sea. Shattered, he kicks her out of his flat. It is mostly the men who are sentimental and possessive in this film.

All the while she's been having an affair with a doctor, a refined and sophisticated fellow who can't cope with her sassy impudence and is driven to bouts of mild sexual sadism. He in turn offers to break up with the young woman he is going with, who is pregnant with his child, and marry Siv but again she says no. It is impossible for her to be faithful to any single man; she is in love with the male gender as a totality. Finally she meets a man who possesses the raw, untamed masculinity she craves ... and he rapes her. On his way out the door she asks if she can see him again but the idea repels him; he doesn't need a woman hanging around. She begins to laugh hysterically, having finally met a man who is just like her, a man who won't be controlled by anyone.

Filming took place that summer in Novaris. Studio publicity was billing it as the most open-hearted and authentic of erotic confessions, "from a woman's point of view," while the yellow press was already describing it as the most daring film ever shot on Danish soil, "half pornographic." Among other things it could be divulged that Persson had "blushed over the whole of her body" during the first takes. She soon came to terms with that part of it. "Luckily," she commented, "everybody was nice and discreet on the set so the embarrassment didn't last long and I didn't waste another thought on it." And yet she felt increasingly uncomfortable playing opposite the line-up of male actors whom Guldbrandsen had cast. They were much older than she was and it was difficult for her to relate to those actors; that girl would have never fallen for those men. On top of it their acting was flat, or else they over-acted. She just couldn't bear to play it straight, and her acting took on a more ironic tone so that she ended up submitting a somewhat distanced and spiteful performance—which turned out to be perfect.

By July a final cut was being prepared. The naughtiest bits had been snipped out and the hope was that the censor board would pass the rest. And so they did, to everyone's surprise, without cutting a frame. *I, a Woman* opened on September 17 and theaters were packed—and reviews the next day were merciless.

The film's sins and transgressions were multiple, according to critics. The dialogue was stiff and banal to a degree that reportedly provoked laughter in the audience. The

Essy Persson gets the rough treatment from a boyfriend in *I, a Woman*.

illusion was further shattered by the fact that it was dubbed in Danish, badly so and out of sync. (Persson did the part in Swedish and never liked the voice they chose for the Danish version, deeming it too old and mature for the character she was playing.) Keith Keller from the paper *Aktuelt* elaborated: "The actors recite Guldbrandsen's romantic/realistic dream-dialogue in the most deranged, old-fashioned theater style. Everyone talks a kind of Danish that hasn't sounded so unnatural in a film since Carl Dreyer's *Gertrud*, although in that case it was supposedly intentional." Another critic remarked that the actors were best when they left off talking and just used their mouths to kiss.

As noted, Guldbrandsen's script followed the book fairly closely with only minor deviations. Deleted, for example, is the scene in the book where a friend of Siv's dies after an illegal abortion. But if he was faithful to the plot he certainly hadn't been faithful to the spirit of it. He had turned erotica and sensuality into prurience; he had distorted and cheapened the book. So said his legion of critics.

Another oft-echoed complaint was that the characters were implausible and superficial, though Essy Persson's acting was invariably praised. She had stopped blushing long enough to submit a thoroughly unique and timeless performance, and maybe a lingering nervousness had even enhanced it.

But when she saw the finished product she was left in a state of shock. This happened on September 16 in the Palads Theater where she and her agent were given a private viewing. A photographer was also on hand to capture for posterity her pained expressions and her tearful dash from the theater when she could bear no more. It wasn't the film per se she objected to but how she looked on the screen, something the shooting process had not prepared her for. She was shocked, she claimed, at how bad she looked and vowed never to watch the film again. The whole affair had so battered her confidence that she refused to go outside and remained locked in her flat with a stack of Chopin records. Perhaps she really was the "sweet, shy, sensitive" girl that the gossip magazines were making her out to be, worried and torn up about what her girlfriends back in Sweden would think. She made it clear she wanted out of the sexploitation genre pronto.

Another wronged woman expressing her disgust with the movie was one Agnethe Thomsen, who had publicly come forth back in March and revealed that she was, in fact, Siv Holm, the one and only author of the book. At a lecture at the Kalundborg high school student union she explained that due to financial difficulties she'd been compelled to sell the film rights to her publisher and hence had no input into how it was shot. Had she been on the set she would have screamed and hollered about all the dirty scenes they were shooting.

"The film is dirty," she told a writer, "because the people who made it had no feel for its erotic dimension but only exploited the sexual aspect for prurient purposes. The film lacks background. It fails to take into account my reasons for writing the novel, namely that after I broke from the prejudices I sought to live in an honest way and to have the reader participate in that honesty."[30]

Not everyone bought what Persson and Holm were saying. How could a movie based on such a hotted-up book turn out to be anything else? And not everyone was enchanted with Persson's performance either. *Aktuelt's* reviewer thought it lacked real heat and was too over-the-top: "the scenes of intercourse are neither pretty nor appetite arousing and the foreplay leading up to them is without appeal, without sensuous excitement. If anyone feels the slightest bit aroused by all these wrenching kisses and all this wild orgasmic cavorting then the awkward and cliché-ridden dialogue will quickly bring them back to earth."[31]

But nothing could dampen the crowd appeal of *I, a Woman* and it ended up selling more tickets than any other movie in the history of Danish cinema to that point.[32] This film and access to "the pill" were the big events that year in Denmark.

Rights were quickly sold to most foreign territories, and as the film played abroad that fall, censors as well as critics took their knives to it. In Norway three of the strongest scenes were cut out. In Sweden it was turned over to a committee composed of experts in social, moral and artistic matters to discuss a course of action. Swedish film critics didn't need to discuss it; they simply thought it stank, and among the general populace it came to be considered a "dirty" film. It was denied entry into Japan for over a year, but when it finally opened in July of 1968 it was in one of Tokyo's biggest theaters and Japanese viewers streamed in to find out what these Nordic women were all about.

At long last a positive review was to be found in Germany where the major daily *Die Welt* took the film seriously, describing it as a daring attempt to explore a young woman's erotic motivations and moral dilemmas.

In the American market, the film had already been reviewed in *Variety* on September 29, 1965, in decidedly negative fashion. "This film makes some pretense at attempting artistic photography and artful dialogue," opined reviewer Kell, "but as 'art' it is a rather ridiculous affair." After outlining the plot and leveling blasts at Ahlberg's direction and Guldbrandsen's dialogue, he closed with praise for Persson's performance. "Only

Essy Persson ... seems happily unaware of the surrounding banality. She plays her role with vigor and talent, radiating sex and displaying an oft-exposed body."

The review caught the eye of New York distributor Radley Metzger. A cultured fellow who collected art and enjoyed ballet, Metzger supplied "sex pictures" to the secondary art-house and independent circuits. He specialized in films with a European flavor and some pretensions to class, served up in a form American audiences could digest while pushing the erotic component to the absolute permissible limit. Some of the films he imported were run-of-the-mill foreign pictures that he just doped up with stock (nude) footage; by editing the skin shots into the movie on American soil he didn't need to slip anything questionable past U.S. customs. At this point just about any European film meant sex to American viewers.

The review in *Variety* intrigued him enough to fly to a snow-bound Copenhagen, and as he would later relate, "They didn't even have a screening print, I had to go to the suburbs to see it."[33] He offered what he considered a fortune for it—$20,000—but someone else had already bought the film, he was told, and they only had one more payment to make before the deal was final. As it turned out, that last payment was never made and Metzger got the movie. Reports on the price vary. Sources in the Danish press say that he paid between $25,000 and $35,000 for U.S. rights and $75,000 for world rights excluding Europe.[34]

Whatever the exact amounts, it would go down as one of the most lopsided deals in film history. Guldbrandsen had sold the film to Metzger for a flat fee and he would get no percentage of eventual profits. Had he retained even a tiny percentage he probably would have become a millionaire many times over, something that pundits in the Danish media would never let him forget.

But the Danish version was too risqué to be released in the States, compelling Metzger—one of the very few distributors with hands-on film cutting experience—to rearrange some footage and re-edit it. By '67 he had it ready to play in American theaters.

It proved immensely controversial. America's beleaguered censors were trying to hold the fort against such films, but the front lines of the cultural battlefield were shifting daily. Screenings were blocked in Kentucky and at drive-in theaters in Indiana, where theater employees were jailed, even though they were all showing a censored print in which four cuts had been made. Meanwhile a Chicago theater showing the same censored version was besieged by a mob of angry housewives. In court proceedings in Memphis, Hartford, Providence and Boston the film was found not obscene. Elsewhere around the country prints were seized and theater owners jailed. All of this fuss helped give *I, a Woman* the allure of the forbidden and sent box office through the roof. Courts inevitably ruled in favor of the film, and it continue to play.

In New York City it opened that spring in 13 theaters and soon it was playing in 44, with subtitles no less, something which usually turned off the general public. Dubbed versions were later prepared for middle America. By October it had been sold to 35 countries with more standing in line.

The film was everywhere. Friends of Essy's even reported to her that they saw it playing in a remote Saharan village: "Essy Persson in *I, a Woman*," announced a gigantic sign. It never played behind the Iron Curtain where it surely would have been seen as proof of capitalist decadence. Metzger would have happily pleaded guilty, but he never consid-

The strip performance scene was deemed overly suggestive and cut from many prints of *I, a Woman*.

ered it to be just another sexploitation picture. "Everybody thought," he noted years later, "that *I, a Woman* made a lot of money because Essy Persson fucked all through the movie, when of course there were so many fuck movies, much hotter pictures actually, around at the time. What happened was that she touched women, there was something in this girl's personality, in her story, that touched an awful lot of women in the audience, and that is really I believe what caused the success of *I, a Woman*."[35]

It played strong into 1968 and by June it had grossed more than three million dollars in the States.

I, a Woman challenged all the assumptions about how big such a movie could go, but to art film purists it signified a disturbing trend. As *Time Magazine* sardonically noted in July of 1968, the film could now be seen in the kind of theaters which "in better times" had shown Fellini and Antonioni. Wasn't *I, a Woman* an art film?

It wanted to be one. Aside from the rude crotch-rubbing, hip-grinding dance number that takes place in a club where Siv and lover steal away for a drink, it was all pensive moments and violins. It exuded the melancholy naturalism of Bergman and *felt* like an art film. But the snob set in their tweeds and wing-tips thought not. For one thing art film directors figured as holy deities, their names often billed above the title, but Mac Ahlberg was completely unknown, and according to various Danish critics (and Persson herself) the film was more a product of Guldbrandsen's incessant meddling. And with it being called superficial and old-fashioned even by trade publications like *Variety*, what was a pipe-fondling, beard-stroking intellectual to do?

But to the unwashed masses it fit the bill; it was from Europe, it had subtitles and it had sex. Despite all the talk about poetry and metaphor, part of the attraction of art films had always been that they delivered more skin than the Hollywood product, and in the early to mid–'60s the term "art film" was loaded with licentious meaning. Witness the emotional exchange between Sue Lyon and James Mason toward the end of *Lolita* when she confesses that she ended up in a beatnik commune in the Southwest where artists, poets, body-builders and other counter culture types indulged in bohemian excess. Here Peter Sellers' character, Clare Quilty, tried to persuade her to be in an art film. "Art film!" exclaims Mason, aghast. It was at that point that she actually left Quilty. The implications of an art film were just too decadent to be contemplated further in a mainstream movie.

I, a Woman was full of nudity and confirmed and reinforced this stereotype. And for all the talk about this being a women's picture, about a woman who takes control of her own sexuality, it was also for men — the kind of men who wear raincoats when it's not raining. They could readily appreciate its central premise, articulated by Persson in the shower scene when she excitedly declares that all women secretly yearn for rape. Here was the missing link between the rarefied art film and the down-and-dirty American sexploitation movie: a *European* sexploitation film.

Metzger would be credited for "breaking down barriers in U.S. exhibition and opening up the conventional theatrical and art-house market to soft-core sexploitation films,"[36] and this was the key movie in that process, a true cross-over hit. It opened a

Siv Holm (Essy Persson) confesses rape fantasies to Heinz (Preben Mahrt) in *I, a Woman*.

new market that American filmmakers like Metzger himself, Joe Sarno, Jack O'Connell and others would soon exploit as they shot films with a European feel for a Stateside audience, straddling art and exploitation for fun and profit. And it didn't hurt with the censors if your film seemed to be from across the pond as they were apt to look more kindly on European art films, with their dark metaphors and poetic understated titles, than on homegrown exploitation pictures that sported monikers like *The Smut Peddler*, *Scum of the Earth* and *Faster, Pussycat! Kill! Kill!* Intent was everything.

I, a Woman was the first major Scandinavian sexploitation blockbuster of the '60s, and it was something more: a pop culture phenomenon that even entered the vocabulary of underground cinema as filmmakers like Andy "*I, a Man*" Warhol and George "*I, an Actress*" Kuchar riffed on its title and toyed with its pretensions. It was reported on as an event, not just a film, and even people who didn't go to the movies knew about it.

According to Metzger it eventually earned four million dollars, a staggering sum at that time. It allowed him to finance his next picture, *Therese and Isabelle*, a somber romantic drama based on Violette Leduc's memoir about two schoolgirls in an uncaring world who find refuge in each other's arms. Persson, who was given the part of the troubled Therese, was introduced to the elderly author who was dressed all in lilac and whom she found to be a very strange woman. Anna Gaël played the role of the older and more experienced Isabelle with wide-eyed, breathy abandon. (The Hungarian-born actress appeared primarily in French films in the '60s and went on to a long career which included a role in Mac Ahlberg's adaptation of the Emile Zola novel, *Nana*.)

Therese and Isabelle was a class production and figured as Metzger's big breakthrough as a filmmaker. Persson was paid more for it than what some of the top stars in Sweden were getting for their films, and was being heralded as the new Harriet Andersson (*Penthouse* had already dubbed her "the new Greta Garbo"). Metzger, too, had only good things to say about her. "Persson was an extraordinary talent," he later recalled, "who thought of herself as a girl who got famous by showing her tits and doing fuck films. And now she had a real part."[37]

Metzger continued to cash in on the mythology of Scandinavian sexuality in films like *Her and She and Him* from 1970, a tale spun on the sexual adventures of an innocent Swedish girl adrift in decadent Paris. This was nothing new as Scandinavians were frequently typed as innocents abroad. For example in the 1966 Aram Emanuel–directed *The Sensualist*, an innocent Danish girl ends up knocking about New York City. This film is cross-referenced in the American Film Institute catalog with waitresses, rape, lesbianism, troilism, striptease, New York City, and Greenwich Village, which pretty much says it all. It was a pattern repeated in countless other films. After whirlwind sex in Paris or New York or fill-in-the-blank city, Inga or Greta or Ulla or Eva was ready to return home to safe, secure Scandinavia.

After *I, a Woman* Persson stayed in safe, secure Copenhagen to shoot *Sonja*, a daffy James Bond parody in which she plays a Swedish secret agent in league with a cartel of Russian villains. Dressed in a body-hugging red outfit, she plays her part with spirited abandon and seems to be having fun while at the same time countering, in eye-popping fashion, some critics' complaints that she didn't have much of a build.

Guldbrandsen might have sold *I, a Woman* to Metzger for a pittance but he still had the rights to the sequel by Thomsen, a.k.a. Siv Holm, and was positioned to spin off endless remakes, follow-ups and films that merely ripped off the title. This he did, quickly producing and releasing *I, a Lover* in 1966 and opening it in the U.S. two years later. It was based on a novel not by *Siv* Holm, but by *Stig* Holm. (There were also the books *I, a Man* parts 1 and 2 by *Sverre* Holm.) Guldbrandsen again wrote the script, and most of the rest of the Novaris crew was back for another turn, including Sven Gyldmark who composed the excellent music score that would hold the film together in the fashion of Jacques Tati's *My Uncle*. The plot concerned a man who snaps out of his marital lethargy only after his love-hungry wife leaves him. He becomes obsessed with sex, dallying with various women and fantasizing that he suddenly sees gals in the street without any clothes on. In the end he meets his wife on a plane and they jet off to an exotic land.

It was a curious follow-up to *I, a Woman*. It was not a sexually liberated film but rather a satire of sexual liberation, a playful ode to voyeurism that more than anything else resembled Russ Meyer's aforementioned and now thoroughly antiquated 1959 "nudie-cutie" *The Immoral Mr. Teas*. It possessed nothing of the spirit or daring of its predecessor. Today it can be appreciated for the camp stylings of its minimalist '60s sets, its effective mood music and the subtle performance of Jørgen Ryg who was back reprising his role as the hapless average Dane, but for those expecting a hot time Essy Persson style it was a crashing disappointment. The presence of Dirch Passer in a secondary role, mugging in his usual style, was further evidence that nothing new was at play here.

Guldbrandsen kept trying to reheat the magic, subsequently pumping out *I, a Nobleman*, *I, a Woman 2* and *I, a Woman 3* (a.k.a. *The Daughter*), all of which will be mentioned in more detail later.

While *I, a Woman* was a contemporary piece, there was a clear trend in the opposite direction: the basing of movies on literary sources set in the past. The other two significant Danish sex films of 1965, *Two Times Two in the Four Poster* and *Soya's 17*, fall into this category.

Two Times Two was a Danish-German co-production. According to critic Carl Nørrested, the German scriptwriter Herbert Reinecker gave the picture a German feel, even though the story was adopted from a text by the French author Pierre Viallet. It took place in the early 1900s in an isolated North Sea villa where the young Count Pierre de Sauterne has decided to spend the summer quietly studying. His plans are disrupted, however, when two girls accompanied by their aunt are forced to seek shelter there during a storm. He allows them in and they return his hospitality ten-fold.

Soya's 17

More successful with the public was *Soya's 17*, made by Palladium Studios which had also produced *Crazy Paradise* back in 1962. Now they were ready to take the folk/sex-comedy to the next level.

Set in the early 1900s, this coming-of-age drama was based on a novel by the Danish writer Carl Erik Soya. Its publication in 1953 had stirred controversy and secured his reputation as a writer of liberated erotica, a reputation that Palladium would continue to exploit in a series of Soya adaptations in which the author's name figured prominently.

This film would prove to be a turning point in the career of one Ole Søltoft, thus

Jacob (Ole Søltoft) gazes gratefully at Hansigne (Susanne Heinrich) after his first sexual encounter in *Soya's 17*.

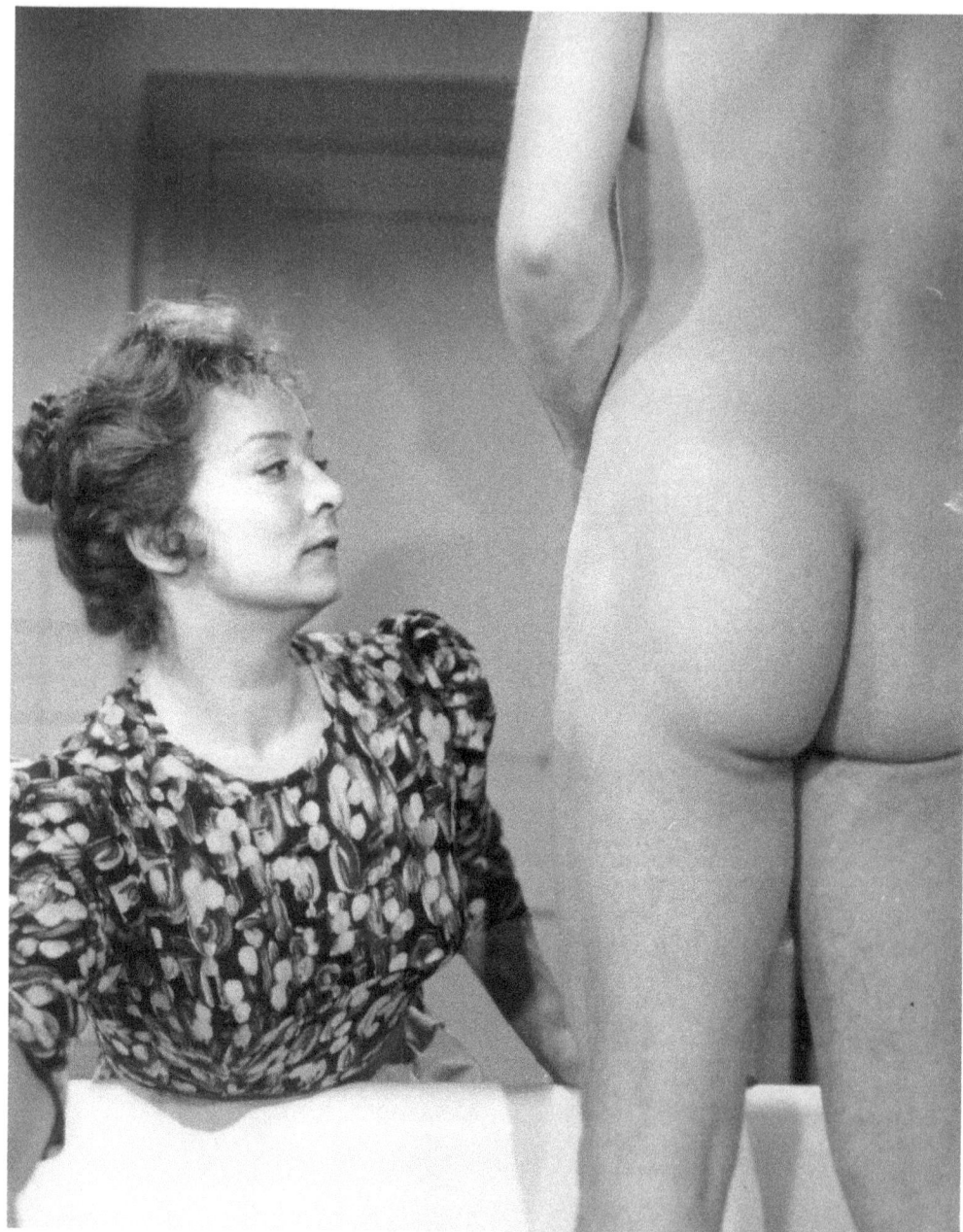

Denmark's unlikely sex star, Ole Søltoft, shows all while Lily Broberg looks on in *Soya's 17* from 1965.

far best known for the 1962 costume drama *The Beloved Family* where he played Benjamin, an earnest young dandy in a top hat. He had also appeared in *Two Times Two in the Four Poster* in a secondary role but now he was the star, playing Jacob, a sexually inexperienced 17-year-old student sent to a small country village to spend the summer with his aunt and uncle. There he falls under the spell of his beautiful cousin Vibeke, but she is so childish and flighty that his advances lead nowhere. Rather it is the buxom servant girl, Hansigne, with whom he has his first sexual experience in the cozy confines of his garret room. She is played by the dark-haired Susanne Heinrich who exudes a more mature sexuality.

Despite the fact that he was playing a 17-year-old at 23, the average looking Søltoft brought plausibility to the part, able as he was to convey a boy-next-door kind of innocence that was just right. Vibeke, played by the 30-year-old Ghita Nørby, was less convincing and in fact a bit pathological.

The stylized period settings, vividly photographed in Technicolor, struck a tone of cheery and idealized nostalgia. It was an entertaining and accessible fantasy that contained only brief nudity and couldn't trouble a single censor, and yet in this context the film's sexual frankness was all the more groundbreaking. For one thing, one of the characters is clearly a closeted homosexual. Also, the sex is unusually adventurous: in their attic tryst, after disrobing to take a position on top of Jacob, Hansigne tells him, "We can also try it this way," and turns her naked backside towards him as she smiles expectantly into the camera and the scene fades. Because it was filmed in such an innocent, storybook style, without a trace of vulgarity, *Soya's 17* could get away with a brazenly suggestive scene like this and still pass as a coming-of-age drama fit for family viewing.

While the rest of the world was waiting for the next ever-more explicit Danish film, this was the country's real achievement in the erotic arena at this stage: not that Danes were about to crash through the porno barrier but that without any big fuss these unique folk/sex-comedy hybrids were allowed to play in a mainstream context and that films that were in no way porn films were able to deal frankly with sexuality.

Although it contributed almost nothing to the growing debate on sexual liberation or censorship, *Soya's 17* became a popular and beloved film in Denmark, Heinrich's performance iconic for a generation of Danish lads. It did relatively minor business outside the country. In the U.S. *Seventeen Magazine* objected to any possible connection and forced a title change from *Seventeen*, as it was known in Denmark, to the confusing *Soya's 17*.

But like *I, a Woman* it did set in motion a swarm of follow-ups and imitations, and it was the film that launched Ole Søltoft's career.

Venom (a.k.a. *Gift*)

"Absolute freedom is an absolute void"
— Knud Leif Thomsen

In February of 1966 Knud Leif Thomsen was back in the press in connection with the censorship controversy forming around his new film *Gift* (which in Danish means either "poison" or "married").

This picture would be his most confrontational and uncompromising, a no-holds-barred attack on the state of society's moral health, which to his mind had deteriorated badly since he'd made *The Duel* four years ago. It appeared his predictions were coming true.

Whether or not the public would respond was anybody's guess. His studio chose to hedge its bets and made him share the risk 50/50, giving him a credit as co-producer.

Possibly they thought it might prove unreleaseable. If this was the case then their fears were well founded, for Thomsen's drama about the destructive effects of pornography itself contained several brief scenes of actual explicit hard-core sex.

The censorship board had demanded that three scenes be cut in order for it to receive a 16-and-older rating, and now the whole issue was playing out in the press before anyone else had even seen the film. Thomsen refused to cut it and took the unusual step of appealing the decision to the justice minister. It seemed unfair that a film as exploitive, in his opinion, as *I, a Woman* had passed without any cuts and now they wanted to take the scissors to his movie.

There was also a political dimension. The film board had granted *Gift* Film Fund support which of course meant that the board had approved the script. The critical importance of these hard-core scenes to the story had been stressed during that initial procedure, and by granting money the board had in essence agreed. So the censorship board was in effect overruling the film board, pitting the cultural ministry against the justice ministry.

There were other less baroque paradoxes at play, most obviously the fact that Thomsen was demanding the right to include hard-core pornography in a film that was preaching the evil of pornography. And by appealing the censor's decision, he was, as many saw it, undermining the last safeguard that prevented the total "pornification" of the culture.

While some accused him of harboring a yen for martyrdom, this was no impulsive provocation on his part. The inclusion of hard-core pornographic footage was essential to the film: he had watched hundreds of hours of vintage 16mm stag films to find the right scenes, selecting examples of what could be termed "clinical pornography" where the mechanics of intercourse were shown without inhibition.

The cuts the censors wanted to make, he claimed, would change the nature of the whole film and introduce an element of leering prurience, something that would only release the poison, not just reveal it. He wanted to confront the audience, not pander to them. His goal was to force the issue, to show the audience the real nature of pornography and in the process reveal how un-sexy it was. This would be a film about pornography and not a pornographic film. That distinction was essential. The fact that the film was a defense of decency entitled him, he felt, to use whatever materials he needed to press his case.

While such reasoning could seem arcane and contradictory to the general public, Thomsen's antipathy towards censorship was, as noted, shared by many Danes. Even critics who disagreed with his views were heartened by his attack on censorship, particularly those on the left. He maintained that censors took the right and the power to make judgments away from the people. And why was film treated so differently from books or paintings or other artworks? If they were deemed in violation of the law the case would be decided in a court, in *public*, but film censorship took place in secret and was decided without debate by faceless officials who assumed the right to safeguard the morality of a public who had not elected them. Such an undemocratic process seemed a throwback to more authoritarian times.

Thomsen wanted to show the film to an unbiased audience and get their feedback, and so when the student association at Copenhagen University offered to screen the as yet uncensored version for the students and an ad-hoc jury of eleven professionals from relevant fields, he agreed. (A number of films banned from commercial exhibition were shown by the student association in what were technically closed screenings, among them Roger Corman's *Wild Angels*, and these were always full.)

When the screening rolled around on February 15, 1966, so many people came that the halls and stairways leading up to the auditorium became impassable. In the crush hundreds had to be turned away, and when the first images flickered on the screen people were sitting on the floor and standing along the walls.

The jury, composed of eleven doctors, authors, psychologists, law professors and the like, found the film not guilty by a vote of nine to two, meaning that the pornographic scenes should be kept intact. The screening opened up a wider debate about censorship in general, or rather lack of debate since all the members of the jury and an overwhelming majority of the audience agreed that censorship of film by the State should be completely abolished or take a different form. Thomsen's film and his outspoken opposition to censorship had clearly caught the spirit of the times, however mixed opinions about the movie itself were.

The effects of pornography in general were also discussed. A doctor by the name of Kurt Flemming who had shown up claimed that it only acted as a stimulant on healthy and mature people, and that assumptions that criminals commit offenses after having seen pornography were baseless.[38] Children were also not damaged, he maintained. Their sexual instincts were already determined by six years of age and they did not understand pornographic films. Yet he felt that "normal people" should not become accustomed to such scenes and they should not be shown in public.

Although it had been made clear that the show at the student union was not a press screening and that writers should not review the film at this point, psychologist Gerhard Nielsen did give Thomsen probably the best review he would ever get, calling it well written, well acted film art of the highest caliber. He furthermore recommended that the justice minister watch it in a theater along with all other government officials and their wives.

By March Thomsen and the board of censors had reached a compromise: *Gift* would not be cut but instead large white crosses would be superimposed over the offending scenes, which totaled about two to three minutes and were all contained in the film-within-a-film. It could then be certified for 16-and-over. How this new method of censorship would affect the film and its message gave occasion for further debate of a fairly theoretical nature.

In the newspaper *S.F. Bladet*, critic Børge Trolle reckoned that the white crosses now turned the film into pornography by the very fact that they obscured the action of the offending scenes:

> There is a point to Thomsen's use of real (clinical) pornography in *Gift*, and it is based on the understanding that pornography inevitably becomes anti-pornographic the moment it is presented to a large public gathering. (Imagine a chapter of Henry Miller read aloud in front of a crowd in the vast Forum auditorium.) Pornographic movies are created to be shown to a very small circle of people. In that setting the movie can affect them ... the reactions of some contingent upon factors that are independent of the film itself (the person one is sitting next to, etc.). Shown in a big theater, the (clinical) pornographic film becomes something akin to a splash of cold water in the face, simply because you know that hundreds of people sitting around you are seeing the same thing.

> Therefore Thomsen is quite correct in asserting that an out-take from a pornographic film can be used for artistic purposes. That he fails to achieve this in the film because it is so bad is another case. His reasoning is correct.... (Now) by obscuring these scenes with white crosses the censors have transformed an anti-pornographic film into pornography!

The actual inclusion of hard-core pornography in a commercial feature film would have been in 1966 inconceivable in any other country. No studio would have made it, no director would have gambled his career on it, no professional actor would have participated and it would not have been allowed to generate such widespread debate. Yet to credit Thomsen with advancing the cause of screen freedom would have been backhanded praise indeed, since he was adamantly opposed to just about everything these freedom seekers believed in. Aside from Trolle, few were willing or able to discern that his main aim was actually much more courageous and at the same time much more basic: to expose the very mechanism of pornography, which is *context*. Now the censors had meddled with the mad professor's formula and the experiment could only go badly wrong.

Gift opened on March 24 and now average Danes could judge for themselves. And although Thomsen said he found the media's fixation with the censorship issue regrettable (and claimed that the censors themselves had mobilized the press), it made the film one of the most eagerly anticipated ever and theaters were packed. In at least one theater in Copenhagen the film was shown with tourist-friendly English subtitles.

It begins with a late-fortyish couple awakening in bed one morning. He is a real-estate agent who cheats his buyers, makes passes at his secretary and gets suggestive with their sexy and well-endowed if simple-minded maid (played by Thomsen's wife, Judy Gringer). She is a housewife with all day to roam the empty rooms of their fine seaside villa and stare despairingly into the mirror. They're deep into a mid-life crisis and a crumbling marriage, and their spoiled daughter Susanne is growing increasingly alienated from them.

As the attractive blonde teenager lounges in a swimsuit on their private beach, studying for her finals, a motorboat approaches and begins to cut around in circles out beyond the dock. The craft is recklessly piloted by a bold young fellow called Per who briefly films her with a 16mm camera. He anchors the boat and swims ashore to pester her with impertinent come-ons. She ignores but does not overtly discourage him. He is self-confident to the point of arrogance but charismatic in a rascally way, and well-spoken, if glib. He urinates on the sign that says "private beach" before following her up to the house and introducing himself to the mother.

Days later he shows up uninvited at the villa for her graduation party, interrupting the father's awkward welcome speech with a gift for Susanne—a copy of *Fanny Hill*. Later that evening he baits the father into a discussion about morality. Provoked, Dad tosses the book into the fireplace. Per in turn places the family Bible in the fire, jovially proclaiming himself the prophet of a new form of Christianity that worships the flesh. He's been preaching this new morality from the first moment he came into their lives, ever ready with a snappy retort or self-serving turn of logic.

Soon, to the parents' displeasure, Per and Susanne are a couple. They hang out at his seedy flat where he shows her hard-core pornographic films on his 16mm projector. In one montage a stallion mounts a mare, a bull enters a cow and then a man takes a woman from behind. The message is clear: we are all basically animals. Susanne is taken aback but not shocked. She seems incapable of being really shocked by anything. She personifies the dim view of modern youth: not a bad kid but emotionally dulled, lazy, without goals and seeing nothing to emulate in her parents.

They go off with his gang to a remote stretch of beach where they smoke pot and Per films the girls as they lounge in swimsuits. He is apparently shooting some sprawling, self-absorbed movie about his life and philosophy. The title: *Me*. While Susanne cavorts with the others, he starts to make out with another girl, pulling her top down as he positions his camera to film the action and putting his hand between her legs to her half-hearted protests. Susanne catches them, she's mad, but ... no big deal.

At his wit's end and assuming their daughter will tire of Per faster in daily doses, the father invites him to move into the villa. Per, a socialist at heart, accepts. Now having completely insinuated himself into the family, he is at leisure to roam the grounds and philosophize about the main evil of modern life which he spits out with contempt: "Blufærdighed," meaning modesty or decency.

He jousts with the father who cannot shake his cool, and comes on to the sexually frustrated mother who keeps a copy of *Kinsey and Women* on her bedside table. She reacts ambiguously at first but then storms off in tears. Per tries to break people by confronting them with the truth — his truth. But he apparently feels nothing himself; he is only "interested" in Susanne, not in love. He tries to shake the old man's convictions about right and wrong and tries to get him to admit these are only relative concepts.

"What do you?" asks the father.

"I dig ... for bodies."

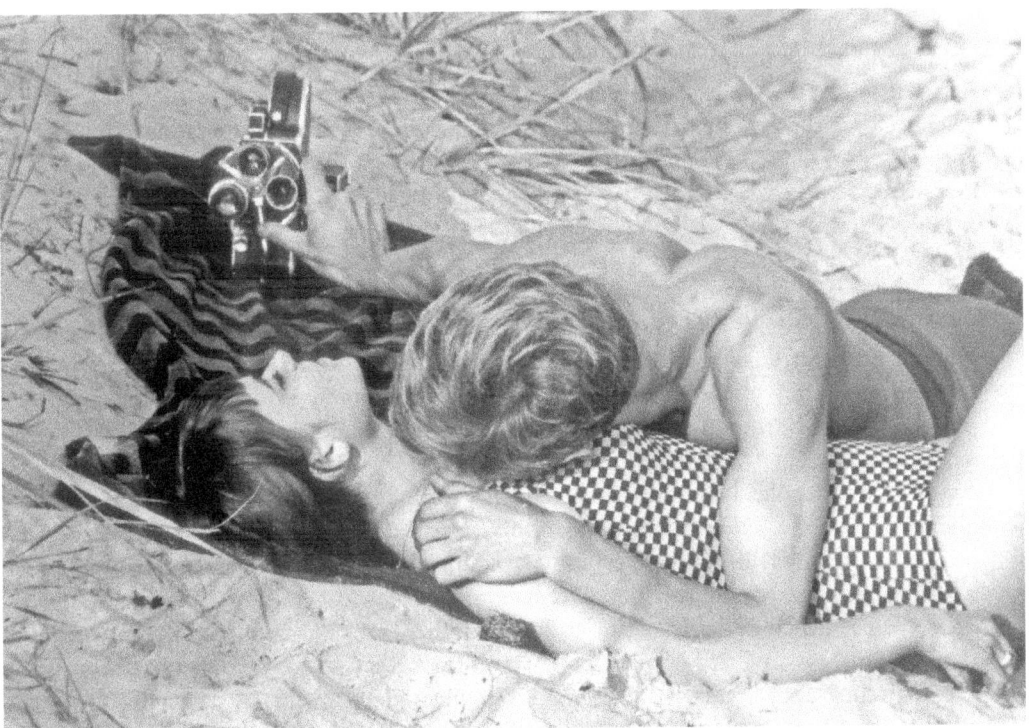

Per (Søren Strømberg) films his own seduction of a teenage girl (Vic Salomonsen) on the beach in *Gift*.

"And that's what you think we are, just corpses?"

One day he is alone with Mom, Susanne having gone off to see her dad at his office to try to talk him into financing Per's film. ("He's sick—surely it will be a sick film." "No—it will be the first *healthy* film.")

Per invites the mother into his room for a film show. He shows her pornographic films. She is embarrassed, repulsed and ashamed. Then he shows her a pornographic film he shot with Susanne. Outraged, she flees his den of depravity and calls her husband at work. He comes home to find Per trying to cajole her into coming out from behind a locked door. He attacks the glibly smiling Per, slapping and dragging him down the grand staircase and throwing him head first out into the yard. He then hurls all his films and equipment out his second-floor window.

Finally the father has been driven to act, not just talk and argue and philosophize. Those are the weapons of the new liberals, the film seems to say, that is how they take control: with endless philosophizing, circular logic and slick talk. Per preys on people who will listen to him and debate and doubt and discuss, but he himself lacks the kind of gut beliefs that drive a man to act.

Susanne has taken a cab home and is distraught to find Per lying in the yard in a pile of films and shattered equipment her father has hurled from an upper-story window. "Don't worry," he tells her, "your father has just been fighting with himself." Susanne rushes up to confront her father, who slaps her across the face and locks her in her room. Firmly clasping his wife's hand, he looks gravely ahead.

Thomsen's message was, according to some, that pornography was a virus that destroyed love and genuine eroticism as surely as the most potent poison, yet he probably intended it to figure in a more metaphorical fashion. Pornography, as a kind of manifesto of unbridled sexual indulgence, could be seen as just a means to an end, a great leveling force that put the rich and poor and people of different generations and races and classes on the same footing, that disproved all the moth-eaten social codes and religions which were only designed to keep people in their place and preserve the power structures, as Per might have expressed it. In this way it could be seen to have obvious parallels with socialism. In its extreme simplicity pornography could be used as an argument to make any set of beliefs or values seem trivial, hypocritical and illogical. This new morality which purportedly held basic human nature highest could be made to seem liberating and humanistic, but in Thomsen's view it was exactly the opposite, the ultimate suppression of individualism, and to his mind these champions of the New Morality who preached sexual liberation as a cure-all had in fact more exploitive and self-serving agendas in play.

Thomsen endlessly referred to them as the "prophets of liberation," the "apostles of liberation" and the "worshippers of liberation." He didn't need to name names since the people he was referring to were prominent enough in the media: people like Sten and Inga Hegeler, Phyllis and Eberhard Kronhausen and Jens Jørgen Thorsen who even once dressed up as Christ and dragged a cross through the streets of Århus in a mockery of the Crucifixion. Now in *Gift* Thomsen had given form to the ultimate prophet of liberation, Per Genitalius: anti–Christ as amateur pornographer toting a hand-held camera and even a Latin-sounding last name.

He had previously elaborated on these themes in a defense published in the daily *Information* back in February:

> The reason I am against pornography is not because I perceive it to be "damaging" but rather because it is an unavoidable consequence of the purely materialistic lifestyle. The young man in the film has chosen flesh as his religion, he is a missionary for that view of life. And he believes — as many on the Left also believe — that if one can just liberate people from modesty they will lose their complexes and become happy.
>
> Here in their recent New Year assessments of 1965, the papers dubbed it "the year of porno," as if that was the culmination. I think things will go much further, and with my film I am trying to jump a few steps ahead and show where we risk ending up. [ED.: "Is that kind of thing legal?" Susanne asks Per in dismay as he shows her a pornographic film. "It will be," he replies.] It is to that end that I wanted to use pornography.
>
> ...I am well aware that there are those who will claim I have something against sexuality and erotica, but it is only the cynical use of erotica I am against. I am afraid that the alternative to conservative ideals which some people — with some justification — battle is not greater freedom but cynicism. Humans are both body and soul and there must be a balance.
>
> I would point out that even though I am against pornography, I don't want to fight it with prohibitions and censorship. I am against every form of censorship. What I believe is that every single person can censor himself. One can, of course, fear that individuals aren't responsible enough to deal with it, and possibly in that case anarchy lurks just around the corner, but I believe that is a risk we must take.

On March 25 the reviews hit the streets, and Thomsen's prediction that critics would slaughter the film proved absolutely correct. Among other things he was accused of reactionary behavior, of being an egomaniac and of fabricating and then attacking a problem that didn't exist. He was also accused of being tone-deaf to the way people really communicated. Others were impressed by his reach — how he rolled up Socialism, pornography and marijuana into the same ball of wax. Still others thought the film was so inept that it didn't deserve to spark a wider debate, but of course it had.

The most common criticism was that the characters, particularly Per, were not realistic. "One might well assume," wrote Christian Braad Thomsen (no relation) in the newspaper *Democraten*, "that *Gift* was made by an Aborigine who had spent all of two days in this country to study us, so despairingly ignorant is Thomsen of his countrymen and the language that we speak here.... There are no young people to be found in Denmark of the type he describes in his film."

Several young viewers interviewed by the press concurred. "You can't believe *Gift* because the characters are so utterly improbable," commented a 20-year-old viewer, "especially Per." "Completely unrealistic," agreed two teens. "The people were caricatures."

But the film was, as Thomsen said, "an attempt to jump a few steps ahead," to see the future, so perhaps Per should have been considered in a more symbolic light.

It is tempting to see it this way. For one thing, nothing is known about his past, where he comes from or how he got to be the way he is. At one point he describes himself as a "man of the future." And in the end he offers no resistance as the father pummels him, and then he tells Susanne not to worry, that her father is only fighting himself. Is he really there at all? And his last name, Genitalius, clearly seems to indicate he's a symbolic figure.

Although the director maintained that Per existed and could be found in Denmark, on another occasion he conceded that perhaps Per "represented a tendency of a time more than a single person." At another point he remarked: "If I am accused of fighting ghosts, that's correct. It is that ghost I have tried to make visible in the form of Per."

And why not? Bergman depicted death as a living figure in *The Seventh Seal*, and Thomsen was giving immorality human form in *Gift*. Maybe Per was indeed the proverbial mystical stranger with uncanny powers who comes and goes leaving everyone changed. The only problem is that he *doesn't* go; at the end he picks himself up off the ground and goes to the door and rings the bell again and again. Perhaps he is human after all and has been defeated or has finally been provoked to violence.

The door doesn't open and the movie ends. Had anyone opened the door, it would have allowed him to start explaining, apologizing, persuading, ... *talking*— his strength. But actions have finally spoken. Would anyone ever take action in Denmark, or would the debating and philosophizing and talking simply go on forever?

If *Gift* makes more sense as a moral parable than as a realistic drama, it wasn't fashionable to see it that way in the Denmark of 1966. Realism was all the rage at the time; that's what "the modern film" was all about and that was what would save Danish cinema. *Gift* was simply out of step with the times and was savaged, in part, for being so.

Still, by boldly dealing with the very latest controversial topic, pornography, it did lay claim to a certain realism or at least topicality. And there were the up-to-date cultural references in *Gift*, like the books (*Kinsey, Fanny Hill*) and certain lines of reasoning that touched on the Danish political situation. Even the film equipment Per works on is the real hand-operated stuff. "Unrealistic" as the characters might be and as low-budget as it undeniably was, *Gift* provides a much better snapshot of the moment than *Weekend* did and reveals much more than almost any other film about the Denmark of its day.

But Thomsen felt himself misunderstood. The film was not meant as a solution for anything. "It is at best a help to self-help, an antidote." It was intended neither as an impassioned defense of conservative dogma nor as an attack on liberalism, but as a warning to both camps. "Materialism and its growing legion of interpreters proclaim the pursuit of carnal pleasure to be the medicine which can cure all human ills, political as well as personal, based on the assumption that there is nothing other than that. That is what Per believes. And his opponent, the father, is close to believing the same thing because he doesn't believe in anything else.... Even in the end when the father eventually counter-attacks, that happens out of desperation and not conviction."[39]

"Doesn't liberality have its positive sides?" asked a writer.

"It *only* has positive sides. What is dangerous about it is that taken point for point it produces a ton of pluses, but the sum of all those pluses is an enormous minus."

Thomsen was not one to tread lightly. He spoke his mind with no effort to be diplomatic. *Gift* was strong because "sometimes the patient needs an operation instead of just medicine." Denmark's leftist cultural-radical front had "terrorized Danish cultural life for the last ten years." The country was embroiled in a "state of ideological war." Socialists were close to animals. And so on.

It was always "us against them" with Thomsen, but against whom? Against everyone, really, or at least every institution. Thomsen was of a libertarian rather than a conservative bent. The conservative press criticized his films as much as the liberal press and he sporadically also lunged out at the right. "I can understand the thinking of the prophets of liberation since undoubtedly the majority of conservatives don't get out of life what they ought to because they are too conditioned by an unquestioning belief in authority and by conformist thought patterns."

Thomsen, at least at this stage of his career, was the kind of reckless warrior that Danish film needs today, sedated as it is by all the awards and commercial success and self-congratulation. Some complain that Danish filmmakers today have nothing to say, nothing on their hearts. Fair enough; films with a fiercely political viewpoint or films that dissent from the trends of the day in the manner of *Gift* are indeed few and far between.

When seen from a contemporary perspective, *Gift* clearly stands out as perhaps the most unusual and oddly compelling film of the era. It has attitude and ideas, it spews righteous wrath and portents of doom. All this is channeled through the character of Per, one of the most darkly intriguing figures in modern Danish cinema, and almost everyone had high praise for Søren Strømberg, the actor who played him. As noted earlier, he had once played in a rock band, and in between acting stints he worked in advertising. These were two professions the fictional Per, with his ability to turn on the charm and to spout slippery rhetoric, would have been good at. He was indeed well cast. (One is reminded that a brash young Tony Blair also led a rock group at one point.)

Yet upon repeated viewings Sisse Reingaard's underplayed performance as the suggestible Susanne strikes one as equally impressive, even though critics at the time complained that she failed to produce "sparks." It would have been a very easy role to overplay and sparks would have been easy to produce, but in all her emotional disengagement she is perfect and emerges as the central enigma of the film and its most lifelike character. She is Per's impassive and noncommittal co-conspirator. She watches his pornographic films with only the slightest trace of visible reaction, but what does she really think?

A spirit of voyeurism and psychological sadism permeates *Gift* and tempts comparisons to Michael Powell's 1960 classic *Peeping Tom*. Although it lacks that film's high-pitched drama, there is a similar feeling of ritual and fetishism about the 16mm equipment that Per surrounds himself with. He is never without his 16mm camera, filming people without their permission, turning it on and propping it in place at just the right angle to capture his foreplay with a girl in the sand. Back in his room he constantly pores over his spools of film, his treasure trove of violated privacies. He is always at work on them, winding them through a viewing machine, applying splices or lacing film into his projector. The flickering of the image on his wall and the clanky, rhythmic sound of the projector as the spectators sit transfixed in darkness, their facial expressions telling the story as much as the filmed images ... this is the classic iconography of voyeurism. And his private shows for invited guests only — Susanne and her mom — always take place in his room, giving it the feel of something adolescent and dirty.

The music contributes to the effect. The movie opens with a discordant and repetitive organ piece that resurfaces throughout the film. It was composed by Niels Viggo Bentzon, who had written music for experimental films going back to 1943's *The Girl and Pan*. Simple and low-tech but effective, it gives the ominous impression that the characters as well as the times are in a state of chaos and disharmony.

A very different feel is conveyed by the other piece of music used, the pop-rock song "My Situation," sung in English by The Matadors. Composed by the 18-year-old recording wunderkind Tommy Petersen, it exudes teen angst in the style of the day, although it is hard to see how it specifically fits the story other than to represent the younger generation.

These are the only two pieces of music and both are repeated throughout, just

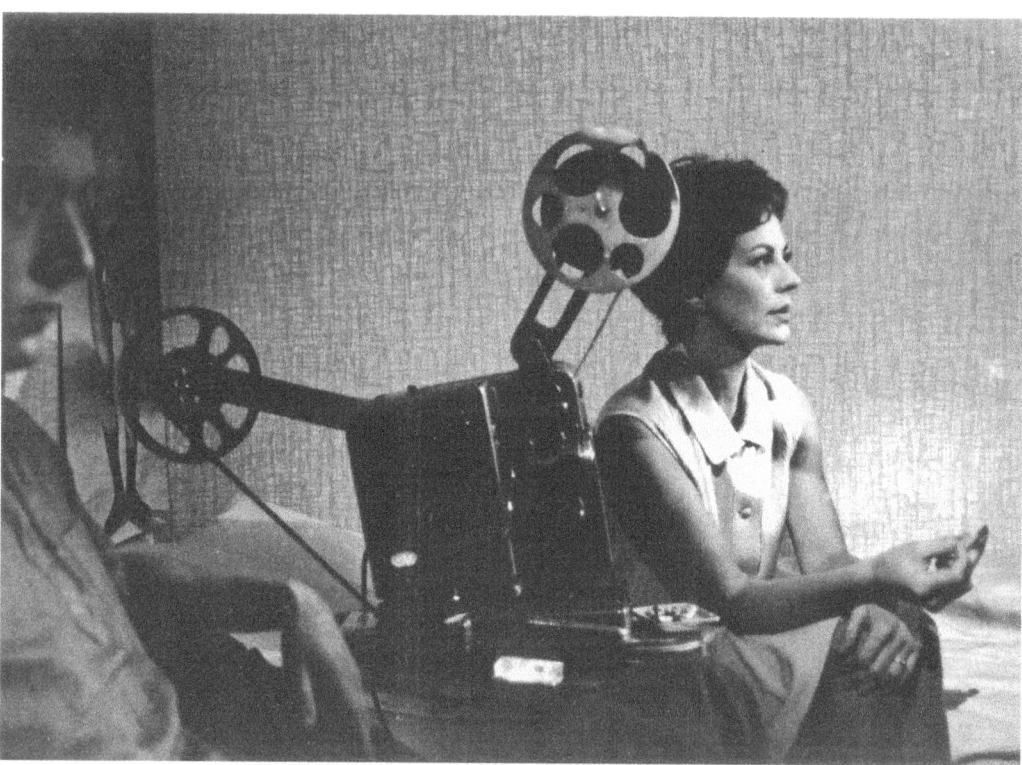

Top: Per (Søren Strømberg) shows Susanne (Sisse Reingaard) porn movies in his room. *Bottom:* Per treats Susanne's mother (Astrid Villaume) to movies starring her daughter.

dropped in at various points. One is tempted to conclude that, unlike radio vet Poul Nyrup, Thomsen really knew nothing about the younger set. He had no affinity for the music and could only find one song to represent a whole generation. This and the lack of any background or mood music makes for a rather barren soundscape, but the starkness is appropriate. To pack it full of the latest teen tunes in the style of Nyrup's gangster trilogy would have been distracting.

The film turned a nice profit for Thomsen in Denmark but he never won a Bodil for it, and it was never considered part of the so-called New Danish Wave. Quite the opposite. The big artistic success in 1966 for Danish film was rather Henning Carlsen's *Hunger*, an adaptation of the Knut Hamsun novel about a starving artist trying to maintain self-respect and integrity in Kristiania (the old name for Oslo) of the 1890s. Like *Weekend*, it was a revolt against the feel-good contentedness of the folk-comedy and it was the film that won the Bodil that year. Additionally its lead actor, Per Oscarsson, won the best actor award for it in Cannes. Finally Denmark once again had a film figure who was internationally acclaimed!

In contrast, Thomsen's movie was sold as the latest sex film from naughty Denmark, rolling out to foreign markets in the same censored version that had played domestically.

In May of 1967 a full page ad in *Continental Film Review* magazine heralded its opening in London at the Jacey Tatler theater in Piccadilly, a membership club of the type where most "sex films" screened. It played under its original title, *Gift*, and was hyped as "the study of a private world," "the Danish film that was banned in Denmark."

It was imported by Anthony Balch, one of the more colorful characters in the movie game. An underground filmmaker himself who moved in Beat circles and counted the likes of William Burroughs and Brion Gysin among his friends and collaborators, his tastes were eclectic. He was the first to bring Tod Browning's *Freaks* to home audiences and introduced Benjamin Christensen's *Häxan* to '60s Britain, condensing it and re-titling it *Witchcraft Through the Ages*. Because Balch was ever on the lookout for the latest in groundbreaking and confrontational cinema, it was a given that the films of Liberated Denmark would attract his attention. ("Balch had a touch for titling," recently recalled friend and fellow film buff Tony Rayns. "He released a nondescript Scandinavian sex film under the title *Skin Skin*— he was proud of that one — and watched it clean up at the Cinephone on Oxford Street."[40])

Gift drew crowds and played in other British theaters as well, but not everybody got the point. An anonymous wag who went to see it at the Cameo Moulin noted, "Packed house at 2 in the afternoon, not a breath of air. The film turned out to be an interminable lump of Danish philosophy, intensely worded and intellectually indigestible. In brief the old story of the struggle between generations with a kind of young amoral Tartuffe taking over a nice bourgeois family. The audience seemed to be having a well earned sleep; or perhaps in the anonymous dark they were quietly indulging their own fantasies. I advise anyone tempted to spend their money on this aphrodisiac rubbish to [think again]."

In January of 1968 it opened in New York, re-dubbed *Venom* for its American release and promoted as the latest Scandinavian "sexation." Critics might have been expected to dismiss it out of hand, and some did, including *The Daily News* which called it awful. But it also won praise, no doubt to the shock of the critical community back in Denmark. *The New York Times* found its generation gap theme to be of particular interest and rated the acting first-class, although scribe Renate Adler wished she could have seen the uncensored version which she figured would have been a very different experience. But it would likely be years, she concluded, before that version could ever be shown in the U.S.

Archer Winston of *The New York Post* compared it to *A Stranger Knocks* and Dreyer's *Day of Wrath*, containing as it did some of the same thematic threads but adding a new element, the young marijuana generation. *Venom*, he declared, ranked high on his list of the year's best foreign films.

Finally, Thomsen received praise from the ever so hip and fashionable *Playboy* which called the film honest and clear-sighted, "a jolt of shock therapy." Their scribe was also intrigued by the film's generation gap theme.

After *Gift* there could be no doubt that Denmark was leading the way into unexplored territory. Barriers were falling day by day and things that would have been shocking only a few years ago were now simply accepted as part of the new times. To some this was cause for celebration, but there was also a widespread sense of insecurity, and to many it seemed as if things were spinning rapidly out of control. The old morality was crumbling, but what would replace it ... if anything?

Loving Couples and *Night Games*

Sweden also had its share of outspoken personalities in the film milieu. The previously mentioned Mai Zetterling was one. She was responsible for that country's scandal film of 1966, *Night Games*.

The slender Nordic beauty had come a long way since she had been cast as the shop girl with loose morals in the Ingmar Bergman–scripted *Torment* over 20 years before. That movie had attracted the attention of British filmmakers and won her a role in the 1947 picture *Frieda*, playing the German bride of an RAF officer (a part for which the blue-eyed and blonde-haired actress was perfectly suited). She continued to appear in British films through the '50s and into the '60s, but grew tired of acting and in 1962 began her directorial career with a short film called *The War Game*. As she told *The Associated Press* in 1973, "I gave up acting because I was not a passive person. I had been infuriated about direction in films again and again. I wanted, for many reasons, to do my own ideas, positive ideas."

Shortly thereafter she returned to Sweden and in 1964 made her feature film directorial debut with *Loving Couples*, a loose adaptation of an Agnes von Krusenstjerna novel. It dealt with three pregnant woman who meet in a birth clinic and begin to reminisce about their sexual pasts, their stories conveyed in flashback. During a midsummer's night they act out an erotic hide-and-seek that includes prostitution, incest and other forms of sexual expression. Breasts are exposed and characters with homosexual and pedophiliac tendencies are part of the mix. Viewers were startled by a number of graphic scenes which included copulating dogs, a dog shot to death, a dead fetus thrown into a garbage can, genuine birthing sequences and so forth. It was a stylistically bold and idiosyncratic work and came to be respected as such by critics, although at the time it caused controversy in Zetterling's otherwise open-minded homeland as well as at Cannes. (By 2006 all was forgiven and the Gothenburg Film Festival honored *Loving Couples* with a tribute revival screening.)

Bizarre characters, among them Lauritz Falk (center, in drag), haunt the castle in *Night Games*.

Zetterling stayed in Sweden to make *Night Games* in 1966. Based on her own novel and shot entirely at Penningby Castle, it was to prove a bigger commercial success and would be even more controversial.

The main character is Jan, a 35-year-old who is still trying to come to grips with his decadent upper-class family. One day he and his girlfriend Mariana return to the castle where he grew up. They wander the silent, empty corridors as the old pictures reawaken memories of his past life, particularly the problematic relationship he had with his eccentric, neurotic mother. The grand dame of the castle, she was fond of arranging lavish orgies to which she liked to invite a bizarre clutch of characters and at which the boy was present. He recalls these overtly erotic scenes. Childbirth is again a main theme; his mother throws a huge party the same evening she is to give birth—but the baby emerges dead. The past and present intertwine as Jan literally walks into scenes from his life as a 12-year-old. He finally liberates himself from his dominating mother during one of her grand parties, and the castle goes up in flames that night. He is now able to start a new life with Mariana.

Night Games was the purest of pure-blown art films, yet its erotic content and catalog of perversions got it banned at Venice, aroused controversy in Sweden and gave its English publicity an exploitation flavor ("*Night Games* is a film about hatred and love among degenerate people..."). When it landed in America, at the San Francisco Film Festival, jury member Shirley Temple Black walked out on it. John Waters, a devoted fan of the film, was witness to that moment and still savors the memory. He obtained the film's poster, and it can be seen hanging on a wall in at least one of his early films.[41]

Zetterling's sense of moral engagement won her comparisons to Buñuel, though like all Swedish filmmakers she found herself forever in the shadow of Bergman. Like Bergman she made deeply personal and symbolic films although she was never considered his equal, according to some because she was a woman. But these two films, at least, were every bit as original and could only have been made by Zetterling ... and only in Sweden.[42]

Part Two

1967–1970: Censorship's Last Stand

I, a Nobleman

Mac Ahlberg and Per Guldbrandsen were back again in 1967 with the third installment of their *I, a Something* trilogy; *I, a Nobleman*. This film was based on the real life story of a celebrated impostor who captivated the Danish public in 1963 when his bizarre double life was suddenly revealed. By day he was a respectable family man, a low-paid accountant in a chemical firm. By night he held court in a stately villa, masquerading as the Marquis *Marcel* de Sade, millionaire and supposed blood descendent of the Marquis de Sade. Here he would lord about in regal dress accompanied by his chauffeur. High society flocked to the lavish parties he threw, all too willing to be duped by his exotic charade.

The illusion was shattered one day when police collared him trying to flee the country with a pistol and a satchel of money he'd defrauded from his company, who had unknowingly financed his extravagant lifestyle.

He was sentenced to four and a half years in prison, and upon his release he was persuaded by Peer Guldbrandsen to participate in some capacity in the making of *I, a Nobleman*, with Gabriel Axel to play his part. Purportedly some actors balked at appearing in a film along with the "real" fake Marquis — a criminal. (He is still around and hamming it at the time of this writing, now living in the Vesterbro neighborhood and posing on occasion for the press in full nobleman attire.)

The tall, courtly Axel, his hair finely bleached and coiffed and his stately Van Dyke well trimmed, was perfectly cast. Having been raised in France, he was able to adopt the right airs and cock the occasional eyebrow with understated patrician flair. It was the kind of role most actors would have over-played, but Axel played it with the appropriate emotional ambiguity of a man destined to function as a conduit for other people's depraved fantasies, people who in the end betray him but are themselves revealed as the real fools.

The film was very different from either of its predecessors. Although clearly a low-budget production, the several fantasy sequences that feature women in historical dress stripping and gyrating to pounding jazz music were well choreographed, beautifully shot in Ahlberg's evocative film noir style, and, not least, bizarre. Seen today, these episodes are delightfully kitsch but they're also very hot, going beyond what would have been permitted elsewhere. A long scene in the mansion where Axel's debauched friends get car-

Gabriel Axel (left) as Marcel de Sade casts a lecherous gaze in *I, a Nobleman*.

ried away with themselves eventually assumes a kind of hallucinogenic character. Axel never participates in the action but instead functions as the impassive catalyst whose presence sets things in motion as his guests work themselves into a lather of inhibition and foolishness.

Among the cast could be found *Weekend*'s Lotte Tarp who was busy burnishing her reputation as Denmark's favorite bimbo with a topless turn as "The Baroness."

Axel was involved, as a director, in the other high profile erotic film made in Denmark that year, *Hagbard and Signe*, an epic love story set in the time of the Vikings. Shot on Iceland and filmed by one of Denmark's best cinematographers, Henning Bendtsen, it featured magnificent scenery and dramatic action montages aplenty, including Kurosawa-inspired sword-fights on horseback. Yet, although the film was the most expensive Danish production to date, critics were underwhelmed. Grandiose and lacking excitement, they said.

The stark naked appearance of former Danish pop princess Gitte Hænning, who at the age of eight had had a hit with the single "I Want to Marry Daddy," stole much of the spotlight. That also earned the picture a condemned rating from the National Catholic Office for Motion Pictures when it opened in the States the following year, but the rating failed to scare off American critics and ticket buyers, who were somewhat more receptive to the film than their Danish counterparts.

Henning Carlsen, fresh off his success with *Hunger*, also made a film with an erotic

A scene from *I, a Nobleman*: Gabriel Axel considers his next move (actress unidentified).

theme in 1967 called *People Meet and Sweet Music Fills the Heart*. Starring the one and only Harriet Andersson, this mystical rumination on the various dynamics of physical and spiritual love was based on a nearly unfilmable, free association novel of the same name by Jens August Schade. Tinted throughout in various colors, the film was ponderous and not really sexy in any sort of earthly sense but was undeniably "art" and won the Bodil. When it opened in 1969 in the U.S. it managed the ultimate mixed review from *Time Magazine* which called it at once boring, roguish and very entertaining.

Gitte Hænning shields chained companion (Russian actor Oleg Widow) in *Hagbard and Signe*.

I Am Curious (Yellow)

"Take out this film in ten years and you will remember, as if it were yesterday, the tiresomely crazy porno years of the 1960s."
—Vilgot Sjöman

"Swedish society has made sex easy and love almost impossible."
—Charles Champlin

But the big erotic sensation that year in Denmark — and the rest of the world — was a Swedish film, *I Am Curious (Yellow)*, directed by Vilgot Sjöman. It would put the issue of film censorship on the front burner in every western country, and this time the lead actress was even blonde.

She was the same blonde Sjöman had used in *491*, Lena Nyman. Ever since the ordeal of that film he felt he owed her. He had tried to find a part for her in his next film, *The Dress*, but she wasn't right for it. He followed up that picture with *My Sister, My Love*, a film that purports to portray incest, and then finally he found another role for Nyman in *I Am Curious (Yellow)*, or rather he decided to mold a film around her. He was in the midst of a creative crisis, and in one crystalline moment at the start of 1965 he decided to clear the decks of all his films-in-progress and make "something young ... something with Lena Nyman."

His experiences with *491* had left him feeling embittered and disillusioned on a number of levels and *I Am Curious (Yellow)* was also an attempt to respond to some of that.

As noted, conservative politicians had used *491* for their own purposes, while his own studio had run scared and bought him out of his contract in order to be done with him. Now he was prepared to bring party politics into a commercial feature film.

He would demand total creative freedom with this picture, not least the freedom to shoot erotic scenes in which the performers didn't have to sheath their bodies in skin-colored tights as they had in *491*. He was determined to depict sexuality in a realistic fashion and to put an end to the kind of fakery that Christina Schollin had turned into an art form in *Dear John*. Though he credited that performance as the best of her career, he fumed about "all this fuss with sheets — the chief weapon of film conventionalism simply accepted by audiences, producers and actors year in and year out." Schollin was a prototypical "sheet virtuoso," with a magic ability to appear in "so many bed scenes without revealing a glimpse of breasts or loins. (Back and bottom having long been part of conventionally accepted nudity.)"[1]

But this new film was about more than creative freedom or nudity. It was an experiment in form and content, an attempt to break down the barriers between reality and fiction and a bid to demystify the filmmaking process. It would be a lot of different things all at once; a rumination on modern youth, a take on the state of Swedish society and a check-list of Sjöman's own personal hang-ups. And not least it was an occasionally poignant story about a confused and conflicted teenage girl who, armed with a tape recorder, youthful indignation and a yen to fantasize, goes out onto the streets to find answers.

Nyman was then a student at the Swedish national school of drama, and because Sjöman had to work around her schedule there, the initial footage was filmed over the summer of 1966. He consulted closely at every turn with her and the small ensemble of professional actors he had gathered together. They had to discuss things since there was no script and since Sjöman, 41 years old at this point, not surprisingly doubted his instincts when it came to depicting modern youth.

The film would be, as he noted over and over again in his notes, a "kaleidoscope." He would cram all of Sweden into it. "The film that's a newspaper," he termed it at one point, only half in jest. It would touch on a plethora of subjects — "let it overflow" — that he and his cast found interesting, disturbing or problematic, and this chaotic approach was reflected in its scattershot free-associative form. Interviews would jumble together with fantasy sequences and slabs of dramatic narrative. There was even a film-within-a-film subplot in which Nyman has an affair with both director and leading man as fictional commercial filmmaking, documentary and whimsical home movie collided.

Sjöman was torn between telling a story and telling a kaleidoscope, and it was harder than anticipated to make it all gel. That fall and winter he began shooting additional scenes in an effort to tie it all together. He ended up with a mountain of footage, and as he sweated through the final phase of editing in June of 1967 he was compelled to cut whole scenes and sub-plots just to get down to a three-and-a-half-hour running time. This led to his decision to make a second film, *I Am Curious (Blue)*—blue and yellow being the two colors of the Swedish flag. It would not be a sequel but a kind of parallel film.

The result was a bold experiment — so bold that Scandinavian cinema would not see anything like it until the emergence of Lars von Trier and his Dogme95 movement in the mid–'90s. *Weekend* has already been mentioned as a precursor to Dogme but in fact the movement's debt to *I Am Curious (Yellow)* is far more extensive.

Aside from scenes in Lena's flat, nestled in a condemned building, almost all shooting was done on location. "Get out of the studio!" Sjöman had exhorted in his notes early on, decrying the fact that nobody in the tradition-bound Swedish film industry was trained in location shooting. His various notations throughout the filming process read like a blueprint of Dogme95: "Draw on the actors' own lives and ways of life for the material" ... "We're playing ourselves" ... "Destroy the script."... He preached the virtues of shooting in available light, and had his actors wear their own clothes and use their own names. He included scenes using people with Down Syndrome, as did Lars von Trier in *The Idiots*. Additionally his camera crew is glimpsed on screen. Like von Trier, he wanted to make the filmmaking process visible.

And he ran into some of the same problems von Trier would grapple with three decades later. This improvisation thing was damned difficult to pull off; Sjöman admits there was only one instance of truly spontaneous filmmaking in his picture. Both directors also found that the shooting of explicit sex scenes was tough for their supposedly liberated cast and crews. And finally both directors shot tons of film. Sjöman could have spoken for von Trier when he said, "I have had to feel my way along, wasting film, making mistakes." All the Dogme "vows of chastity" had one general aim: to allow a film to change and grow right up to the moment the prints were struck. "Keep the doors open to the end," Sjöman had declared.

Yet in some fundamental ways *I Am Curious (Yellow)* was antithetical to Dogme. It was staged to a large degree, and with its fantasy sequences and disrupted narrative flow it wasn't strictly shot in the "here and now." And Sjöman himself and his personal fixations were very much front and center. In fact the fictional Nyman was as much Sjöman as Nyman. Dogme was an attempt to take the director's ego out of the equation to the point that he or she wouldn't even be credited, but there was no way that Sjöman's name could be left off the credits. This was his film in bold strokes.

He himself had termed it "reconstructed reality," and reconstructed it was, but did that make it any less real? Real life itself is no standard narrative; it's composed of disconnected daydreams, random musings and interrupted sub-plots. Some of this random spirit is represented in the film by the fleeting appearance of texts: slogans, graffiti, banners, posters, words simply printed out. Today this use of texts seems like a prescient satire of the "sound bite" culture to come.

Journalists from the whole world were invited to attend the premiere in Stockholm in November of 1967. Many were taken aback by the sex. There was frequent male and female nudity, scenes of oral-genital contact and at least seven instances of (apparent) sexual intercourse. One Yugoslavian critic was surprised by something else: the fact that apparently in Sweden the revolution was being waged only in the sexual sphere. (It would be left to another Yugoslavian, the Belgrade-born filmmaker Dušan Makavejev, to show how revolution, politics and sexuality were inextricably intertwined.)

The censorship board didn't know how to rule on the film and requested an opinion from a higher authority, a seven-member advisory panel. The panel decided the film should be allowed, calling it "an artistic work that for a Swedish film is characterized by an unusual moral and political engagement." The board went along.

"We had reservations about elements of violence," noted panel member Anne Marie Thunberg, "but not about the sex. We didn't find it exciting in the context of the film. If we had found the sexual scenes exciting, we would have had to recommend that they be cut."[2]

There was anger in Parliament at the film due to the politics expressed and the fact that the up-and-coming politician Olof Palme (to become Swedish prime minister on February 10, 1969, and later to be assassinated) appeared in it, talking freely. Like other interviewees he did not know he was to appear in a "porn film," and because of it his career was temporarily placed in jeopardy. Another unwitting participant was Martin Luther King who talked on camera (to Sjöman) while he was in Stockholm on a visit. As King later wrote to a Swedish colleague, he never had and never would participate in or support pornographic or extremely political films or publications of any kind. Other lesser known personages appeared without their consent, and at least one sued.[3]

The panel's recommendation was criticized by unhappy officials, including Eric Skoglund, the head of the censorship board. He had dissented against their decision and now he warned that indecent or pornographic films would be able to seek legal sanction by laying claim to artistic merit. He feared this would embolden sleaze merchants to test the censor's tolerance by releasing a lot of more or less pornographic films. Nevertheless the picture was certified for 15-and-over. (In February of 2003 the film was shown in the U.S. at a retrospective of Grove Press releases that took place at the Harvard Film Archives, and the minimum age was set at 18 — and strictly enforced.)

Sjöman had again managed to divide the public and create a scandal. Many attacked him, including some Swedish leftist groups. No wonder; the movie could be, as one writer noted, seen as a "devastating attack on the shallowness of the counter-culture,"[4] primarily due to Nyman's character who struck many as empty-headed and hypocritical, lacking the strength of her noisily advertised convictions. But wasn't this the way young folks really acted? Compulsive, emotional, at times inarticulate, half-cocked and too fed up with adults to bother with their good advice? Could it be both? Could the film simultaneously function as an attack on the status quo as well as the counter-culture? Could it be, in today's lingo, a *mocku-* as well as a *docu*-mentary? Many of the American critics who claimed to understand its political dimension called it a sophomoric leftist rant ... or was it a satire on sophomoric leftist ranting? If it lacked sophistication perhaps that was the intent: "make propaganda coarse and crude ... throw it in the public's face," Sjöman had mused in his notes.

In any case the criticism from the left came as a blow to Sjöman and led to his loss of "political innocence" as he termed it. But others supported him, including Bergman, who called it a masterpiece.

That was odd since Sjöman claimed his film was a rebellion against all that Bergman represented as a filmmaker.

People on both sides of the issue claimed that it made the censorship board redundant. How much further could a film go?

In Denmark *I Am Curious (Yellow)* passed without any cuts, and this was something of a surprise since Jean Genet's *Un Chant d'amour* had just been totally banned. Sjöman's film opened there on December 11, about a month after its Swedish release.

How would Danes relate to this film? Would it generate as much interest in Denmark as it had in Sweden? "Probably not," reckoned reviewer Knud Voeler.[5] "The film is distinctly Swedish in its attitude and slant. But it is, in its rejection of all forms of Puritanism, prejudice and convention — and in spite of its brutality — well-intentioned enough, and we can learn as much from this film as if it were one of our own."

Politiken's Herbert Steinthal thought that it had plenty of local relevance: "*I Am Curi-*

ous (Yellow) concerns itself with Swedes and their lack of engagement, their apathy to the outside world ... and with their self-satisfied welfare state mentality. But Denmark is not so far away. The parallels are so obvious that with some small adjustments the film could very easily be about us." Steinthal was also surprised that a Swede had been capable of such a teasing sense of humor. It was not a quality Danes ascribed to their neighbors across the Øresund Strait whom they generally viewed as dour and reserved.

In Norway the film was totally banned. Between 1963 and 1967 twenty-two films were prohibited by censors there, but those who wanted to could always drive to Sweden to see the movies. In 1963 Norwegians had taken bus tours to Sweden to see the uncut version of *The Silence,* and now it was being reported that students from Trondheim were driving 300 kilometers to the Swedish border to see *I Am Curious (Yellow).*

In America the film was distributed by Grove Press, the renegade publishing house run by leftist maverick Barney Rosset. Founded in 1951, Grove had published the works of D.H. Lawrence, Henry Miller, Hubert Selby, William Burroughs and other literary rebels, and had repeatedly beaten back government attempts to ban these books. In the mid-1960s Rosset became involved in film, commissioning screenplays from some of his writers and even producing a short film by Samuel Beckett. It was natural that the company would become interested in distributing movies; that was where the biggest First Amendment battles would now be fought.

While on a junket to the Frankfurt book fair in 1967, Rosset heard about the film and the controversy it had caused in Sweden and flew to Stockholm to see it. He found it to be a "very powerful political statement ... the first thing that I had ever seen that was based on women's rights in an upper middle-class country." He purchased American rights for 100,000 dollars and left Stockholm with a print.

As could be expected, U.S. Customs officers insisted on seeing the film before allowing it to enter the country. This was in January of 1968. Their finding was also as one might have expected: importation was denied on the grounds that the film was obscene, primarily due to (apparent) acts of fellatio and cunnilingus and brief shots of an exposed if flaccid male member. A trial by jury loomed.

Rosset enlisted the aid of attorney Edward de Grazia who had won prior cases for books by Burroughs and Miller. A select group of officials and professional people who were to testify at the trial then gathered in a dank little screening room in the Treasury Department building on Varick Street in downtown Manhattan. Sitting on folding metal chairs, they watched the film. This small audience consisted mostly of Rosset's team of expert witnesses. They included respected film reviewers and professors as well as the likes of Dr. Howard Moody of the Judson Memorial Church and literary heavyweight Norman Mailer. At the trial they gave moving testimony. Critic Hollis Alpert argued that it was a "devastating retort to the screen's traditional way of handling erotic material," and the film reaped similar praise from the others.

Sjöman himself came over to testify and to try to explain as best he could a complicated film. He was seen by many has a prophet of sexual liberation, but for this part he was clearly miscast. He despised coarseness and had been raised in a Puritan manner, and with his Amish-style beard, close cropped hair and thick-framed glasses he resembled more than anything a Quaker elder (he had even briefly studied at a Quaker school in Philadelphia back in 1956). He was cut from very different cloth than the Danish "porn evangelists" Thomsen had warned of, and upon even the most cursory of glances it was clear his film was not preaching sexual liberation.

He stated that his intention with the film was to portray Sweden at that very moment in time via the viewpoint of a female character — "a new kind of female" — who demanded the same freedoms that men had always had. Did it have any social importance? That was the central issue. Certainly it had lots of politics. It was loaded with politics. But if there was a serious political message Sjöman seemed to constantly undercut it with ironic asides and deflecting maneuvers. Where did a serious political message stop and satire begin?

Fine points like these were lost on the government prosecutor who preferred instead to grill Sjöman as to whether Lena Nyman's lips had actually touched her lover's penis in perhaps the most crucial scene from a legal standpoint. (He didn't know.)

All was for naught. The prosecutor, as Alpert noted, "had been cleverer than he seemed during the course of the testimony. He made his case simply by showing the jury the film."[6] — and they unanimously found it obscene.

This was not necessarily bad news for Rosset since he could now take the case to the appeals court where judges were routinely setting aside obscenity convictions. With any luck a forceful verdict could establish precedent and make it easier for future "questionable" films to screen. The U.S. Court of Appeals for the Second Circuit did indeed reverse the decision that fall of 1968, ruling two to one that the film merited constitutional protection and could be exhibited.

The government decided not to appeal, but in any event this ruling only applied to New York, Connecticut and Vermont. That was good enough for Grove, which launched the film in two modest-sized Manhattan theaters on March 10, 1969. One of them was the Evergreen, the company's own venue in Greenwich Village. The massive publicity the movie had received throughout 1968 made it the most eagerly awaited film of the day, a movie that people scalped tickets for. Ads for the film published in New York papers in May of 1969 merely instructed the public on "how to see *I Am Curious (Yellow)* without standing in line" and didn't even bother to promote it. That was hardly necessary.

The crush to see the film was news in itself, even when people were trying to get *out* of theaters. People like Jackie Onassis, who showed up at the Cinema 57 Rendezvous with husband Aristotle and then walked out halfway though the picture. Her great escape sent her straight into a gaggle of paparazzi that had been dogging her and she apparently ended up decking one of the shutterbugs. Pics of the sprawled cameraman adorned papers the following day and made it seem that the movie was so shocking it literally knocked folks for a loop.

The buzz around the picture was nothing short of sensational, but Sjöman's intentions had been anything but, and many complained the whole thing was unutterable boredom.

In conveying sexuality Sjöman rejected the overheated exaggerations that usually dominated erotic depictions in cinema, and his leading lady was appropriately unsensational. She was the antithesis of the bad girl types who populated American exploitation cinema, usually either victimized bimbos or out-of-control nymphomaniacs. She liked sex, wanted it and had it in all different situations but was really just an average girl, and this confused a lot of viewers and somehow made the film unsexy. In the context of exploitation cinema — the operative dynamic in American film culture — sex could never be just a normal, healthy activity, even if Nyman for much of the film seemed to be anywhere but in a healthy place.

Her unwillingness or inability to play the stereotypical blonde seemed to incur the wrath of many American critics. Rex Reed, writing for *The New York Times*, was particularly scathing. In his view the film was "pseudo-pornography at its ugliest and least titillating," with various sexual acts "by people who are not only so physically repulsive that to be even slightly titillated by their grotesqueness would suggest to me the need for consultation with a reputable psychiatrist, but by people who actually seem to hate what they are doing." Leonard Gross, the European editor of *Look Magazine*, largely agreed: "Sjöman makes something violent and frightening out of what is normally delightful and affirming.... The first sex scenes are rollicking fun ... but the sex soon turns sour, vulgar, selfish and violent."[7] Reed, like others, felt that the politics was cheap cover for the sex and it drove him up a wall to think that porn might be masquerading as art. In truth it seems that Sjöman's greatest crime was that he hadn't given us attractive looking people in the usual situations, and in refusing to do so he revealed just how bound erotic cinema was to a set of immutable conventions.

Pity the poor Swede. He hadn't set out to make a "sex film" but the Americans insisted on seeing it as one and were now slamming him for failing to deliver the goods. For their part, American sexploitation directors were green with envy. This was the kind of breakthrough they had long dreamed of, and now it had been achieved by a European film that they didn't understand and that in their opinion wasn't even sexy. William Rotsler, director of films such as *Suburban Pagans* and *House of Pain and Pleasure*, dismissed it as "deadly dull and about as erotic as a flooded gopher hole" in his book *Contemporary Erotic Cinema*.

Others took a more nuanced view: Kenneth Turan and Stephen Zito in *Sinema* credited Nyman with a "rare ability to project warmth, intellectual confusion and basic goodness of character," but concurred that she was no sex goddess.

A Danish critic had noted way back on occasion of the Stockholm premiere in November of 1967 that this picture was anything but what people were led to expect. How true. Even in Scandinavia teenage lads had lined up to see the first "porn film," but Americans seemed to find a sex film that wasn't a sex film particularly base and unforgivable. Additionally the Swedish twist to the political and social topics at play, such as non-violence, feminism, prison reform and the class society, made the issues seem remote for those who were paying attention. A lot of folks apparently weren't; at a show in New York the subtitles were projected below the screen for the whole duration of the film, and hence impossible to read, and nobody complained.

Many who rushed the turnstiles in the spring of 1969 were baffled and disappointed. It became something of a popu-

Lena Nyman in *I Am Curious (Yellow)*.

lar wisdom in the trade that the film ruined the market for any more of these "experimental" Scandinavian sex films. Sjöman himself was the first victim as *I Am Curious (Blue)*, released a year after ...*Yellow*, met with overwhelming indifference.

But the hype, much of it supplied by seething conservatives, was still bringing in record crowds. At one point a Maryland attorney claimed that if the film were allow to screen in that state it would lead directly to "couples copulating in the aisles." Who could ask for a better advertisement?

By May Grove had opened the film in Philadelphia to block-long lines and scalpers selling two-dollar tickets for ten bucks a pop. Big theater chains were offering vast sums of money to get the film, willing to risk police raids and lawsuits for a stake in this bonanza. Grove picked their spots carefully for more openings, and in six months the film grossed more than four million dollars on just 25 screens. Over the weekend of November 26, 1969, it became the first foreign-language film to top the American charts and remained the most successful foreign picture for the next two decades. Along with *Easy Rider* it was the youth-culture phenomenon of the year and made it easier for other sexually frank films like *Midnight Cowboy* and *Straw Dogs* to be accepted by mainstream audiences.

There would be more lawsuits, plenty of them. American censorship was exceedingly patchwork and outside the realm of the Second Circuit Appeals Court the film was fair game. States and localities—and individuals—could still sue, and they did. Local sheriffs could decide the film was obscene and close down theaters and arrest theater employees, and they did. It was like the wild west. In some places it was judged obscene and in other places not. Grove adapted a novel twist to their defense efforts by offering local First Amendment attorneys a cut of the box office for every day they could keep the film playing in their town.

It was all more grist for the mills of free-speechers and moral crusaders alike, the latter continuing to attack the film with a bitterness that in retrospect hardly seems merited. Everybody had an opinion. A Superior Court judge in conservative Phoenix spoke for many when he declared that the film "had no plot, no economic message and no religious dogma. Its only message is immoral copulation, public fornication and illicit habits." Sjöman had predicted all of this back in the spring of 1967: "If this film has been properly made," he wrote in his book *I Was Curious*, "20 to 30 percent will highly approve of it; the rest will think that it's 'worth discussing,' 'goddamn rubbish,' 'staggeringly inartistic,' 'unnecessarily vulgar,' 'unsurpassed speculation [exploitation] with an eye to profit' and wonder 'what's gotten into Sjöman?,' etc."

Chaos reigned, and activists on both sides of the issue prayed for a Supreme Court decision to clear the air.

I Am Curious (Yellow) was a watershed event in American popular culture and helped set in motion the country's wider sex revolution. Magazines featured the film prominently in countless photo-laden articles on the growing preoccupation with sex in cinema, theater and art, while TV comedians made dirty, innuendo-laden jokes that belied claims that America was becoming more sophisticated and open-minded about sexuality. Elsewhere books like *Portnoy's Complaint* were flying off the shelves and TV commercials were getting suggestive to an unprecedented degree ("Take it off— take it *all* off," demanded a Swedish beauty queen in a shaving cream commercial).

Conservative America counter-attacked.

Senator Everett Dirksen cited *I Am Curious (Yellow)* as yet one more reason why lawmakers should support his bill to limit Supreme Court power in obscenity hearings. A reporter asked him if he had actually seen the film himself. "Lord, no," came his curt reply. Anti-obscenity rallies in Miami, Detroit and elsewhere drew tens of thousands of supporters and the blessings of Richard Nixon. Raids against films, books and magazines with sexual content were on the rise. In Chicago prints of Jack Smith's underground film *Flaming Creatures* were seized; three cinemas were padlocked and a movie house manager arrested. And small theater companies were going even further. New York police stormed a playhouse on the Lower East Side and arrested ten actors and the manager for their involvement in a production of *Che* which featured full nudity and various forms of sexual activity including a genuine act of fellatio, as *Life Magazine* reported. Another theater was closed on sodomy charges after staging a play that contained a scene where a nun was raped by a gorilla[8] (or, we can assume, an actor in a gorilla suit).

The sex revolution had become a three-ring circus and in all the hullabaloo the real issues were being distorted. Few free-speech supporters wanted to give sleazy pornographers unfettered access to American minds and movie screens. Instead they reasoned that a freer market would make available more thoughtful and serious films on the subject and put an end to the exploitationists' monopoly on erotic cinema. When given a choice, went the theory, people would choose quality erotic films that dealt with sexuality in a mature and artistic manner, like the European stuff. And then the sleazoids would be out of business. In a perfect world this might have worked, but more highly regarded filmmakers and their producers were being scared away from the subject by all the lawsuits, protests and nastiness.

For the moment it was a perfect world for theaters running *I Am Curious (Yellow)* to full houses week after week, and it was a perfect world for Grove Press; they had "gone public" just before the film's release and their stock had tripled in value. The movie would go on to be cut, banned and condemned ... and do huge business. *I, a Woman* had made 4 million dollars; *I Am Curious (Yellow)* earned well over 10 million, with some sources putting the figure as high as 20 million.

Lena Nyman was paid a total of 56,000 Swedish crowns for both ...*Yellow* and ...*Blue*, and when a writer asked her how it made her feel to know the film was earning a vast fortune in America, she replied that it didn't bother her in the least. "Money isn't important. One can get by perfectly without a crown." What did hurt her, she would recall many years later, were the personal attacks. Not everybody was as positive about her as Norman Mailer had been. "I love that girl!" he'd exclaimed after seeing both ...*Yellow* and ...*Blue*, adding that it was a shame that Sweden did not, like Norway, have a three-colored flag.[9]

Nyman was also criticized in Sweden, but, never the shrinking violet, she fired back at her detractors in the press. Yet some amount of damage had obviously been done since according to Sjöman she never again allowed herself to improvise in a film or theater play.

The legal travails of *I Am Curious (Yellow)* took a decisive turn when cases in Boston and Maryland worked their way up to the U.S. Supreme Court in March of 1971. The justices deadlocked 4–4 after Justice William O. Douglas, whose book *Points of Rebellion* had been excerpted in Rosset's *Evergreen Review*, disqualified himself on conflict-of-interest grounds.

The film had been in the public eye now for four years!

To the disappointment of free-speech advocates, the decision set no precedent. (That wouldn't happen until several years later when the concept of "community standards" was established as a defining factor for a film's legal status.) "The Court view," wrote Charles Champlin for *The Los Angeles Times*, "seemed to be that certain material could be ruled to be obscene for immature audiences but not legally obscene for viewing by consenting adults." A landmark non-decision.

But things had changed radically since the film had first come to the attention of American audiences. Grindhouse and storefront theaters in many cities were now playing, with impunity, the hardest of hard-core pornography—films made in the good old U.S.A. and hence safe from the clutches of customs agents. Even Hollywood films were getting more explicit. *I Am Curious (Yellow)*, that snapshot of the moment of Sweden in 1966, now seemed like a quaint artifact from a much more innocent era.

Grove Press, for their part, had fought the good fight for screen freedom and had spent a fortune in legal fees doing so, but it seemed that their efforts had largely just paved the way for fast-buck exploiters who were now pumping out hard-core factory-grade pornography, no subtitles needed. (That sleaze merchants had grossly exploited the freedoms that artists had struggled to win was a dynamic also playing out in literature. As Erica Jong would state after the publication of *Fear of Flying* in 1973, "The freedom which permitted genuine writers to describe the powerful sexual feelings which most of us experience also permitted pornographers to make a fortune out of shit. And it didn't take long before it was hard to discern the difference between garbage and literature."[10])

In the time honored tradition of exploitation cinema, countless directors tried to cut in on a piece of Sjöman's action. This resulted in sex films like *I Am Furious*, *I Am Curious but Not Yellow*, *I Am Curious Beaver*, *I Am Curious Tahiti*, *I Am Curious Gay* and *The Curious Female*, but the film's influence was not really felt on a deeper level, although some of its stylistic innovations (multiple narrative lines, flash graphics, a cinéma vérité approach) did crop up in a number of American films in superficial ways. It was certainly not a movie that spawned any imitations in Sweden, and the three notable erotic films of the following year (1968) adhered to well established formulas.

Nothing could be more "well established" than basing a film on one of the classics of erotic literature, and no classic had the impact of *Fanny Hill*. In fact it had already been done, by Russ Meyer, in 1964.

That didn't dissuade Mac Ahlberg from shooting his own updated version in 1968. It took place in modern-day Stockholm, and curvaceous redhead Diana Kjaer played the title role decked out in the latest mod fashions. Ahlberg had much more freedom to show skin than Meyer, whose version was criticized for being too tame and puerile, but many felt that Ahlberg's film also failed to do the novel justice and lacked among other things a sense of daring. The critic from *Playboy*, for example, found it too "cleaned up" and saw little resemblance between this Fanny and her bawdy English namesake. Ahlberg's trademark artful photography was much in evidence and some beautiful Swedish landscapes were on display, but not the unhinged sex that might have been anticipated. Nonetheless, Ahlberg's *Fanny Hill* did well at the box office.

The film was apparently made for the American market, hence toned down, and seen from a Danish perspective this *Fanny Hill* was not particularly arousing. Just a bit of "Swedish flirtation with 'frisind,'" commented one Danish writer.

A "*flirtation* with frisind?" Weren't Swedes intrinsically in possession of a free mind? Hadn't they invented it? Yes and no. *Frisind* as it was now being defined was not a state of being but a state of doing, and inasmuch as the term denoted a revolutionary orientation — that was distinctly Danish. Swedes were perhaps just too *laissez-faire* to get it exactly right. They knew how to produce pornography, but did they really understand true liberation?

Yet another "summer film" graced screens in 1968, *One Swedish Summer*, as it was titled for the American market. In the UK it was tagged with a straight translation of the Swedish title: "*...As the Naked Wind from the Sea.*" It was another coming-of-age story set in the cradle of the Swedish countryside but was notable for its lavish abundance of male and female full frontal nudity and plot twists that touched on S&M, voyeurism, incest and other sexual aberrations that in particular afflicted a trio of beauties who carnally consort with the leading lad. One of the gals was raped by a priest, and she gets off by reliving this episode.

But the Swedish film of that year that made the biggest splash abroad, particularly in the States, was *Inga*, a deft balancing act between art and exploitation that was the handiwork of the 47-year-old American director Joseph W. Sarno.

Inga

Like many exploitation filmmakers of his generation, Sarno learned the trade in the service during the Second World War. When the war ended, however, tight union control kept most of these service-trained cinematographers out of Hollywood and they were obliged to film commercials, industrial promos and documentaries to make a living. As the '50s wore on Sarno and others of his ilk like Russ Meyer turned to the making of exploitation movies which was a bull market. In 1959 Sarno began talks with producers that would eventually lead to the making of *Sin in the Suburbs*, a loose adaptation of a fact-based story from *Coronet Magazine*. This would prove to be the kick-off to one of the most prolific careers in American exploitation cinema. Through the early to mid–'60s Sarno and his actress wife Peggy Steffans cranked out a slew of films like *Sinners a la Carte*, *Love Rebellion*, *The Love Merchant* and *Naked Fog*.

In the late '60s, driven by his opposition to the Vietnam War and his urge "to get away from Nixon," as he stated in an interview, he moved to Sweden. Over the next ten years he pumped out sex films with Swedish actors and themes that were tailored for the American market. All were fashioned to exploit the by-now well entrenched myth of Sweden as a sexual Shangri-La.

He made pictures like *Love in the Third Position*, *Veil of Lust* and *To Ingrid My Love, Lisa*. *Swedish Wildcats* was one of his better known films from this period, if somewhat atypical. It took place in a Copenhagen brothel staffed with lusty Swedish prostitutes. Why Danish girls weren't on site instead remains a mystery. Either it attests to the fact that Swedish gals were more desirable, or, more likely, to the fact that so many folks in America actually thought Copenhagen was the capital of Sweden (as Danes like to joke). To the average American Joe the two countries were in fact pretty much interchangeable.[11] Copenhagen probably had more star power than Stockholm, and Sweden, as noted, was synonymous with sex to a greater degree than Denmark since "Danish" was inevitably equated with pastries. And any American can toss off a rough approximation of a sing-

Party girl attempts to seduce Karl (Casten Lassen) in *Inga*.

song Swedish accent, but generally they have no idea that Danish sounds completely different. Scandinavia is a jumble of stereotypes to outsiders, so why not for the sake of convenience move Copenhagen across the Øresund Strait to Sweden? Then one would have the best of both worlds. If one can say that a kind of simplified "porno geography" exists parallel to the real thing, then that is where you would find Copenhagen, in Sweden, where all the blonde girls wear long braids and are milk maids — which in itself seems to be more of a German or Swiss cliché. (John Waters gleefully serves up this far-off-the-mark Swedish stereotype in his film *Cry Baby*.)

Sometimes, though, a Swedish film ended up exploiting the allure of Denmark. Like the 1973 movie *Baksmälla*, which means hangover in Swedish. Its international English title was *Tenderness* but in the UK it was called *Danish Love*. So much for the art of titling. No matter; Sarno dedicated himself to nurturing the myth of Scandinavia as a sexual utopia, and every time a blonde Nordic girl of any nationality gets harassed on an Italian street corner, he deserves some of the credit.

And no movie he made was more influential in this respect than his first, *Inga*.

Innocent by comparison to his later fare, particularly his forays into hard-core, *Inga* was first and foremost an attempt to exploit the success of *I, a Woman*—*I, a Virgin (Jag, en Oskuld)* being its Swedish title. It too was something of a hybrid, but while its understated titling, pace and storyline suggested art-house, it lacked the virtuoso camerawork of a Mac Ahlberg and was not helmed by a name director. It was filmed for a pittance, was poorly dubbed and had a wah-wah fuzz-guitar soundtrack. If *I, a Woman* was an art-house pretender, *Inga* couldn't manage even that and was fit only for exhibition on the exploitation circuit. All to its advantage, for here it proved the right film at the right time and became a huge hit.

Perhaps after all the "roughies, "ghoulies" and "kinkies"[12] that had buffeted American movie goers through the mid–'60s, a gentle, naturalistic Swedish film was just what the doctor ordered. It opened in the U.S. only a year after *I, a Woman* and apparently appealed to the same audience. In both movies a female who made her own choices was the central character. Maybe that's why it became a hit. Or maybe the credit for *Inga*'s success in America owed more to Jerry Gross, whose Cinemation releasing company distributed the film there in the most lurid and sensational manner possible.

In Sweden masturbation and intercourse sequences were considerably condensed, meddling that Bergman hadn't been forced to suffer in *The Silence* five years earlier. Producers made the most of the situation by proclaiming on the film's poster that its "strong erotic scenes" had proven too much for the censors. It didn't help; *Inga* was released only in three prints in Sweden, was not a success and was apparently not released in Denmark at all. The Swedish press hated it. That was nothing new — they hated most of these sex

Innocent Inga (Marie Liljedahl) discovers sex with Karl.

films—but beyond the issue of quality or lack thereof they found it, as Lasse Bergström noted in *Expressen*, hardly sinful enough. "To hardened Swedes," he wrote, "it is neither sinful nor innocent." It was fit only for those "Puritan temples of porn to be found on 42nd street in New York," he sniffed. Ah, those Americans....

But it did manage to launch the career of lithe, dark-haired Maria Liljedahl, a former ballerina who exuded the right mix of innocence and sexual curiosity. She played the naive young Inga who ignites the flame of lust in all the men she encounters while at the same time trying to cope with her own budding desires. In the end she is led astray by her manipulative though not unsympathetic aunt Greta, over the hill at 30, who pimps her out to a family friend. But for all her conniving Greta ends up the tragic figure after Inga follows her heart and runs off with her boyfriend.

This was a new Sweden served up for the hip generation, the film offering a whole new take on sex. Compare it to the antiquated *Teenage Mother* shot only a year before. Here a Swedish teacher employed in a small-town high school offers a sex education course and scandal ensues when a female student feigns pregnancy to trap her boyfriend. Said teacher is now accused of corrupting the students. This was a plot straight out of the '30s or '40s! Dusty artifacts like *Teenage Mother* were living on borrowed time.

Sweden: Heaven or Hell?

Joe Sarno was hardly the only foreign filmmaker who saw potential in the land of milk and honey and Volvos: the veteran Italian director Luigi Scattini was also attracted by the possibilities and that same year he released a mondo film,[15] *Sweden: Heaven or Hell?*

The title sought to convey the purported schizophrenia of Swedish life. As narration informed: "Sweden can boast the healthiest children who are the least childlike children in the world. The oldest and loneliest old folks and the freest living and unhappiest women you'll ever meet. Stockholm, Sweden: Heaven or hell?"

As we have seen, the stereotype of Sweden as a cold and soulless welfare state where people believed in nothing and had no passion for life, except in the summer when they had too much passion, went back decades. This was a popular wisdom broadly accepted as fact and the Italians had not invented it. Now, however, in light of Sweden's growing reputation as a sexual paradise, it was gaining new strength.

There was a moral underpinning to such a view. People from other cultures were convinced there had to be a dark side to it all and one needn't look any further than the country's suicide statistics. Despite all the beautiful blonde women and the free sex, Swedes seemed fated to commit suicide or die elderly and alone, well fed but spiritually malnourished. So went the popular notion.

Scattini seeks to illustrate the brutality that lurks beneath the surface of what is outwardly a gentle and free society. In one scene down-and-outers drink anti-freeze and eat shoe polish to dull the pain while others try to lose themselves in a spasm of drugs and sex. In another episode an innocent boat excursion turns into total debauchery, or so we are encouraged to believe.

The viewer is led to assume that Swedes utilize pornography in their sex education and that meter maids moonlight as porn models. At one point we find ourselves in a bar where Swedish gals chose black guys over Swedish men since they are "more primitive, more to the point." (The assumption that Scandinavian women had a thing for black guys or vice versa can actually be found in a number of films and became something of a stereotype. In Larry Buchanan's *Free, White and 21* from 1963 a beautiful Swedish girl called Greta Mae Hansen comes to Texas as a Freedom Rider. She checks into the YWCA but her friendship with local black residents makes her unpopular there and she is forced to move to another hotel where the black proprietor (possibly) rapes her. A mondo film from the following year entitled *Malamondo* features what was then a somewhat controversial scene; the marriage of a white woman and black man in Sweden. In *Watermelon Man*, a racial satire from 1970, a white insurance agent wakes up black one morning; one result is that his blonde Norwegian secretary suddenly finds him much more interesting. Also in 1970, interracial relationships would be depicted in Peer Guldbrandsen's *The Daughter*.)

In the classic mondo tradition everything in *Sweden: Heaven or Hell?* is given as lurid a twist as possible and many of the scenes of this supposed documentary, particularly those of a suicide and a gang rape, are clearly faked. On the positive side, Piero Umiliani contributes an excellent soundtrack which in recent years has gained more renown than the film itself. Highlights include "You Tried to Warn Me," sung by Lydia McDonald, and Alessandro Alessandroni's "I Cantori Moderni." Oddly, the most famous song is the nonsense-syllable number "Mah na Mah na," which was appropriated and popularized by the *Muppets* TV show.

Sweden figured prominently in other mondo films as well. In *Women of the World* from 1963, a feminist scenario is played out as a Swedish clergywoman celebrates mass. In *Mondo Teeno* from 1967 the changing morality was starkly underlined when an unmarried Swedish mother claims that the man she eventually chooses to marry will accept the child as his own. A con job from the year before, *The Forbidden*, purports to capture sexual behavior throughout Denmark and Sweden, among other countries, but things are not as they appear; the film was made by the notorious duo of Bob Cresse and Lee Frost, and many of the scenes were actually filmed in America and then mulched into an unidentified French feature. The above-mentioned Italian-produced *Malamondo* also did its part to reinforce the stereotype of a gloomy people by including a scene of Swedish students openly contemplating suicide.

Myths, some enshrined in mondo films and some not, continue to shape the perception of Scandinavian women with Italian men. This became all too apparent to Danish journalist Sigrid Rasmussen who in July of 2007 found herself in Milan, posted by *Berlingske Tidende* to write a story about illegal immigration. In the course of her research she became engaged in conversation with a group of men who were hanging out in front of the city's train station. When they became aware of her nationality one fellow piped up and asked if all Danish women were lesbians. "Everyone knows that the polar winds increase a person's level of testosterone," he stated with unshakable conviction. His pals backed him up and they could not be persuaded otherwise. Then, on one of her trips back to Copenhagen, Rasmussen fell into conversation with an Italian pilot who had been to Denmark many times. He began by praising the country, in particular the statuesque blondes and music festivals. But quickly he changed his tune, maintaining that "Danes are constantly depressed because of lack of sun ... and the women are as cold as ice. Danish women are beautiful and liberated but liberated in a false way. They become lonely. They don't understand how to enjoy life and be happy. It's not their fault — it's because of the climate." His opinions were intractable and he claimed the country's high suicide rate proved his assertions.

Danish Blue

> *"The endless liberality [frigjorthed] all around us has deprived us of the ability to be shocked ... and hardly anyone is curious anymore."*
> —The paper *Vendsyssel Tidende*, August 18, 1968

After *Hagbard and Signe* in 1967, Gabriel Axel was back again the next year with a very different and more personal film entitled *Danish Blue*, a documentary that examined the nature of pornography and also attacked those in positions of authority who attempted to suppress it. Following his big historical epic he wanted to make a more topical film and involve himself with real life issues.

As it was, he knew nothing about pornography, but all the recent outcry about indecent magazines had caught his attention. He made the acquaintance of a collector of erotic films and watched one after another on a 16mm projector. He was decidedly old school, convinced that true eroticism happened above the waist, and the one scene he remembered most of all was the blissful expression on a woman's face.[14] As he stated in program notes, he wanted to present a more liberated view of pornography in the hope that higher quality product would come into existence when the first wave had passed.

He contacted Leo Madsen to discuss the film further. A German-Jewish refugee who had lost both parents in World War II, young Madsen had been adopted by a well known Danish barrister, but as the years passed he became something of the family's black sheep. It's hard to imagine that he made his adoptive parents any prouder when in the mid–'60s he became known as Denmark's "porno king." The controversial magazine *Weekend Sex* was his flagship publication and cash cow.

For some time Madsen had been producing short sex films for screenings in private clubs, but now, angry over the mass confiscations of his magazines that took place throughout 1967, he decided to make a feature film that would blow the lid off the issue and hopefully nudge toward extinction the law known in Denmark simply as "Paragraph 234," created in 1930 in an effort to protect public morality. After *I Am Curious (Yellow)* was permitted to screen uncut in Denmark it was clear to him that film was far and away the most liberal medium.

He allowed Axel to film the making of a porn movie in his studio, but they did not collaborate further and went on to make their own films, Axel plunging into what at first went under the working title of *Say You Love Me*, and Madsen going on to produce *Look Out, Little Man!* Madsen's film ended up as no hard-hitting exposé after all but instead turned out to be an idiotic mix of low comedy and soft porn.

Look Out, Little Man! premiered January 8, 1968, in the industrial harbor town of Kalundborg and went on to screen in other provincial outposts. By the time it hit Copenhagen Madsen had spliced in some XXX-rated copulation scenes that he claimed were necessary to understand the story but which drew protests from many of the actors. The censors at first prohibited the film but then reconsidered and allowed it to screen uncut with—as per *Gift*—large crosses over the offending scenes.

It frequently double-billed with *Who Said Scandalized?*, a 35-minute documentary independently produced by freelance journalist Thorkild Voss. In the film Voss took issue with Denmark's porn legislation. He interviewed hundreds of people on the subject, including Inge and Sten Hegeler, and filmed the making of a porn movie in Leo Madsen's studio. Madsen also engaged in verbal fisticuffs in front of the cameras with a pro-censorship advocate. On another occasion, Voss filmed a debate he arranged with the Conservative Student Association in Århus, and afterwards he showed them a genuine porno film. This was indeed a more innocent time when simply handing someone a pornographic magazine or showing them a porn film was full of all kinds of profound implications. Pornography was the fuel of great debates.

While also taking aim at the censors, Axel's film, now called *Danish Blue*, was a more creative, playful and subjective take on the topic. It was more jazzed up than Voss' film where the sex and nudity was intentionally presented so coldly that it could not possibly arouse. The Film Fund refused to grant *Danish Blue* any support but there was little danger that Axel would go broke when one considered how well Danish sex films were performing abroad.

Axel had another thing going for his film: the assistance of attractive Gurli Taschner. A fashion model and pop impresario in her late twenties, Taschner had been much in the news the previous year after receiving a four month suspended sentence for producing pornographic films. She had been scapegoated by the authorities and it was all very unfair, went one line of thinking. Perhaps, as it was even suggested in the press, she was the first "porno martyr." She was in any event an interesting figure in her own right. A book about her, *I, Gurli*, had been published by Stig Vendelkær. Peer Guldbrandsen had wanted her to play the lead in her own life story, but that idea fell by the wayside and instead he introduced her to Axel.

In *Danish Blue* Taschner functions as a kind of bridging device, appearing in between episodes to pontificate about the liberating power of pornography and to share insights she gained from counseling the sexually troubled. We also see her in the act of shooting a porn film, flitting about the room with her Bolex as she feeds her actors dialogue before every sequence and badgers them to "do something." Elsewhere Axel inventories a cross-section of ancient erotic artworks, offers up his own parody of an old stag film and takes an inside look at the making of a pornographic movie in Madsen's studio. The female model from Madsen's porn film is later pictured at home with her husband and kids, living a normal, average life. In another episode we join a rowdy mixed audience of teens as they watch a porn film and display a range of emotions. Some professional actors were used in *Danish Blue*, among them Birgit Brüel from *Weekend* who surfaces as a well-endowed dame in the silent film parody and manages to "project eroticism also with her clothes on," as one reviewer put it.

Danish Blue mixed color with black and white and the farcical with the serious, the tone fluctuating from naughtiness to humor to sermonizing and straightforward hygienic advice. And it was relatively chaste, featuring full-frontal nudity and plenty of insinuation but no live-action coupling. It had a sense of playful whimsy about it and yet attempted to deal in straightforward fashion with the basic issues of why people buy and consume pornography and how it affects their sex lives. In one rather bizarre vignette a despondent gray-bearded Walt Whitman type, representing the loneliness of old age, drinks out of a water pipe and then fantasizes about licking a young woman's breast.

Even detractors found the movie fun in spots and it was widely credited as the first film to approach the issue with humor. That and the fact that it was produced by a respected director and was made to a passable technical standard no doubt helped convince censors to approve it without any cuts. It marked a break with the moodiness and pessimism of the traditional Scandinavian sex film and can be considered an early forerunner of what Swedes would call "glad porn" (Happy Porn—glad porr in Swedish), about which more will shortly be said.

Eberhard Kronhausen, whose erotic art exhibit was pictured in the film, gave it his blessings and personally recommended to Grove Press that they distribute the movie in America. Five other distributors eventually entered the bidding but Grove was flush with profits from *I Am Curious (Yellow)* and came out on top, offering more money than any distributor ever had for a Danish film. Axel was guaranteed 70,000 crowns even if legal challenges in the States prevented it from screening, and 300,000 more as soon as it came on the American market. His residuals were pegged at 40 percent.[15] This was a vastly better deal than *I, a Woman* had received or even *I Am Curious (Yellow)*.

Grove was also well positioned to market literary spin-offs of its films and published a lavishly illustrated book about the movie, also called *Danish Blue*, in 1970. For *I Am Curious (Yellow)* they had published Sjöman's *I Was Curious: The Diary of the Making of a Film* in 1968, as well as the script itself which was spiced up with 250 photos.

Gurli Taschner and Gabriel Axel fit the description of Knud Leif Thomsen's "porno evangelists" to a tee, and the incessant pro-porn slant of their arguments irritated some

A scene from *Danish Blue:* Aage Fønss as a rococo count in the company of three "graces."

reviewers when the film opened domestically on July 29. Axel had said he wanted to stir up debate on the subject with this film, but many criticized it for its lack of objectivity and nuance.

Several reviewers also pointed out that in Denmark, at least, the film was already outdated. "Does this film come too late?" wondered one writer. "Paragraph 234 will probably be laid to rest in the next session of Parliament by a conservative Justice Minister, which hardly anyone would have predicted just ten years ago.... Gabriel Axel should have made this movie some years back. Then it would have been a real provocation."[16]

"Axel bravely rips the clothing off the naked ones," sarcastically stated another scribe, "allowing people to talk about what everybody already talks about, clearing a passage for the wave of pornography that has already passed." He was accused in other quarters, as Knud Leif Thomsen had been, of creating and then attacking a problem that didn't really exist, of creating fictional characters or situations to prove a point he was bent on proving.

Others were troubled by the film's assertion that pornography was not for "normal" people but only for the lonely, the old and the sickly. Why pick on the lonely? wondered a writer. Why assume they all have a hidden need for pornography? The film maintained that pornography had therapeutic value and was no more objectionable than any other kind of medicine, and that people could eventually get "better." For all the film's purported liberality this was an oddly moralistic, almost puritanical message.

Additionally some thought that Axel wasn't dealing straight. If it was just the lonely, sick and elderly who needed pornography then who were all these people filling the theaters night after night? The film was couched in a kind of intellectual and moral elitism, but maybe he was just pandering after all.

Still others found it intrinsically sexist. The sequence that pictured examples of ancient erotic art like Greek vases, figurines and so forth was spotlighted by one reviewer. "One shouldn't overlook the fact that the majority of these examples of erotic art that Gabriel uses as documentation in the film originate from countries or times when women had no equality but were merely obedient repressed beings who existed to work, procreate and provide pleasure."[17]

Perhaps there was also a generation gap as well as a gender gap. Axel himself was 50 at this point. "Porn is dirty.... It's just something for the older generation," stated a group of teens in the press (and in the film itself).

A special screening was arranged in Norway which Axel attended. He discussed the movie afterwards with critics who wondered how censorship could still exist in Denmark if *this* was permitted. There was some hope that the film might finally break the sex barrier there, but it didn't, one of the reasons being that in Norway most cinemas are owned by the townships in which they're located. This arrangement functioned as a kind of bulwark against smut coming up from Denmark and Sweden, as the government decided in most cases which movies would be imported, distributed and booked. Thus specific movies could be excluded without engaging the mechanisms of censorship.

Danish Blue was invited to Cannes in 1969 by a group of young upstart French film directors who rented two cinemas in Paris where the film was screened to much hoopla. A special showing also later took place at the Berlin Film Festival.

Danish Blue was sold to a lot of countries. It was also banned in a lot of countries, but predictably not in Sweden, or (surprisingly!) in America where it was allowed to screen without any cuts. In Denmark even part-time writers from provincial papers had taken a rigorously critical view of the film, but in America and other European countries it received almost unqualified praise and was held up as a revolutionary example of a liberated view of sex. Even Amos Vogel, author of *Film as a Subversive Art* (the 1974 landmark study of transgressive cinema), gave it his blessings. In most countries any loosening of censorship was viewed as a good thing and any film that advanced the cause was to be applauded.

In Denmark, though, which was several years ahead of the curve, it was seen as the end, not the beginning. On June 2, 1967, censorship of the written word had been abolished and demand for so-called indecent literature had actually declined as a result. Many expected the same would happen with motion pictures once film censorship was abolished. As writer Hans Andersen declared, there was no need for more of these films. "If our porno legislation is abolished there will be little interest in the case—and thereby a film of this type will be the last."

Without a Stitch

"To refrain from sexual enjoyment is no more moral than to refrain from picking flowers, reading books or skiing."
—a quote from author Jens Bjørneboe
posted in theaters showing *Without a Stitch*.

Response to this new atmosphere of freedom was still very much evolving, as evidenced by another much talked about film from 1968, *Without a Stitch*, which arrived a month later and also stressed a happy and carefree approach to sex but dropped the documentary premise.

It was based on a novel published (and immediately banned) in Norway in 1966. The author was Jens Bjørneboe, a controversial figure who had been a painter, sailor, vagabond and teacher and whose political convictions had compelled him at one point to emigrate to Sweden. Published pseudonymously under the tag "a Norwegian writer," the novel told the story of a high school senior called Lilian whose lone attempt at sex with her boyfriend goes awry. Fearing she's frigid, she seeks the counsel of doctor Petersen who specializes in female sexual dysfunction. He cures her, not least with large doses of philosophy, telling her among other things that the term "sexual morality" is a misnomer because there is no one single sexual morality, and that essentially all is permitted as long as you don't harm others. Armed with his advice, Lilian celebrates graduation by throwing herself into a summer hitchhiking tour of Europe which leads to numerous and diverse erotic encounters.

The book was published in Denmark in 1967 by Stig Vendelkær's company which had now established itself as something of a counterpart to Rosset's Grove Press. Palladium quickly acquired the rights for a screen version and hired Annelise Meineche to direct, hoping they could recapture some of the box office magic of *Soya's 17*. The film, like the book, would set the story in various European locales and that would also make it more exportable.

Anne Grete Nissen, a 21-year-old engineer's daughter and Roskilde University student, was chosen to star after they saw her perform in a student farce entitled *I Am Not Curious but Yellow and Blue All Over*, a parody of Sjöman's *I Am Curious* films.

Nissen's parents already knew Bjørneboe's novel and reportedly had no objections to their daughter's participation, although she did delete her last name from all publicity, billing simply as Anne Grete—"pronounced 'Great'!" as ads in America would helpfully inform. (It was claimed she dropped "Nissen" in deference to an older colleague with the same surname.)

Various location photography throughout Europe was necessary, and a shooting crew soon departed for points south on a trip that would prove to be something of an adventure in its own right. In Paris, as they were setting up a shot on the Champs Elysées, the statuesque Nissen caused a stir when passers-by objected to her outfit. It was just a knitted dress she'd purchased in a regular Copenhagen department store, a dress that wouldn't have raised eyebrows in Denmark, but it riled Parisians who thought the gaps in the weave were too big and revealed too much. In Hamburg a number of scenes were shot on the Reeperbahn, the city's notorious red-light district, and these came closest to imparting a bit of realism in what was otherwise a very staged movie. At one point, with cameras rolling, Nissen crossed a busy street and ran into a horny sailor on the far sidewalk who thought she was one of the neighborhood's regular prostitutes. He came on to her quite aggressively, only to glance up and see a small crowd of crew and plainclothes officers rushing to her defense. At that point he gave her a quick kiss and absconded. While the star took it all in stride, the local papers were full of reports of more serious incidents in the Reeperbahn—a girl missing, a strangling and a deadly punch-up—that did little to calm their nerves.

Shooting wrapped back in Denmark and the film was finished and submitted to the censors, who immediately slapped a total ban on it. Lilian's sexual escapades were just too much. In a scene in Sweden, for example, a fellow picks her up hitchhiking, has sex with her in his van and then pays her to act in a porn film, the whole thing transpiring with all the sunny abandon of *Mary Poppins*. She travels further to encounter a Copenhagen lesbian who arranges a threesome, a kindly German gentleman who insists they whip each other and a gay British lad who drives her to Italy in his sports car, sodomizes her and arranges another threesome with his straight friend ... and so on.

Although *Without a Stitch* did not show genitals or penetration, many were under the impression that it revealed a lot more than *I Am Curious (Yellow)*. Not much more, really, but it implied just about everything.

The ban was appealed and officials backtracked and allowed it to screen with four minor deletions. These cuts were so insignificant that it seemed that adult film censorship in Denmark had now for all intents and purposes ceased to exist. Nor were the cuts a disadvantage for Palladium as they enabled the company to release an "uncensored" version a year later after film censorship had been officially rescinded.

Without a Stitch opened on September 2 and at least one paper refused to run ads for it, but that hardly mattered; crowds were massive. And critics were merciless. Lacks humor, wit and quality, some said; unintentionally funny with crowds laughing in all the wrong places, noted others. Nothing but factory-grade porn, concluded just about everyone. It was evident that a lot of critics were getting tired of all these porn films, which they felt were degrading the reputation of Danish cinema in general.

But in spite of its transparently exploitive intentions, the film was anything but vacuous entertainment. In today's world where sexual abuse by authority figures is no longer countenanced, Lilian's sessions with Doctor Petersen, who fondles, copulates and performs cunnilingus on her, can only make one cringe. The Danish medial establishment, suggested one scribe, was the real victim of the film.

But never fear: His ministrations were all in the name of science and a liberated ideology. At least one of the scenes where Lilian has contact with Doctor Petersen had to be reshot; in that take it appeared they might have a romantic attachment to each other, and their relationship had to be of a purely clinical nature.

Better, perhaps, that they actually felt something for each other. A lot of time is spent on these scenes at the doctor's office where a sterile, hygienic approach to sex is stressed. Possibly the filmmakers thought that putting a sober, educational gloss on it would smooth it with the censors, but instead it turns out to be every woman's worst-case-scenario trip to the gynecologist and Lilian's total compliance only disturbs.

Nissen's performance has an unsettlingly robotic feel to it, particularly when she ventures out into the wider world. She behaves like a life-size Barbie doll; functional, bendable, gamely upbeat and always smiling, and yet somehow numb and eerily vacant. Whenever she finds herself recoiling from unwanted advances she hears the doctor's Svengali-like voice inside her head reminding her that all is permitted as long as no one is hurt by the experience. She considers it and then overrules her own natural reactions to the situation and jumps into bed. She is not even really promiscuous since that implies that one has made a decision. The decisions are not hers to make because she is being guided by a philosophy, not by free will.

Lilian was just a character in a movie, but some began to fear that this was precisely the kind of person the sex revolution was churning out; sex robots, people who had become obedient to an ideology and had lost their free will. And this was not at all the message of the book. Quite the contrary.

Bjørneboe's novel was an attack on the conservative dogmas that shaped Norwegian thinking and a political attack on various authority figures — attacks that were completely dropped in the film — but more importantly it was a call for equality between the sexes, springing from a belief that young women should have the same freedom to experience and discover things as young men. This aspect of the book is marginally retained in the film but makes no sense. Lilian is constantly going into book shops to buy books, but not many people bought tickets to the movie just to see her read. And if she has discovered any new ideas in these books or has changed in any way, this is not evident in her behavior or demeanor. Nissen was not the actress to tilt the movie back in a more nuanced or thoughtful direction and it was too late in any case. The unwitting message of the film may well be that if one's only experiences are of the physical variety then one never will really grow or evolve.

In short, a book that was written to advance the cause of humanism and individualism in a Norwegian context became something quite different when relocated to ultra-liberal Denmark and reinterpreted by filmmakers eager to sell tickets. They transformed it into an advertisement for Danish sexual liberation, and under cover of promoting individualism it instead promoted a new kind of conformity, one that came complete with its own set of dogmas and assumed wisdoms. No film preached the prophecies of this new "religion of the flesh," as Thomsen had termed it, more determinedly than this one.

An interesting rebuttal to the film was issued by reviewer Rolf Bagger in the September 3 edition of *B.T.*:

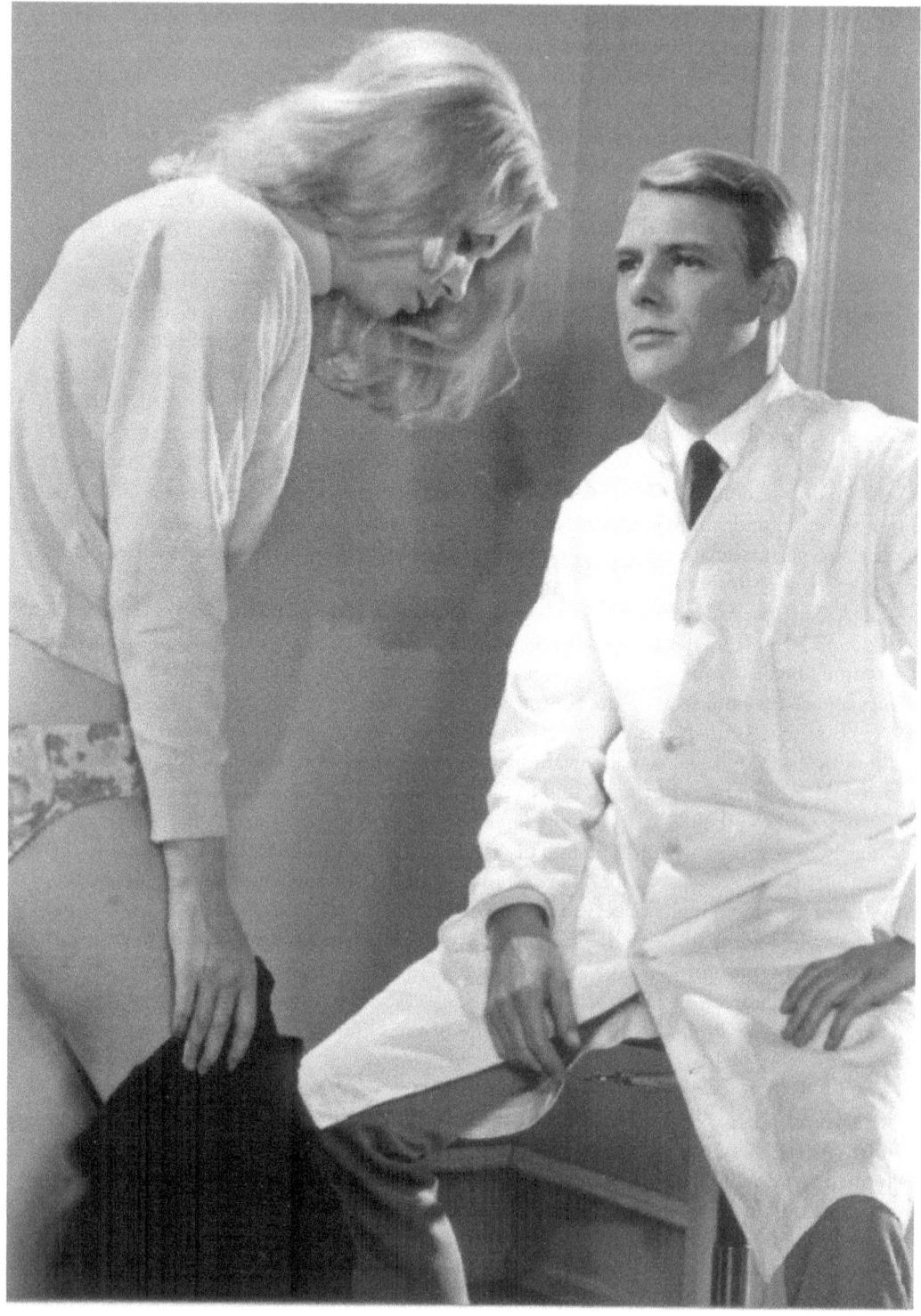

Lilian (Anne Grete Nissen) disrobes for a clinically-minded Dr. Petersen (played by Ib Mossin).

> The sex revolution is about to eat its own children as all revolutions do. People fight for a freedom and afterwards force upon the world their kind of freedom — in freedom's holy name. *Without a Stitch*, under supposedly liberal cover, is an extremely reactionary film which tries to convince the whole world that we are all the same in both a human and a sexual definition. Modesty is today seen as something that people suffer from, something that can be surgically removed. Afterwards a person must be sexually re-educated (with frequent indulgence in diverse sexual acts mandatory).
>
> The film takes a deplorably ambiguous position on prostitution, etc., and its attitude towards homosexuality alarms. It denies the existence of real homosexuality by suggesting that it is just a cozy supplement. In addition to the fact that the film is shabbily made, it is so ambiguous, hypocritical and cold that it induces nausea.
>
> If these are the kind of sexual attitudes that the future is bringing then we are in fact entering a scary stone age. We have great need for freedom in our erotic life — freedom to be ourselves. Therefore all genuinely open-minded people ought to distance themselves from this film. A new counter-revolution can begin, and shall we start by calling this torrent of supposed liberated thinking "sexual fascism"? In that world there is only room for regimented, cold, over-sexed human beings. To arms, friends!

The film's merit as an erotic fantasy was quite another case, however: Except for the brief whipping scene, the movie had a playful and rollicking spirit about it. Nissen was ever in motion, and clothed or unclothed brought a compelling physicality to her part. Her threesome with the Copenhagen lesbian, Lise, and her straight male friend, Jan, a count who is played by *Gift*'s Søren Strømberg, was notable. They meet, goof about and caper their way through a brief but very bizarre dance number before ending up freeze-framed on a bed in a suggestive *ménage à trois* pose. It is perhaps Nissen's hottest moment precisely because she is *partially* dressed, clad in a skimpy kitchen apron that rides up her impressive curves. A few more of these dance numbers and the film could have gone down in cult history as one of the most eccentric musicals ever.

What the bluenoses in America would make of the film could only be imagined, but Jack Harris of V.I.P. Distribution could smell another hit and figured that importing it was worth the gamble. It was something new on the erotic front and set itself apart from most American-produced sexploitation films which traded in violence and perversion and aspired to be as dirty as possible. It too traded in "perversion" but in a somehow more viewer-friendly manner due to its exotic locales, lush color cinematography and cheery optimism. Its message might have chilled some, but Americans could easily take a pass on that and if the subtitles fell off the screen again it probably wouldn't much matter. It was another one of these uncanny Danish hybrids, an attempt to "remake a famous provo-plus-porno[18] novel into witty entertainment for the whole family," as reviewer Keith Keller put it. The authors of these erotic novels invariably hated the movies that were made out of them, but such nuances were lost on Stateside viewers.

Immediately seized by customs upon arrival into the United States, *Without a Stitch* spent the remainder of 1969 tied up in federal court on obscenity charges. It finally came to a jury trial and was surprisingly found not guilty in December.

It opened in January of 1970 in Loew's flagship theater on Broadway where it earned a smashing 150,000 dollars over the course of its five week run there. Now even the biggest showcase theaters were willing to play soft-core porn films as long as they paid off, and in the city as a whole there were over 600 theaters that had started to play sexploitation movies.

Anne Grete Nissen (lower) and Joan Gamst get cozy in *Without a Stitch*.

"You have never seen it photographed before!" headed the full page ad that Harris took out in *The Village Voice* on January 8. "This is the first film to enter the U.S. from Denmark since its liberalization of permissiveness!" The December 10 *Hollywood Reporter* article that announced the court decision was also included in the advertisement, pasted in over a photo-still of the movie's Stockholm porn shoot scene that pictured a crew training lights and camera on a naked couple.

Then came the hot-sell: "Denmark — the country that already has gained a reputation of being the world's most permissive — has gone one step further.... American audiences of the '70s may be astounded and shocked by Denmark's newest motion-picture, *Without a Stitch*, [which] makes *Curious Yellow* instantly obsolete. But more so, it's a *good* movie. One that American audiences will *like*, understand and enjoy. Women will empathize and identify with the beautiful heroine. Men will immediately love her" (emphasis original).

American critics certainly loved her. Anne Grete was sweet and well-built, gushed both *The New York Times* and *The New York Post*. *The Village Voice* thought it an "immense improvement on the two biggest sexploitation swindles of 1969, *Juliette de Sade* and *Fanny Hill*," — both Swedish (partially shot on Danish sets) — but still deemed it silly exploitation.

The film was also acclaimed in underground circles, with Al Goldstein, publisher of the pioneering sex tabloid *Screw*, penning a predictably crude tribute. He had been eagerly following developments in Scandinavian cinema. *I, a Woman* had previously caught his attention: It was phony, he conceded, but it had "tits and ass and a good looking female lead." In June of 1969 he flew to Copenhagen to check out the scene for himself. *Without a Stitch* was his main discovery. He found it far superior to "dreadful dreck" like *I Am Curious (Yellow)* and predicted that "if this type of skin-flick ever reaches America, the whole corrupt field will be made obsolete by actually giving the viewer his money's worth." He dedicated the whole of issue #23 to "Sexual Freedom in Scandinavia," but all the copies of that edition of *Screw* were confiscated *en masse* by the authorities when they hit the streets and his dispatch from Copenhagen ended up in *The Los Angeles Free Press* instead.

While the film was now free to play uncut, that didn't preclude other lawsuits, and over the course of the next two years it was dragged back into court in a number of states. A California case gave Associate Justice Roy L. Herndon opportunity to weigh in with one of the nastiest reviews the film would ever get: "The English language does not provide adjectives sufficient to describe the utter rottenness of this sordid product of subhuman depravity and greed that portrays every known form of sexual perversion."[19] Apparently Jack Valenti, head of the MPAA, shared Herndon's views. The film, he said, was pornographic trash and unsuited to be advertised in poster display cases. The film's distributor claimed Valenti had stepped over the line by trying to persuade theater owners to boycott it, and sued him.[20]

With movie attendance falling off across the board, *Without a Stitch* earned but half as much as the four million dollars *I, a Woman* had grossed in the U.S., but it had impact beyond its numbers. This time America suddenly found itself in the unlikely position of being on the forefront of screen freedom. And the legal issues it stirred continued to roll on. As late as 1975 it was being hauled up in front of the Supreme Court in connection with a lawsuit filed by one Clark Ewing. Ewing had earlier brought charges against a theater in Lucas County, Ohio, claiming it constituted a nuisance simply because it had shown *Without a Stitch* (under Ohio law any place that showed filmed obscenity was deemed a nuisance), and his appeal worked its way up to the Supreme Court, which ultimately dismissed it. The legal apparatus in America moved slowly, and just as with *A Stranger Knocks*, *I Am Curious (Yellow)* and a host of other Scandinavian films, *Without a Stitch* had long ceased to have any relevance by the time its day in court arrived. And back in Denmark hardly anyone remembered it at all.

Oddly the film had been cut for its Swedish release. The censor board there had once again asked the advisory panel for their opinion, and since they felt that this film was a corrupting influence on young people they recommended a total ban. The board in turn decided to let it pass with a number of cuts. This was seen as odd in Denmark since Sweden was, after all, "the fatherland of sexual liberation," as one Danish critic put it, and besides, the film had passed uncut in Denmark and hadn't led to mass fornication in the streets. (Maybe now it would be Swedes taking bus tours to Denmark.) At the same time the advisory panel had been asked to give an opinion on *One Swedish Summer* and they had no objections and the board passed it uncut, even though it was full of naked bodies and youthful sexuality. Danes saw favoritism at play. "And after all the sex films Sweden has sent us!" sniffed one Danish writer.

Swedish critics savaged *Without a Stitch* even more fiercely than their Danish colleagues had, resulting in record-breaking bad press.

While *Danish Blue* and *Without a Stitch* figured as the high profile erotic films of 1968, *I, a Woman 2* was also produced and released that year in Denmark. Gio Petré replaced Essy Persson in the lead with Mac Ahlberg returning as director-cinematographer.

This was Guldbrandsen's real follow-up to *I, a Woman*, based on Agnethe Thomsen's 1963 sequel *The Marriage*. It picked up the action with Siv now married to an antiques dealer who exploits her, photographing her nude and selling the pictures under the counter. She must also make herself sexually available when her husband invites an important associate home. When she learns that he forced his first wife to become a prostitute and that he was also an SS officer during the war she leaves him and begins a relationship with a doctor. The Nazi theme was not popular in Germany and upon release there all references to her husband's war record were deleted. In America a new ending was shot where Siv has a rendezvous with a black man.

Danish censors wanted to cut some scenes but Guldbrandsen appealed. As a compromise the scenes in question were replaced with still photos, but these photographs revealed even more details and this attempt at censorship was widely ridiculed.

Although the film did well in foreign territories, reviews were negative. Al Goldstein, for one, hated it. He found the dialogue clichéd and Petré too old for the part. Worst of all he found the Nazi theme beyond the pale, "bad taste incarnate." (This from the publisher of *Screw*.) He noted that audiences actually booed the film. To Goldstein the revolution would someday start in a movie theater "when audiences get sick and tired of being bilked by greedy and dishonest film producers." Back in Denmark Guldbrandsen and Ahlberg were unrepentant and planning yet another sequel.

Out in the real world there was trouble in the air. Students in cities all over Europe were taking to the streets in revolt, setting up barricades, torching cars and occupying the offices of universities. Filmmakers were also rebelling as they discarded accepted wisdom about style, form and content and sought to connect with the newly resurgent spirit of youth. So far in Denmark no film had really captured the spirit of the times, but a new one tried: *A Strange Romance*. It constituted the directorial debut of a young medical student named Nils Malmros who sank his own money into it and got his friends and fellow students from Århus to participate. Inspired by François Truffaut's *Jules and Jim*, it was shot in an experimental style that borrowed various techniques from the New

Wave, including the restlessly moving camera that underscored the back-and-forth of animated and sometimes philosophical discussions about the problems of young love.

In the summer of 1968 it was shown at the Århus student film club and was received so enthusiastically that a commercial cinema in Zealand opened it. But *talking* about sex was not what the general public wanted at this point and its run only lasted two days. Nils Malmros himself would go on to become a commercial filmmaker of considerable importance.

Also in 1968, Saga studios tried to get hip with their own social-realist take on youth rebellion, *I Love Blue*. Complete with inner monologues and other experimental techniques, this tale about a wayward 15-year-old girl who becomes pregnant was their nod to *frisind* and owed a clear debt to J.D. Salinger's *Catcher in the Rye*. An intriguing if flawed film, it was if nothing else another brave attempt to break with the folk-comedy tradition.

Meanwhile out on the streets a somewhat more frivolous manifestation of the sex revolution was all the rage: toplessness. This could be openly enjoyed in amusement parks as well as in topless clubs. Through the summer of 1968 a topless all-girl pop band called the Lady Birds capitalized on the craze in a string of performances at Fjordvilla amusement park in Roskilde. On September 8 they got top billing over a group of shaggy-haired musicians from London who were then touring Scandinavia under the name The New Yardbirds but were in fact the first functioning edition of Led Zeppelin. On September 15 at the Liseberg amusement park in Gothenburg, Sweden, this early version of Zeppelin played second fiddle to topless dancers *and* a fireworks display. They were advertised as "The Yard Birds popband" in the smallest block lettering on the bill. Jimmy Page, Robert Plant, John Bonham and John Paul Jones toiled away on the tiny stage as families with children in tow and teens out on a first date strolled by largely oblivious, more interested in their cotton candy. Not until the Lady Birds came on would a real crowd gather.

In November the four guitar-slinging gals traveled to England to perform, but their tour ran aground in Plymouth where outraged citizens and at least two city council members attempted to shut down their show at a joint called Ronnie's Club. Noting that Ronnie's was a membership club and not officially accessible to the public, authorities allowed the show to go on.

The previous year both Norway and Denmark had followed Sweden's example and appointed committees to come up with recommendations about film censorship.

In Norway as in Sweden there was particular concern about the increasing violence in movies and the potentially damaging impact that could have on 16- and 17-year-olds. This concern prompted Norway to raise the minimum age for adult films to 18 when the new Norwegian Censorship Law of 1969 was adopted. The new law also kept intact the basic concepts of *moralsk nedbrytende* (films that are morally subversive or destructive) and *krenker ærbarhet* (films that violate decency) which in both Norway and Denmark had underpinned the philosophy of film censorship since the 1910s. Sigurd Evensmo, a member of the censorship oversight committee, voiced disappointment over the fact that Norwegian censorship still hinged on such concepts. He would have preferred a more enlightened approach, something closer to the Swedish model that treated sexuality more as a mental health issue.

In Denmark it was the banning of books that drove the censorship issue, and in particular it was the obscenity prosecutions of the novel *Fanny Hill* in 1964 and 1965, both of which ended in acquittal, that galvanized opposition to censorship. The old laws that prohibited so-called pornographic literature were obviously antiquated and the authorities were forced to change with the times. The first committee established in 1966 to study this issue had consulted with educators, psychiatrists and criminologists and then recommended that pornographic writings be decriminalized. In March of 1967 the Danish Parliament adopted their recommendations on a 159 to 13 vote.

A second committee was established in 1967 to consider whether *image* censorship should be repealed, and they were also unable to find any evidence that sexually explicit printed pictures or movies had a negative effect on psychologically stable adults. They ended up concluding that pictorial pornography should be decriminalized, having given somewhat more weight to freedom of speech issues than the Swedish and Norwegian committees. It was now generally expected that decriminalization would soon happen, even as police were conducting sweeping raids on adult book shops and storage facilities.

In 1968 the Danish justice minister, K. Axel Nielsen, who had battled with Thomsen over *Gift* and had (against his will) presided over the liberation of the written word, was replaced by the elderly Knud Thestrup. The son of a small town veterinarian, he had risen up through the ranks of the Konservative Folkeparti, and although he seemed an unlikely figure to suddenly be sitting in judgment of this new morality, many of his viewpoints were very much within the mainstream of Danish thinking. He viewed pornography as an aesthetic and not an ethical issue, and he felt the State had no right to interfere with the private lives of its citizens. He and many others also believed that the allure of pornography lay in the fact that it was prohibited and that demand for it would fade once it was legalized, just as demand for "dirty books" had fallen off after the abolition of written censorship. *Fanny Hill* would hardly have become such a famous book, he maintained in a speech, had it not been the subject of so many highly publicized court cases.

Finally, Thestrup wanted to give the police more effective means by which to combat the most flagrant obscenity violations, and he felt that the law as it stood was unenforceable because it was impossible to legally define what was obscene. He thereby deleted the second and third sections of paragraph 234 in the Criminal Code, which specifically prohibited the dissemination of *utugtig* (immoral, obscene, pornographic) pictures, and elsewhere replaced the term with the much broader *anstødelig* (objectionable, offensive). The die was cast. All the committees and all the experts agreed that censorship should be abolished and now Thestrup put in place the mechanisms.

The Danish Parliament at that point had no genuine right wing, and the legislation sailed through on a 125 to 25 vote. The new law was signed by the king and the justice minister on June 4 and went into effect on July 1. This would go down in history as the day that pornography was "set free." (Film censorship for adults, those 16 and over, was a somewhat separate issue and had in accord with the committee's recommendation already been abolished by Parliament on March 18.)

"Thestrup was deaf to the tornado out of which the porno wave sprang," noted historian Paul Hammerich, as Copenhagen turned X-rated almost overnight. "My people are about to sink into a moral cesspool," railed pastor Christian Bartholdy, while across town the sounds of hundreds of accordions echoed down the main walking street as young hymn-singing Christians marched in protest. In September a group of West Jutland anti-pornography activists calling themselves The Enemies of Porno erected a memorial to the cause in a public park. Upon it was inscribed:

Here Rests Danish Decency
Suffocated in the Summer of 1969
It Will Come to Life Again
When the People Awaken

In October the hippie-like Jens Theander with his long hair, beard and peace-and-love demeanor and his brother Peter, clean cut and usually clad in a tailor made suit, organized SEX-69, a massive porn trade fair held in a cavernous Copenhagen convention center. They had entered the field back in 1966 with an aim to publish "the first, the biggest and the most pornographic magazine in the world." Like the competition, they had initially been forced to resort to underground production to avoid the police and had to store and sell their magazines in secret. By now they were up to issue #86, which they published in full process-color with a storyline translated into three languages. This legislation now gave their business, Color Climax, momentum beyond their wildest dreams.

Two hundred foreign journalists covered the week-long event which racked up around 100,000 paid admissions and figured as a kind of coming out party for Liberated Denmark. Charter buses from as far away as Morocco joined the thousands of other arriving vehicles to paralyze inner-city traffic. A thousand people a day had to be turned away. Inside the hall porno happenings sprang into motion as nearly naked women strolled about and gawkers trundled their way through a sea of pornographic magazines, inflatable dolls and dildos. Madame Tussaud's "Chamber of Sexual Horrors" was icing on the cake.

Religious organizations protested, fearing that Denmark would now become a supplier of pornographic goods to the global market, which was exactly what a lot of Danish businessmen hoped for. Customs authorities all over the world began to batten down the hatches as small mountains of suspicious packages from Denmark began to flood their sorting centers. Pornographers like the Algerian-born globe-trotting playboy Alberto Ferro, a.k.a. Lasse Braun, set up shop as the last vestiges of soft-core porn quickly gave way to that of a much harder variety. Down at the Danish-German border by Flensburg a kind of pink zone materialized as porn shops sprang up on the Danish side to serve German motorists, many of whom had driven hundreds of miles to sample their wares.

Further west, towards the North Sea coast country, rural villages like Lydersholm and Rudbøl suddenly found themselves on the front lines of the porn revolution. On one side of the road fields of corn and rye waved in the late summer breezes as they always had, while on the other side — the Danish side — circus-like billboards picturing naked women were thrown up and tents were pitched and stocked with all kinds of sexual paraphernalia. A kind of gold-rush mentality ruled as any Danish farmer with a dusty patch of land on the German border could now make fast money renting it out to the flesh merchants of Copenhagen. Soon caravans of Volkswagens, boxy Opels and Porsches were kicking up dust on the narrow lanes and roads, creating a ruckus not seen in these quaint environs since the Nazi invasion of 1940.

While that unique state of mind called Danish *frisind* could not be exported, porno could be, and was, by the tons. Porn soon ranked second only to agriculture as an export commodity. In just a two month period Italian postal authorities confiscated 100,000 pornographic magazines from Denmark, pressing their storage capacity. Italians had all the wrong ideas about Danes, claimed a Danish woman residing in Italy who expressed her dismay in a letter printed in a Danish paper under the heading "Our Foul Reputation." She pointed out that an Italian weekly magazine called *Epaca* was printing article after article about the "easy morals" of the Danes.

The British were not so successful as the Italians at intercepting mail-borne porn. The Danish embassy in London was beginning to receive complaints from traumatized Brits who had received porn from Denmark. In one case it seems a woman was so shocked that she suffered a nervous breakdown and had to be admitted to a clinic.[21]

Others just had to get a closer look. They came to investigate in person, not just common gawkers but important opinion-makers and officials from foreign governments. Two of Britain's best known moral crusaders, Mary Whitehouse and Lord Langford, made the trip. Years later Whitehouse would recall the horror of nipping out of her hotel to get a paper, only to find that a booklet she absently browsed through at the counter had porn inside. "I don't think I'll ever forget that," she would state.

The balding Lord Langford, for his part, was heading up an official commission investigating the phenomenon of pornography. He was more courageous and struck out boldly into Copenhagen's porn jungle to visit a couple of live sex clubs, afterwards reporting that they were even more "ghastly" than he had feared. A tête-à-tête with Jens Theander captured on film shows the Danish porn wunderkind earnestly explaining how they now intended to make a more high quality product. He hands Langford a copy of one of their new magazines and the Brit seems grateful.[22]

Other Danes, particularly those who lived in the conservative, religious hinterlands of Jutland, were appalled by the way people were behaving in their capital city, plastered as it suddenly was with all sorts of lurid come-ons and from all reports and rumors populated by a new tribe of sexual heathens.

And the rest of Scandinavia found it just as unsettling, not least many middle-class Norwegians who were generally steeped in more rural and traditional values. Although no "asphalt jungle" in the American sense, Copenhagen had long been the only true urban environment in Scandinavia, and now, swamped in a wave of smut and permissiveness, it gained an even more sinister reputation. To worried parents from Stockholm to Oslo it loomed as the incarnation of Sin City, a veritable den of vice and depravity, and this dark vision was captured in a remarkable Norwegian film from that year entitled *Heaven and Hell*.

Heaven and Hell

The film begins predictably enough as a cast of stock types are introduced. There is the swarthy Zatek, an unmistakably foreign looking drug dealer teasing the blade of his knife through a candle flame. There is the hip psychologist, Orheim, prototype of the radical '60s academic who lectures to enthusiastic applause at a high school that marijuana is not dangerous. And there clapping along in the audience are the main characters, Eva and Arne, basically just good kids from the leafy suburbs of Oslo.

Before you can say reefer madness they are grooving at a psychedelic nightclub, the Club 13, sharing a joint as a rock band plays in the background. Eva gets dreamy and trippy. Another boy in their party breaks out into uncontrollable laughter for no reason ... only to suddenly fall silent again, entranced by the profundity of random objects.

Eva (Sigrid Huun) watches Arne (Lillebjørn Nilsen) smoke hash in *Heaven and Hell*.

Later Eva and Arne smoke hash on a hill in the sunshine, lying on their backs in the cool grass as they watch the trees spin. They casually embrace ... Arne reaches under Eva's skirt ... she slaps his hand away, laughing. It's all just normal teenage behavior.

But hash costs money and they end up pawning a watch on their way back to the Club 13. Once there Eva is ushered into the back room where Zatek plies his nefarious trade. She wants to buy more dope but doesn't have enough cash. Zatek arranges to meet her later that night at his pad to discuss the matter.

That evening they smoke hash and dance. He comes on to her. The ultra-naïve Eva seems oblivious to Zatek's real intentions and playfully slips out of his embrace, but the hash takes effect and she is rendered vacant and defenseless. She smiles distantly as he undresses her, laughing as she stares into a distorted mirror to see their naked bodies pressed together. She fingers his hippie medallion with stoned absorption as he lays her on her back and places himself on top of her.

Suddenly she understands. "No! No!" she screams, but it's too late. Her eyes glaze over in deadened, hollow acquiescence, and she begins to return his affection.

In this scene Eva is shown in full frontal nudity. This was a daring gambit by the director Øyvind Vennerød in light of strict Norwegian censorship, but it works in the context of this film. It effectively illustrates her descent into a state of moral indifference and is in no way titillating. Drugs have dulled Eva's sparkling personality and deprived her of free will as virtue and self-respect are cast to the winds; dope has turned her into a whore. The film is really about the destruction of innocence and virtue, which owes as much to insidious philosophies as to the drug itself. Here was the kind of movie that could only have been made by a fire and brimstone moralist.

Afterwards Eva goes over to Arne's house. He's angry—why is she so late? He slaps her.

Things go from bad to worse: they smoke hash, stay out all night and lie to her parents, and at one point Arne is even stabbed by Zatek.

Eva's teacher tells her dad that she smokes hash. He goes to the Club 13 where Orheim is giving a pro-drugs speech to a packed crowd. He argues with Orheim who shouts him down. The audience cheers on their prophet and the father is thrown out of the club.

Dad searches the city streets for Eva but she's nowhere to be found, having taken refuge in the kind of ghastly drug den that only exists in the imagination of a crusading movie director. By dawn's early light her father and the police burst in. She is lifeless, apathetic and uncomprehending. A zombie.

The heat is on Zatek who hastily closes shop and splits for Stockholm.

Eva is admitted to a rehab clinic. She starts to recover. Life there is good and she gradually again begins to show signs of that warm, spontaneous and cheerful girl we used to know. Happy and smiling, dressed in a white sports outfit, she plays badminton with the handsome attendant.

Then an ominous letter arrives from Arne that provokes mixed emotions. He is coming to help her escape. The next night he steals money from his mom's bedside table and goes to get her. Eva's mother screams hysterically when she gets the call from the clinic telling her that Eva has disappeared.

And worst of all, Eva and Arne are now in ... (sound of bongos) ... Copenhagen!

Familiar landmarks of the Danish capital appear in the background as the two young people aimlessly wander the streets, eventually making contact with a group of grubby, long haired hippies dressed in ratty fur coats. Arne hands over all of his money in exchange for a promise of lodgings and they all pile into a microbus and speed away.

That night they find themselves at some kind of bizarre hippie happening populated by the most far-out stereotypes imaginable. In one corner a shaggy-haired tripper cackles psychotically to himself as a wild freaky blonde, fueled by the music, the drugs and her own wanton Danish nature, breaks into a spontaneous striptease and ends up fondling herself. As a driving bongo beat fills the air another dope-addled hippie gently slaps away

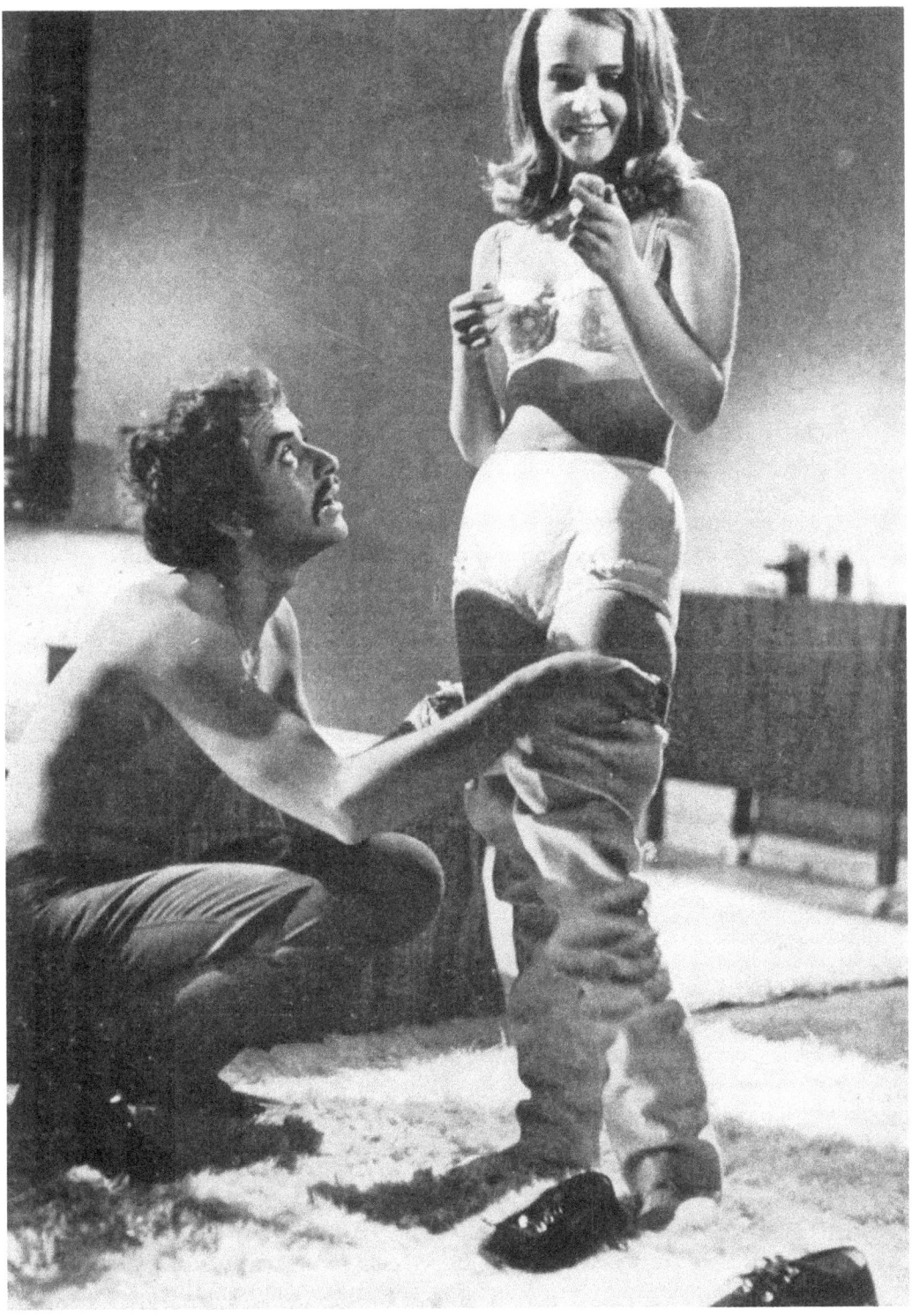

In a doped haze Eva is undressed by Zatek, played by Per Tofte.

on his girlfriend like she's a musical instrument. And Eva gets a present: a shot of heroin. Soon the cops burst in and Eva and Arne manage to flee. So much for a place to stay.

They find a seedy hotel room for 100 crowns a night. Eva pays and now they're both broke.

Back home in Oslo, her mom has had a nervous breakdown and lies incapacitated in a hospital bed. Orheim's depraved theories have contributed to all this, and Eva's Dad goes to confront him in his office. He just laughs. The father attacks him, beating him around the room and smashing an ashtray over his head. The false prophet falls dead to the floor. Now he's a murderer. A whole family destroyed!

In the garret room of their dive hotel, Eva and Arne have a nasty fight as they face the reality of being broke. Arne goes out to find the hippies who took all his money and runs into them on the sidewalk, playing flutes and drums. They refuse to give him his dough back, telling him to go and pimp out Eva.

He returns to the hotel and tells her she has to do it. She's horrified and refuses. He slaps her around and pushes her down the staircase and out onto the street. She hangs around until an older man eventually approaches her and soon they are speeding back to his house in a cab.

Lounge music floats from his stereo as he mixes drinks and tries to set a price with Eva who can scarcely comprehend her situation. She gulps her cocktail, choking on it, slowly dancing herself further into a state of numbness ... stepping out of her clothes. He undresses and lays her down on the bed. After suffering a brief pang of conscience, he positions his fat naked body on top of her and begins to hump away. She lies there feeling nothing, staring blankly at the wad of cash she still holds clutched in her fist.

Eva flees his house the next morning, vomiting over a garden fence before catching a cab back to the hotel where Arne meets her on the staircase. She wordlessly thrusts the cash at him, brushes off an attempted kiss and continues up to the room. He dashes out to buy some LSD with the money while she kills time by staring at her lifeless reflection in the mirror.

He returns. He's got it. Things don't seem so bad after all and amid giggles they cheerfully gulp down some tabs. They lie together on the bed, smoking and chatting happily and waiting for it to kick in. They kiss. They are still only teenagers and still in love in some way, but tragically their future has dissolved in a puff of hash smoke and their embrace is marked not by the innocent longing of young love but by the furtive desperation of two lost souls.

Suddenly Eva becomes hysterical and delirious, striking out at Arne. The next second she is silent again, staring intensely at her hand. Arne himself is now having a terrifying hallucination. He squeezes back up against the headboard, a horrified expression on his face. Something is coming. In his tortured brain he sees a snake. The snake kills and eats a white rat. He clutches at his throat. He gets off the bed and begins to gracefully flap his arms up and down like a great bird preparing to fly. He flaps around the room and over to the window. He climbs out onto the steep, sloping shingled roof, still flapping his arms as if about to launch into flight.

Seconds later Eva wanders over to the window and gazes out. She sees his body sprawled on the cobblestones below and a vague, far-away smile forms on her lips. As she turns back inside the room, reality hits home and she starts screaming wildly as the vision of a crumbling skull consumes her.

"Heaven or Hell" was too pussyfooted a title for the Danish distributor, Nordisk, who retitled the picture *The Way to Hell*. They then launched it in classic have-it-both-ways exploitation fashion, packing its program booklet with sanctimonious lectures about the evils of hash as well as stills of a naked Eva being seduced by Zatek.

> As known, there are many different opinions as to the effects of hash smoking. Some very liberal minded psychiatrists, psychologists and pedagogues maintain that hash is not a narcotic and ought to be legalized. They overlook the fact that it is [a drug that is] forbidden in all NATO countries in compliance with a pact entered into with WHO [the World Health Organization].
>
> In Norway the esteemed doctor Victor Borg, who is well acquainted with rising drug abuse and the unhappiness it causes, has together with director Øjvind Vennerød chosen to utilize film as the medium which can best reach out to youth. The result is this film, *The Way to Hell*. Denmark is also experiencing a shocking drug problem of epidemic proportions. For many young people without sufficient psychic and physical resistance, hash is a mortal danger since continued use leads to addiction and the consumption of stronger drugs, with degradation and misery to follow.
>
> The intention of this film is to spread information and stir thought. Few addicts can be cured, and the authorities are powerless in the face of this immense drug problem that has become a serious burden to the social system. This story of two young and likable people is ripped straight out of the real world. They become, like many of their friends, depend-

Eva and Arne seek shelter in a Copenhagen drug den.

ent on drugs and apathetic. They slide listlessly down the slippery slope, driven into criminality and prostitution — for them hash is THE WAY TO HELL!

A work of bruising realism? Back in Norway critics thought not. They faulted the film for its simplistic dialogue and the actors' wooden delivery as well as the lack of nuance and realism. It's unlikely the bad press phased Vennerød since this was obviously a labor of personal conviction and urgency. However obvious its failings as a piece of film art, it remains an eye opening look at the dark side of Liberated Denmark, albeit viewed from a great distance and through a very distorted looking-glass. A fascinating piece of popular mythology nonetheless.

Sensuela

Like Copenhagen, Stockholm also spread fear into the hearts of over-protective parents and figured as Sin City in a number of films — but who could have guessed that Helsinki in conservative Finland also loomed large as a city of lost souls? It did, at least in one film, the amazing *Sensuela*.

This was the all-consuming work of obsession by Teuvo Tulio, a Russian émigré who had been active in Finnish cinema going back to the silent period when he had performed as a suave leading man in the Valentino mold. Later as a director he became noted for a series of cheaply produced though stylish melodramas that went against the grain of realism dominating the country's filmmaking traditions. These pictures usually involved country girls who came to the big city and ended up being exploited, and *Sensuela* was in this vein. Yet the film remained only a tantalizing rumor in Finland for many years, as towards the end of his life Tulio became an embittered recluse and prevented *Sensuela* from being broadcast on television or distributed on video. Not until after his death in 2000 did this film again see the light of day.

Although its year of production is listed as 1975 Tulio had started shooting it in bits and pieces as early as 1964. Apparently his priorities and focus shifted along the way as a story originally set in impoverished postwar Finland ended up sporting all the pop-art excesses of the swinging '60s and the degenerate early '70s. Tulio was clearly caught up in all the hype of the sexual revolution that he saw taking shape elsewhere in Scandinavia and in Britain, and his plan was to explore its emotional dynamics in the context of the clash of cultures native to Finland.

The film begins as a *National Geographic*–tinged ode to the beauty of Finnish nature and the traditional values of the Laplanders, but its documentary tone quickly morphs into melodrama and the story of pure-hearted Laila begins to unfold. A spunky, nature-loving gal, she is lured into leaving the close-knit tribal life of reindeer herding and sled racing in the snow-bound valleys of the far north by Hans, her German lover, who in shades of Antonioni's *Blow-up* is a fashion photographer. She first met him at the end of World War II when as a Nazi pilot he bailed out of his burning plane, parachuting into a snowy field not far from her village. While recovering from an injured leg he learned to speak Finnish (with some German words thrown in — spoken with a Finnish accent). All rather improbable, and now on top of it after the war he has returned to Finland and lives and swings in Helsinki, the late '40s and '50s lost in the chronology.

Reunited with Laila, he spirits her away to the big city where she becomes a part of his life and a main motif in his risqué photography. He throws a wild party. Two blondes engage in frenzied topless dancing as hipsters wander about in absurd outfits that approximate someone's strange idea of mod fashion. Hans' apartment, saturated in primary colors and hung with kitsch examples of modern art, has the arranged artificiality of a department store window display and looks more like a stage set for an absurdist play than an informed attempt to recreate a swinger's pad. Various couples look for empty rooms they can have sex in while others dance. One cad pours a cocktail into a girl's panties. Another party guest discovers a nude couple under a blanket in the 69 position. Most of the film is accompanied by lumbering classical music that harkens back to a scoring style reminiscent of the early sound era, heavy on the violins, but now a rockish instrumental cuts in and later we are treated to a slab of guitar laden power pop inexplicably set to a scene of Laila washing dishes.

Dashing Hans has lots of girlfriends and it soon becomes clear Laila is just another one of his play toys. She flees his pad only to end up toiling in a series of dead-end jobs — but at least he has helped her discover the world of carnal pleasure. Her sexual awakening is conveyed in a series of long trance-like scenes, scored with classical music and so stylized as to seem symbolic or dreamlike. To say this languid pace runs counter to the rapid-fire expectations of the MTV generation is an understatement, but it is effective on its own terms. Sex is conveyed by the sensuous curves of two entwined bodies and the groping of hands filmed in close-up against a dark backdrop. For Laila the experience is something to be savored and indulged in and not rushed through; hence the emergence of her alter ego, Sensuela.

The sexual frankness and at times vulgarity of certain scenes suggest that as shooting wore on Tulio fell deeply under the spell of the times. Increasingly explicit scenes and elements were undoubtedly added as barriers and inhibitions fell. After decades of only being able to allude to physical passion Tulio now had the freedom to visualize it, but he did so tastefully and without resort to explicitly pornographic imagery, as befits a man of the old school. His heroine is a romantic at heart, swooning over a stuffed teddy bear her new boyfriend wins for her at the circus. Even Greta, a kind-hearted prostitute with whom she now shares a flat, decorates her den of sin with a giant teddy bear.

The film has many oddly charming moments but is also voyeuristic and prurient. For example one of the party-goers enters a room to find a naked couple fornicating on the floor. They yell at him to leave but he can't resist going back to spy again, and we viewers are treated to yet another prolonged peek. At one point Greta is brutalized by Laila's angry father, Aslak, who demands to know the whereabouts of his daughter. He shoves her around the room as her robe opens and her breasts are exposed. The scene is repeated when Laila's boyfriend attempts to get the same information out of her, and she is again shoved to the floor in a state of undress and humiliation. Nudity is usually not portrayed as a state of shame in the film, but here, to this character, nakedness is shameful. Greta's immoral behavior is sure to be brutally punished in accord with the almost biblical logic that infuses the film.

One is hard-pressed to name another movie that has such a fairy-tale like innocence about it and yet at the same time is so sleazy. This is a morality tale writ large, and unlike the Danish directors at ground zero of the sexual revolution, Tulio was under no pressure to address nuances and ambiguities. This was in any case a youth phenomenon, and he

Laila (Marianne Mardi) finds erotic bliss in the arms of her new boyfriend, Pekka (Ismo Saario), in *Sensuela*.

was 63 when the film was released. It's as if he were observing the '60s from the vantage point of the '30s.

The film is "old fashioned" in its filmic style as well as its moral orientation. Many of the sequences are filmed in standard "two-shot," actors spouting dialogue as they face each other in front of a painted backdrop. At one point they stand in front of a sky backdrop and one can see their shadows. These mostly amateur actors ("name" actors reportedly quit as shooting wore on) deliver game but unpolished performances, imbuing *Sensuela* with the kind of disarming naïveté found in the films of Ed Wood.

And like Wood, Tulio's rock-bottom budget forced him to be inventive with his make-up and special effects. A plane pictured in flight is a crude superimposition moving at a snail's pace against a sky backdrop. A brawl between Hans and a rival is conducted at a speeded-up pace with fake blood applied to faces in increasing quantities. Elsewhere we see a wolf howling and a reindeer buck braying in agony after castration. These are actually stuffed heads being held aloft, and one suspects the tormented sounds are produced by a studio hireling screeching into a tape recorder, but it's hard to be sure what we are actually seeing and hearing.

The film is full of such bizarre moments, and as the plot thickens even the quaint Laplanders in their colorfully embroidered outfits and peculiar four-pointed Lapp "wind hats" (not a far cry from the headgear of medieval court jesters) take on an otherworldly quality. In the snowy wilds they pass for authentic, but in the city it's another matter and they begin to strike those viewers unschooled in Finnish folk customs as clownish. This effect is particularly pronounced in scenes where Aslak, in full traditional garb, pursues Laila through modern day Helsinki, enraged after seeing her in a nude pin-up calendar (which is actually rather modest). These costumes give the movie the feel of low-budget science-fiction, and indeed, Aslak and Hans might as well be from different planets — planets about to collide.

One is tempted to write the film off as trash, but to dismiss it so easily would be a mistake. It is if nothing else bold and audacious. As in *Heaven and Hell* a trusting and innocent young girl is brought low in a cold uncaring city, but the scope of *Sensuela* is epic in comparison, spanning continents, eras and cultures. It required enormous amounts of either courage or foolhardiness to launch into such an ambitious story with means so limited and to stay with it for a decade. The end result is many things all at once: ethnic travelogue, psycho-sexual melodrama and lurid exploitation fantasy full of overwrought characters who perpetrate ghastly evil. Yet for all its exaggerations and technical snafus it also displays elements of real quality. The cinematography for example is often accomplished. While interior shots are constrained by small sets, many of the outdoor shots are thoughtfully composed and evocative. And if one can accept the film's rudimentary language the story works and engages.

It also packs a message, or rather a number of them, but they are mixed. We are predictably led to understand that the purity of country life in the outdoors is superior to the materialist temptations of big city living, but there is also a feminist thread that runs through the story. Laila not only discovers sex but evolves to the point where she demands her own pleasure, insisting at one point on being on top. She becomes much more savvy and determined than she would have had she stayed with her tribe. She becomes a fighter and a survivor if ultimately a cynic, an individual caught between two implacable cultural forces, the traditional and the modern, both of which are oppressively male dominated. At her lowest point as a prostitute she argues that behind every fallen woman is a man who has caused the fall. At another point, Greta delivers an angry lecture dismissing all men as conniving scum who are only after her ass. In fact the language can be quite earthy and vulgar.

If Tulio disparages the values of the sexual revolution as destructive and egocentric, he deals traditional Laplander life an even harder blow, ascribing to Aslak an unbending moral absolutism. A skilled herdsman who castrates reindeer bucks with nothing but a knife and his own teeth, he does the same to the duplicitous Hans in the middle of a go-

go dance party. The film flashes back to the (stuffed) reindeer buck braying in agony to remind us of Aslak's prowess in this department. With scenes like this the whole astonishing patchwork of a film is difficult to process at first glance.

Laila has fallen far in Helsinki, but in the end it is her fate to fall even further, and as the film nears it's conclusion we find her in Copenhagen. This happens after her suicidal contemplations on a bridge are interrupted by a statuesque man who tells her she is too pretty to throw it all away. But alas, he turns out to be not just a brutal pimp but a performing sadist. Soon she is part of his act which they take on the road to a live sex club in the Danish capital. Here he whips her mercilessly as she grovels on the floor. Then she stands and he strikes off her bikini with precisely aimed lashes, leaving her stark naked to gather up one by one the coins tossed on stage by the ridiculing male patrons.

First Prize Irene

If Brits, Norwegians *and* Finns were alarmed by the prospect of finding themselves adrift among the fleshpots of Copenhagen, Italians seemed to be intrigued by the idea. They were geographically and culturally far enough removed to view the whole situation with the kind of detached fascination that people exhibit when they visit a freak show. Amazed, that is, but not particularly scared or offended. They had already turned a fascinated gaze toward Sweden the year before in *Sweden: Heaven or Hell*, and now here in 1969 was a film about Denmark that summed up this particular attitude in spades, *First Prize Irene*. (Its original Italian title hints at something a bit more to the point: *Danimarca — L'incredibile Realtà della Nuova Morale*.)

It was shot by Renzo Ragazzi who had previously toiled as second-unit director on a string of westerns, pulpy space adventures and other genre pictures helmed by better known compatriots like Margheriti and Tessari. The film resembles a classic mondo production in its episodic construction and pseudo-documentary approach but lacks the killer instinct of the more extreme examples of the genre. It was not attempting to spotlight the violent or grotesque practices of the natives, in this case Danes. Quite the contrary; it was attempting to show how normal and at peace they were with their way of life and how organically this new sexual liberality fit into the broader concept of Danishness. That in itself was the shock, that a country like Denmark existed and that Danes went about their daily routines so unshocked by it all.

Ragazzi plays on the stereotype of Denmark as a cozy, old-fashioned little country of straw-roofed cottages, carefully tended flower gardens and postmen garbed in trademark red jackets who wheel through cobblestone streets on bicycles. In accord with this he strives to create a gentler tone, eschewing the sensationalism typical of the mondo genre in favor of a naturalism that results in endless references to Hans Christian Andersen. But underneath the country's quaint exterior things seem to be in turmoil: The film starts with a quote from the Hans Christian Andersen tale *The Drop of Water*, in which a troll views the Danish coast inside a drop of water. The twist here is that the drop of water, placed under a microscope, is in total chaos, prompting the narrator to exclaim that "it can only be Copenhagen!"

Every possible cliché and fantasy about Danes is hauled out. In one sequence a flock of Danish gals cavort nude out in the woods, laughing and rejoicing in their nakedness and shaking long tresses of blonde hair. This is intercut with scenes of deer gracefully bounding through the wilds while a '60s a cappella vocal arrangement emphasizes the exotic yet harmonious character of the images. The narrator supplies the subtext: it's natural for Danes to be naked together since the "tyrannical Danish climate" makes them yearn for the fleeting freedom of summer.

Yet the film also serves as an interesting and accurate snapshot of sexy Denmark in a more innocent phase just before the arrival of hard-core porn refigured the landscape. And there is not a frame of hard core in this film. That would have ruined the playful and innocent tone and precluded theatrical exhibition in all except the Scandinavian territories. The only exception is a snippet of dialogue in Danish, left untranslated for obvious reasons, that can be heard under the narration in a telephone sex scene. Nevertheless, while the film carefully skirts explicit content, what it implies is "hard" enough.

In one scene a boy arrives at a typical Danish home to visit his girlfriend. He is escorted up to her room by the mother. The two engage in normal teenage trivialities and then possibly (off screen) have sex. After a while another boy arrives and is led up to the girl's room. The two lads are casually introduced and shake hands without the slightest trace of hostility. Then the mother, wondering how her daughter will deal with the situation, politely sees the first boy to the door. The narrator goes on to say that the girl knows exactly what to do; she simply says goodbye to the first boy and seduces the newcomer, and at a much earlier age than her mother would have. This dramatization contains no nudity whatsoever, and the tone is casual and playful, but the message is not to be mistaken: this new morality is not just a hippie phenomenon but is also invading average middle-class Danish homes. These people are that relaxed about sex. The title itself, *First Prize Irene*, which refers to a contest sponsored by a contact bureau that gives away a real live woman, reinforces this theme.

In another scene a girl strips naked in a phone booth and is quickly joined by her (fully clothed) boyfriend for some heavy petting. The camera pans back to reveal pedestrians on a busy street who don't pay it any notice. Later a (fully clothed) young couple playfully enact various sexual positions out in a public park amid giggles and horseplay while a cheesy Farfisa organ-accented pop tune percolates along on the soundtrack.

Conversely, situations that are ordinary enough are made to appear lurid. A beach party of graduating high school students is made to look like a drunken orgy. The narrator, for his part, ponders the apolitical nature of Danish youth. "Will these young people become anarchists or revolutionaries? Hardly. They will in all likelihood just become perfect members of the consumer society. Danes do not believe that sex and drugs are connected to social rebellion." Later a dramatized sequence at a summer house ends in boozing and indiscriminate sex among married couples, harking back to the stereotypes about Danish "weekend morality" enshrined in films like *Weekend*.

For long stretches the film veers entirely away from sex, no doubt sorely testing the patience of the majority of the audience, and turns into a kind of tourist board promotional about Danish social customs. In one sequence some officers board a boat and motor out to rescue an ailing duck bobbing about in a canal. "What a gentle little country" seems to be the conclusion.

More topical and controversial aspects of Danish life also get screen time as hippie collectives, homosexuality and drugs and booze (we see a drunk babble and flap his arms like a bird) are discussed, although not in any sort of systematic or objective fashion.

Throughout the various vignettes the narrator theorizes about the Danish mentality while indulging in sweeping generalizations. Shakespeare's Hamlet as well as Hans Christian Andersen, he declares, could only have been Danes, so possessed were they by bleak and gloomy dispositions. Social exclusion and loneliness are very much sub-themes of the film. At one point aging parents visit their daughter and her family, but the young folks just want to get rid of the oldsters as soon as possible, finally telling them, "There is just no room for you here tonight." They call a cab which takes them back to their towering modernistic high-rise complex, leading the narrator to surmise that this new Denmark has become a "ghetto of the elderly." In light of all this the free sex movement is depicted as little more than a palliative for the alienated and dispirited citizens of the modern welfare state. (This was also very much the message of *Sweden: Heaven or Hell?*)

Yet *First Prize Irene* is also ambivalent. It also asserts that only in such a highly developed country could such a liberated culture arise. It concludes by noting that the lark has replaced the stork as the emblematic bird of Denmark, the lark being free and playful as opposed to the more traditional, family bound stork. The narrator wonders if other countries will follow Denmark's example.

While *First Prize Irene* takes refuge in stereotypes every bit as hackneyed as those that informed Øyvind Vennerød's *Heaven and Hell*, it at least attempts to understand its subject and the result is an intriguing period artifact that even manages some glimpses of genuine insight.

The Language of Love

Things were taking a very different turn in Sweden where, also in 1969, veteran director Torgny Wickman released a film called *The Language of Love*. Clinically objective and fiercely sober-minded, it would be one of the first commercial features to show unobscured intercourse on the silver screen. And while nothing indicates that Vennerød's *Heaven and Hell* was ever shown outside Scandinavia, *The Language of Love* would play or end up in court almost everywhere and confirm impressions of Sweden as a land of a thousand sexual positions. No surprise that it was to Stockholm that Zatek chose to flee.

Wickman was no porn film hack. He had been active in the Swedish film industry going back to the '30s and '40s when it was in the throes of modernization, and by the '50s he headed his own production company, Svensk Journal Film. During those years he directed countless short films and documentaries. He shot everything: commercials, travelogues, instructional films and artist portraits, making his feature film debut in 1954 with *Girl Without a Name*, a picture that is still rerun on television today. And now he was making a sex film, in the same manner that so-called legitimate directors in Denmark like Gabriel Axel had ventured into the genre.

Explicit sex on film was nothing new. It had been available going back to the 1910s, in the form of stag films, silent black and white shorts of ten minutes or less that were strictly illegal and were produced and circulated down through the decades in the most clandestine of circumstances. But the dissemination of pornography in '60s Scandinavia was quite a different thing and Sweden was clearly in the lead. While the abolition of censorship in Denmark was attracting all the attention, Swedish pornographers had all along been pretty much free to produce whatever they wanted. Unlike the UK and Den-

Torgny Wickman (lower right) and Sten Hegeler (lower left) check sound levels in *The Language of Love*. (Models unidentified.)

mark, for example, Sweden had never been a signatory to the League of Nations pact that specifically prohibited the production, distribution and export of pornography. It had been a purely domestic issue there and what laws did exist to regulate the trade were so vaguely worded as to be of little consequence. Hence as the demand for explicit 8 and 16mm shorts and magazines exploded in the mid–'60s, Swedish producers dominated the market. Among the first was the flamboyant Berth Milton, a former car dealer who founded *Private Magazine* in 1965 and brought hard-core to that country at a stage when Denmark was still a comparative police state.

But pornography was still very much a low and dirty enterprise, still forbidden, hidden away and stigmatized almost everywhere else, and in this context *The Language of Love* was all the more groundbreaking. Suddenly here was a commercial feature film that would play in theaters to a wide public, be advertised, debated, reviewed and reported on. It would shake up the debate, cause scandals and challenge censorship rulings far and wide. All in the good name of science.

Wickman claimed that his film had educational value and was not pornography. He did have qualified experts on board, notably Inge and Sten Hegeler upon whose book, *The ABZ's of Love*, the film was based. Following its publication back in 1961 the couple had become increasingly visible as spokespersons for the liberated generation, and in 1965 they were invited by the women's magazine *Femina* to edit a write-in advice column headed "There Is No Such Thing as a Frigid Woman." The topic was highly controversial and letters poured in that dealt with all aspects of sexuality. This was too much for the magazine's publisher, who fired them, saying he wanted a column that to a greater degree concerned itself with "the mind."

Two months later they were employed in the same capacity for the tabloid *E.B.*, dispensing advice every Monday that caused the timid to blush beet red. The column became a great success and was responsible in no small way for bringing sex into the open in Denmark. It was also reprinted in Swedish and Norwegian papers. Inge and Sten quit, however, when the paper's editor objected to one of their replies to a letter. In any case the column gave Wickman the idea of making a film about sexuality based on the sober and educational approach to the subject they had popularized.

The movie would resemble a kind of liberated TV talk show, and like television it would be shot with multiple camera set-ups. Inge and Sten were joined on couches by the progressive Swedish gynecologist Sture Cullhed and the short but redoubtable lady doctor Maj-Britt Bergström-Walan. Puffing away on cigarettes, the four dispensed maddeningly rational advice on various types of sexual practices, although fellatio, male masturbation and so-called deviations were avoided as Wickman felt all that merited a film of its own. As the experts talked, demonstrations of the various acts and positions were provided by living, breathing "non-professional volunteers" and further illustrated by diagrams and split-screen and animation techniques.

To stress that the acts weren't faked, multiple shots were shown together. For example a demonstration of female masturbation appears in a three-picture display; a close-up and mid-distance shots from different angles. This clinical approach and all the dispassionate level-headed advice made it seem less than arousing, and Wickman figured that the split-screen sequences made it even less so since a film about sex that actually aroused people was to be avoided.

The crew showed up on the first day somewhat dispirited, assuming they were there to shoot regular old porn. Yet Wickman chose to begin by filming the panel discussion which they reportedly found fascinating. As he recalled, "there was an almost devotional atmosphere in the studio when we actually began to shoot the sex scenes"[23] — devotional enough that one model was reportedly so absorbed by her own masturbatory performance that she kept at it even after the director yelled "cut" and obtained a second orgasm. Or so the story went.

Other actors were less thrilled. Advance promotion focused on the authentic nature of the film, but one Margaretha Henriksson loudly objected, asserting in the press that the "authentic sex scenes" were anything but and that the actors had in fact been acting. She maintained such promotional claims had caused her parents to despair and had ruined her good reputation. The producers hotly denied any fakery.

Swedish censor boss Erik Skoglund saw the film twice and was apparently so shaken that he had to take three days off. Initially he and his fellow board members wanted to completely ban the film, but later they relented and passed it without cuts, cleared for anyone 15 and over. It became a massive hit.

Denmark was the only other country where the uncensored version was permitted to screen and it became the hottest attraction there since *Doctor Zhivago*.

Sweden had created the mythology of a free and open-minded Scandinavia and a Swede had made this film, but now Denmark was taking things even further, as head-

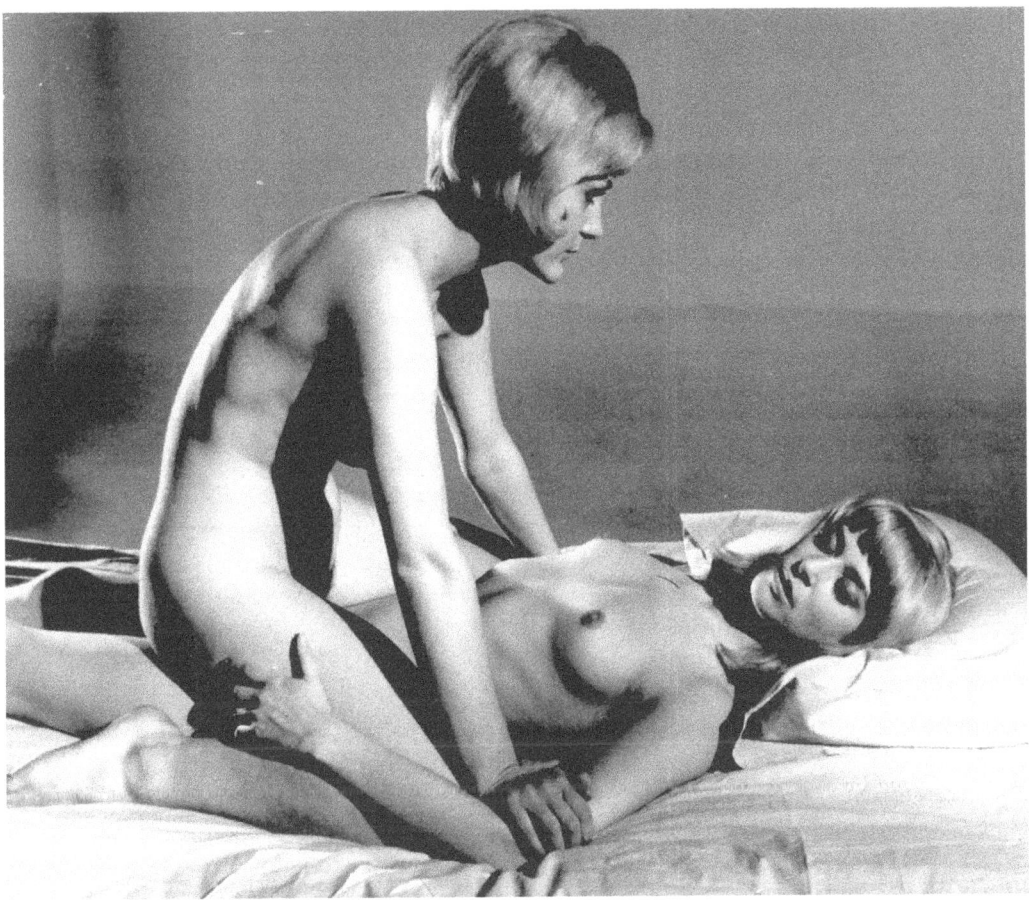

A scene from *The Language of Love* visualizes what many women really dream about while having sex with men — other women.

lines from Danish papers of November 1969 seem to confirm. Here it was revealed that seven kids from a sixth grade class, all approximately 12 years old, had been taken to see the film by their teacher, Ole Kjær. They'd been invited by a local radio station that wanted to record their reactions.

"In my opinion," stated Kjær, "the film shouldn't have been prohibited for children. Are they unable to suffer the sight of how people live and relate to each other? That, in any case, can't be kept a secret from them."[24] After the screening the students were in agreement that the film wasn't at all shocking and that they were glad they'd seen it.

Another teacher took his 16-year-old students to see the movie (it was 16-and-over for adult films in Denmark) at the behest of *E.B.*, who then published some reactions. Among those who weighed in was a lad called Thorleif. "It bothered me a bit that all the performers were 18, 19 ... 20 years old. It would have been nice to see 15- and 16-year-olds. It's hard for the older generation to accept that people that age have sex." He added that it was nice to see completely normal couples performing in the love scenes. "One of the young fellows had pimples all over his face. That's comforting."[25]

Though the film was popular there was dissent. Some critics found it to be artificial, unpleasant and absurd, and a theater owner in Nyborg was obliged to remove promotional stills from his display case after passersby took offense and called the police, but in Denmark the film did not cause a panic. The producers even tried to get the age limit for adult films dropped from 16 to 12, and lobbied for the film to be included in the sex-education curriculum of public schools. It was eventually shown in 11 Danish schools for kids under the age of confirmation (13 to 14) without the authorities stepping in to stop the screenings.

Even if some thought this was going too far, kids in Denmark had rights too and had to reach their own conclusions. This widely held belief was also reflected that same year via the publication of *The Little Red School Book*,[26] a user-friendly guide about how to survive (high) school. It had been written by two Danish teachers and was soon translated into a number of languages. Fashioned as a take-off on Mao's *Little Red Book*, it delivered straightforward advice to students on a range of subjects including sex, drug use, tests, teacher's duties, discipline, and so on. Detractors believed it enabled and encouraged kids to challenge the authority of the school system; advocates believed it encouraged students to think for themselves and take responsibility for their own lives. Although freely available in America, it caused significant controversy in Australia and in the UK where, after a high profile court case, it was only permitted to be published in a censored version.

The Language of Love raised a similar storm in the UK, enflaming the passions of many thousands of Brits who protested against it in Trafalgar Square at the instigation of clean living pop star Cliff Richards. To moral crusaders in Britain, as in America, Sweden was no example to follow. "Sweden — more porno, more suicide, more alcoholism and more gonorrhea every year!" proclaimed banners. In Norway it was shown with the genital regions blocked out.

In the U.S. the film was seized by customs and came to figure in yet another high profile court case on film freedom. (The publicity value of such trials was not lost on envious Americans, some of whom even sent their films out of the country so they could re-enter and be seized by customs.) All the usual suspects once again gathered in the uncomfortable little screening room on Varick Street. Critic Hollis Alpert, by now a veteran of these customs-house screenings, found it "deadly dull a great deal of the time."[27] but raised a good point when he commented in same article that "the film is presumably not harmful to the judges, attorneys, witnesses and juries that view the seized films. It is only 'the community' that is supposed to be in danger." What indeed was this diffuse concept called "the community"? It had to be endlessly and fiercely defended by individuals who themselves of course were sophisticated enough not to take offense. The court never interacted with those whose sensibilities they were supposed to be protecting, but functioned rather as a forum for the debate of theories: freedom of speech versus a concept that was just as theoretical in nature, "community standards."

Legal proceedings lasted over a year and a half, with Bergström-Walan brought over from Sweden to testify in federal district court. The government's council screened the now legendary *I Am Curious (Yellow)* for the jury in an effort to show how much more shockingly explicit and numerous the sex scenes were in *The Language of Love*— and they agreed, eventually finding it obscene.

The verdict was immediately appealed, and as so often happened the decision was reversed by the court of appeals, which maintained that the film dealt with sex "in a manner that advocates ideas," and that its aim was to identify and offer solutions for sexual problems.

While *The Language of Love* was at the time of its production clearly more explicit than other adult films, things were happening fast, and by the time of its belated American release in 1971 it had lots of competition. Soft-core cinema was by now virtually obsolete. This was partly due to the fact that the MPAA ratings system, in effect since 1968, did not differentiate between soft-core and hard-core and thus tended to drive the cautious away from both forms of exhibition. In any case, however, these developments were inevitable. For decades everything had been leading up to this moment. The art of the tease was dead; the forbidden fruit was no longer forbidden and people wanted a taste.

Many of these early hard-core features and featurettes were pseudo documentaries that professed educational intent — "white-coaters" as they were called in the trade in reference to white gowns traditionally worn by doctors — and *The Language of Love* was a prototype of this genre. No matter that most of them were shabby in the extreme and featured "experts" of dubious authenticity whose stilted lectures functioned merely as an excuse to show hard-core sex. Few complained — they were getting what they came for.

In 1971 Wickman released a Danish version of *The Language of Love*, entitled *More About the Language of Love*. This was a more radical take on the subject and featured chapters on homosexuality, pornography, sex and children, sex and the aged, and how the blind and the handicapped relate to sex. Here Inge and Sten Hegeler were joined by doctor Preben Hertoft and other Danish experts.

There would be five sequels in all, resulting in a total of six *Language of Love* films.

The original *Language of Love* had another brush with fame when excerpts were shown in the movie *Taxi Driver* in 1976. That is the pornographic film (shown in glimpses)

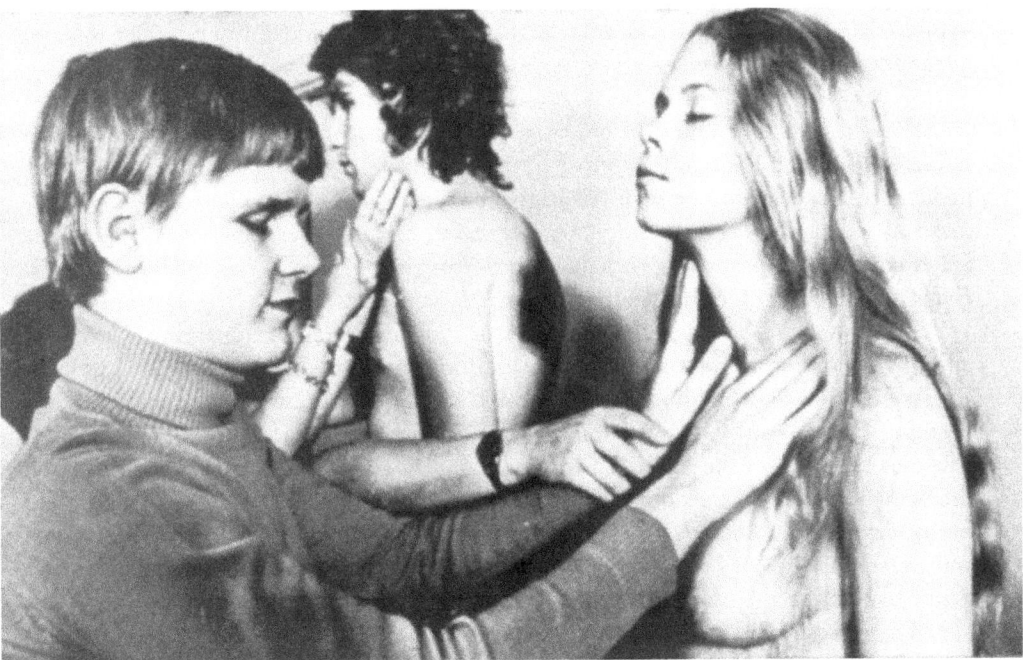

A blind boy uses his other senses in *More About the Language of Love*.

to which Robert De Niro takes Cybill Shepherd in the most disastrous first date in movie history. This was a good measure of the gulf between cultures: in America it was deemed vile pornography, the stuff of grindhouse nightmares, while in Denmark it was shown to kids as young as 12 by their teachers.

Also in 1969, Wickman made another film, completely different and actually shot before *The Language of Love*. *Swedish and Underage* was a drama about a 14-year-old girl called Eva. She lives in Stockholm, but when she moves to a small town things start to unravel. She becomes alienated from her foster parents and her school mates who bully her and look down on her. She ends up on the streets, selling her body for cash or a bit of friendliness or some chocolates. The men folk of the small town exploit her mercilessly and even the social authorities treat her badly. In the end she is subjected to court proceedings presided over by the town's mayor who has also exploited her. What hypocrisy!

The export titles—*Eva: Diary of a Half Virgin* and *Eva: Was Everything but Legal* as well as *Swedish and Underage*—are all cons in the classic tradition and hardly hint at the serious, not to say depressing, subject matter that the original Swedish tag (in literal translation *Eva: The Ostracized*) more accurately conveys. Wickman was attempting social criticism here, but of course being the work of Torgny Wickman the film contained sex and nudity—although these scenes are not frequent and are not conveyed in a particularly exploitative manner. Released in a clothed version for countries with stricter censorship, the film was not a big hit but is considered one of Wickman's best.

It included several notable performances, including one by Inger Sundh who plays Eva's friend Berit. Together they seek escape from their bleak fates by creating a fantasy world. Eva was played by the 22-year-old theater school graduate Solvig Andersson in her debut performance. She was deemed to have star potential on the basis of this film and subsequently got lots of work, including the lead in Wickman's 1973 porn-horror hybrid, *Fear Has 1,000 Eyes*, but never managed or perhaps wanted to claw her way out of the sexploitation ghetto.

Back in Denmark a number of Danish-American co-productions were taking shape as everyone waited for censorship to fall. The Bronx-born Brandon Chase (often credited as Lee Beale) would be involved in two of them: *Threesome (Think of the Possibilities)* and *Relations—The Love Story from Denmark*. His previous experience back in the States consisted of producing rock-bottom horror titles (*Blood of the Zombie*, 1961, and *Four for the Morgue*, 1963) and directing a single sexploiter, *Girl in Trouble* from 1963.

And now here he was in the summer of 1969 in Denmark, directing *Threesome*, officially the first film to be shot after the abolition of censorship. Co-produced by New York's V.I. Films and Guldbrandsen's Novaris Studios, it was cast mostly with English-speaking Danes (Poul Glargaard among them), and had echoes of Antonioni's *Blowup*. The plot centered on the American wife of a Danish fashion designer who finds herself shocked by the sexual freedom in Denmark and the amount of nudity involved in her husband's work, but loosens up after witnessing a couple making love at a party. She then embarks on a series of bisexual affairs that lead her to edge of emotional collapse and a temporary stay in the psych ward.

The film was clearly tailored as an export item and had only a single closed screening in Denmark before crossing the Atlantic to lay siege to America, where it was billed as the next stage in the evolutionary process begun with *I Am Curious (Yellow)* and *With-*

out a Stitch. "*Threesome,*" shouted the ad copy, "is the first film made in Denmark since that country abolished all censorship. *Threesome* was seized by U.S. customs and, as in the case of *I am Curious* and *Without a Stitch*, was finally released by the U.S. Attorney's office *without a single cut!*" Being seized by U.S. customs was a badge of honor for foreign sexploitation films, but it was not surprising that *Threesome* emerged from the process uncut since, like the other two films, it contained no actual scenes of hard-core sex.

It garnered some good reviews. "A sex film of the strongest kind ... totally revealing ... goes as far as possible ... sex and quality combined," wrote *Backstage*. "A sense of style and a thoroughly professional job ... give-all-take-all erotic encounters ... masses of female nudity and intimacy ... superior technical know-how added to basically nude dramatics," chimed in *Variety*. Also in the UK there was praise to be had, with London's *Cinema Magazine* calling it a "high-powered lesbian drama" that "smacked of Bergman" and was "certainly the best film yet in the fast moving new vogue of Scandinavian-American co-productions."

Its Danish cast apparently thought otherwise and were alarmed when it finally opened in Denmark in 1972; supposedly they had been promised that would never happen.

Relations—The Love Story from Denmark

According to some sources Brandon Chase co-directed the more ambitious if dour *Relations—The Love Story from Denmark*, shot about the same time and also aimed at an American audience, although Danish sources list only the Swede Hans Abramson as director. Abramson had already caused a stir in his homeland with *For the Sake of Friendship* in 1965 and *Stimulantia* in 1967 and would now flavor this new project with some typically downbeat Swedish social realism.

Based on the novel *Nu (Now)* by Johannes Allen, *Relations* had been pre-sold to America and England where there was growing demand for Scandinavian sex pictures. It was, in fact, a pretty sorry advertisement for "naughty Denmark," bleakly depicting as it did a well-to-do factory owner's doomed romance with a 16-year-old girl of the streets.

Yet unlike most of the competition it attempted social commentary. It confronted the ambiguities of the times and the limits of *frisind* with more courage than most while its de-glamorized presentation of the Vesterbro underworld harked back to the kind of social realism that had been hailed as the hope of Danish cinema in the early '60s.

(What ever became of that much ballyhooed New Wave, anyhow? After *Weekend* Palle Kjærulff-Schmidt and Klaus Rifbjerg collaborated on a number of other semi-experimental features which, particularly in the case of *Two* (1964), owed a continuing debt to the French New Wave, but it quickly became clear that these films had limited appeal in foreign markets where the big scores were waiting. Danish studios and directors, with an eye on the box office, were less interested in challenging filmic conventions than in chasing the chimera of *frigjorthed*, the seductive if illusive concept of total freedom for which Denmark was becoming famous.)

While the elfin 25-year-old Gertie Jung was credible as the 16-year-old Sonja, neither she nor Bjørn Puggaard-Müller, who played her lover, the factory boss Pegel, managed to infuse the story with real pathos. Pegel is especially inert, an ultimately hopeless figure who generates little sympathy or engagement.

Bjørn Puggaard-Müller in a scene from *Relations — The Love Story from Denmark*.

With all that said, Abramson nonetheless managed to paint a compellingly rough-hewn picture of Sonja's world, mysteries intact, and to convey to some degree the feel of the Vesterbro bars, cafes and tenements. The film is rendered in drab colors and a minimalist, melancholy score is employed to capture that certain bleakness that is intrinsically Danish.

As in Knud Leif Thomsen's *Gift*, this well-do-to businessman is no hero and not a man to envy but rather a character who symbolizes the spiritual drift of modern times. Mired in a dysfunctional marriage, he conducts joyless affairs of convenience behind his wife's back only to find himself "in lust" with Sonja after a chance encounter. She exploits him for money, loans never to be paid back, but he doesn't seem to much mind. Why shouldn't she? His wife also drains him of cash and at least Sonja gives him something in return.

He discovers hidden sides to her life, including the fact that she poses for pornographic photographs. Her world and her values are inconceivable to him, however well articulated and natural her explanations sound, and the more he tries to understand her, to control her, to make her over, the more confused and disheartened he becomes and the more his life unravels. Yet as troubled as he is by her lifestyle, his own existence seems to be just as much of a dead-end.

Relations is, in its own dour way, also a rumination on *frigjorthed* or the lack thereof in daily life and on the chasm between generations and between the rich and the poor. Disingenuously pitched in Denmark as daring erotica, the film opened there on Septem-

Stine (Sisse Reingaard) helps Jens (Ole Busck) hit the books in *Stine and the Boys* from 1969.

ber 22, 1969, while the country was all shook up over the "liberation of pornography" and it managed to strike a discordant if largely unheard note. In America, where it opened in 1971, it was predictably pitched as borderline porn. Jung even went over to shoot additional scenes of a more explicit nature. It was, in the fine tradition of *Weekend*, *Venom*, *Swedish and Underage* and *I Am Curious (Yellow)*, yet another sex film that wasn't a sex film. Hiding in all these sexy porn movies was some fascinating social commentary, if anybody noticed.

In the realm of what could be considered erotic offerings in 1969, Danish directors also produced a couple of actually quite sincere and sensitive films about young love: *Smile Emil* and *Stine and the Boys*. The latter was a loose adaptation of the novel *I, a Girl* directed by Finn Karlsson. Critics praised him for depicting realities of the teen world without resorting to mawkish or cloying affectation, and *Venom*'s fetching Sisse Reingaard was excellent as Stine. The film, the first by a director to graduate from the newly founded Danish film school, had a spontaneous and poetic honesty about it and was seen as an indication that new and vital forces were at play in Danish cinema. Karlsson was now considered a rising star.

Christa

Although it wouldn't grace Danish screens for several years, there was at that point another film being shot that would embody the mythology of Liberated Denmark as no other. It was the brainchild of one Jack O'Connell, an American who had come to Denmark that spring to find his dream girl. He'd previously produced commercials for American television and a pair of feature films on the counter-culture, *Greenwich Village Story* in 1963 and *Revolution*, about the hippies of San Francisco's Haight-Ashbury district, in 1968. Now he was going to make a film about today's liberated woman. And not surprisingly he had come to Denmark to find her. And she would be called Christa.

"Christa can only be a Danish girl," he told a writer. "In my opinion Danish women possess a more fully developed awareness of themselves as women and as independent human beings than women elsewhere. Although Swedish girls are just as militant as their Danish sisters in their insistence on being themselves (and the one girl I've met who was the closest to being a 'Christa' was Swedish), Danish girls demand their rights and pursue their opportunities more as a matter of course. Therefore Christa must be Danish and the film must be shot in Denmark."[28]

Christa would be liberated, intelligent, friendly, warm and at peace with herself. O'Connell had been working on the script for three years, and Christa would be his own personal fantasy brought to life on the screen, much the same way that the movies of Russ Meyer were the manifestations of his own personal fantasies. He would make his fantasy the world's fantasy. Christa, said O'Connell, would become just as iconic and representative of womanhood as Michelangelo's David was of manhood. He set up shop in Denmark, partnering with Lanterna film which would help solve practical problems and supply him with a production manager.

He searched for several months for Christa, canvassing the model agencies and watching Danish films. At various points he had Lisbet Lundquist and Sisse Reingaard in his sights, but finally after considering over 200 women he settled on Birte Tove Sørensen.

She was not a complete unknown. In 1962, at 17, she had been discovered by a photographer on Hornbæk beach. He snapped some pictures. They ended up on the front page of *E.B.* and that led to a modeling career. She was one of the first to pose nude for a modeling assignment (in 1968) but she was also a practical minded girl who had earned a degree in nursing and gotten work on the operating ward. Now at 24 the blonde with the Barbie doll figure was O'Connell's "it girl." She was photogenic, she projected and she seemed every inch the free-living woman of tomorrow.

The film would be about a liberated Danish stewardess who beds a dashing assortment of well-to-do male passengers, in the process introducing them to free-loving Denmark and blowing their minds. Her part called for lots of nudity, but according to producer Benny Korzen there was more to the nudity than just ... nudity. "Christa feels free when she goes around naked, and the nude scenes should preferably transpire without calling attention to the fact that she is naked. Her nudity is an organic extension of her mentality — she wants to liberate herself and clothes are unpleasantly constraining."[29]

All in vain, as Sørensen, soon to be known simply as Birte Tove, was singularly unsuccessful in getting viewers to look past her lack of clothing.

All the new legislation, sex-advice columns, hot movies and expanding crop of media personalities spouting slogans about sexual freedom had officially given birth to Liberated Denmark, and the foreign press was eager to pick up on it. In March of 1970 the second annual porn trade fair, pitched as "sex for the millions," was held in Hans Christian Andersen's home town of Odense. Even *The New York Times* was there. "Danes Open a Four-day Sex Show That Shows All," announced headlines in the March 20, 1970, edition.

But as the '70s dawned Denmark seemed afflicted by a case of split personality. There was the sunny liberated paradise of sexy, easy-loving blondes that was being aggressively sold to foreign audiences; and then there was the rainy everyday that Danes actually lived in, which was vastly more complicated and where this supposed new utopia was difficult to define or access. They and their country were being grossly typecast by filmmakers claiming to have discovered a sexual paradise on earth and it was almost embarrassing. Was there a single Dane who hadn't at some point been stopped on the street by a camera crew asking them what they thought about pornography? Judging by the plenitude of such scenes in a rash of recent movies, one wouldn't think so.

Thus far Liberated Denmark had been almost exclusively depicted by folks from the foreign and domestic film industry — accent on *industry*— and hardly any of the commercial features had managed to capture the pulse of the times. This dubious trend would continue as increasingly films would be shot in Denmark but tailored largely for foreign audiences eager to buy into a picture that was largely imaginary. It was becoming difficult to even define what a Danish film was anymore. If foreign directors weren't using the place as a staging ground for their own fantasies then Danish directors were stealing themes from successful foreign pictures and transplanting them to Danish settings with a staggering lack of subtlety and finesse. It was creating something of an identity crisis.

The most breathtaking example of this hack-and-paste approach arrived only two months into the new decade.

The Daughter

"This film is just for yahoos — and Americans."
— Feb. 10, 1970, excerpt of review of *The Daughter*

I, a Woman 2 had been a success for Guldbrandsen in the States. Gio Petré, the Swedish sexploitation star who had replaced Essy Persson in the lead, had been sent to America to promote it and that had gone well. She had been interviewed on radio and TV and photographed for magazines like *Playboy* and *Life*. By the summer of 1969 the movie was playing in 41 theaters in New York alone. The original *I, a Woman* had been re-released twice since 1967 and was also at this point on screens. According to Guldbrandsen the two films had played a total of 104 theaters in New York — "and at the same time, even."

There was strong demand for a follow-up in the U.S. and elsewhere, strong enough to allow him to pre-sell a third installment to numerous territories. Now all he needed to do was make it. First, however, he needed a good idea and that was easier said than done since only two *I, a Woman* books had been written.

Back in September of 1965 Siv Holm, a.k.a. Agnethe Thomsen, had mentioned to a journalist that she had finished a third volume of the series which was set in the countryside where she had ended up living a peaceful and happy life. Apparently this book

Glassy-eyed stares and pot smoking in *The Daughter*.

was never published, but in any case quiet times out in the country was specifically *not* what Guldbrandsen wanted. He wanted Hell's Angels beating up hippies, racism, lesbianism, drugs, the generation gap — all the combustible ingredients of a searing youth-problem picture that would attract young viewers the world 'round the way that American directors had managed to do.

Times had changed by leaps and bounds since the original film had come out; a woman who just slept around was now so passé. There was so much more to explore and exploit, and Guldbrandsen set to it, throwing himself into a completely original story that he entitled *Three Kinds of Love*. Having already written scripts to 45 films by this point, he hardly broke a sweat. But since this movie was technically a continuation of the *I, a Woman* series (released in some territories as *I, a Woman 3*), the character of Siv Holm again had to be present.

It was intended that Petré would also star in part three but in August of 1969 tragedy struck when her two children died in a fire and she canceled out. Gun Falck, another Swedish actress, was then signed to replace her. The focus of the film, however, was Siv's daughter, Birthe. That part went to the 17-year-old fashion model Inger Sundh who had previously starred in *Swedish and Underage* and *Inga 2*. She would now perform in a series of daring sexual situations that already had publicity shills tagging her "the new Essy Persson."

The plot of *The Daughter* was nothing if not ambitious. It begins when Birthe arrives home several days early from her Swiss boarding school to find her mother, who works as a nurse, in bed with a doctor from the hospital. The child has lived a protected life thus far and she's shocked. Furthermore the house is littered with the flotsam of this new sexual revolution: vibrators, sex toys and even a pornographic record which she discovers and plays the next day to her horror. When she finds pornographic photos of her mother in the closet, that's the last straw and she flees traumatized into the night-time streets of Copenhagen.

That evening she is accosted by two obnoxious hippies, Egon and Max, who drag her along to a mod nightclub full of strobe lights, go-go dancers and rock music. (Egon is played by Søren Strømberg. It's a far cry from his role in *Gift*, but perhaps not so far since his portrayal of the hippie is anything but flattering.) Egon gets distracted and she briefly meets Stephen, a black medical student from America whose lesbian cousin, the well-built Lisa, happens to be a go-go dancer at the same club and also has eyes for blonde Birthe.

Suddenly a biker gang attacks. They smash up the club and brutalize the hippies. Out in the parking lot Stephen and Lisa manage to escape, climbing into a cab as the bikers shower them with racist invective. Egon and Birthe make their way to a shadowy dope den frequented by longhairs. There Max picks out a mournful tune on his guitar as another hippie accompanies him on harmonica. Kids are smoking hash from big pipes. A couple has casual sex while others stare off into the distance. Egon attempts to have sex with Birthe, but she is repulsed and starts screaming and must be rescued by Stephen who has driven over thinking she might need help.

Back at his flat, Birthe is still shook up, her face tear-streaked and one breast exposed after the mauling. Lisa accuses her cousin of trying to rape her and consoles her ... a bit too physically. Birthe is given a room of her own and falls asleep. The next morning Stephen goes to the hospital where he works, coincidentally enough, in the same department as Birthe's now worried-to-death mother. Meanwhile Lisa seduces Birthe and they have sex.

That evening they all gather again at the nightclub and hang out by the bar while Lisa does her go-go routine on stage. Egon and Max confront Stephen who is plainly in love with Birthe. They accuse him in laughably bad English of stealing their women. (It was much easier to put together an English speaking cast of locals in Denmark or Sweden than anywhere else in Europe, and although this was ideal for co-productions or films made for the U.S. market it resulted in a lot of bad English.) Stephen slugs Max, much to pacifist Egon's astonishment, and then leaves with Birthe.

They return to the apartment. That night tensions rise when Lisa gets back from the club and Stephen realizes the two women are in love. He leaves in anger and goes to visit Siv who is "a real woman who loves men." Once there he is again the sober and rational gentleman and they try to understand what's happened.

That night Lisa and Birthe again make prolonged interracial lesbian love, which constitutes almost the whole of the film's erotic content. In a bizarre twist, Lisa brandishes a nude photo of Siv she found in Birthe's purse and uses it as a prop in their sexual play: "pretend I am this woman, she is the one you really want...."

This leads to a strange flashback that regurgitates snippets of basically all of the film's action and Birthe comes to realize that it is Stephen she really loves. She now goes to find

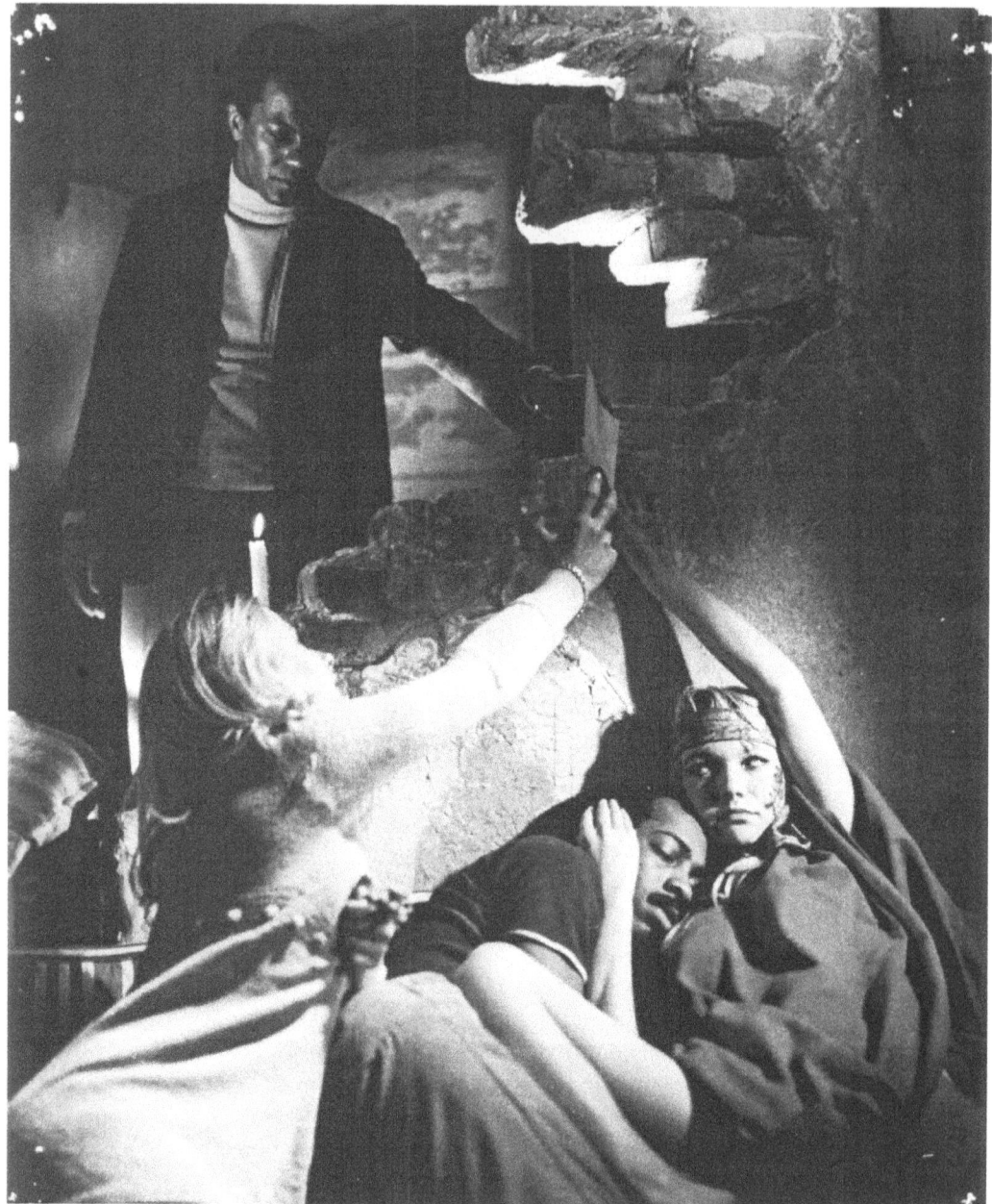

A scene from *The Daughter*: Stephen (Tom Scott) ventures into the lair of the hippies to save Birthe.

him. There is a quick church wedding for the two while Lisa looks on forlornly from a distance. Siv tries to put on a brave face but confides to her lover that she's still apprehensive about her daughter marrying a Negro.

One of the most lurid exploitation films ever made in Denmark, *The Daughter* is a muddle of issues, characters and slabs of dubious psychology culled from the tabloids and the outré limits of Peer Guldbrandsen's imagination. He sought authenticity by employing real hippies and bikers and by frequently using a documentary-like shooting style. And he got it in bits and pieces, but the actors were never able to stand up against the preposterous script and the result is pure soap opera.

For one, the issues hardly corresponded to the reality in Denmark. Of course there were bikers and they did cause occasional havoc, most famously at the premiere of John Wayne's *The Green Berets* at the Saga Theater, in May of 1969, when they attacked *en masse* hundreds of left-wingers protesting the film. This brawl became known as "the Saga War." Bikers famously detested hippies and leftists and this also led to real friction on the set, but these bikers had little resemblance to Sonny Barger's Hell's Angels. While the brief scenes of motorcycles roaring through the night-time streets of Copenhagen spiced up the film, these helmeted hellions were for the most part idiotic rather than menacing.

And the racial issues that are batted about, mainly in exchanges between the black actors Tom Scott and Ellen Faison, who played Stephen and Lisa and had been brought over from America by Guldbrandsen, were overwrought and absurd. The concept, tone and story had been imported wholesale from the U.S. so that it would be a hit — in the U.S. Of course there were blacks in Denmark at this point, including a population of American draft-dodgers and conscientious objectors, but not many. The grafting of distinctly American themes onto a Danish setting made the film ungainly enough, and with all the actors speaking their own languages for the most part — Danish, Swedish and English, and bad English when spoken by other than Scott and Faison — it felt all the more constructed. And even in the common-language exchanges between Scott and Faison (English) and Falck and Sundh (Swedish) the dialogue was wooden and the acting flat.

Whether Guldbrandsen knew anything about racism was an open question, but in fact he had actually once written a book about it, *White Ecstasy (Hvid Ekstase)*. The first Danish publisher he had submitted it to reportedly said it was excellent but had one major drawback: the author was white. So Guldbrandsen sent it to another publisher claiming it was written by a black man named S.V. Gold and that he had merely translated it. They published it, with the critic of one major paper declaring that it was a book that could only have been written by a Negro.

Guldbrandsen was accused of presenting a distorted and unfairly negative portrait of bikers, if that was possible, and hippies, the latter cast not only as jerks and sexual predators but as racists. "I intend to show that people from both the Right and the Left are intolerant," he commented in the press. "That can also be done in long-haired, so-called artistic films but what's the use when no one bothers to see them?"

Not since *Weekend* had such an unflattering portrait of Danes, in this case the counter-culture, been disseminated to the wider world. Niels, one of the real hippies hired to appear, was not happy about the way the film portrayed them, particularly when they mock a girl for being a lesbian and hurl racist comments at Tom. "Hippies are certainly more tolerant than most and only a person who doesn't know the milieu at all could manage to write such scene.... That dialogue was in any case delivered by a professional actor, and the real hippies who were involved were not told anything about the background of the film." A biker known as The Führer told a reporter that despite their behavior in the film they really didn't have anything against blacks either. "We were paid to be in the film and to say the dialogue they gave us. The whole thing is total exploitation in any case, and it's okay as long as it pays off in America."[30]

Turning out in full regalia for the sold-out premiere, the bikers whistled and stomped on the floor when they appeared on screen and wisecracked their way through the sex scenes to the amusement of the rest of the audience. "It's a good thing they have protective covering on the seats ... hands off the zippers, boys, you're making noise ... watch out for the gals when you leave — they're all lesbians now!"

Grindhouse cinema had come to Denmark.

This being the first Ahlberg-Guldbrandsen film in color, it did present unique visual possibilities which they exploited to the full, most notably in the freaky opening scene. Here a ravishing blonde floats naked in different positions, suspended in the air as swirls of smoke and liquid slide effects bubble up around her and snowflakes fall. A lonely harmonica warbles as the opening credits appear. She rubs and fondles her body, lost in a pleasurable trance. A snake appears and crawls along her naked flesh ... another naked woman sucks one of her breasts ... but suddenly what has been a dream turns into a nightmare as she awakens screaming in a hospital bed.

Despite scenes like this and other inventive stagings that Ahlberg had obviously taken time and care with, it lacked the finesse and polish of his previous black and white work. There were no performances of the caliber of Axel's in *I, a Nobleman*. Sundh as Birthe gives some very natural turns and seems to be the only actor not paralyzed by the bad script, displaying in flashes an appropriately snotty defiance, but still on whole the acting has a thoroughly sedated quality.

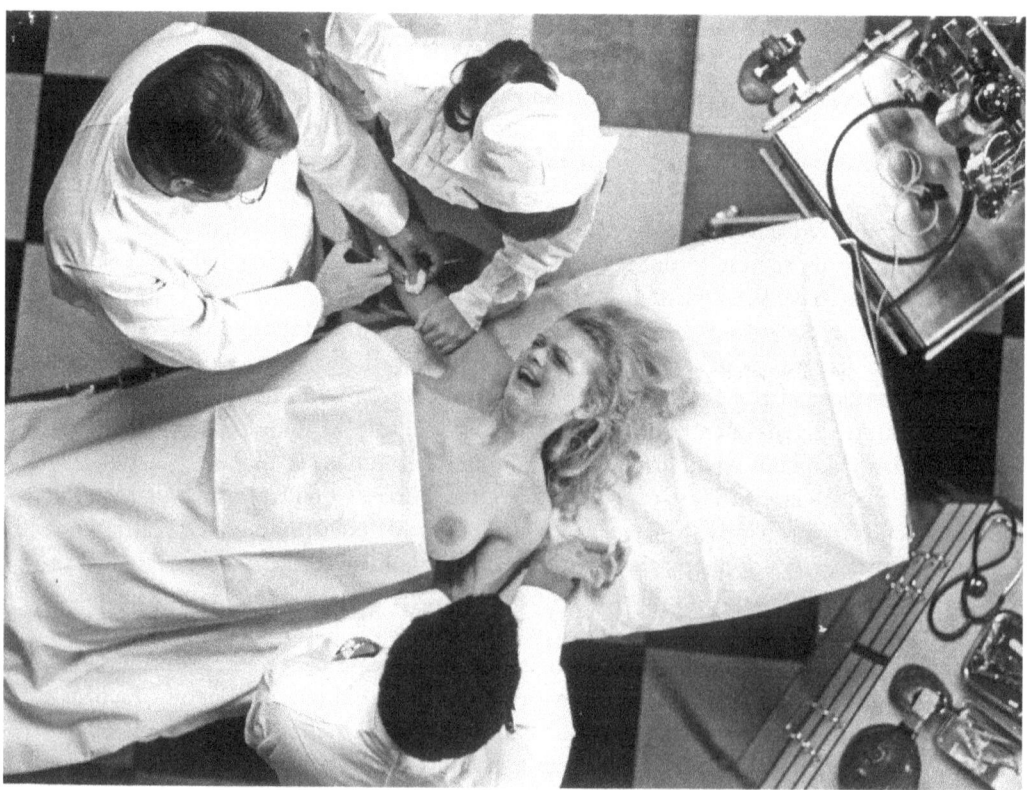

Inger Sundh awakes from an acid nightmare in *The Daughter*.

Still the film manages a number of hauntingly effective and atmospheric moments, such as those that transpire in the smoke-wreathed lair of the hippies. And a sequence where Klaus Pagh and Gun Falck examine sex toys, page through the personal ads in a paper and discuss the new sexual liberality serves as an almost journalistic snapshot of the moment. As awesomely wooden as *The Daughter* is, it depicts the (pop culture) mythology of the times in a suitably sensationalized fashion and gets to the heart of the matter with a recklessness that only exploitation cinema, devoid of all pretensions, can manage. Despite its confusing mix of documentary and melodrama, it was much more plugged into the reality of the times than carefully staged, hermetically sealed studio fictions like *Without a Stitch* and the soon to be discussed *Bedside Manner*.

The Daughter represented the most exploitive extremes of these new trends that had internationalized Danish cinema, and even though these developments were largely driven by raw capitalism they also managed to open up the field to more artistic directors. The access to new markets pumped money, energy and ideas into Danish cinema and made a lot of very unlikely films possible, not all of them exploitation pictures.

Without Kin, a feature length collection of six experimental short films, was a good example of the new opportunities opening up in production and exhibition for so-called underground directors. One of the films included scenes of a female cross-bearing Jesus figure dashing stark naked through the Danish stock exchange as grey-suited traders look on glassy-eyed in various states of incomprehension and shock. It was an art happening and this image became iconic of the times, much better known than the movie to which it belonged. Other shorts dish out S/M and nudity and there is even a mini-spaghetti western, Danish style. *Without Kin* no doubt strained the patience of many a viewer, but at the same time it exemplified what was possible and illustrated how new ideas and aesthetics, expressed in underground short films that normally only played at galleries, were starting to make inroads in commercial filmmaking and exhibition.

These were exciting times. The predictability that had characterized Danish cinema for decades had given way to a new spirit of experimentation. Things loosened up overnight as whacko artists, rogue producers and social researchers on a mission crashed the party. Movies were not just being made by studios anymore.

Quiet Days in Clichy

The rowdiest gate-crasher was artist and general shit-disturber Jens Jørgen Thorsen, and he was to have the honor of being the first to turn a Henry Miller novel into a movie.

Thorsen had long been a fan of Miller's writing and when the author had come over to Sweden in 1961 to visit the painter Børge Sornum, they met, became friends and started a correspondence. In 1967, with several short films behind him, Thorsen suggested to Miller that he make a movie of his novel *Quiet Days in Clichy*. This was an account of Miller's bohemian adventures in Paris back in the early '30s when he was trying to make it as a writer, and a main (but not exclusive) focus of the book were the numerous erotic encounters he and his flat-mate Carl had with a parade of strange and alluring women.

Over the years Miller had turned down countless offers to make his books into movies, but he reacted positively to Thorsen's proposal and after an exchange of letters agreed to look at his script. He claimed it was the best adaptation he had seen thus far and eventually gave his Danish friend approval to make the film. At about the same time, Paramount had begun adapting another of his novels, *Tropic of Cancer*, for the screen, and he sold the rights to Thorsen for but a tiny fraction of what he was charging them. Not that Thorsen needed charity; he had the solid financial backing of the SBA Agency, a major booker of rock and jazz acts throughout Scandinavia. They probably had something to do with getting Country Joe McDonald (sans The Fish) to supply the film's music. (Best known for the "FUCK" chant at Woodstock, McDonald would deliver a theme song so smutty that it was banned from radio in many countries.)

Miller also gave his blessings to the casting of Paul Valjean as the young version of himself, Joey, as he was called in the book. A balding 34-year-old American dancer and choreographer living in Denmark, Valjean bore a striking resemblance to the young Miller. But there seemed to be far more interest in who would be cast in the female roles. That was bound to generate controversy, the women of a Miller novel!

It was at one point reported that Thorsen was on the verge of signing Lena Nyman to play the lead. He loved her performance in *I Am Curious (Yellow)*, which was then taking the U.S. by storm, although he had little good to say about the movie itself. He could not see how it constituted any genuine breakthrough in screen freedom since it did not show any real sex. As he would later say, he made *Quiet Days in Clichy* as a protest against Sjöman's fakery, his "cock-tease freedom," as he put it.[31] His film would show the real stuff, he promised.

Anyway, Nyman never signed.

Lotte Tarp said no to the role of Nys, the Rubinesque beauty Joey falls for. One writer suggested that Janis Joplin, whom SBA had under contract for concerts in Europe, should play that part. That also never went anywhere but all this gave the papers something to talk about. The women who did eventually sign on were for the most part newcomers or non-actors.

Thorsen had simplified the book's action and moved it up to the present day. Through May and June of '69 they filmed interior scenes in Denmark. In Paris cameraman Jesper Høm shot a lot of footage around Place de Clichy and the adjoining Montmartre district where Miller had roomed and rambled. He managed to create an appropriately gray and dilapidated portrait of the city while avoiding the clichés that Paris tempts, and his cinematography was praised even by many who disliked the movie. At one point the 78-year-old author himself visited the set.

Quiet Days in Clichy premiered at the Cannes Film Festival on May 8, 1970, and even though it was playing outside competition, interest was massive and reviews were overwhelmingly positive.

Back in Denmark Thorsen found himself embroiled in an unexpected controversy. A Danish writer who had seen the film in Cannes suspected him of pulling a fast one with his actresses by adding frames showing penetration to make it appear they were having actual intercourse. Did the women know that? He called them all up to ask, and managed to whip the issue into the talk of the op-ed pages for the next three weeks until the film opened in Denmark.

Susanne Krage, who played the character of Christine, the blonde bombshell from Denmark who shows up to dally with the boys in the concluding scene, was against the practice — if it had happened. None of them really knew since Thorsen hadn't shown them a final cut yet. Krage added that it was regrettable that most of the girls were new to the

Jens Jørgen Thorsen (left) confers with Henry Miller on the Paris set of *Quiet Days in Clichy*.

game and not members of the actor's union, and therefore not able to do much about Thorsen's editing. (The irony of Krage's character—the only woman in the film to find herself repelled by Joey and Carl's lifestyle—was not lost on writers who wondered if it would be at all possible in today's Denmark to find a woman capable of being shocked.)

Ex-teacher and fashion model Louise White, the daft "Surrealist girl" who in the opening scene has sex with both Carl and Joey while puffing away on a cigarette fixed in a long-stemmed holder, was also upset about the alleged sequences and sued the filmmakers for 10,000 crowns. She refused to discuss it further with the press, however, since in the meantime she had found something more important to consume her time: Scientology.[32]

There was lots of discussion in the media as to how much sex the actors actually had with each other, if it was "real" and if it really mattered at all. Apparently there had only been two penetration inserts,[33] both of these clipped into White's scene near the start. No doubt Thorsen wanted to establish the film's hard-core credentials early on and show this was no "cock-tease" fakery. In any case White withdrew her suit before the premiere, having, according to reports, agreed to the inserts.[34]

Beyond the personal issues at play, all this raised debate about the nature of Denmark's fabled open-mindedness. "That the discussion is taking place at all," noted reviewer Claus Rdde, "indicates nothing has changed and that we still hold sexuality in unapproachable awe. It is hard for us to accept intercourse as a film topic on a par with other human activities such as vacuum cleaning, sports, eating, etc. Therefore we also find it difficult to come to terms with the fact that intercourse on film is an illusion, just as the whole film is an illusion."[35] Others noted that there was still a long way to go before a film with explicit sexuality could be taken in stride and evaluated on the same basis as all other films.

All this sex talk was more than any press agent could have hoped for, and the opening in Copenhagen's Dagmar theater on June 1 resulted in one sold out show after another. Across the country it sold 100,000 tickets in the first three weeks of June. It even gave Warner Bros. the jitters; their film *Woodstock* was scheduled to be the next premiere at the Dagmar but it looked like *Clichy* might pack the joint for months! It was predicted that everyone connected to the film would become millionaires, including one Dirch Passer who had co-financed it and was pleased as punch about its success. Stig Vendelkær, whose publishing house had been in steady decline since the abolition of written censorship, jumped on the bandwagon and reissued Miller's book with the slogan "See the film, read the book."

All this discussion about penetration frames and whether the film was more hardcore than *I Am Curious (Yellow)* had tended to obscure the more essential issue of treatment. It was not so much what the film showed but *how*. It had lots of nudity, it had exposed genitals and it had penetrative hard-core action in the form of the aforementioned added frames, but despite all that, was it a "porn" film at all? Some thought not. "The question of porn is completely irrelevant," weighed in theater critic Jens Kruuse. "The film has nothing to do with porno — it's a wonderful film full of vitality and *joie de vivre*."

It had humor and spirit in a genre where most films were turgid and lifeless affairs and where most of the humor was of the unintentional variety. It was playful and sloppy, a balmy slapstick celebration of vulgarity, excess and carnal indulgence that ran counter to what were in fact the very puritanical conventions of commercial pornography which stipulated that the humor must never interfere with the sex. In *Quiet Days in Clichy* the sex was not treated with an iota of seriousness, mystery or reverence. A case in point is the legendary scene where Joey takes a messy wine-soaked bath with two party gals he brings home, a wild romp that comes to an abrupt halt when he pisses in the bath water. This was hardly the stuff of pornographic fantasy. All involved claimed they were not making a porn film and that was indeed true enough.

In its depiction of sex as fun, sex as jubilation, sex as a complete loon, it was unique, but as to whether that made it an enlightened or progressive film was another matter entirely, and some thought it just the opposite. "The whole film is permeated by the most reactionary male attitudes toward women.... Its attitude to sexual morality is 'way out' and is anything but liberated and progressive," wrote Suzanne Giese, one of the few female voices to be heard on the subject.[36]

Granted, the book was written well before there was any widespread consciousness about sexual equality, but that was small comfort to sensitive souls who in these liberated times found themselves suddenly confronted by Miller's old school chauvinism which Thorsen did nothing to soften. The word "cunt" is literally everywhere, for example. It's uttered with gusto in almost every other sentence and scrawled like graffiti over the opening credits with a playful defiance that recalls the old Lenny Bruce maxim about naughty words losing their power to offend if repeated often enough. "That's your cunt, this is my cunt," proclaims Carl by way of introducing their girlfriends. All this in the good cause of attacking the prudish and repressive powers-that-be, of course; all in the name of the good fight. But was that Miller's fight? Maybe not. For Miller personal honesty had always been paramount and, as journalist Helge Kristensen noted, "he hates all this modern 'sexual freedom' nonsense."

There was scant comfort for the feminist minded. The young nymphomaniac Colette, who cooks and cleans up the house, is characterized in the theme song as having "all her brains between her legs" because she's a sloppy housekeeper who "spoils the coffee and burns the eggs." She is also just about the only girl who doesn't ask for money after sex, or doesn't simply have it handed to her as a matter of course. Although attitudes among Danish women had changed radically between 1968 and 1970 as a spirit of feminism took hold, this change had yet to be reflected in the movies that were being made.

Nonetheless, *Quiet Days in Clichy* was widely heralded as a manifestation of the new liberal attitude. It was seen as a breakthrough for screen freedom and was considered the first post-censorship film with artistic merit. Thorsen was after all an artist. And it nurtured a delightful sense of solidarity among viewers right from the opening bell. "Before the film begins," related a journalist, "a neutral female voice warns the audience that 'the film you are about to see' contains several 'unusual' scenes. People glance about to see if there is anyone who hasn't realized that beforehand. The pleasant voice then announces that modest patrons in the audience who might suffer offense from these scenes can, if they leave the room right now, get their money back. The crowd is all abuzz as everybody looks around to see if anyone has the courage to get up. It's high tourist season in Copenhagen and the message has been delivered in English. It is then repeated in French and German to endless jubilation in the audience. We nod knowingly to each other. The crowd has been sorted and the avant-garde remains. That is all of us."

Some found the film permeated by the militant liberality of the day which they deemed incompatible with the laid-back naturalism of Miller. Additionally the good atmosphere that Thorsen had sought to create seemed at odds with the tone of desperation that was also part and parcel of the book and made it a tragicomedy. This tone was nowhere to be found in the movie. The frustration and angst that Joey experiences is overshadowed by the deadpan humor that Valjean seems to exude as a matter of course.

To purists Miller's book was not pornography; the sex was rather an expression of the character's appetite for life and a source of joy and stories and experiences that could offer respite in the face of overwhelming despair. For his part, Miller praised the film for its joviality and its Rabelaisian qualities.[37]

The movie caused another stink when excerpts were shown on Danish TV in connection with the premiere. It was one thing to play it in a theater, but to bring it into the living rooms of middle-class Denmark was something else entirely and graphic proof to some that this new freedom was being grossly abused. Speaking from the pulpit, a priest in North Zealand called upon Danes to rise up in protest against pornographic texts and broadcasts which, he declared, violated the sanctity of family life under cover of a distorted interpretation of open-mindedness.

The international success that the Cannes screening had set in motion made a lot of Danish film people proud, but how Danish the movie was—shot largely in Paris, in English, and aimed at an international market—was debatable.

It was eventually sold to 87 countries but censor boards blocked it in many places. Sweden passed it uncut and it was extremely popular and critically praised there. It was also a big hit in Germany, even though the Berlin Film Festival got weak knees and canceled their in-competition screening at the last minute, claiming that its appearance in

Quiet Days in Clichy— Left to right: unidentified "party girl," Carl (Wayne John Rodda), Christine (Susanne Krage) and Joey (Paul Valjean).

Cannes disqualified it. The German distributor, on the other hand, had been so thrilled about it that he had insisted on drawing up and signing a contract on the spot — on a napkin. The normally cutting-edge Edinburgh Film Festival turned it down, claiming that local authorities would seize the print and take away their license to exhibit films if they showed it. It remained officially forbidden in Scotland but did later play at the London Film Festival.

Ironically, it was still banned in France where Miller's novels had first been published. "The French were the first to accept my work," the author protested in a telegram to French authorities, "and gave me the courage to continue. What's happened?"

As *Le Nouvel Observateur*'s film critic Michael Mardore reported, French censors considered the film "too advanced for the current state of French morality." Oddly, a reissue of Miller's book *Sexus* had just finished a run on the French best seller list. This brought into focus the gap that still existed between books and movies, and between Danish and French cultural norms. (France was a good five or six years behind Denmark in the evolution of screen explicitness; not until 1975 did the first hard-core feature open in Paris, Alex de Renzy's *History of the Blue Movie,* and it was not until later that same year that the first French-made hard-core film saw the light of day.)

But the biggest score was waiting in the States. There had been keen interest from numerous American distributors even before Thorsen & Co. had started shooting. The film had "can't miss" written all over it: the daring novel by Henry Miller that couldn't be published until 1956 because no publisher was brave enough to print it, and couldn't be filmed until 1970 because no country would permit a filmmaker the freedom to do so.

Grove Press won out in June of 1969 by offering Thorsen the biggest sum ever for a Danish film, and on the most advantageous terms.[38] Grove had been the first to publish Miller's books in the U.S., thus the film was a natural for them, and in September of the following year Rosset met with Anders Stefansen of SBA and Thorsen to iron out details as they prepared for the American release. Grove had thus far paid 100,000 dollars for the American rights and the Danes would get an additional 10 percent of ticket sales.

Expectations were sky-high. Back in December of 1969 SBA had placed a full page ad in *Variety*:

> *Quiet Days in Clichy* by Henry Miller
> Filmed on location in Paris
> the biggest potential money-maker of 1970
> Direct from Scandinavia.

I Am Curious (Yellow) was at that point at the top of the charts in America, and they reckoned that if they could get it into the country *Clichy* might do even better. As expected it was seized by customs and forced to defend itself in a court of law. To everyone's surprise it passed the test rather quickly, a federal judge ruling that it possessed artistic value.

The first omens were not good; *The New York Times* and *Time Magazine* slammed it. Sjöman had also gotten bad reviews, and Grove could have brushed the press aside if lines had started forming outside theaters ... but they never did.

By November Grove was reported to be on the verge of bankruptcy and in all likelihood Thorsen would never get a dime out of the company. Their attempts to release *I Am Curious (Yellow)* in the American heartland had resulted in endless lawsuits and the court expenses had cost them dearly, while at the same time the talk was that they had taken on more films (400 at one point) than they could handle. And while film distribution was not their only financial woe, they had clearly gambled too heavily on titles that didn't pay off. For example they sent *Danish Blue* back to Denmark after only grossing 25,000 dollars on it.[39]

Thorsen was also mad about the version Grove had released in America. "What irritates me personally is that they released a terrible version of the film into the market. They tinkered with the lighting/exposure and cut 16 minutes, not particularly from the naughty scenes but in such a way as to obliterate the atmosphere. They also tampered with the sound. I saw that version in New York and can easily understand why the reviewers suggested that Miller should sue us for damages."[40]

He eventually got *Clichy* back into eight cinemas, yet ticket sales never picked up and it went out not with a bang but with a whimper.

Its failure in the U.S. was a shock, but it owed to a number of factors including timing. Coming in the wake of *I Am Curious (Yellow)* was no advantage. Like Sjöman's movie it was also very much an underground film — the nexus between the underground short and the feature film, as Thorsen boasted — and eminently unsuited to a general American public lured in by promises of sex. Many still felt swindled by *I Am Curious (Yellow)* and were in no mood for another experimental non-narrative. *Quiet Days in Clichy* was long, it was very episodic and it was non-synch sound, resulting in an obviously (or "wretchedly" as the writer from *Time Magazine* put it) dubbed finished product of a type for which viewers had less and less patience. It might have been ahead of its time in its unconventional depiction of sex but it was behind its time in a purely technical sense. It was on all counts simply not palatable to mainstream American audiences.

In early 1971 *Variety* offered its own prognosis: Despite the publicity it attracted, it was simply not naughty enough to compete with the very latest adult films and not good enough to succeed in the bigger theaters. Finally and perhaps most importantly it was in black and white. Films not made in color were considered by that point almost impossible to sell.

Thorsen could still console himself with the success he was having elsewhere. In Montreal people waiting to see it had stood in a line that wrapped around the block three times. In Denmark, Sweden and Germany it had been a huge hit. Nobody in Spain or Italy dared to import it, but it finally opened in France, due to the active intervention of the newly appointed French cultural minister Jacques Duhamel in February of 1971. It drew big crowds, earned highly positive reviews and helped to shatter the French sex barrier in the process, albeit in a version cut by 20 minutes. (The original version screened in Cannes was very long and the film was tightened up although not necessarily cleaned up for exhibition almost everywhere, including Denmark.) *L'Expressen* called it the first Danish film worth seeing since Dreyer's *Gertrud* in 1964 and recommended that France follow Denmark's lead and completely abolish film censorship (for viewers 18 and older).

Along the Champs Elysées it was obvious which theaters were showing *Quiet Days in Clichy* by the mile-long lines, and midnight shows were quickly added to the bill at some venues.

"For Frenchmen the film is a shock," wrote Paris correspondent Gunnar Larsen. "Frenchmen have seen sex films before but they've mostly been Swedish films of such poor quality and so severely cut that they made little impression.... There is lots of talk that this is the first time that women's pubic hair has been permitted to be shown. Thus far that has not existed in the French film world."[41]

Censorship in Denmark — A New Approach

Perhaps *Quiet Days in Clichy* would have done better in America had it more shamelessly advertised its Danish origins. That would have sold tickets. For example, while it was struggling to draw a crowd in Manhattan, John Lamb's *Sexual Freedom in Denmark* had been playing for 32 weeks, making a mint at The Cameo over on 8th Avenue.

Lamb's good fortune was brought to a sudden halt when his picture was busted for obscenity, but prosecuting these films was getting more difficult by the minute. At the trial defense lawyers screened other contemporary erotic movies that had recently been found not obscene and the court dismissed the complaint against it, ruling that it was protected by the First and Fourteenth amendments. The decision had immense importance, establishing a workable precedent and clearing the way for the release of other pornographic films.

Producer Alex de Renzy brought out his own movie, *Censorship in Denmark — A New Approach*, at roughly the same time. A very different type of fellow than the old-school Lamb, he had worked a variety of jobs outside the film business, having been among other things an instructor at an Air Force survival school and a croupier in Reno and Vegas.

Moving to San Francisco in the '60s, he broke into movies after landing a job with Gordon News Films, and he used their camera to shoot short sex films after hours. When somebody stole the camera he used the insurance money to pay for his first feature film. He could see this was the coming thing and in 1968 leased a shabby 50-seat theater in San Francisco's Tenderloin district, renamed it The Screening Room and dumped in over a hundred grand to renovate and enlarge it and to fend off periodic busts by the city. Up on the screen were the movies he himself shot, a new production every month. At first he cast them with prostitutes and later hippies who responded to ads he placed in the *Berkeley Barb* underground paper and promises of 50 bucks a film. It was a mom and pop operation without the mom.

Desperately needing product, he joined a whole flock of other American skin flick producers and flew over to Copenhagen to attend SEX 69. While there he roamed the city with his camera and shot vast amounts of footage, anything that reflected light, and interviewed anybody who would talk to him.

He took it all back to the Bay Area and began shaping it into a film. He knew it would run into trouble with the authorities so he padded it out with scenes of tourist attractions and took pains to stress the documentary aspect, shooting much of the hard-core action directly off Danish movie screens instead of making duplicate negatives of the original material. This would allow him to claim it was a documentary *about* pornography — not a "porn film."

He opened *Censorship in Denmark* at The Screening Room and business boomed. (Since he had taken over the venue weekly grosses had jumped from an average of 100 bucks to 8,000.) He also got theaters in Los Angeles and New York to run it and eventually moved the San Francisco engagement to a bigger house in the upscale Marina district to pull in a more mainstream crowd. It was busted once in Los Angeles and twice in San Francisco but courts in these localities refused to close the show, and in six months a film that cost 15,000 dollars to produce grossed 800,000.

In the key New York market it was also a money spinner but ran into trouble when three theaters in suburban Essex County, New Jersey, put it on the bill. Local authorities took notice; the theater managers were arrested and the prints were seized. This led to a trial that also contributed to establishing a precedent, but the issues at play here hinged more on the technical question of how much latitude the authorities had to seize prints, and thereby automatically shut down a show, before any legal decision had been reached.

Consequently in a purely legal sense it was Lamb's film rather than de Renzy's that brought an effective end to censorship and paved the way in America for the screening of hard-core pornography, but according to Turan and Zito in *Sinema*, *Censorship in Denmark* had considerably greater impact. Lamb's film, they note, "was far less notorious and successful, probably because it confined itself to strictly educational material." The tone was deadly serious and the action was delivered "in an orderly and almost antiseptic manner." Simply put, it lacked "hard breathing prurient sex." Both productions featured similar Danish-originated material, but de Renzy's film had hard-breathing prurient sex in spades. Depicting intercourse on screen had been the Holy Grail of exploitation cinema, fuelling the dreams of hucksters and con-men for decades, but it was not just what was shown but how it was shown. There was a difference. Audiences knew the difference, and even *Time Magazine* knew the difference, criticizing educationally oriented porn for depicting sex in a way that was "crude, loveless and even passionless." As their scribe put it, "These films are really horror movies — repellent not so much for their immorality as for their inhumanity."

De Renzy treated the subject with raw honesty. Turan and Zito point to an interview he conducted for the film with Tony, a young woman who acted in sex films with her boyfriend. "Tony is nude during the interview with de Renzy but she is completely dignified and unselfconscious about her nudity and the nature of her employment. She talks about herself (she is 18, does not take drugs and likes sex and rock music) and admits that she really enjoys working in sex films, but only when she appears with her boyfriend. This highly personal and touching monologue is inter-cut with footage from a very hardcore film that Tony and her boyfriend had previously made ... and the impact of this words-and-action portrait is calculatedly powerful."

This type of hard-cut editing was de Renzy's trademark, resulting in a brashly unapologetic and in-your-face style of porn which he took to almost brutal extremes in a companion production of the following year. It seems he had also come back from Copenhagen lugging a 30 minute Danish production indelicately entitled *Animal Lover*. It offered unblinking depictions of Bodil Joensen engaged in explicit frolics with her barnyard companions. He couldn't do anything with a 30 minute film so he apparently shot, commissioned or simply hijacked another 30 minutes of domestically generated lecture footage to serve as a kind of framing device. Here a scurrilous professor-type lectures in singularly unconvincing fashion on the growing popularity of sex with animals, and in a harrowing turn interviews a young woman who confesses to having been kidnapped and forced into bestiality slavery in the Middle East. The authenticity of this lecture-interview is highly dubious to say the least and has clearly been fashioned to join up with a different film, but no matter; de Renzy patched it all together with some on-the-street interviews he'd shot in Copenhagen, kept the original title and unveiled the whole unsavory cocktail to the paying public on his home turf in San Francisco. Yet it proved too much even in America's most liberal city in this most permissive of eras, and the citizenry rose up in arms and forced it to close. What might pass in radically *laissez-aller* Denmark without raising an eyebrow was still too far beyond the pale for Americans.

But that fiasco was still a year away and for the time being it was a win-win situation for de Renzy. His refusal to talk down to audiences by loading his film with educational banalities caught the attention of the press on a national scale and his honest approach won him at least the grudging respect of writers.

"Highly interesting, well-paced and technically adept," reported *Variety*. *The New York Times* weighed in on June 17th with a review penned by esteemed critic Vincent Canby who called it "an impolite film that makes very little pretense of being anything else." Turan and Zito noted that this was "the first time a major critic from a major newspaper took notice, much less sympathetic notice, of a film that graphically showed intercourse, fellatio and cunnilingus."

Curiosity about Danish sexual morality was at a fever pitch and Canby followed up with a more in-depth exploration of the subject a few days later in the Sunday edition. Right next to a review of Rudolf Nureyev's latest ballet he now opined not only about *Censorship in Denmark* and *Sexual Freedom in Denmark* but also about *Wide-Open Copenhagen '70*. The latter was originally entitled *Pornography: Copenhagen '70*, but advertisers demanded the P-word be dropped, just as they had demanded de Renzy jettison his original title of *Pornography in Denmark*. Along with the usual interviews and obligatory behind-the-scenes peek at the making of a porn film, *Wide-Open* featured a visit to a porn convention of the type that was now taking place in almost all Danish cities. It also profiled an actress who participated in daily group sex performances, revealing her to be a married mom with two children who commuted everyday to her job. Just regular folks.

Censorship in Denmark was the most talked about of the three, gracing screens that had previously revealed nothing more risqué than the occasional flash of breast. Hardcore had been available in marginal "mini" and "shoebox" cinemas in San Francisco and New York since mid-1969, but not in mainstream theaters that served a vastly larger public, and it was in this context that these Danish-fixated movies pioneered new territory. Respectable venues were now willing to screen porn, the legitimate press was willing to review it and "decent" middle-class folks were willing to go see it. This was in fact the unheralded beginnings of "porn chic" which wouldn't be officially proclaimed for another couple of years. These pictures paved the way for the next generation of porn classics like *Deep Throat* and *Behind the Green Door* and opened up the mainstream theatrical market for ever more daring European co-productions like *The Last Tango in Paris*. Denmark was helping America get laid, and porn was no longer just for perverts.

It was the culmination of a particular evolution. From *A Stranger Knocks* to *I, a Woman* to *Without a Stitch*, Danish films had contributed to important advances in American screen freedom, and although these newer films weren't made by Danes this fascination with Danish sexual morality was ongoing.

This was nothing less than a revolution in American film and social culture and Alex de Renzy was leading the charge. He was the man of the moment, the personification of pornographer as equal parts hipster, freedom fighter and all-American self-made millionaire indulging every whim. It was an image enshrined in the July 1970 issue of *Time Magazine*. In an article headed "Sex Trip" the yacht-owning, Porsche-driving smut king was portrayed as a man who had taken the low road all the way up to a luxury hilltop estate in Marin County where he now lived with one of his former actresses and a private secretary — both pregnant by him. Add to that at least five earlier offspring he was supporting.

"I guess you could say I'm on a sex trip," he quipped to *Time*.

"So," concluded the magazine, "is a growing portion of the movie-going public."

Bedside Manner

Back in Denmark they were taking the high road and literary adaptations were now all the vogue. While Thorsen was doing Henry Miller, Annelise Meineche was doing Agnar Mykle, the controversial Norwegian writer who had published *The Song of the Red Ruby* back in 1956. The book had been seized by the authorities, put on trial and found obscene, and yet was "acquitted" upon appeal. With all that publicity its success was assured, but outside Norway it met further resistance; in Denmark a reading over the radio was halted, in Finland copies were burned.

The book was a sequel to Mykle's earlier work from 1954, *Lasso Round the Moon*, a coming-of-age story about a sexually precocious young man, Ask Burlefot. *The Song of the Red Ruby* picks up the action with Ask attending college in Oslo and openly describes his many sexual experiences.

Ole Søltoft gets bashful with Birte Tove in *Bedside Manner*.

In Meineche's screen version, Ask Burlefot was played by the omnipresent Ole Søltoft who would transform yet again from a shy young lad into a grown man knowledgeable in the mysteries of love and life. In the book Ask is an angry young man and an avowed socialist, but Meineche glossed over such unpleasantness in order to concentrate on the erotic dimension. Angry young man becomes sexy young man. Additionally the period and setting—Denmark or Norway?—were uncertain and it was all a bit of a muddle.

The erotic scenes were just as daring as those in *Without a Stitch*, establishing the unlikely Søltoft as a sex star, but they went no further despite porno having been "liberated" in 1969. It was, all considered, a rather lame film for Palladium to be releasing on the cusp of the sexual revolution. (Oddly, a re-edited version of the film that surfaced in the 80's did have a number of inserted scenes where an obviously older Søltoft was performing in explicit situations.) It failed to recapture any of the magic that Søltoft, Meineche and Palladium had generated five years before with *Soya's 17*, although the promise of racy scenes and the presence of a number of popular actors drew crowds. It was also a hit in Norway where the censors approved it for play in an uncut version.

Agnar Mykle was considerably less pleased, calling it an act of vandalism against his book and even going so far as to declare war on Denmark!

There were many trends at play in 1970, the year pornography was legalized in Sweden (though film censorship technically remained in place there — and as late as 1995 a scene of violence was censored out of Martin Scorsese's *Casino*). Filmmakers continued to grind out "White Coaters" and travelogue-style documentaries while adaptations of books were also in vogue. And there were films like *Quiet Days in Clichy* that were quite unto themselves.

And now Swedish producers were also trying their hand at comedies. In contrast to the Danish folk- and sex-comedies which often had a bit of dramatic range to them, these were slapstick, screwball affairs. *Do You Believe in Swedish Sin?* and *The Lustful Vicar* were two of the most notable examples.

Do you Believe in Swedish Sin? deals with a German sociologist who travels to Sweden to find out whether "Swedish sin" is a myth or a reality. He ends up doing much of his research in a women's dormitory with predictably randy results. This Swedish-German co-production was launched with a laugh-guarantee that promised the customer his money back if the film didn't make him split his sides. Germans were particularly fascinated by Sweden and this gave rise to the term "Schweden film" there, meaning simply of course porn film. (Moreover in Japan if one visited a so-called Swedish shop one was paying a visit to an adult bookstore.)

Another comedy, *The Lustful Vicar*, was directed by Torgny Wickman. This was the tale of a priest cursed by a witch that one of his forefathers had burned on a bonfire. The priest is fated to suffer an erection that never subsides, even after all the town's womenfolk have had their go at him. Among the actresses featured were Anne Grete Nissen, who played "Barbo, the evil witch," and Magali Noël, a Turkish-born vixen who acted in the films of Fellini (*Satyricon, Amarcord*) and many other famous directors. Dirch Passer also had a part.

Both of the above mentioned movies were produced by Inge Ivarson, a force to be reckoned with in the field of Swedish sexploitation. He also produced *The Language of Love* and its many spin-offs as well as *Swedish and Underage, I, the Body* and many others. It's hard to think of any foreign producers who dominated the field in their respective countries the way that Ivarson dominated in Sweden.

But the Swedish comedies lacked something that Danish comedies had, something fully evident in a key release of 1970, *Bedside Manner*.

In the years to come Danish porn comedies would prove they could be just as loony as the Swedish or British competition, but perhaps at least the *Bedside* series, of which this was the kick-off, benefited from the fact that it was still somewhat rooted in the folk-comedy tradition. Or perhaps the films just benefited from the fact that one slightly dumpy, boyish fellow by the name of Ole Søltoft was usually the male lead, and that he and co-star Birte Tove created a certain chemistry.

In *Bedside Manner* Søltoft again played a shy and sexually inexperienced character, the teacher Max Mikkelsen. He finds himself in line for a position as headmaster at an upper-class boarding school but must be married to get the job. The previous headmaster has a pair of fetching young daughters and they conspire to get the likable Max hitched, giving occasion for all sorts of suggestive soft-core foolery.

With *Soya's 17* and *The Song of the Red Ruby* and now this, Søltoft had become Denmark's favorite virgin. "He doesn't seem to be a particularly fast learner," noted a scribe.[42] "He was already taught about the mysteries of erotica by a host of pretty gals way back in *Soya's 17*. And yet now at about the age of 30 he appears in *Bedside Manner* as the same naive character and has to be taught the same lessons all over again by an even friskier group of women." Already critics were complaining that Søltoft was being unmercifully typecast, but it was with his full complicity.

The two lovely daughters were played by Nissen and Tove, the later as yet unknown to audiences. While she had been frequently naked in the thus far unreleased *Christa*, she was happy to remain more or less fully clothed here.

Too fully clothed, in the estimation of several reviewers who were hard-pressed to hide their disappointment when the film opened in Denmark at the end of August. "It's a big drawback that the naughty women aren't remotely naughty enough," sighed one writer. Others felt equally short-changed, asking whether this was all the much bally-hooed sex revolution could deliver.

A further evolution of the folk-sex-comedy, *Bedside Manner* owed its success to the fact that the sex didn't obliterate plot and characterization. Frivolous entertainment that it undeniably was, it confirmed theories that story and character development had a place even in porn and its mix of sincerity and light-heartedness struck a chord.

"People have become dead tired of hard-core erotica in cinema," opined the Swedish film distributor Conny Plånborg in an attempt to explain the film's phenomenal success in his country.[43] "Now there should be porno with humor, porno one can laugh at." That was the kind of porn that Swedes were apparently not particularly good at producing. "It is said," Plånborg noted, "that Danes are a cheerful people, although I think that's something of an exaggeration apart from when it comes to the making of light films. In that area they have something that we unfortunately lack here. For example look at all the success that *Soya's 17* and *Quiet Days in Clichy* achieved in Sweden."

Bedside Manner was a huge draw there and today stands at 19 on their all-time movie hit list, selling over 1.5 million tickets. It even earned footnote status in Swedish politics when it came to light that the Social Democrats in Märsta had screened it at a party meeting. The session opened with ten minutes of information about party policy, then the film was shown on a 16mm projector and after that coffee was served and the politicians took questions.[44]

The film also did massive box office in Denmark. In some places it became the stuff of legend — on Bornholm, for example, where half the population of the island ended up seeing it at the lone cinema in Rønne.

Bedside Manner even played well in England where they had their own similar softcore films such as those that comprised the *Carry On* series. The arts magazine *What's On* weighed in on the picture when it opened in London in February of 1971. "The whole thing is done with such outrageous honesty, with lots of smiles, with hardly a single noticeable leer, that one just accepts it for what it is: happy titillation embroidered with broad comedy."

Broad comedy it was, sans the usual low slapstick that had plagued Danish cinema over the last many years. It was unashamedly sex-obsessed and prurient to the core, but thanks to the Everyman quality of Ole Søltoft it was also disarming and somehow affecting. Plånborg was right, this was an unlikely cocktail that only the Danes seemed able to throw together, and it functioned as a kind of antidote to the hard-core films that now dominated screens and were becoming increasingly dirty. This was sex without dirt. No one had to shield their faces when they went into a theater to see it. This really was porn for the whole family. And with occasional, albeit superficial, references to things like sexual equality and flower power, it had trace elements of a contemporary consciousness.

A film that was really much more interesting if hardly as successful was Gabriel Axel's Danish-French co-production *Amour*, which opened just a week after *Bedside Manner*. Composed of three self-standing chapters, it was an attempt to explore different film styles, to elaborate on themes from his earlier movies and in part to recreate the charm and spice of the naughty French postcard.

The first act takes place in a Viking village, a setting borrowed from *Hagbard and Signe*. A young girl's marriage to an older man goes sour after she falls in love with a boy her own age. Her husband is enraged and vows to kill them both if they persist. One morning she escapes from their hut to meet up with her lover. They flee on horseback, only to be encircled by the husband and his two henchmen. Long sword fight sequences followed, undoubtedly disappointing viewers who had expected pornographic content, but then again that was not Axel's forte.

The second chapter, which critics liked best, was a mildly erotic bedroom farce filmed in the silent movie style, an elaboration of the movie-within-a-movie that had appeared in *Danish Blue*. It was not just another tepid stag-film parody but rather an ambitious piano-driven two-reeler, a rousing and risqué tale about a woman, her husband, her lover and various interested masculine parties. It was well made and very funny on its own terms, but again, for 1971 was scandalously chaste. It was an homage to the old timey comic cavortings of the Keystone Cops rather than the kind of taboo-shattering exploration of Danish open-mindedness that the times seemed to demand ... and again, porn aficionados must have been crestfallen.

Chapter three, shot in Paris with French actors speaking in their native tongue, was set in the 1840s and depicted lovers who dally to the Romantic period poetry of Alfred de Musset and Lamartine. This chapter is the most interesting from a purely erotic standpoint and for the first time moments of nudity are glimpsed. Here Axel conveys a romantic conception of sexuality which exalts in carnality but without explicit situations which would have pre-empted mood, atmosphere and fantasy. The timeless argument that it is sexier to allude to sex than to show it is often just cover for a puritanical point of view, but sometimes it rings true and this is one instance. And Axel does show: physicality is an important part of the set up. The characters become engaged in each other's bodies and auras in a gradual, sensual and relaxed manner.

In the context of the fast moving early '70s all this was hopelessly square and this chapter of *Amour* passed virtually unnoticed, but it was in its own way unique, if only because it eschewed the popular dogmas of the time and focused on defining sensuality, not sociology. It was no manifesto; there was nothing here for the anti-censorship crowd to champion.

Also of interest is the film's opening sequence where two couples prepare for a night on the town, with the younger pair splitting off to go dancing at a topless go-go club. This brief dance scene in the club visualizes to some degree the notion of what a Swinging Copenhagen would have looked like.

Meanwhile the older couple enjoy a formal dinner and converse about universal and timeless sexual dynamics, and this framing conversation provides the segue between time periods, underscoring the film's obvious message that nothing has changed.

A scene from the French segment of Gabriel Axel's *Amour*.

All told, a well made if exceedingly fractured film that remains very much its parts rather than the sum of. It premiered that spring in Cannes, outside competition, and opened domestically in time to draw on the summer tourist trade. It did well enough in Denmark thanks to the subject matter and a cast that included home-grown favorites such as Ghita Nørby, Dirch Passer and Ove Sprogøe.[45]

Part Three

1971 and Beyond: Total Freedom in Fact and Fiction

By 1971 evidence of the new freedom was everywhere on display in the Danish Capital. In advertising key attractions, even the most respectable tourist guides ran pictures of sex shops next to Tivoli and the Little Mermaid. The main walking street was becoming a kind of pink zone. Leo Madsen proudly opened the first "sex supermarket" there and soon he had lots of competition. There was even a vending machine at the airport to supply harried travelers on the run with porn magazines. Copenhagen had been transformed, but not exactly into paradise. More like a giant pornographic freak show.

"Within a few months," as Paul Hammerich wrote,

> the walking street, Istedgade and surrounding areas were transformed into a Gomorra of porno cafes with top-or-bottomless waitresses and phosphorous phallic window displays. The sounds of cracking whips and faked moans of pleasure could be heard coming from porn theaters offering 18 hours of non-stop lechery. There were windowless clubs with bad coffee, professional bouncers and dark colored mirrors on the ceilings. They featured half-dead live shows on boxing mattresses where doped students struggled to arouse their passions ... where black Vietnam War deserters could earn a living and where girls from the poor end of town performed with chained up dogs only a century after the death penalty for sexual activity with animals had been repealed. And there were the claustrophobic massage parlors heavy with the stultifying smell of aerosol deodorants.... The streets swarmed with under-aged prostitute-addicts, foreign pimps, boy hustlers, pushers, rental shark gorillas, customs tax cheats and pick-pockets. Young Christians brandishing Bibles and disturbance-squad officers with beeping walkie-talkies added to the mix along with camera-bedecked Japanese businessmen, UN observers and Swedish drunks."[1]

All this the sweet fruit of liberation.

Just how liberated Danes actually were was debatable. Some maintained that only a small segment of society was liberated, but there was no doubt that when it came to the viewing of pornography they were extremely liberated. In fact the whole country seemed to have gone porn-crazy. It wasn't just limited to tourists and it wasn't just limited to Copenhagen.

Hammerich went on:

> From Brønderslev down to the German border, Jutlanders could choose from around ten theaters that screened primitive 8mm porno films after the regular shows. Even Harry

Porno explosion: just one of many adult book shops that populated the Danish Capital at the dawn of the '70s.

Jepsen from Brørup, known for his quality programming, did it. Gunnar Skadelund from the Kinograpen near Aalborg showed porn at midnight to earn income for new initiatives. "Support culture — see a porn film" went the slogan, and the money rolled in. From all over the island of Funen people streamed into the theater in Otterup to see films like *Orgasm in the Bathroom*, *Sweat-dripping Love* and *The Pussy That Dreamed*.[2] Zealanders seemed to prefer experiencing advanced sex in special clubs where they had to pay high membership fees as well as a hefty charge at the door."[3]

Some theaters in Copenhagen exclusively showed explicit films, but there were only a few. Back in 1966 the Hawaii Bio had been doing live shows, probably something on the order of burlesque, and in '69 they started playing porn. Soon they split their auditorium up into two theaters and started showing films non-stop. (They eventually subdivided these spaces with individual cabins for private service, and that has enabled them to survive to this day.)

Most notable, however, was the Carlton, which flourished under the able guidance of Ove Brusendorff. They had long specialized in erotic fare and were well positioned to exploit the abolition of censorship in 1969. Sometime later the Nygade theater and Cinema 3 came on the scene. Then there was a venue called Studio 1-2. When commercials opened the show, with lights only dimmed, the place was empty, but the moment the lights went down and the feature started the place was suddenly full. The desire not to be recognized at such a low attraction soon went by the wayside, however, and things changed. Copenhagen was no place for false modesty.

"Porn has become an essential part of our repertoire," commented E. Larsen, boss of the mainstream Scala theater in 1971. "These films attract a broad public, not just special groups. All considered, people have a completely different and more relaxed attitude to sex films since the legislation that freed pornography. People no longer sneak into the cinema. It's become quite normal to see a porno film. It's just like going to see any other movie."[4]

With 8mm and 16mm film widely accepted as screening formats in cinemas the process of making movies was still in the hands of the common man. Almost anyone from anywhere who owned a Bolex camera or could borrow one could make a picture that had a faint hope of being theatrically exhibited. Any aspiring American documentarian or smut peddler, for example, who was able to cover the cost of plane fare could come back from Denmark lugging enough footage to fashion into a playable feature film, no matter what he shot. If it came in under an hour it could always be padded out with the obligatory shots of the Little Mermaid, Town Hall Square or the changing of the Royal Guard. Naughty images of adult bookshop window displays on gritty Istedgade street could also be thrown in for good measure. Still more padding could be obtained with shots of a narrator, microphone in hand, pontificating on the phenomenon of Danish open-mindedness, and he could interview passers-by and ask them what they thought about pornography. Everybody did it. If that was all a budding filmmaker came back with, the hard-core pornographic sequences could be shot in his back room and labs in liberal San Francisco would process the footage. And if he couldn't even afford to fly to Copenhagen he could just stick the city's name somewhere in the title.

There was certainly already a tradition for that. U.S. exploitation maven Herschell Gordon Lewis tagged his 1968 soft-core film *The Psychic* with the alternative title of *Copenhagen's Psychic Loves*. Another dubious item was *Ride Hard, Ride Wild* from 1970. *Easy Rider* was still raking in money and Denmark was at the moment a very sellable brand, so why not make a *Danish* biker movie? But that would be expensive, and also ridiculous if the bikers in *The Daughter* were any indication of what one could expect. So why not just splash "new from Denmark!" all over the advertising and stay home and churn out the usual pap? In this case producers chose that option. It could be hard to determine the actual point of origin of footage, and fraud was the order of the day.

Other examples include *Doctors from OH! Copenhagen*, titled to exploit the controversial nude play *Oh! Calcutta!* that opened off–Broadway in 1969 and attracted massive press, and *The Girl from Denmark* which involved an allegedly Danish lass—stress on "allegedly"—embarked on a quest for total sexual freedom. Here a nameless American porn actress pretends to be from Denmark even though from her accent and all other evidence she hails from the lower end of Sunset Boulevard. She has just arrived in Los Angeles to visit a film director who is an old friend of the family. Long ago he co-produced some sex films with her dad in Denmark. So much for the paper thin plot; before you know it she's showing the uptight Americans all about wife-swapping, lesbianism, tossing off your clothes to get a dull party in gear and taking baths together. Denmark and its vaunted open-mindedness remain vague concepts, with our starlet at one point seeming to forget what country she's supposed to be from, but there can be little doubt

Vox pop: armed with microphone, filmmaker grills pedestrians about porn.

that this tall leggy blonde was cast to embody what folks perceived to be Danish qualities, and her happy, upbeat and carefree attitude about all things sexual is similarly in character.

The film is as cheaply made as possible. It's glacially paced and studded with flubbed lines, ad-libbing, bad sound-sync, telephones that ring for no reason and a primitive home-made musical score that includes a couple of atrocious Beatles covers. It's a stellar example of disposable porn cinema at its most disposable and yet still manages a crude home-movie type of charm, saved to some degree by the fact that we are seeing "real people" and not actors.

Another porn film that played the Danish card was the Spence Crilly–directed *Danish and Blue* (not to be confused with Axel's *Danish Blue*), one of the first of the sex club travelogues. It opened in Dallas in 1970 and told the tale of the sexually troubled Johnny, an American who supposedly travels to Denmark to encounter a black female impersonator, lesbian group sex and the sight of a woman pleasured by two studs clad in Viking garb. He buys porn and returns to his hotel room where he meets Ketti, one of the sex performers, but fumbles his attempt to have intercourse with her. She turns him on to a lady sexologist. The two women cure him and he returns to America an experienced and virile lover.

Part of the same early wave of squalid Scandinavian-fixated frauds was *Sex Circus* from 1969. A hottie called Erika who was once employed as a lion tamer in a Swedish circus comes to New York to open a sex club based on her act. She staffs her show with prostitutes (whom she personally instructs in the erotic arts) and stages far-out orgies for her kinky customers. A girl whom she has beaten for being uncooperative grabs a whip at one point and gets her revenge, ripping off Erika's clothes and dragging her to the center of the party where she is violated by all present.

All of the above were rock-bottom productions made in America or made specifically for the American market. They were produced on the lowest of budgets and pumped out in days, the prints sometimes sold straight to theaters for cold cash. In most cases they disappeared quickly without leaving a trace, a kind of disposable cinema. So many films like this were churned out in 1970 alone that it's impossible to know if there aren't 100 more such titles lurking out there. They've fallen through the cracks of even the most definitive data bases, and even if credits can be obtained they're often fake.

Danish filmmakers, as we have seen, were also quick to exploit the possibilities and had long been doing so with short films aimed at the home use market. Now in the rush to get any kind of porn up on the screen filmmakers were cobbling together these shorts into feature packages. Ole Ege had his 54 minute *Pornography—A Musical,* a compilation of ten shorts which opened theatrically at the Carlton in 1971. The sound technician Ole Ørsted of Venus Films pitched a package of 25 shorts to audiences as a so-called cultural-historical document in 1972 under the title *That's How They Do It!* It included a *Snow White and the Seven Dwarves* porn cartoon and commentary by Søren Strømberg. Ørsted followed it up the next year with *That's How They Do It—Again!* In 1973 he released *Porn All Over the World,* a title inspired by the wave of mondo films coming out of Italy and one that this compilation of uninspired American porn shorts, again accompanied by commentary from Strømberg, hardly lived up to. "Imaginable and unimaginable things from all over the world take place," boasted the press release, "from a naughty Negro girl on a water-mattress to an Indian who lays a white girl."

Porn was the happening thing and everyone seemed to be shooting it, from amateurs armed with home movie cameras to hired hacks cranking out peep-show loops to old hands from the industry who dreamed of a last big score before retiring. Never before had filmmakers needed to invest so little in a film to potentially make so much back. Today it is almost inevitable that if a stash of old films is discovered in a musty trunk in an attic or basement in Denmark, it's porn — the dusty relics of those gold-rush days.

Graduates from the Danish film school also explored the phenomenon of pornography. One of them was Nils Vest who had previously worked as assistant director on *Christa* and would go on to make two of the more significant documentaries of 1971, *Sex Galore* and *Who's Doing What to Whom? Sex Galore* is a record of his investigations into the world of massage clinics, live shows and adult book shops over the course of the fall of 1970. "We only had one intention," he stated, "to take stock of the milieu and the people involved in this new industry in as honest and objective a fashion as possible at this point in time when the summer 'tourist trace' was over." He refused to editorialize on the phenomenon and managed to extract some candid observations from the parties involved, even giving space to the Association of Young Christians who spoke out against pornography.

Filmed in a single day in September of 1970, *Who's Doing What to Whom?* was a more complicated proposition: a documentary about the shooting of a porno film. We follow Bent Næsby as he shoots a film called *Do It Yourself,* and then we watch the finished production. Vest perceived his film as a study in the subjectivity of documentary filmmaking. "All films are lies," he would say, "and afterwards it is just a question of the degree of deception. Porno films are among the most deceptive."[5] He considered his film to be in the mold of Andy Warhol's *Flesh* and also claimed Jean-Luc Godard as an inspiration. According to Carl Nørrested, the film attempts to function as a political manifesto and figures as the only experimental pornographic film of the era. The notion that pornography somehow begets or equates freedom was contradicted by all on-screen evidence as Næsby desperately challenges his actors to "try to look like this makes you happy" and "act as if it's nice." Critic Ib Monty thought it was excellent as an industrial product-promotional of the type that advertised other Danish goods and services like bacon and handicrafts.

While the 28 feature films released in Denmark in 1971 seemed to be about the limit of what the domestic theatrical market could bear (its annual output usually hovering around 20), the export market appeared insatiable. And as we've seen, if the censors in the countries concerned allowed them to play the profits could be immense. It is no surprise, then, that a lot of films continued to be made specifically for the American market.

But even in America the streets were not always paved with gold. A good example was producer Bent Tømming's oddly titled *Vilde Porno Lyster* which literally translates into *Wild Porno Desires*. It was made for the American market and there it was entitled *The Blue Balloon*, perhaps in an effort to sucker in the art film crowd. Tømming shipped it over to the States, lost track of it and never saw a dime in profits. On a visit to the U.S. in 1974 he accidentally came across the print in a film lab and had to cough up 3000 bucks to get it back.

Back in Denmark, he managed to get it a theatrical opening that same year. Not long after, the field choked with better produced competition, it disappeared for good. Today it ranks as one of the more obscure Danish feature films ever made, a testament to how wide open the playing field was at that point.

Although its cartoonish cocktail-napkin style promo art led one to believe it was a hilarious sex comedy, the English language plot synopsis offered in the press packet paints a very different picture—one of unrelenting sordidness. Penned in a fractured and primitive prose style, it trades in all the luridness that epitomizes exploitation cinema and gives short shift to anything that resembles Danish open-mindedness. As the press synopsis reads:

> The girl in the title role, Lisbeth Olsen, has a marvelous wispy quality of beauty. As a young naive bride, she is perfect. The opening love scene on a secluded beach is beautifully photographed and very moving. Both she and her mate bring reality to this frank, sexually stimulating sequence. The sex scenes are real.
> After he leaves for the army, she is comforted at the bus station by an evil abductress who drugs her without her knowledge and takes her to a farmhouse where she performs lesbian acts upon the helplessly drugged youngster. The sordid surroundings of the farmhouse provide a neat counter-point to the pure, simple surroundings our heroine was accustomed to before.
> The lesbian, through narcotics, succeeds in destroying the girl's will to fight off her sexual advances. She sells the young girl's favors to one man after another, sometimes to two or more at once.

Each vivid detail is chronicled and faultlessly brought forth on the screen. New lows are reached through continued use of drugs. The lesbian continues her hold by threatening to expose her to her husband by sending him photos taken of her in some very compromising poses.

Reaching the lowest rung of the ladder, our little lady turns into an alley tramp, a common whore. The transformation from fresh, young innocent bride into a heavily painted whore is complete.

But there is a sudden tear-jerking end to this film. Her husband returns from the wars and in a drunken state commissions the painted whore to do him in the alley. This develops into a brutal and cruel encounter that makes the audience writhe in their seats, hoping to kill the pig. But as he turns to leave her, she tears off her wig and with tears streaming down her face she calls to him. The recognition slowly creeps into his glazed head and he sweeps her into his arms as the camera slowly fades back, leaving the lovers to recapture lost tenderness.

All in all, the Blue Balloon has everything you'd want in a movie, even a moral about the dangers of drugs.

Tømming's other film from 1971, *The Birthday Party*, was a shade more upbeat. Here a girl named Lisbeth has a boyfriend who seems more interested in his secretary. To get back in his good graces she arranges an orgy on his birthday and all ends well. Like *The Blue Balloon* this was a Danish-American co-production cast with uncredited Danish actors who spoke English and it was again aimed at the American market. It was not released in Denmark until 1977.

The aforementioned *Christa* was finally unveiled to the world in 1971 at Cannes. It wouldn't open in Denmark until 1972, by then almost past its sell-by date and looking hopelessly behind the times. Birte Tove, director Jack O'Connell's woman of tomorrow, was suddenly the woman of yesterday and left to fear that she would be made to look the fool in fashions from 1969.

Her male foils in the film were played by stars of some renown from various European countries, but the females had to be Danish. In their white vinyl miniskirted uniforms, complete with racing caps and sun visors, the stewardesses of Astron Airlines serve cocktails, spin records, and, since it is legal to light up in international airspace, provide hash pipes for their passengers. The rock band Manfred Mann contributed soundtrack music, and there is even a version of "Beautiful People" which fairly sums up O'Connell's take on the situation.

The popular myth that stewardesses are wild women was fuelled by films like *Christa*, but in spite of all the nudity the end result was pretty chaste. There is one brief scene in the more risqué Danish version that contains fleeting glimpses of hard-core imagery. This occurs when easy-going Christa and boyfriend pop into a porn shop to examine the goods, but it seems out of place in a movie that is for the most part actually quite wholesome. And, as Christa rationally explains to her male companion, porn doesn't turn her on anyway. She is at peace with her own sexuality.

"Tourists will pour into Denmark to meet Christa Petersen," predicted writer Henrik Iversen who saw the film at Cannes. He reckoned the rose-colored picture it painted of his homeland — a nudist paradise as well as a land of enlightenment where "freedom smiles like a toothpaste commercial"— could only have been conceived by an outsider. He found it to be so likeably naive that even "the ridiculous dialogue" somehow came off as charming and innocent. It was a movie without anything that resembled a good performance but one that "would have been spoiled by good performances."[6] True enough, the naiveté of Tove's acting does actually make the character work after a fashion.

Yet free love for Christa was but a means to a very conventional end, to find a rich husband. O'Connell was a good bit older and no doubt squarer than those of the love generation he was depicting, and this was really just an old-fashioned story of a sweet young gal on the winding road that finally led to true love and marriage—albeit one performed in the nude. On top of it he hadn't completely understood everything about sex and enlightenment in socialist Denmark, a reviewer would remark, since Christa only checks out the male passengers in the first-class section.

Although she lived in a hippie commune, maybe Christa Petersen wasn't so liberated after all. And maybe Birte Tove wasn't either. She didn't relate at all to the feminist dialogue her character spouted ("morality was created by men to control the sexuality of women"), and was shocked that O'Connell smoked hash. At one point he showed up at her house stone drunk and she threw him out.[7] Later, when the film opened in America, Hugh Hefner offered to run a photo-spread on her in *Playboy* to help promote it if she would agree to pose for additional pictures. She didn't agree. Back home in Denmark such modesty seemed in short supply as the porno wave gathered.

The film had been fashioned as a tribute to all things Danish, but could the country possibly be as idyllic or the women as endlessly sensual, gentle and wise as O'Connell portrayed it? As the reviewer from the American magazine *Applause* noted, "The ads imply that if everyone was as spaced out, sweet, sensuous, healthy, sane, happy and loving as Christa the world would be a wonderful place—and it can all come true in Denmark. What I want to know is, what happens to ugly Danish girls with illegitimate babies?"

AIP, the American distributor, was unhappy with the title which they felt was not evocative enough and considered switching it to *Danish Fly Girls*, but then someone in their office pointed out that the public might unduly connect Danish to pastry, and so they simply changed the title to *Swedish Fly Girls* instead. And that's how it became known. As studio boss Sam Arkoff recalled in his autobiography, "*Swedish Fly Girls* made a respectable showing in theaters, and with a mild 'R' rating it became a gigantic hit playing the hotel circuit. There was a little bit of nudity in it—enough to win over a lot of tired businessmen who would dial it up on their hotel TVs late at night. It played for years on closed-circuit TVs that way and became a big grosser in hotel chains. Maybe it was the title that attracted viewers."[8]

Christa did lead to something for Tove: an offer from ABC-TV to make a series. She went back over to the U.S., but the whole deal collapsed one day when she was invited out to go sailing with the program boss and his mother. She showed up in an old teeshirt and jeans to find the mother impeccably dressed, and the TV exec proceeded to lecture her that she must never again leave the house without make-up or she'd never get anywhere in *this* country! That same night she called up her boyfriend and told him she was catching the next plane and to pick her up at the airport.

However unrealistic the film was, today it functions as both a kind of Rosetta Stone of all the dated rationales and slogans used in service of the wider sexual revolution and a check list of the more specific stereotypes that were being applied to Denmark. At least one starry eyed middle-aged American guy believed it all. For Jack O'Connell, Denmark was the perfect place for this revolution to start.

The Swinging Stewardesses

An uncannily similar take on sex-obsessed Copenhagen can be seen in yet another stewardess film from 1971, *The Swinging Stewardesses*. Here an ensemble of lusty lasses gets laid in Zürich, Rome, Copenhagen and Munich, the locations forming separate chapters.

In the opening scene a randy stewardess goes into the cockpit to have sex with the pilot as he sits at his controls, and it becomes immediately clear that we have embarked upon a witless two-dimensional exploitation fantasy. (*Christa* at least attempted to portray the psychology of an individual and the society in which she lived.) Still, in glancing blows it does allude to the fact that there was some kind of revolution going on.

Just before departure the lucky stewardess who gets assigned the run to Copenhagen is tossed a set of keys to a mystery flat in said city by a co-worker. Upon landing she cabs there to find herself in the midst of some kind of hippie sex-commune, but unlike the similar setting in *Christa* this has nary a trace of bohemian squalor and her lover-to-be is a self-obsessed body builder.

The next morning the other resident stud takes her out on a tour of the town which leads to a flirtatious romp amongst all the familiar tourist sites: town hall square, the Little Mermaid and Nyhavn canal. Quickly enough they are passing sex clubs and porn book shops and we're given user-friendly facts and figures (there are exactly 24 sex clubs, etc.). They drop into a book shop to encounter a groovy topless sales chick who is full of level-headed advice about what kind of magazines the lady might like. Although her character is not Danish, she is, like Christa, sexually experienced and shrugs off the dirty books and magazines. Guys think it's adventurous to take a girl into a porn shop, but this type of girl is not impressed. Rather it appears to be the men, perhaps less experienced or less secure in this brave new world, who seem to have a need to demonstrate that they are "with it."

That evening back at the commune they are joined by another sexually liberated female, played by German starlet Ingrid Steeger, and the four of them watch a porn film on a 16mm projector. We experience the hypnotic atmosphere of such an event, but soon our lanky, libidinous stewardess is complaining about the staid nature of said slab of celluloid which contains only fleeting moments of explicit imagery. Still it is hot enough to eventually turn on both couples who repair to separate rooms to engage in (off-screen) sex play. Steeger exudes the most energy and vivaciousness and although she only has several brief scenes they are among the hottest. (After racking up credits in countless such sexploitation films, she broke through to a much wider public a few years later on television where she played a kind of nude German version of Goldie Hawn.)

As in *Christa*, Denmark is presented as a land of free sex and hippie tolerance, but Steeger doesn't waste her time mouthing philosophies and instead gives forth with a torrent of flippant over-sexed gibberish that is no doubt a treat for viewers who savor crudely dubbed dialogue.

It is not really until the last chapter that the filmmakers attempt political sermonizing, and that happens in Munich. Here a different stewardess has ended up exploring the club scene with a gay co-pilot who spouts anti-capitalist witticisms and takes her back to his pad which turns out to be a commune full of revolutionaries. The most bizarre scenes in the movie take place here as she (apparently) takes LSD and is treated to nude dance routines that depict sex from a radical socialist perspective. It's all rather jaw-dropping and incoherent, but obviously the filmmakers had something on their minds, and the movie is ultimately more than just the mindless soft-core travelogue it initially appears to be.

But it was Copenhagen, not Munich, that was attracting the sexual pilgrims of the new age.

Prominent among those who emigrated to Denmark in search of the elixir of open-mindedness was the American couple Phyllis and Eberhard Kronhausen, professional psychologists who specialized in human sexuality. Both were members of the Council of Psychoanalytic Psychotherapists and both were ardent apostles of this "religion of the flesh."

And they were nothing if not outspoken. At a professional convention in Zürich in 1957 their lecture on family therapy sparked controversy, and the next year Phyllis became the first psychologist to testify as an expert witness at a pornography trial in the U.S. Court of Appeals in California.

While they drew inevitable comparisons to the husband-and-wife team of Inge and Sten Hegeler, they had a somewhat more international profile and were more active in different fields: they had published books (*Pornography and the Law*, *The Sexually Responsive Woman*) and had assembled one of the most extensive collections of erotic art in the world. In 1968 that collection was exhibited to overflow crowds in museums in Hamburg, Lund, Stockholm and Århus, the latter exhibit featuring briefly in *Danish Blue*.

And they made movies. Their first, in 1962, was the ten minute *Psychomontage* which presented a series of deceptively simple scenarios that reveal how predisposed the human mind is to see erotic intent behind just about any action. A finger unexpectedly enters the frame ... a tongue licks an orange ... and so on, all of it appearing somehow sexual.

In 1969 they made their first feature.

Freedom to Love

"Can group sex save a marriage?"
— promotional blurb from *Freedom to Love*

After years of living the expatriate life in Paris, the Kronhausens moved to Germany at the end of the '60s and it was there they made their first commercial feature film, the semi-documentary *Freedom to Love*. It was, as the film's press material put it, "the logical next step in their inexhaustible battle against prejudice, hypocrisy and antiquated sexual attitudes."

The film consisted of an episodic array of dramatic re-enactments that dealt with topics like homosexuality, group sex, the sexual urges of children and so forth, and along with the more clinical *The Language of Love* helped to usher in the documentary approach to pornography. Interviews with the likes of Hugh Hefner, Kenneth Tynan, and Inga and Sten Hegeler were interspersed throughout.

In the surreal opening sequence a group of older, formally dressed people sit around tables eating while two young lovers have intercourse on a podium in the background. One of the oldsters pauses to complain that morality today is in decline, that the younger generation doesn't know what decency is and that they only think about sex.

In another scene two small girls search for a lost ball. They come upon a house and look through the window to observe a lesbian couple making love. Back home in the bedroom of one of the girls, surrounded by toy animals, rocking horses and dolls, they begin to re-enact what they've seen, kissing and cuddling. They are discovered and the two sets of parents respond very differently. One girl gets a slap and is sent to bed by her mom and dad who decide to call the police and report the lesbians. In the other girl's home a sober discussion takes place about women who make each other happy but cannot have babies together.

Freedom to Love contained some of the strongest scenes yet in a commercial feature film and censors almost everywhere demanded deletions. In Germany authorities would only approve it in a black and white version. Only in Denmark was it released uncut. "For the first time in the history of film," boasted a tagline in the Danish press kit, "151 meters of continuous group sex — authentic footage." "Make love — not babies" sounded another slogan from publicity materials, this a quote by the Kronhausens themselves that played on the popular saying, "Make love — not war."

The film was clearly fashioned as an attack on America and its hypocritical sexual morality, and it was clearly going to have trouble getting released there as well. That was a culture, noted Lizzie Bundgaard (writing for *E.B.* in July of 1970), where you had to be 18 to be considered an adult and in some states 21. The rather long interview sequences that broke up the action would probably irritate Danish viewers, she noted, but the Kronhausens wouldn't have a ghost of a chance getting the film exhibited in America if they didn't indulge in the same duplicity of which they accused their own culture. "Scenes of copulation must be disguised as 'art' in order to get through ... precisely the kind of hypocrisy the film claims to protest.... According to the law sexual scenes can have artistic merit, but, if they are too sexy and stimulating, people get offended and it is judged to be pornography. That is, in effect, saying that it is indecent to become sexually aroused, and that's nonsense!" Bundgaard could well scoff at the Americans since in Denmark this was no longer an issue. In many ways the sexual revolution in Denmark had complicated rather than simplified things, but at least this form of hypocrisy had been laid to rest.

Having moved to Europe to escape the repressiveness of America only to find France and Germany too uptight, it was natural that now the Kronhausens would consider moving to Denmark to continue their research. And so they did, in 1970. They were motivated by the same spirit of adventure and curiosity that had drawn western anthropologists into the African jungles decades earlier to study the strange love rituals of dark skinned natives. Now Denmark was the land of mystery, the place where strange and exotic things were happening, and pioneering sociologists needn't go so far afield. And while there was no racial component at play in the films they produced, they do display a kind of cultural prejudice and they are marked by the same kind of lurid voyeurism and stereotyping that had characterized earlier so-called shock travelogues such as *Naked Amazon* and *Malamu*.

While the pseudo-documentaries produced by the sociological safaris of the '30s and '40s exemplified the essence of exploitation cinema, these new films which sought to probe the mores behind Danish sexuality were of a much more clinical nature, though no less exploitive for it. Ironically the only place these increasingly explicit new films could be shown uncut was Denmark itself. The Kronhausen's next film, *Why?*, was a prime example. It was, as a Danish journalist wrote, "a film that could never have been made, let alone shown in a mainstream cinema, in any other country on earth."

Danes considered themselves enlightened, but were there no limits? How much more did they need to learn about themselves? And how much of all this did they believe?

Why?

Why Do They Do It? (Hvorfor Gør De Det?) was the film's Danish title, shortened to *Why?* for the export market. It was something of a follow-up to *Freedom to Love* but went much further, indicating just how far things had come in a couple of years. Focusing on the phenomenon of Copenhagen's live sex clubs, it purported to show how normal sex performers really were and that this was just honest work. *Why?* would stand as the most radical advancement of this philosophy and give form to the Liberated Individual. And by now things had progressed so far that they didn't need to justify their actions with any sort of politics. Censorship had been abolished, so what was there to fight? The most radical thing about these people was how *average* they were.

Why? was divided into three chapters. The first featured a lesbian couple, Effie and Marianne. The masculine Effie had been adopted as a child by a Danish couple and had never known her real parents, a black GI stationed in Germany and a Polish housekeeper working for a German family. Marianne, a petite blonde, was a bored housewife out with her husband for some drinks on the night they met Effie at a club. The two women danced a bit and unbeknownst to the husband the pretty mulatto seduced his wife in the ladies' room. Effie was in the picture after that. The husband didn't mind as he imagined it might lead to a threesome, but instead it led to Marianne's dumping him, taking the baby and moving in with Effie.

Now they needed money to survive. In another time and place they might have been compelled to take waitressing jobs, but this was Denmark in 1970, so instead they created a lesbian live show act. They performed it at the Movie Club, with "Bridge Over Troubled Waters" providing the background music, and made good money. It was there they came to the Kronhausens' attention.

The second chapter focuses on two heterosexual married couples, Alex and Lisa and Connie and Fleming. They live normal middle-class lives — aside from the fact that they perform at sex clubs.

All three of the above mentioned couples then demonstrated their specialties at a large live show arranged by the Kronhausens at the Copenhagen University student union hall. Approximately 400 students, many of them foreign, showed up to witness the proceedings with a mix of emotions (including boredom) as the couples performed on mats placed on a makeshift padded stage. The show was put together, staged and filmed by the Kronhausens as a centerpiece for their movie, and the resultant panel discussion and reactions from students provides much of the interview material that is sprinkled in. Ib Monty felt the spectators were the real story, and that the question was not "Why do they do it?" but "Why do they sit there and watch it?"

The third episode starred Bodil Joensen, outré porn celebrity of the moment whose activities with her animals on a run-down farm in West Zealand had been the source of many scandalous tabloid stories. She had already appeared in a number of films, including *Sex Galore* and Ole Ege's *Bodil, a Summer Day in 1970*, and now she was to figure in *Why?*— one more exhibit in the Kronhausen's treatise on sexual freedom. To some the fact

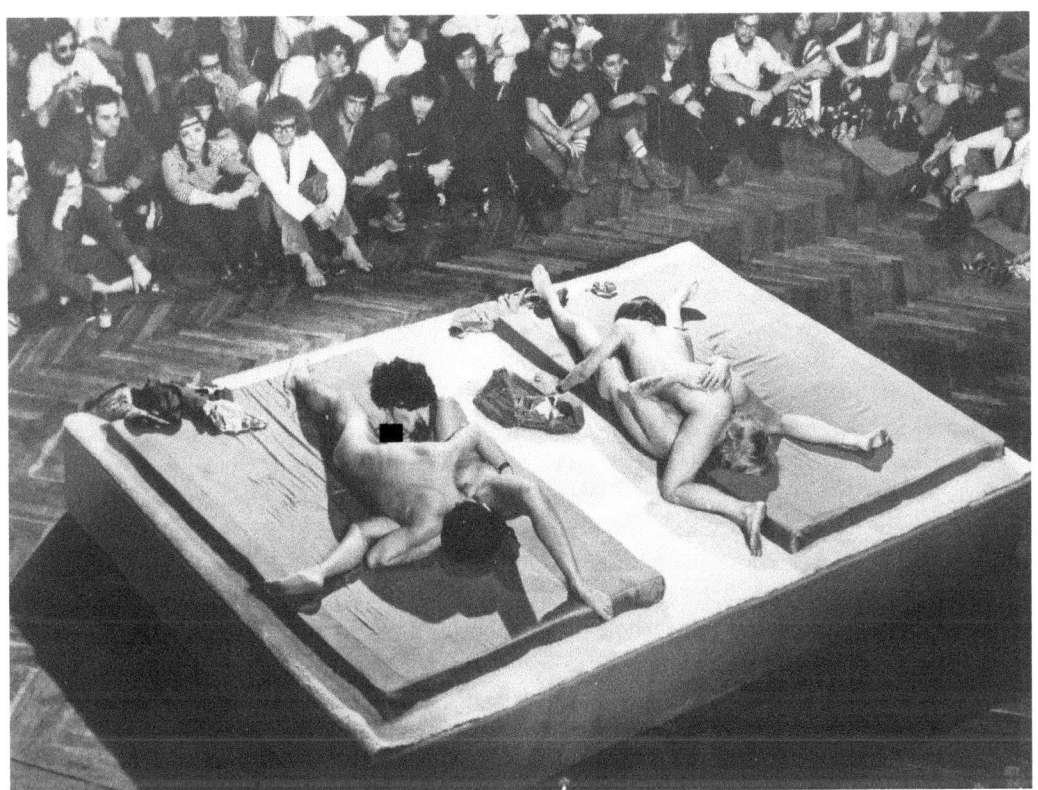

Students look on with a mix of emotions as couples perform public sex in *Why?*

that Bodil was allowed to do these things and to make a living at it was not a sign of freedom but a sign of a wider social collapse. This was obviously the most controversial part of the film. And not all Danes were as blasé about it as the Kronhausens supposed; on the first day of filming the restaurant across the road from her farm denied their crew permission even to park their vehicles in the lot.

Even members of their own shooting crew found the visit to her filthy farmhouse a distressing experience. They set up their equipment in her manure-laden barn and shot her grappling in a dirty stall with Sofus, her bull, and the next day she performed with her collie in the house. In their book *The Sex People: Erotic Performers and Their Bold New Worlds* (1975), the Kronhausens elaborate on the making of the film and reveal that their shooting assistant Karen was so traumatized that she threatened to quit the production and report Bodil to the social welfare authorities.

Perhaps not surprisingly some considered Bodil mentally ill, and rumors that she was feeble-minded or in prison or had committed suicide flourished. In earlier decades, she would have been a prime candidate for incarceration on Sprogø, a small island between Funen and Zealand that from 1923 to 1961 functioned as a kind of internment camp for "morally defective" women. How much had changed in ten years! Women who fit that description could now become media superstars. (The island is now a link in the two-bridge span that connects Zealand and Funen. Clustered on a wooded, windswept hill, the original buildings and lighthouse are easily visible to passing motorists.)

By now Danes were used to being attributed supernatural powers of open-mindedness by foreign advocates of sexual liberation, but the Kronhausens took this line of thought further than ever with *Why?*, and to some it was a dubious blessing indeed. No sexual act was unnatural if it was engaged in by two people — or one person and one animal — as long as they loved each other. Their preachy, almost born-again tone could be hard to stomach. "In long interviews," noted a writer, "the Kronhausens tell us that it is a state of happiness incarnate to be so liberated. They make the point again and again, wagging their fingers in our faces.... It all makes one yearn for the old repressive times when everything was forbidden...."[9]

And even in these most liberated of times among a populace more or less inured to pornography, the poster displays were too much for some people. Like Niels Nielsen from Heddinge, for example, a priest and head of the local school parent organization, who demanded that poster displays for the film, which incorporated the most brazenly explicit stills, be removed from the local theater display cases. And so they were.

The only participant in the film credited with a good performance or the ability to act was the lesbian Effie Schou. She'd broken up with Marianne on the last day of shooting. This owed partly to the fact that Marianne had been on the set and witnessed the (enacted) rape of Schou by several men, a scene that the Kronhausens wanted for the film. It had "upset Marianne's whole mental equilibrium," as they related in *The Sex People*.

Other re-enacted scenes also deeply affected the women, or had the potential to affect them. The re-enactment of their first meeting at the Golden Pheasant Club had to be shot with Ebe, a professional actor, standing in for Marianne's ex-husband, who perhaps understandably turned down the Kronhausens offer to play himself. That disappointed them. As they detailed in their book, "We were most unhappy about not having used it as an opportunity for real psychodrama, with perhaps Ebe taking the role of the husband and expressing 'his' feelings and thoughts during that night. It might have resulted in an even more dramatic sequence and possibly been highly therapeutic for the two girls. But pressure of time and certain technical considerations unfortunately didn't allow for it."

Schou had left Copenhagen by the time the film opened on January 29, 1971. She had moved to the small town of Herning, where she had enrolled in a boarding school for window-display designers. Now, however, as the star of a porn film she got an icy reception. It became clear she couldn't stay and so she returned to Copenhagen, hoping to find another film role, one in which a black Danish woman could be a natural part of the action.

Why? provoked dissent even among the liberated. "The porn industry has nothing directly to do with *frigjorthed*," protested one writer. As for the full title, "Why Do They Do It?," the Kronhausens purported to answer this question in the movie: "They do it because they love each other." Yet as many pointed out, they did it, from all evidence — usually flatly stated — for the money.

Those who had accused *Without a Stitch* of diagnosing everyone to be sick with an illness called modesty, and then prescribing one mass cure, could say the same about *Why?* If the Kronhausens' assistant Karen had been appalled by the activities of Bodil, it owed, as they implied in their book, to her Catholic upbringing and her being "uptight about sex."

The next film to explore Danish open-mindedness would be directed by a Danish woman, and one had to wonder if she would get any closer to the truth.

24 Hours with Ilse

"Watching porno makes people happy and free..."
— Ilse Damsgaard

As previously noted, the country's film industry was a small one and professionals had to go where the work was. This was one reason why so many "respectable" directors, actors and technicians participated in porn films. The 45-year-old Annelise Hovmand, who had been making films since 1948 and had even won a Bodil for *Be Dear to Me* in 1957, was one such decidedly respectable director. From 1964 to 1968 she had been a member of the film board, and by this point she also operated a cinema.

While scouting an actress for her next film, Hovmand happened to catch the performance of Miss Lutzi at Private Club, a live sex show venue, and she suddenly realized she'd found the perfect female lead—for a completely different movie. Having wanted to make a film on the subject of Danish sexual liberation for a couple of years now, she saw her opportunity and persuaded Miss Lutzi (real name: Ilse Damsgaard) to make a film about a day in the life of a sex show performer.

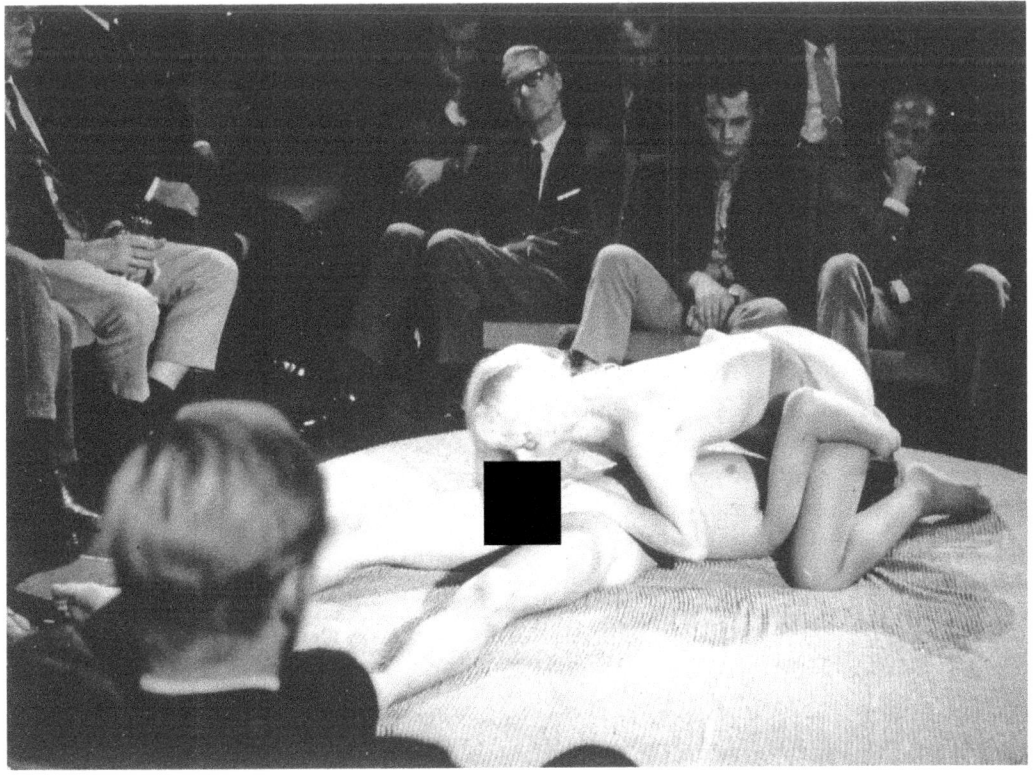

Well-dressed spectators look on grimly in a scene from *24 Hours with Ilse*.

It would be all about this so-called Danish open-mindedness, and it didn't really matter that the dark haired Austrian-born Damsgaard wasn't your stereotypical Danish blonde; she had a certain openness about her and with those expressive eyes had an ability to project that was perfect for film. And she was for all intents and purposes Danish, having moved to Denmark at age six.

She had always loved to dance, at 17 performing professionally, first as a go-go dancer then at private parties, then as a stripper. This was high art to her, not porn, although she was also no stranger to that, having appeared in explicit situations on film for Ole Ege. Up to this point she had performed in various clubs in Europe and had fans who claimed she was one of the best. Sometimes she modeled on the side. That spring (1970) she had married a German fellow and it seemed she had "found herself" and "had it together," in the parlance of the times.

Hovmand's film purported to be a day in the life of Ilse Damsgaard. She would play herself and be herself, and most of the other characters would be played by non-actors and people who looked like the right types. Two participants with acting experience were *Weekend*'s Birgit Brüel, who played her mother in a brief scene, and Lisbet Lundquist who played Hanne, a lesbian performer with a drinking and jealousy problem.

"Denmark's eternal schoolgirl"—that was the phrase one writer used to describe Lindquist. She was the quintessential Danish blonde and she would take her clothes off; in short she was exactly the kind of actress that directors were now looking to cast. She got to meet lots of them and it wasn't always a pleasant experience. She had previously acted in *Quiet Days in Clichy* and *The Song of the Red Ruby*, playing, respectively, the hysterical Jeanne who ends up running half naked down the street, and a nude dancer called Synnøve. Critics called the latter role a catastrophe while she herself termed it a "dark chapter."

Fairly thankless roles thus far, and now she was cast as a drunken lesbian sex performer. Yet pretty much everyone agreed that she submitted the best performance in *24 Hours with Ilse*, as the film was officially titled, for whatever that was worth.

Hovmand saw Damsgaard as a new social phenomenon, the epitome of the modern liberated woman who was taking charge of her own sexuality. Yet she also supposedly intended the film to be an unvarnished look at the milieu, a milieu not without its problematic aspects. That would be examined via the conflicts that arose between Ilse and her husband and between Ilse and Hanne. She wanted to pose questions. Are we as liberated as we think? Has pornography become a natural and integrated part of our lives in these liberated times or is our attitude to these things really unchanged? Are we liberated or just curious? And is it perhaps only a small group of people who are psychologically equipped to live a sexually-liberated lifestyle?

The film's supposedly critical approach to the subject was a clear departure from the unabashed advocacy that pervaded the documentaries of the Kronhausens, and many applauded that. Yet in Damsgaard's frequent appearances in the press she was every inch the Kronhausens' new liberated sexual being come to life, expressing herself with the same naive straightforwardness that would characterize her performance in the film. "I just want people to be happy, to do what they want, to enjoy each other and to be good to each other." And, "Watching porno makes people happy and free.... We are, as it turns out, all the same. Why must we always hide our feelings when we can be honest? People are so inhibited, they don't have the courage to say what they mean. I believe that when I strip the audience becomes less inhibited, I get closer to them. There is so much hatred and awfulness in the world, why must it be like that? It is nice when two people make love, whether they do it up on stage or out in a public park."

Shooting began in October of 1970, largely on the premises of Private Club, but it was not without problems. According to reports, none of the actors had seen a script or had been told what the film was about, and now some of them felt they had been lured into a "porn film" under false pretenses. It must have been particularly sobering for Lisbet Lundquist; only a few months before she had been pictured in the press with a huge grin as she inked a contract with producer Benny Korzen. Now on the set she was suddenly told to strip naked and perform a lesbian act with Helli Louise. Both she and Louise refused.[10] (In the same article it was reported that Laterna Film was on the brink of bankruptcy after losing money on an expensive production of *King Lear* and now hoped two porn films, *Christa* being the other, would put money in the coffers.)

The actors at that early stage weren't sure if the film was being made to show in theaters or private clubs, but from all indications it was theaters—*American* theaters. The dialogue was largely in English, Korzen was a producer brought over from America, and there was a kind of narrative framing device that involved an American journalist couple who had come to Denmark to write an article entitled "Sex in Scandinavia."

For all its claims to be a serious examination of the issues, its March 31 (1971) premiere was promoted with taglines that screamed pure exploitation: "Striptease, live show attractions and other daring scenes for the price of a movie ticket!"

Some deal, grumbled a sizable chunk of the audience who found it to be less than arousing. The actual sex scenes didn't total much more than ten minutes of screen time and it wasn't as daring as other films from that year, though ticket buyers got more than their money's worth of philosophy, particularly in the last scene in which Ilse is presented as a kind of porno prophet. "The film seems to say that in a few years when we are all making love in public we'll be able to look back and appreciate Ilse's avant-garde attitude to sex," noted Ib Monty. Perhaps rather than a prophet she was a kind of female Christ figure. She was selfless; she liked to perform more than she liked to have sex herself, or so she said. And she was convinced her porno performances could cure the sick and lonely—strength and healing through pornography. That she was attempting to perform these miracles in the temple of financial exploitation, the live sex club, perhaps only further attested to her naïveté. Monty went on to note that in spite of all of its liberal philosophizing, or perhaps because of it, the film was probably more reactionary and repressed than the audience it hoped to convert, the audience that came to see all this wild sex for the price of a mere movie ticket.

It was paradoxical that so many of the recent porn films tried so hard not to be porn films, and *as* porn films these documentaries and semi-documentaries were indeed rather tepid affairs. There was a very clear difference between films that advocated explicit sexual behavior and those that just showed it. Furthermore, all this preaching about a new liberal way could be construed as something of a dodge, and all this rationalization and justification was starting to resemble a kind of Puritanism. Pornography apparently could not exist for its own sake but had to refer to something more profound and universal. Where was the simple joy of hedonism?

Purely as a piece of narrative drama the film was uneven. Aside from Lundquist, the performers weren't particularly adept at acting while at the same time they lacked the ability to be natural in front of the cameras. Ilse, for her part, was unable to manage scripted dialogue with much finesse and her husband in the film, Cy Nicklin, a British folk-singer living in Denmark, contributed to the confusion by speaking a mix of broken Danish and English. Yet while the film fails as pure documentary, it seems, perhaps because of its faults, somehow inexplicably genuine. There is a kind of naturalness about Ilse as she goes through a typical day paying a visit to her agent, chatting with the American journalists over lunch and making arrangements with fellow performers to participate that night in a special private party which she is to host.

Damsgaard and the other actors were there at the premiere to sign autographs and hobnob. Ilse was everywhere in the press at that point, offering to strip for the King as well as Nixon ("He'd love it..."). She was the toast of Liberated Copenhagen, queen for a day or a month, meeting celebrities such as Ghita Nørby who was herself stripping at the Royal Theater in a production of *The Ruling Class*. And when the film played at Cannes that May it attracted huge interest and praise from perhaps the hippest filmmaker of the moment, Roman Polanski. And then it was over.

Lisbet Lundquist escaped the sex film ghetto the following year with a part in a children's picture. Annelise Hovmand didn't make another commercial film until 1991, and then only because the original director became ill. Unable to get another film role, Damsgaard disappeared from the Copenhagen scene, but not before threatening to sue the producers for the 50,000 crowns that her lawyer estimated she should have been paid for the three months of full time work she had put in. Instead she had only reportedly gotten 5,200 crowns, in contrast to the sum of 150,000 plus perks and expenses that Hovmand had received. So much for equality. And so much for the healing power of idealism. The final disposition of the suit is unknown, but in any case she left town, she and her husband moving to Berlin around the end of 1972. In 1974 reporter Ole Jacobsen went down to try and find out what had become of her.

He found her in a flat with a bruised arm, two dogs and Walter, her 70-year-old

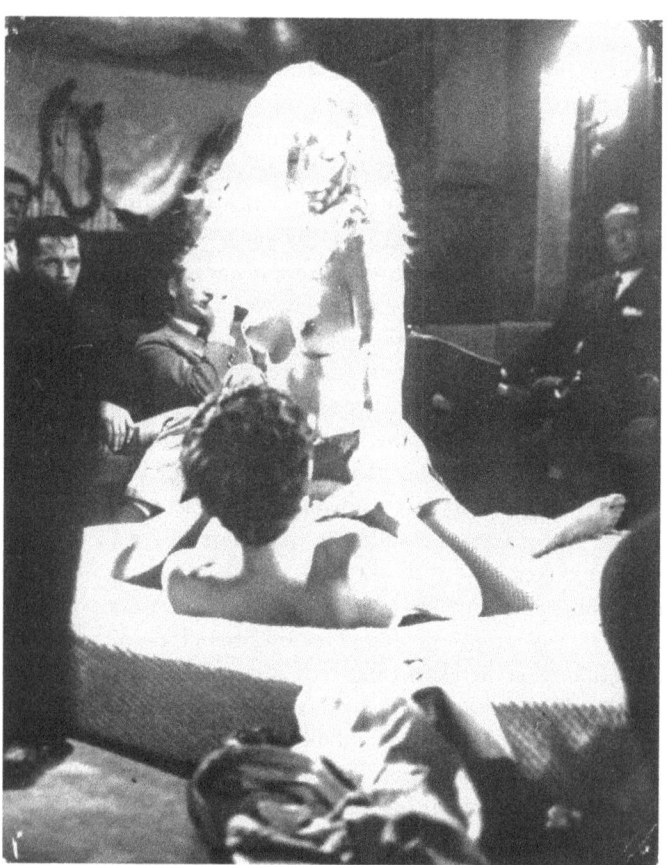

Wild sex at discount prices in *24 Hours with Ilse*.

"slave," whom she ordered about the house on trivial assignments as Jacobsen tried to get a bead on her state of mind, something made even more difficult by the fact that the phone kept ringing. It was her husband Mike, calling up to find out what she was doing and with whom.

"Twenty-four hours with Ilse in Berlin," Jacobsen would write, "is a nerve-wracking experience that takes place on the edge of reality," so changeable were her moods and so cryptic her answers.

The conversation wound on in fits and starts. She ordered Walter to get her a drink — and fast! She claimed (unconvincingly) she was happy, denied she was a prostitute ("I wouldn't sleep with these sick fucks") and instructed Jacobsen to write that she had three or four butlers waiting on her beck and call ... only to suddenly confess how lonely she was and how difficult it was to survive in the S&M underworld of Berlin. She'd had two or three friends but they had stolen shoes and clothing from her. And she complained about all the weight she'd gained ... but she was sure she could lose it again if she stopped drinking schnapps for a while. She couldn't go into detail about a lot of it and he really wouldn't understand anyway. And good thing they were speaking Danish as Walter wasn't to be party to all her doubts and worries. She had to remain "Domina" for his sake. And for her sake, too, since she was moving tomorrow and had to borrow the rent money from him.[11]

Even now at their peak there were signs that Copenhagen's live sex clubs, places like Club Venus, Club Green, Movie Club, Club Satisfaction and Private Club, were living on borrowed time, so heavily dependent had they grown on the tourist trade. And the police were starting to clamp down. Life was no bed of roses for the female performers either, compelled as they were to give hand-jobs, a.k.a. "Swedish massages," to any paying customer who desired it. They all despised this part of the job but in these competitive times the owners were keen to offer customers all possible extras.[12]

The grimmer realities of the clubs had been glossed over in *Why?* and *24 Hours with Ilse*, and another film from 1971, *Sex in Copenhagen*, likewise chose to depict the live sex scene in superficial and idealized terms.

Tailored for the U.S. market, *Sex in Copenhagen* opens with an American

A male sex performer in action at Copenhagen's Club Venus.

couple arriving in Copenhagen. They soon split up. He goes on to meet a live show girl who treats him to a night in a club, which results in a Swedish massage, while the wife goes shopping. She is pursued by a cut-rate Romeo who eventually beds her, out in the woods no less. These encounters having inflamed their passions, the Americans later meet up in their hotel room more than ready to make love. A happy ending in the never-never land of pornographic Copenhagen.

The film was shot mostly in Club Venus and doubles as a kind of user's guide to sex clubs, giving sober information on prices, conditions and the goods on offer. It includes, among other things, an interview with a female performer who relates how she came to be employed there. But there was really nothing exceptional about this picture, filmed in murky black and white and not even all that explicit. "The funniest thing about this film," opined a writer, "are the old geezers in the audience at the live shows. Strange they don't keel over from heart attacks or choke on their cigarettes during the exciting bits." Otherwise it was largely ignored by the press and none of the cast or crew were credited aside from one Erling Wolter who had produced, written and shot it.

Audiences at live shows were composed mainly of single older males who could afford the steep ticket prices. This sometimes made for a sea of elderly men in black suits sitting row upon row in straight-backed chairs and staring ahead with stony expressions. Wealthy, lonely, elderly businessmen watching stoned hippies have sex. But this was not always the case, and sometimes private shows were arranged for a hipper clientele. Such was the case in November of 1972 when rock star Alice Cooper visited such a club.

Photographer Jørgen Angel was on hand to shoot pics and recalls the evening.

> I arrived at the hotel where Alice Cooper was staying to take some photos. He invited me to join him and the band plus the support act, Flo & Eddie, on a night on the town. It turned out that they had booked a private show at one of the many live show clubs in the red light district of Copenhagen. It was a small, sleazy joint. Half the room was taken up by the stage — a king size mattress. The sound system was an old, red portable gramophone that you would have found in a teenager's room years earlier. At one point when the heat was on on the 'stage' the pickup got stuck in the groove. The rock artists very much enjoyed the performances by the mattress artists. The latter involved the former in the show from time to time. Alice was trying to hide from my camera. First by hiding his head behind a curtain. Realizing he would miss the work of art, he then tried to hide behind a beer bottle.

Facts: Copenhagen Sex-Report

"...makes me wanna puke."
— response from a part-time male porn actor when asked about his profession.

This peculiar brand of spectatorship can also be observed in *Facts: Copenhagen Sex-Report*. It was shot in 1971 by the German director Werner M. Lenz who had previously worked on sexploitation films such as *Your Husband, the Unknown Creature* (1970) and *Guess Who's Sleeping with Us Tonight?* (1969). Produced in a German and a "harder" Danish version, *Facts* was yet another exploration of the city's live sex show milieu.

The film is very similar to *Danish Blue* but with the extra ingredient of in-your-face explicitness. All the usual suspects, from Bent Næsby and Jens Theander to prominent religious and government figures, are interviewed and all the usual arguments are voiced.

Facts: Copenhagen Sex-Report

Rock star Alice Cooper (third from left) and entourage, including Mark Volman of Flo and Eddie (in white shirt), visit a live sex club in 1972 (photograph courtesy Jørgen Angel).

The "man in the street" is also queried *ad infinitum*. The most startling testimonials, however, are submitted by several pretty young girls who talk openly about acting in porn films while explicit close-ups of their deeds are superimposed over the conversation. It is a jolting technique that makes for a bizarre viewing experience.

Some of the girls are students; at least one is a single mother who brings her toddler along to the interview. He disrupts the session, playing with the microphone cord and happily jabbering away. He delivers the real message here, rebutting by his mere presence the myth that all porn actors are village idiots or addicts or hardened professionals. His mom is just a single mother trying to get by, and with all his mischief-making the kid seems normal enough. How could that be so bad? It's a radical proposition and one that we've heard before: that these folks aren't really any different than the rest of us. Any one of these girls could be the neighbor's daughter — or your own. But the spirit of tolerance also has limits; one girl whose face is blocked out to hide her identity draws a finger across her throat when asked what her father would do if he found out what she was up to.

Though it bogs down on occasion with too many talking-head interview sequences, *Facts* is otherwise well paced and exudes some amount of cinematic flair. As a documentation of the live sex show scene it is unflinching. Our first encounter is with a pretty black woman, largely nude, who teases and engages various men in the audience, unzipping flies to grope their privates one moment then thrusting a naked breast into a face

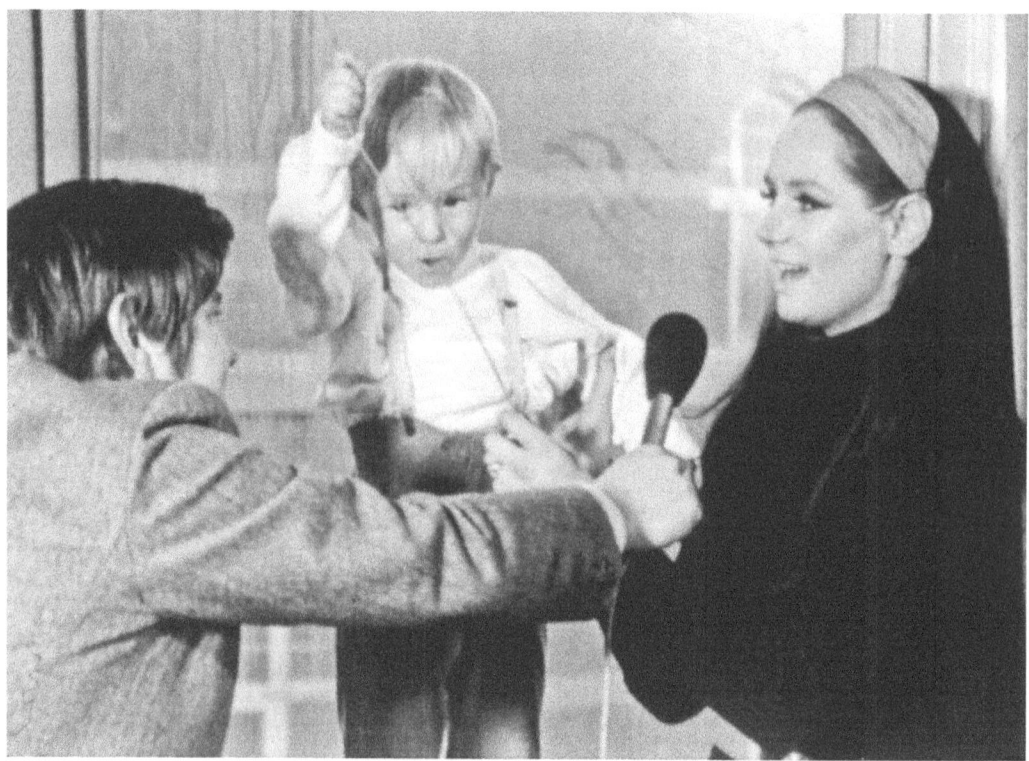

Porn actress brings her rambunctious young son along to an interview.

the next. She buries one patron's head in her crotch and later spreads her legs as another audience member helps her insert a vibrator. Then there is some lesbian action with two white girls. After that we are treated to a special show where a couple of men from the audience are invited up onto a bed. Friendly topless go-go dancing hostesses try their best to produce erections, but one volunteer flunks the test and is sent packing in shame.

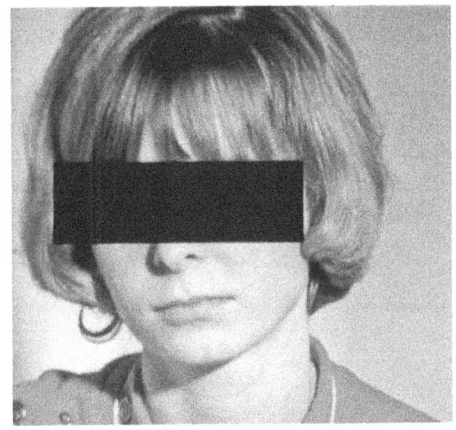

Erotic actress has identity shielded in *Facts: Copenhagen Sex Report*.

The audience, possibly arranged to some extent for the shoot, is more mixed than usual and includes two women, one a grandmotherly dame who appears by turns aghast and sweetly indulgent. In the back a man is either asleep or passed out. Another wears sunglasses, perhaps to shield his identity. And there are the stone-faced loners who appear to be businessmen. It's a small crowd, and the intimate atmosphere is spiced up with a steady stream of schmaltzy romantic instrumentals and French torch songs. At one point a sex act is serenaded by an instrumental version of "Greensleeves," heavy on horns and harpsichord. It's pure kitsch, hard-core style, all at once funny, tacky, grotesque, beyond vulgar and just plain bizarre ... voyeurism to the second power as we watch people watch the performers. Later we watch people watching a pornographic movie.

The film touches on most aspects of the Copenhagen porn scene as it then existed. The interviews with the erotic performers seem candid and genuine, names appearing along with faces, and the picture they paint is not always pretty. Most of them say flat out that they do it just for the money, and one male performer who also serves in the military says that the whole thing makes him want to vomit. The film does not sermonize for free love in the manner of *Why?* (to some degree because the interviewers are so artless and clumsy), nor does it shy away from negative aspects of the scene.

This contributes to a more objective if still formulaic presentation, but at the same time raises the question of whether a hard-core pornographic exploitation film (porn being exploitation by definition) can also be a valid and credible documentary with educational value. Can a film also be what it is attempting to investigate? It clearly wallows in what it claims to take a critical stance on, but at a time when so many similar films hid behind phony rationales and false modesty, maybe that was good, even if it also neatly coincided with its *raison d'être*, to make money. Did it have an agenda? Sure, to present its subject matter in an intriguing light. But then again most classic documentaries also do this.

How authentic the interviews and situations are is impossible to determine. Fraud was the order of the day in the sex documentary genre at this point, particularly with the American-produced films that were full of staged situations and phony medical experts reading from cue cards. Taking into account the difficulties inherent in making an objective documentary about sexuality—a subject about which no one on earth can be 100 percent objective—it deserves credit for whatever degree of honesty it manages, motivated by whatever factors. More important to porn connoisseurs of the period, it delivered what

Danish ad art for *Facts: Copenhagen Sex-Report*: Danish script reads "We go behind the curtains...."

it promised. And more. It did its best to be as extreme, explicit and freaky as possible and that, rather than dogmatic rationalizations (which it also contains), was what people wanted in 1971. It was no fraud. No one could complain that it didn't deliver the goods.

Reportedly there exists a 1973 film on the same subject called *Live Show in Kopenhagen*, but unfortunately this writer has not been able to view it. It was supposedly produced by Lasse Braun and is said to be a mix of interviews and performances. Also of note was a Swedish-made picture called *Report from Stockholm's Sex Swamp (Rapport Från Stockholms Sexträsk)* from 1973. It covered similar ground as *Facts* but was not nearly as explicit or kinky.

Finally there were at least a couple of 1973 films that were not attempting to enlighten anybody: *Danish Dentist on the Job* and *Love Me Darling*.

Danish Dentist on the Job figured as the second installment of Ole Søltoft's soft-core *Bedside* series and was very loosely based on another Erik Soya novel. Effie Schou finally found herself a part here, and much of the cast from *Bedside Manner* was back for more: Tove, Strømberg, Jung, Puggaard-Müller and perhaps the most unlikely actor ever to appear in a porn film, Gotha Andersen, about whom more will shortly be said. Called by one critic the weakest installment of the series, it broke no new ground. Then again this type of film wasn't about breaking ground but about delivering on a formula, and it accomplished that with a flair and workmanship for which the Danes were becoming renowned.

Love Me Darling was yet another erotic anthology filmed by Gabriel Axel, another episodic ode to sexual dalliance through the ages. An amorous couple called Adam and Eva engage in various erotic adventures in a castle in 1740, in a public bath in 1900, in a pub in 1932, etc., these historical vignettes again rendered in Axel's customary retro style.

Critics didn't swoon over it; he had worn out his welcome with this type of film and his quaint and humorous take on sex was quickly becoming passé. But it did okay with the paying public, no doubt because of the presence of the popular Birte Tove as Eva.

Axel himself would go on to make one more porn film the following year, a comedy called *Soft Shoulders, Sharp Curves* that he shot in Germany. After that he left the genre for good.

As for Germany, things were loosening up by degrees and some adventurous cinemas were screening discreet late-night bills of Danish porn and making a mint. Smut from Denmark kept a whole circuit of struggling kinos in business, just as it had in the home country. One of the most noted figures of '60s and '70s German avant-garde cinema, Wilhelm Hein, was running a theater in Cologne at the time and fondly recalls that the sizable profits he made showing Danish sex films gave him the financial freedom to show more risky experimental and underground fare.

The allure of Danish sexual freedom continued to have staying power on the American market as well.

Porno—Made in Denmark, from 1972, was the next movie to take viewers down the pornographic rabbit hole. It was a typically low-budget production, a variation on the by now all too familiar scenario of an American couple visiting Copenhagen to sample the city's erotic attractions. There was virtually no press on the film, but it wasn't really necessary since the title, which was only in English, said it all. Furthermore, tourists and home-grown porn aficionados who would go to such a movie were oblivious to critical appraisals. And there was little left to say about such films; they were utterly predictable. It would have been hard to praise the actors, had there been any good performances, since their names were never divulged; they were referred to only as "nice gals, naughty gals, nice men and not so nice men." Nor was the writer, director or cinematographer credited. Reviewers had been showing impatience with the porno wave for three or four years now and predicting its demise, and they could manage little more than blanket dismissals for this kind of picture. It's a surprise that it even opened in Denmark, but it was in any case probably targeted exclusively at the tourist trade.

Yet hard-core pornography didn't have to be an anonymous and shadowy affair. After all, this was Denmark; what was there to hide? Absolutely nothing, in the case of the year's most celebrated release, *Bordello*, a film helmed by ex-cheesecake photographer Ole Ege who was now offering viewers the real thing minus all the sanctimony and pedagogy. *Here* was the joy of hedonism.

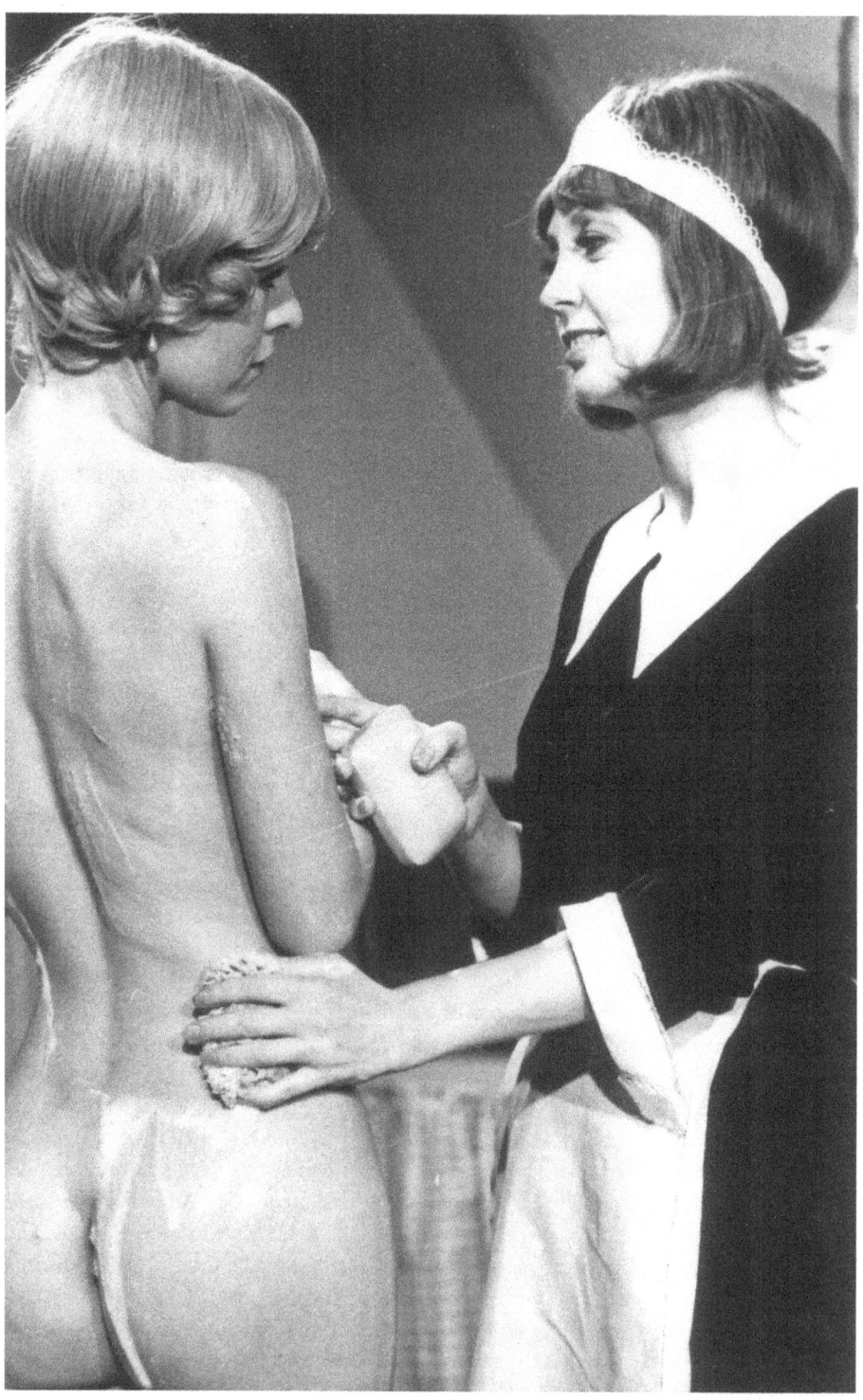

A tender moment shared between Birte Tove (left) and Annie Birgit Garde in Gabriel Axel's *Love Me Darling*.

Bordello

*"I can't allow myself to perform in the actual sex scenes.
I don't think the parents would be too thrilled about that."*
—School teacher and actor Gotha Andersen
commenting on his participation in *Bordello*.

Written and directed by Ege, who also photographed it with the assistance of an able young film school grad named Morten Arnfred, *Bordello* was a disconcerting mixture of old-fashioned slapstick, the hardest of hard-core porn and the artiest of arty pretensions.

Set at the turn of the century, the film opens when a young girl from the provinces ventures into Copenhagen and ends up in a high-class bordello. This is told mostly with the aid of old still photos and narration and gives the viewer the impression that the film has a story. The bordello's owner has just died and the house is to be inherited by his son, a young priest living in Wyoming. Ignorant of its present function, he now returns to claim his inheritance.

Very soon all traces of a plot vanish, save for the screwball antics of two Keystone-style cops who appear sporadically to search the house and indulge in slapstick foolery of the most idiotic sort. There is much goofing and mugging, particularly by the head copper who is played by one Gotha Andersen. A grade school teacher by day, Andersen — with his rubbery face, bushy eyebrows and port-wine nose — was already familiar to Danes via the numerous bit parts he'd played in film, TV and live theater. Nor was he any stranger to porn, having already appeared in *Love Me Darling* and *Danish Dentist on the Job* the year prior (1971). This was his first plunge into hard-core, and, although he didn't have a "performing" part, his appearances were sandwiched in between all manner of explicit sex scenes. At one point in particular an extremely rude XXX close-up suddenly cuts to a shot of his dopey grinning face as he mugs on cue. This whole sub-plot with the police is beyond irritating, distracts from the sex and manages to give all comedy a bad name.

When asked by a writer what the film was about, Andersen had to confess he had no idea, and no wonder. The promising opening quickly gives way to an endless series of random scenes in a big old house (Ege's own villa) where groups of high-born gentlemen and ladies of pleasure garbed in historic finery lounge about. They dally with antique erotic props and indulge in oblique rituals before shedding clothes to engage in the obligatory variety of sexual acts, all scored to the music of Johann Strauss. At times Ege manages to create intriguing atmosphere and now and then the women, who are for the most part attractive, generate some erotic energy, but this grab-bag of a film is wildly uneven and in spots the photography is so bad that the bodies resemble corpses more than anything else.

While dispensing with the plot could have been a good move had it been intentional, *Bordello* is ultimately doomed by the lack of continuity, the inconsistent photography and the insufferable low comedy of Andersen. While the incorporation of humor in pornographic films has always been problematic, here it just didn't come together at all.

Ege himself stressed in interviews that he was attempting to convey screen sex with humor and high-spiritedness rather than through the prism of violence and sadism. He wanted to make it human and to make it fun, but many found his film to be artificial, dishonest and vulgar. "In advance comments," noted one reviewer, "Ege himself has said that 'pornography has unfortunately acquired an odious reputation because its visual component is removed from reality'—[with this film] that statement has come back to haunt him. It is people like Ege who are about to ruin the true and therefore healthy pornography."[13]

If these were the kinds of movies that the repeal of censorship had given birth to, went the thinking in some quarters, then there was good reason to be disappointed. Filmmakers now had total freedom to depict sexuality in positive and realistic ways and yet it seemed that nobody had managed to get it quite right. Sex was a good and positive thing ... why was that so hard to capture on film?

Lots of people were wondering about that, including Germaine Greer, who the following year penned an editorial on the subject for an underground paper called *Suck*. She gave Danish porn a mixed report card while taking a slam at what she perceived to be the dishonesty of underground films that others were so eagerly hailing as revolutionary achievements:

> Removal of restraints in Denmark produced glossier porn, better lit, better shot, but the flesh was still meaty, lit up all pink like a butcher's shop, and the plots were vestigial, the characters depersonalized. But at least the commercial porno films were aimed at a sexual response, however desolate and specific. The underground films were not even genital: either they celebrated sex in narcissistic and "artistic" ways or they offered a sort of commentary on decadent social mores. The hypocrisy of getting kicks out of the depiction of depraved sex while retaining the right to disapprove of it or satirize it was the worst turn-off of all.

When *Bordello* opened in Copenhagen on October 7 it did so in a theater on the walking street, the Metropol, a venue that up to that point was best known for its annual screening of the Walt Disney Christmas special. It earned good notices in *Politiken* and several other dailies (as well as, later on, in *Variety*) even though some papers were now refusing to review hard-core films. But this movie was impossible to ignore, thanks not least to one Simon Spies. Multi-millionaire founder of cut-rate package vacations in Denmark and celebrity-at-large, his beyond caddish behavior at the launch party created a huge scandal and reaped the film tons of free publicity.

As it happened, press photographers at the opening were baiting the actresses on hand to shed some clothes, and Spies, a squat caveman-like figure with an unruly mass of hair and a bushy beard, thought it was such a good idea that he also started to undress. Soon he was rolling naked on the floor with two nude actresses as well-dressed attendees looked on in disbelief, some trying to break it up. Ege himself tossed Dixie cups of water and ice cubes on him but to no avail. As flashbulbs popped, Spies actually managed to perform intercourse, the graphic proof paraded the next day on the front page of the never shy tabloid *E.B.* He was already known as an inveterate playboy but this was simply too far beyond the pale and would go down as one of *the* scandals of the decade.

For any other type of product this kind of publicity might have been something to avoid, but for *Bordello* it was a huge boost and shows were packed, also at the Mercur cinema, owned by none other than ... Simon Spies. (He was no typical corporate mogul in any sense; back in 1963 he had donated a considerable sum of money to a group of experimental filmmakers. To his compatriots in the business world this was perhaps an even more unfathomable act.)

The film ran for six months at the Metropol, breaking box office records and establishing the hard-core-meets-hilarity formula that producer Anders Sandberg would appropriate the following year when he made the first of his "Astrological" films.

It played at Cannes in May where it attracted more attention than many of the official entries, and two extra shows had to be added. It ended up being sold to lots of foreign territories, but everywhere except Denmark it was screened in a censored version.

Bordello was many things but "porn for the whole family" it was not and sensitive souls were forced to seek refuge in theaters playing lighter fare, stuff like the erotic comedy *How to Behave in a Fourposter Bed*. Here a countess seeks to introduce her shy nephew to the mysteries of the opposite sex by entrusting him to a relative who runs a girl's finishing school. This figured as Merry Studio's somewhat more elegantly directed if really quite modest answer to Palladium's *Bedside* series and starred Dirch Passer, hamming it up as usual, and a number of known fashion models. They kept their clothes on for the most part and it was primarily in the dialog that things got randy.

Two more installments of the *Bedside* series were released in 1972: *Bedside Head* and *Bedside Highway*. The formula was now firmly established and would result in a total of eight films. All were produced by Palladium and directed by John Hilbard, and they all starred Ole Søltoft, except for *Bedside Highway* where Søren Strømberg filled in after

Historic theme on display in Ole Ege's *Bordello*.

Søltoft collapsed from exhaustion brought on by an excessive workload. Another plus were the many well known and popular folk-comedy actors cast in secondary roles.

As the advertising never failed to stress, these were *lystspils*—high-spirited, light-hearted dramas that were "festive," "funny" and most of all "naughty." They appealed to viewers tired of being lectured about how liberated they were and who were not into hard-core porn. While the previous documentaries in large part had focused on sexual deviations, the sex here was of the standard heterosexual variety, and what lesbian action invariably occurred was fashioned for the benefit of the men folk.

In these *Bedside* films the tables were turned and the women were the sexual aggressors, using their wiles on men who were either impotent or unwilling for some reason or other but who eventually came around. Sex-obsessed women were hardly new to erotic cinema but these *Bedside* gals differed dramatically from the standard exploitation archetypes. They were not prostitutes or defiled women but just healthy lasses who naturally loved sex, and unlike the sexually ravenous women of a Russ Meyer film, for example, they would never humiliate let alone karate-chop, beat up or kill men. It was pure male fantasy: men never had to feel inadequate even if they were. The gals understood and would do all they could to be helpful and didn't demand anything beyond a good romp in the hay. Sex rarely had negative consequences and entailed no deeper emotional complications. It was just a sign of a healthy passion for life.

The plots of the first films were loosely based on the writings of Carl Erik Soya but they were never much more than excuses for some soft-core blarney.

In *Bedside Head* (1972) Søltoft reprised his role as the headmaster of a boy's boarding school. Seeking funds to make the school co-educational, he and the lads temporarily turn it into a hotel where guests can imbibe of an aphrodisiac they've invented.

Bedside Highway, also from 1972, pitted highway department bureaucrat Søren Strømberg against a small-town community through whose land the government intended to build a road. But things get tricky for Søren when some attractive local ladies use their charms to lure him into a series of compromising situations. In this episode the accent was more on light comedy than sex play.

In *Between the Sheets* from 1973 a woman inherits a company that is worth a fortune but inheritance taxes threaten to bankrupt her unless she and her lawyer can concoct some kind of devious plan. And of course they can, conniving to marry her off to a fellow whose dad runs a competing firm. Actor Karl Stegger was cast as a loose-living playboy business mogul clearly inspired by Simon Spies whom Stegger physically resembled.

Thus far all the Bedside films had depicted men and women nude. Women were glimpsed in full frontal nudity and in all kinds of positions, while the men were mostly viewed from behind, and intercourse was only alluded to. But the next installment, *Come to My Bedside* from 1975, departed from the formula by including hard-core sex scenes, and now there suddenly appeared unobscured close-ups of sexual activity as well as the variety of sexual situations that characterized hard-core pornography. Yet its story, about a newly wed couple who can only satisfy each other after experimentation with other partners, was more coherent than what was passed off as plot in most hard-core porn films and the acting and production values were better.

Introducing hard-core to the *Bedside* series seemed sacrilegious to some while others thought it merely redundant since there already was a hard-core glad porn series up and running in which all the films were named after an astrological constellation, a connecting thread that was lost in the foreign language titling of export versions. For the most part, though, *Come to My Bedside* earned good notices. Reviewers generally thought the naughty story was realized with some degree of elegance, that it was fun and that it was not hypocritical like the soft-core films were. A film that delivered what it promised deserved credit.

Birte Tove, who played the female lead in the first five *Bedside* films, was here replaced by Vivi Rau who had already appeared in explicit situations in other movies and was willing to go further. She would go on to star in the rest of the series. At 31 Tove claimed it was time to give younger actresses a chance and was happy enough to step aside.

Sexy Girls of Denmark

In any case Birte Tove had other irons in the fire.

She had appeared in *Zero Population Growth* with Oliver Reed in 1972, and in 1973 made *Sexy Girls of Denmark* with the Shaw Brothers of Hong Kong. It was by no means one of their best, but from a sociological standpoint this tale of a young Chinese man (Li Ching) sent to Liberated Denmark to conduct business on his father's behalf is fascinating.

Upon his arrival he is almost raped by a secretary from one of the firms competing for his business. The shameless Caucasian hussy, played by Ulla Jessen of *Bedside* fame, corners him in his hotel room and disrobes. This shocks him and he passes out on the floor. Awakening to find her on top of him, he manages to flee to the bathroom. "Jeez," he exclaims in a sweat, "the girls here are so hot ... she's a lot too hot for me!" When Jessen inexplicably decides to take a bath, occasioning more nudity, he escapes into the hall and makes his way down to the lobby where he falls into the somewhat gentler clutches of Birte Tove. She invites him to a party and soon he is dancing with various women. That leads to an embarrassing erection. Eventually he and Tove end up back in his hotel room for a night of erotic bliss.

However extreme it was in other areas, Hong Kong cinema tended to be morally very conservative and depicted sexual situations with infantile innuendo and slapstick goofiness. Like seemingly everyone else, the Shaw Brothers were fascinated by the phenomenon of Liberated Denmark, yet they were perhaps the least equipped to understand it or explore the subject with any nuance or insight. Tove is by word and deed the embodiment of the liberated Danish woman, at first a seductive and sympathetic figure but ultimately every bit as alien as any of the space creatures that populated so many of their other films.

Li Ching is sure they will now marry since they've slept together, and writes home with the news, enclosing a picture of his "movie star" girlfriend. His father is shocked when he opens the letter, recognizing her as the star of one of his treasured porno films. The powerful mother figure now dispatches one of her daughters to straighten the boy out.

Upon her arrival, Li Ching takes his sister over to Tove's studio only to walk in on a rape scene. At first he attempts to beat up the male actor, played with sinister menace by Poul Glargaard, and then he tries to persuade Tove to walk away with him from this terrible job. She refuses, declaring that she loves her work. The director has had enough and sends Li Ching and his sister packing.

Later he goes to Tove's house to apologize. After all, this is a bad way to start a relationship. She tells him flat out that there is no relationship, let alone a marriage, and she insists on the freedom to go to bed with whomever, whenever. Glargaard now appears with just a towel wrapped around his waist; apparently they'd been having sex when Li Ching came in.

He's crestfallen, but soon finds solace and true love in the arms of a Chinese businesswoman who is employed by one of the firms hoping to sign a contract with him. She's not just another piece of bait but rather a nice proper Chinese gal who plays all the endless stupid little teasing games and doesn't sleep with him until they are both drunk out of their minds. On evidence of this film a woman in Hong Kong could only honorably go to bed with a man if she was rip-roaring drunk. This was apparently somehow more moral than just taking your clothes off.

With the other Caucasian women in the film appearing as little more than anatomically-correct window dressing it was left to Tove to play the typical liberated Danish blonde and to articulate the simple free-living philosophies that one expected. She had a lot of practice and spouts all the predictable rationales and slogans in her typical peace-love-everything's-beautiful fashion, turning the character into something of a parody, at least when seen from a contemporary perspective.

Directors of all different persuasions had fantasized on film about Liberated Denmark but never before from such a remote vantage point. If Scandinavian open-mindedness was seen by Americans and Europeans as an ideal worth striving for, here it was depicted more like some kind of virus that had seeped into the water supply.

Despite the fact that it was shot in Copenhagen and featured Danish actors, including Søltoft in a short scene as a leering, cigar-chomping executive, it never opened in Denmark. And for good reason; it was all too tame for the times, the most explicit scene being a sloppy French kiss between the two Chinese lovers. Women were nude, but usually while in the act of taking baths or showers. A Chinese girl refuses to drop her towel and take a shower in the company of her Caucasian sisters, as if they might infect her with immorality. And when Tove embraces Li Ching she is invariably partially clothed.

Sporting enjoyable psychedelic-lite touches and period stylings, Tove's Asian debut endures as an entertaining if silly curiosity, although the dearth of martial arts scenes will disappoint Hong Kong action fans. It is mainly valuable as yet another shining example of how Liberated Denmark was perceived in the wider world.

Adventure in Denmark

Sexy Girls of Denmark was released in Far East markets in March of 1973, but the Asian appetite for all things Danish was hardly sated and that June a similar film opened called *Adventure in Denmark*. Like its predecessor it was fated to become part of that parallel universe of films about Denmark that never actually opened there, films of whose existence Danes were (and largely still are) completely unaware.

Shot on the streets of Copenhagen that previous December, it was, like *Sexy Girls of Denmark*, too tame to play as a sex film in Danish theaters although it was considerably more suggestive and kung-fu packed. In one scene George, the more comical of the two male leads (played by James Yi Lui), falls in with three wild chicks and follows them back to their pad where they all down schnapps and dance to psychedelic acid-rock music. As they dance the gals fling off their clothes and have their way with him in various situations. Danish women are like that, you know. No big deal.

The film's trophy blonde was Lise-Lotte Norup, a well built 21-year-old who had first come to the attention of audiences two years prior for her gutsy performance in the black comedy *Curtains for Mrs. Knudsen*. Here, playing the vulgar and uninhibited girlfriend, she had thrown her all into a couple of hot nude scenes that stopped just short of triple-X. In quick succession she was signed to a pair of *Bedside* films and her typecasting as the country's new blonde hottie was complete. To fans she was the real thing. She seemed experienced beyond her tender years and radiated sluttier vibes than the more porcelain-like Birte Tove. Tove you could take home to meet your mother—not Norup. She made sex dirty again and came armed with a striking array of come-hither looks and sultry scowls, all so effectively on display in *Adventure in Denmark* that one almost doesn't notice she is never actually nude.

The plot was uncannily similar to *Sexy Girls in Denmark*. Again a startled Asian man finds himself adrift in the sexual paradise called Copenhagen. He encounters a bevy of willing beauties, prominent among them Ingrid (Norup) who emerges naked from a cold dip in a lake. They get to know each other. They run slow motion through a field, goof about affectionately in a restaurant and eventually have sex. Later, curled up on her couch, they indulge in some classic Danish coziness, candles burning while George cuddles with a dog and she strums a guitar. Then she tells him she loves him. It's all too perfect. Naturally he assumes they'll be married and is all the more shocked when upon a subsequent visit to her house he finds her having sex with another man, neither taking much note of his appearance. They cease their foreplay long enough for the tattooed biker type to toss him out of the room. One never knows where one stands with these Danish women! In an environment of total sexual freedom nothing means anything anymore; all the codes and signals of how men and women relate to each other have vanished.

While George is being gang-tackled by the hussies of Copenhagen, his more serious traveling companion falls properly in love with the prim Chinese travel bureau host via shy hand-holding and the exchange of glances so furtive that their romance develops at an excruciating snail's pace. Asian courting rituals are clearly very different than the Danish variety, but there can't be much courting if one never speaks to a woman, and George never really speaks to Ingrid. Part of this owes to the fact that the film was apparently shot without sound and all the effects and dialogue were laid on in the studio back in Hong Kong. The Cantonese dialogue was easy to dub, but the few phrases of English and Danish one does hear are delivered in comically off-the-mark cadences. Without dialogue there is no way for George to communicate with these women other than a series of winks and nods and lascivious grins and grunts, in contrast to *Sexy Girls in Denmark* where Birte Tove has reams of dialogue to get her point across. For his part Yi Lui is obliged to wildly goof and mug his way through the film in silent comedy style, to play the hopeless but not unsympathetic foil to his more athletic and kung-fu savvy partner, and it's a pity because in his few serious moments he conveys something of the depth and soulful ambiguity of an Asian Dustin Hoffman.

Returning to Hong Kong a defeated man, George ends up lecturing with great zeal about the dangerous effects of Danish sexual permissiveness at a "moral reconstruction society" in what is clearly a satiric jab at the sanctimoniousness of Chinese social codes.

The film contains a number of clues as to how Asians related to Denmark or at least the idea of it. In one scene George collides with a blonde on a bicycle who takes him home to massage his wounds. This of course leads to sex, but it is interrupted by the entrance of her husband who is dressed in tweeds and a cap and resembles a character out of Sherlock Holmes. (Apparently lacking an idea of what the Danish patriarch looked like, they just chose an archaic British one.) Being the gutless philanderer he is and having already been flattened by a mistress's husband in Hong Kong, George is terrified. But this is not Hong Kong and the husband merely shakes his hand and bids him to help himself to his wife. No such thing as jealously in this country.

On another occasion George enters a porn shop where he briefly flips through a magazine before putting it back with an expression of embarrassment and mild repulsion. He's not really shocked, it just does nothing for him, it's too weird, too gross. It doesn't have anything to do with sex as he knows it. He likes the girls but not the porn and isn't entirely sure what the two have to do with each other. The girls like it well enough, though. Flash back to his encounter with the three party babes. After brandishing a whip and laughing hysterically one of them impatiently points to the line figures in a pornographic pamphlet and demands that he do *that*, as if a whole generation were taking their cue from pornography.

For his part George approaches sex like a big kid, jumping up and down and yelling yahoo when he realizes he's about to get laid. A sophisticated exploration of sexuality this film was not, but it is interesting in its portrayal of sex as completely detached from love or genuine emotion. For these Caucasian girls sex is either just a wild cheap thrill or something purely mechanical, but rarely does anything genuinely sexy come from it. George rolls and tumbles around with naked women but oddly this doesn't seem to lead to anything and is erotic only in glimpses at best. It all has an exaggerated play-acting quality about it, and this was probably by design to get it past stricter Asian censors. When eventually some chemistry develops between George and a fetchingly arrayed Lise-Lotte Norup, and there seems to be some genuine heat building, the scene turns out to be just the set up for another comic twist. By mistake George has taken a purgative instead of a potency pill, and after several false starts a disgusted Ms. Norup is done with him and kicks him out of bed.

And after this movie Norup was also done with her short-lived Hong Kong adventure and today claims she doesn't even remember it. Not so Birte Tove who went on to make two more films with the Shaw Brothers.

The second one was to be filmed in Hong Kong, and at the end of the summer of 1973 she flew over for an extended stay that was to last almost a year. She was under the assumption she would appear in a version of *For Whom the Bells Toll* but instead ended up in *Bamboo House of Dolls*, a sadistic tale of rape and abuse of Caucasian nurses in a World War II Japanese prison camp. This picture did get a release in Tove's homeland in the spring of 1976 and was utterly ignored by reviewers.

"Tremendously exciting," raved the film's press kit, "a raw and ruthless film about the sadistic torture and rape of nurses imprisoned in a World War II bamboo hell. While shards of glass press into her naked body, a (blind) nurse is raped by sadistic Japanese

Birte Tove (left) and unidentified players in the Shaw Brothers' *Bamboo House of Dolls.*

guards.... Satanic brutality and bloody sadism.... An intense film about the total degradation of innocent women."

Tove, credited as Bik Dai Do Foo in the film's Asian release, was less enthusiastic, mortified in fact. She claimed in the Danish press that she hadn't even bothered to watch the finished film and refused to comment on it in hopes that it might be hushed to death.

She also made a third film for the Shaw Brothers, *The Mini Skirt Gang* (1975), of which virtually nothing is known (by this writer) except that it involves men being beaten senseless by beautiful women.

While Tove's Hong Kong experience wasn't much of a career boost, she had undeniably wowed 'em in the Far East. Crowds at her public appearances were often so enthusiastic that police had to hold them back. "You ah sexy," everyone told her in broken English, even normally impassive film company bosses. She was even hotter news than Elizabeth Taylor, whose arrival in the city at one point earned only a small photo in the back section of *The Hong Kong Times* while Tove got the whole front page. "She was so furious," remembers Tove, "that she scolded her film company and then left Hong Kong in a rage."[14]

And yet on at least one occasion her reputation worked against her. Visiting an orphanage on a free day, she met a little Chinese boy and took him to her heart, but efforts to adopt him were in vain; there could be no talk of a sexy Caucasian movie star becoming his mother.

Although her boyfriend had flown over regularly for visits, homesickness eventually got the best of her and she moved back to Denmark to resume her career there.

Birte Tove wields clippers in *The Mini Skirt Gang*.

Not everyone was happy to see her, certainly not the country's growing legion of feminists. She was every car mechanic's wet dream and in their eyes the personification of sexual exploitation. They even published a dispatch entitled *The Birte Tove Report* which took measure of the sorry state of current sexual attitudes and stereotypes.

Her career reached its modest peak in 1975 when she gave a game performance in the first installment of a folk-comedy series called *Girls at Arms*. That same year she tested for a major part but didn't get it, reportedly because she had been in the *Bedside* films. It was a huge blow. She went straight home and without even taking off her coat or boots crawled into bed, curled up under the duvet in the fetal position and cried her eyes out.[15]

Birte Tove's absence from the *Bedside* films was mourned by many, but Vivi Rau possessed a unique sensuality all her own. As a critic put it, "Rau represents to a greater degree [than Tove] the fantasy of seeing the neighbor's sweet but rather ordinary daughter without any clothes on...."

Rau also eventually felt herself typecast. As the headline of a 1976 interview announced, "Vivi Rau would happily perform with her clothes on." She did get a "legit" role that same year in a comedy before leaving the film world to open her own fashion boutique.

The last two *Bedside* films, *Danish Escort Girls* and *Bedside Sailors*, were released in 1976. In the former Rau plays a young housewife neglected by her businessman husband, Adam (Ole Søltoft). Out of boredom she becomes an escort girl who is soon booked to participate in an orgy her husband has arranged to curry favor with a delegation of government officials. By now Søltoft's hammed-up acting style was impossible to ignore and marred the film for some viewers, while Rau managed a more natural performance. "Sex entertainment for the whole family," declared a reviewer, showing there was still life to be had in old slogans.

Bedside Sailors was spun on the story of a gal who fills in for her boyfriend on ship duty after their wild sex lands him in the hospital. She finds the seafaring life to be an extremely chauvinistic one as the "case of mistaken identity" gags come in rapid succession. Finally docking in Hamburg, the sailors pile into a bordello. *Bedside Sailors* was actually one of the better *Bedside* films but falling ticket sales convinced Palladium to put the series to sleep.

Movies made specifically for the American market now constituted a significant portion of Denmark's sex film production, and these pictures were usually very different in tone and approach from the films made with a primarily Danish public in mind. The Americanized movies were, by comparison, downbeat exploitation-style affairs that stressed guilt, perversion, depravity and sadism, while Danish glad porn took audiences in a completely different if not necessarily more enlightened direction.

There were also Danish-Swedish co-productions tempered for Anglo-Saxon sensibilities or lack thereof. *The Keyhole*, written and directed by Paul Gerber in 1974, was one. An American living in Denmark, Gerber had been the cinematographer on de Renzy's *Censorship in Denmark* and had since gone on to write and direct hard-core, bottom-of-the-barrel fare like *The Coming Thing*, *School Girl* and *Bad Barbara*. Erstwhile *Penthouse* centerfold Marie Ekorre played the female lead in *The Keyhole*, a somewhat more ambitious production, while the rest of the cast was local talent.

The film bore on a subject that had actually become kind of *passé* in the midst of so many historically-themed porn films: modern Danish open-mindedness. It told the tale of a fellow charged with the task of penning an honest and believable porn film about "real people." The writer's girlfriend suggests they use her parents as models, but as they spy on the couple they find out that their sex life is anything but routine and the script that results is so racy that the producer rejects it as unrealistic. Real people couldn't be like that. A hard-core comedy, as it were, and clearly a notch or several above Gerber's previous films.

The Sinful Dwarf

Bent Tømming also resurfaced that year, producing what was, in the words of one writer, "the most repulsive film ever shot in Denmark"—*The Sinful Dwarf*. A low-budget tale of sexual bondage, abuse and voyeurism, it starred real life dwarf Torben Bille as a character called Olaf. Bille had worked a circus act and had minor bit parts in a handful of Danish features, but none of that could have prepared the public for the depravity of *The Sinful Dwarf*.

The film is set in a decrepit boarding house that Olaf runs together with his alcoholic mother, a washed up cabaret performer by the name of Lila Lash. Up in the attic they keep women imprisoned, injecting them with heroin and leaving them chained naked on dirty mattresses to be mauled and raped by men who pay for the privilege. Olaf watches it all through a peep-hole. So far so bad.

Voyeuristic Olaf (Torben Bille) spies on naked sex-slaves in the attic in *The Sinful Dwarf*.

Olaf is caught in some repressed limbo between man and child and his stunted condition is a physical manifestation of this. He now functions as his mother's brutal henchman, gamboling about on a cane, sent out on various nefarious errands such as fetching the latest batch of heroin from a toy maker called Santa Claus.

Although it is only sketchily alluded to, he is the malformed product of a traumatic childhood that his mother inflicted on him, and now he is a little monster, a sadistic pervert who lives out his emotional life in the wind-me-up world of children's toys. They figure in the surreal opening and closing credits and appear throughout the film as a kind of Greek chorus. Olaf is ever fondling and arranging fluffy teddy bears (in which heroin is hidden), toy poodles, etc. They mechanically clatter around in the background when scenes of sex and violence transpire, imbuing the film with a perverse sentimentality and hinting at a deeper psychological subtext that is otherwise hardly explored. Some thought has clearly been given to this aspect of the story, but lacking the time, money or ambition to flesh it out the filmmakers simply try to explain it by cramming the film with cute toys, and this goulash of cuddly stuffed animals and sadistic pornography is a bizarre cocktail indeed.

One dark night a British couple named Peter and Mary rent one of the mice-infested rooms out of desperation. We assume they are British because they have British accents, but no attempt is made to establish character or setting. They have sex that night as Olaf spies on them through a peep-hole carved into a photograph of an infant and a dog that hangs in their room. (This is a photograph of a sculpture made by 19th century artist Katinka Kondrup and further advances the theme of warped adolescence.) Afterwards Mary is unable to sleep, kept awake by creaking sounds as men seeking sex climb the stairs to the attic. And downstairs, in what was once a nightclub, Mom gives balmy off-key song performances as Olaf bangs away on the piano. But the old lush is also prone to bouts of temper, at one point donning her leather outfit and going up to whip one of the girls bloody.

Forced to kill time in their shabby room while Peter is out job hunting, Mary's curiosity gets the best of her and she ventures up to the attic where she hears a captured girl screaming. She promises to help the girl escape but is quickly discovered and overpowered, and ends up stripped naked and chained to the wall with the rest of them. Later she is also injected with heroin and raped by a customer. Olaf too eventually has a go at her, abusing her with his walking stick and then throwing himself on her in a slobbering fit of excitement, evoking from the actress an expression of revulsion that couldn't have been anything less than genuine. Indeed, as one Danish critic ventures, "You almost get the impression that the film crew was rough on her and that she was in real agony. It certainly appears that Torben Bille enjoyed torturing her."

Meanwhile Peter puts two-and-two together and returns with the cops. They raid the house and violence ensues. In the bizarre closing scene Olaf lies on the blood splattered pavement, his dying spasms not unlike the mechanical jerkings of his beloved toys.

The acting ranges from naturalistic to nonchalant and the low-budget chemistry is never threatened by a professional performance. Anne Sheldon Williams as the mom is suitably daft (and in one scene inexplicably topless) while Torben Bille is unforgettable, but perhaps even more notable is the British actress pseudonymously credited as Anne Sparrow who plays Mary, Peter's pretty blonde wife. Whether she was a trained actress is unknown, but, from all evidence, unlikely. Her naïve way with dialogue and the straightforward earnestness with which she delivers it is perfectly in sync with the gullible wide-eyed Mary, someone so detached and trusting that she just might end up in a situation like this. Her devotion to husband Peter, a cardboard character if ever there was one, is without limit. Upon being freed from her nightmare of captivity in the attic she declares in her chipper English accent that now that she and Peter are together again everything will be all right. In light of the fact that she's just been kidnapped, drugged and raped by a sadistic cane wielding dwarf, such a declaration is perhaps a bit premature, but there is almost no psychological dimension to her character so such an utterance seems, in the logic of exploitation cinema, appropriate.

She is the eternally innocent female in the tradition of the novels of Marquis de Sade; like a typical de Sade character, she can suffer the most appalling degradation at the hands of men but her belief in true love always allows her to repair herself and hope — and be defiled — again. Maybe the filmmakers didn't have de Sade in mind and her suffering nature just owes to the trite dialogue she was given and a script without any nuance at all, but still she comes across as the perfect victim. This is movingly demonstrated in a closing scene in the attic where, chained and naked, she writhes in abject agony.

The Sinful Dwarf tried its best to be dark, sordid and twisted. It succeeded. Its scenes of perversion and brutality are unapologetic and lingering. If that brutality is somewhat less harrowing than it might be due to the film's low budget and tendency to avoid explicit detail, the hard-core sex scenes by contrast do deliver. Scored to driving rock instrumentals, these sequences quicken the overall pace of the film and are not merely inserts or genital close-ups. Rather they tend to show the outlines of entwined naked bodies engaged in the throes of rampant sex, and are all the more effective for it.

Like other low-budget films that must make do without professional actors or expensive sets or production values, it evinces traces of inadvertent reality. Still, the bulk of the film plays out as a dirty fantasy with a capital D. In one scene a captive woman is sexually receptive to the advances of her rapist and they have a wild session, suggesting that even after days of being chained, drugged, semi-starved and left to wallow naked on a filthy mattress, women can still enjoy hot sex.

Another scene that was often shortened in the tamer export versions is Olaf's rape of Mary with his walking stick. The explicit details are (fortunately) left off screen, but still it's a harrowing encounter thanks to the camera's fixation on his grinning sweat-dripping mug. Some of the milder scenes are even more voyeuristic. In one sequence we see Mary strip out of her clothes and get into her nightgown, breasts jiggling free. It's natural enough that people get into their night clothes before going to bed but even this comparatively matter-of-fact scene manages to reek of prurience. We the viewers are put in a position of being every bit as voyeuristic as Olaf, if not as premeditated about it. The entire movie might as well be watched through a peep-hole.

Like the films of Poul Nyrup in the mid–'60s and Peer Guldbrandsen's *The Daughter* in 1970, *The Sinful Dwarf* fell like an alien object in the Danish landscape. It came from another planet and that planet was called 42nd street. A U.S.–Danish co-production, it had more in common with American grindhouse cinema and is most often compared to Joel Reed's sick black comedy *Bloodsucking Freaks* (1976) which was the epitome

Opposite: Danish promo art for *The Sinful Dwarf.* Danish text reads: "The scary, exciting Danish porno-thriller.... What was the mystical Dwarf's perverse secret?"

of a 42nd street picture. Based on the concept of the blood splattered Grand Guignol, it starred real life dwarf Luis De Jesus and proffered scads of naked women, but lacked the hard-core component of *The Sinful Dwarf* and came out three years later.

Aside from the fact that *The Sinful Dwarf* could not have been made anywhere else than Denmark, there was little that was particularly Danish about it. It was clearly tailored for the export market and was released in the U.S. a year before it came out on home turf. It was shot in a way as to minimize its Copenhagen setting and contained no familiar locations, no signs in Danish and very little distinctive architecture. In fact there were almost no exterior scenes. A number of extras speak with Danish accents and to Danes at least its setting is revealed in various ways, but no country is mentioned in the film and, with a mix of British, U.S. and Danish accents it has an oddly generic feel.

Little is known about the production of the film although the financing appears to have been precarious, thanks in part to the erratic behavior of the American producer. He lodged himself in the penthouse suite at Copenhagen's exclusive Hotel Sheraton and led a festive existence there until the bill came due, at which point he skipped town without a trace. Apparently the making of a perverse porn film loaded with S&M and torture was just an excuse for good times in Liberated Denmark.

If the identities of some of the foreign participants remain shrouded in mystery, in Denmark at least some of actors were well known. Amongst the chained-up women were porn vets Lisbeth Olsen and Jette Koplev who had orgied with Simon Spies at the launch party of *Bordello* the year prior. Also recognizable was Gerda Madsen who played Winnie, Lila's drinking partner. She was a well known figure who had first performed live theatre in 1920 and whose film roles stretched back to 1937. Danish critics were startled by her participation in this travesty. Some also voiced disgust that Bille would exploit his handicap in such a manner.

In addition to the U.S. the film opened in various other countries although true to form the Swedish censors deemed it to be utter trash and denied it a release. They'd stick to Danish glad porn, thank you very much.

Two months later Tømming released another film called *Cynthia's Sister*. This was a slightly more mainstream erotic drama that told the tale of a washed-up fashion model called Cynthia who moves into a manor house with her little sister and rich husband. Cynthia tries to seduce everyone in sight and in her attempts to ruin the marriage she joins forces with the husband's brother, but in the end their nefarious scheme backfires.

Directed by Arnold Baxter, this was another American-Danish co-production and starred actors from both countries. While it was not quite as extreme as *The Sinful Dwarf*, it was still a sadistic little item. "Possessed by a satanic force...," shouted a blurb, "she awakened her sister's abnormal desires to bait a trap of death!"

The Danish cast included Gertie Jung, Poul Glargaard and Preben Mahrt, but only Glargaard had a performing part in the sex scenes. He would go on to be best remembered for his role as a shop owner in the popular Christmas show from 1979, *Christmas in the Old Town*, though he also had bit parts in the hugely popular *The Olsen Gang* films. That he could survive his stint in porn, which included among other films *Danish Blue*, *I, a Woman 2* and *3* and *Bordello*, and keep his career intact and go on to participate in

Opposite: Danish ad art for *Cynthia's Sister*. Danish text reads: "Delicious Danish sex film in "knaldende" (fucking) color."

mainstream fare is yet another testament to the relative freedom that Danish actors enjoyed and the refusal of the industry and the broader public to hold them morally accountable. The men, in any case.

That fewer actresses who had "performing" parts survived the era and kept their careers going no doubt indicates there was a double standard at play, but the fact that most of them got into it as fashion models or strippers and not as trained actors was also undoubtedly a factor. A prominent exception was Ulla Jessen. She appeared in six out of the eight *Bedside* films and played a particularly slutty part in *Sexy Girls in Denmark*—a dead-end role if ever there was one—yet went on to act in two of the more mainstream *Girls at Arms* pictures and became a very popular figure in the world of live theater, involved in the production of musicals, operas, children's theater and cabaret.

Many Swedish actors also survived participation in porn to achieve mainstream success, the most prominent example being Stellan Skarsgård. He acted in a number of sex films in the mid-'70s (*Anita: Swedish Nymphet*, *Swedish Sex Games* and *Taboo*) and still went on to become the respected world class actor he is today.

Sweden continued to remain the quintessential Scandinavian country and a somewhat more marketable brand location than Denmark, thanks in part to the international success Swedish pop bands had in the '70s. Sweden had ABBA—Denmark's biggest rock bands over the same period were Gasolin and Savage Rose.[16] As a consequence a lot of German, American and even Danish producers shot co-productions in Sweden to exploit the myth of Swedish Sin. Denmark still had advantages—virtually no film was too violent, tasteless or explicit to get a domestic release there—but things were also getting relatively sleazier in Sweden although sexual violence remained taboo.

This had been happening for a while. Case in point: Joe Sarno's color follow-up to *Inga*, *Inga and Greta*. Made only a year later, in 1969, it was considerably more decadent and explicit, a harbinger of things to come. In this picture Inga was again played by Maria Liljedahl while Aunt Greta was played by Inger Sundh who was to star in *The Daughter* the following year. Sundh had steamy lesbian scenes in both pictures, something that was virtually *de rigueur* at this point. Of interest to rock aficionados was the fact that Tommy Blom of Tages, a '60s (Swedish) mod band famed for hits like "Sleep Little Girl" and "Every Raindrop Means a Lot," played her love interest. Additionally the picture's title track, "Inga's Theme," was recorded by Benny Andersson and Björn Ulvaeus who were yet to form ABBA.

Inga and Greta was released in the U.S. on an X-rated double-bill with the original *Inga*, the whole thing hyped as a "3 hour super-sexy Inga-thon"—but not until 1972. By that time they were up against competition like *Deep Throat* and hopelessly dated.

Liljedahl was destined for a short but productive career in pan–European exploitation. After *Inga and Greta* she shot a pair of sex films in Germany, *Grimm's Fairy Tales for Adults* (in which she played Snow White) and *The Three-Cornered Bed*, and in 1970 she starred in the Italian horror film *Dorian Gray*.

That same year she returned to Sweden to shoot *Ann and Eve* together with the ever-in-demand Gio Petré. This Swedish-Yugoslavian co-production was directed by the one and only Arne Mattsson of *One Summer of Happiness* fame. Shot largely in the Adriatic, it was a sexploitation film in the classic mold. Here the film critic Eve, played by a now blonde Liljedahl, tries to get over the trauma of having driven her movie director lover to suicide with her devastating reviews. She takes a vacation with an innocent friend, Ann.

Eve encourages Ann to obtain as much sexual experience as possible before she gets married, and they both throw themselves into a whirl of sexual activity with fishermen, truck drivers, a lesbian singer, a hotel porter and so forth.

Mattsson was also trying to say something about this dirty business of film criticism, and at one point a master director in the mold of Fellini or Bergman surfaces and argues that Eve's film critiques are destructive and have no value or meaning. The official take on Mattsson is that his career was in sharp decline at this point, had been for some time, and that "the last decades of his life were embittered by a constant feud with Swedish film critics, many of whom he regarded almost as personal enemies."[17] In this film he was clearly trying to say something about that although few could take it seriously. In any case *Ann and Eve* was aimed at the broader European market and its success showed that Swedish Sin had never been more popular.

Liljedahl's last performance was in Jesus Franco's gothic sex-and-horror drama *Eugenie ... the Story of Her Journey into Perversion*. She plays a virginal young innocent who arrives at a secluded island only to fall into the clutches of a wealthy older woman who has a perverse attraction to the Marquis de Sade. She's beaten, drugged and forced to drink blood and participate in orgies. In the end she wakes up and it's all just a dream.

For an actress who had debuted just a couple of years prior as the innocent Inga, she had come a long way fast and was right at home in Franco's world of demonic decadence. She was later hailed by *Playboy* as their sex star of 1971— all too much after the fact, as it turned out, since she quit acting completely after the Franco film and (at time of writing) has never made a comeback.

At this point a new generation of erotic stars was coming of age in Sweden. Marie Forså was one, getting her start in a 1970 German sex comedy that the English-speaking market tagged *Golden Bananas*. (The German title was *Liebesmarkt in Dänemark*, which means *Love Market in Denmark*.) But the brightest star of this new era was unquestionably Christina Lindberg from the west coast city of Gothenburg. Like Liljedahl she was dark-haired and called to mind a sexually precocious schoolgirl gone "bad."

Like others before her, she was discovered (in 1969) on a beach by a photographer. The pictures were printed in various papers and led to more photo shoots, modeling jobs and meetings with filmmakers — and a trip to the principal's office since she was still in high school. As she recalled the episode: "They weren't exactly happy about it, the female teachers in particular were upset.... Things didn't get any better so I took a 'leave of absence.'"[18]

She put her free time to good use, appearing in a film called *Maid in Sweden* where she played a schoolgirl who is up to all kinds of tacky monkey business, like spying on her sister while she has sex. She still had a few things to learn: there was a scene in a bar where she got too much to drink, since they were using real booze, and starting cracking jokes up at the microphone, but she did okay. Dialogue was her weak point but in any case her voice was dubbed into English for this Swedish-American co-production.

What Are You Doing After the Orgy? (1970) was her next film, and it was more of a real part. She played Anna Bella, a teenage girl who lives a peaceful life with her father on one of the islands off Stockholm. Everything changes when her long lost mother shows up again and turns their seaside idyll upside-down by transforming the bath-house into a bordello and offering her daughter to dirty old men. After a while her dad can't take it anymore and works out a plan to get rid of the wife.

The film screened at the Edinburgh film festival, hyped with the slogan "Swedes make it all worthwhile!" It was Lindbergh's breakthrough; soon she was being photographed for *Lui* and *Penthouse* magazines and suddenly she had money. She could now go to the coolest clubs and discos where she was often on the guest list anyway. She was "porno chic" before the term was coined and threw herself into something of a jet-set lifestyle. And it had all happened so fast; in just a couple of years she had gone from being just another bimbo on the beach to being an internationally known actress.

Her next film, *The Depraved*, about the abduction and kidnapping of a 17-year-old girl named Lena, served to further her career in exploitation and to show that Sweden could also make lurid "roughies" in the American style. Hitchhiking home from a party, Lena is grabbed by a gang of sickos who rape her and force her to pose for pornographic photos. Finally she gets her revenge and the blood flows. The film had an unusually rough edge for a Swedish picture and it also had Heinz Hopf who specialized in villainous roles. He and Lindberg played opposite in a number of films and have become affectionately known to retro buffs as the king and queen of Swedish sleaze.

With a wild soundtrack and enough sex to get it banned in 27 countries (as its promotion proudly boasted), *The Depraved* made waves. It was launched at the 1971 edition of the Cannes film festival. Birte Tove's *Christa* was also there, helping to focus attention on Scandinavian sex cinema, but *The Depraved* had a completely different spirit. Lindberg herself made the trip down and was installed in a luxury hotel called The Majestique while the rest of the team ended up in cheaper digs down the beach. She was besieged by the paparazzi, constantly photographed in ultra-revealing poses and outfits. Her official meeting with the press turned into a mob scene. As she recalled it, "I was going to meet the press out on a pier over the water. After having signed about a thousand invitations, which were given out to select people, I was lowered down from a rented helicopter to the pier topless! There were hundreds of photographers — who all got what they wanted!"[19]

Young Playthings

In 1972 Lindberg did an about-face, signing on to act in Joe Sarno's ultra-bizarre *Young Playthings*.

Like most of Sarno's films, it was primarily made for the American market. In fact it never even opened in Sweden — strange since Lindberg was hot property there at that point and virtually unknown in the States. Shot in Stockholm and based on a traditional Swedish fairy-tale, it was filmed with English dialogue and the taglines were 100 percent exploitation: "They're the erotic toys of the mindless generation ... trapped in a never-never land of distorted sexual practices. Wind them up and they'll turn you on ... satisfaction guaranteed."

Lindberg got top billing for her role as Gunilla, the sweet, shy wife of Janne, a traveling businessman. She's patient and trusting while he is away on trips, unaware that the sexually aggressive Nora, her closest friend, is having an affair with him. The types seem clearly cast from the outset but Gunilla is not your average victim and her contemplative, introverted nature is not to be mistaken for simplemindedness. To the contrary.

The situation makes Nora feel guilty and she confesses this to Janne. He is in a quandary; he loves them both and can't bear to lose either. When his mistress brings up the possibility of a ménage à trois he's doubtful that his wife will go along with it. Nora is not to be so easily dissuaded and devises a plan: Janne will go off on a fabricated business trip while the two women move into a vacation house where Nora will prepare her friend for the experience.

But Nora gets far more than she bargained for when they move into the rented summer house and encounter the mysterious Britt, played by Margaretha Hellström. This inscrutable stranger spends all her time collecting and repairing broken toys which she then sells to those who will appreciate them. As it turns out, this is something that she also does with human beings.

With Britt in the lead the three of them soon embark upon a journey of sexual discovery. Their encounters quickly become surreal, taking on the character of pantomimes or a kind of soft-core pornographic cabaret. For this they have donned a series of bizarre costumes that usually reveal their breasts, while their faces are daubed with white clown make-up.

The fourth key participant in their erotic role-playing is Julia, Britt's sister. She never appears in the flesh and is only glimpsed once, in a picture with her sister, but dominates the proceedings via a series of tape-recorded instructions that guide the other three. Julia has supposedly gone insane after a disastrous relationship with a man, though some doubt lingers as to whether she even exists, or is perhaps just Britt's alter ego. The fantasy sequences are intercut with outdoor scenes that are shot in real-time and represent reality, and eventually the two planes of existence merge and it is revealed how superficial and dishonest the emotional mechanizations of the real world are.

It turns out that Britt presides over a larger circle of people, a sort of psychic sexual encounter group which Nora and Gunilla now join. All of them are attempting a return to the infantile self through the portal of fantasy. Yet while return to childlike openness is encouraged, the central mode of communication is still a sexual one.

The film was composed of several philosophical strands. One of them embraced the belief that people should seek to return to a childlike state that represented purity and innocence. This idea was very popular in the early '70s (advocated by Charles Manson among others). The film also advanced the premise that the bourgeois lifestyle was riddled with hypocrisy. On the other hand it was crammed with the kind of soft-core sex that was ideal for hotel pay TV and the grindhouse circuit where viewers just wanted to see naked women and shrugged off the film's deeper intentions. And Sarno, a former psychology major and literary classics buff, had deeper intentions. Story elements that refer to 19th century seafaring lore can be found, as can references to tales from Medieval times, all of it enacted in ultra low-budget fashion by the girls.

Janne eventually comes back and joins Nora and Gunilla in their rented house. The three of them now spend their days and nights exploring uncharted erotic territory, and he too is soon introduced to Britt and the group.

But things get ugly one night when Julia's taped voice angrily orders Britt punished, and she is placed upon a giant vibrating dildo attached to a wooden horse. She is ill the next day and claims that Julia has escaped from a mental institution and is pursuing her. Dark forces have been unleashed and the group is dispersed across the city to find her. Gunilla and Janne intend to leave but Gunilla is stabbed by Nora before they can do so ... Nora having been handed the knife by Britt.

Nora confesses her act to Britt, and Britt decides that that evening's fantasy enactment shall be *The Saga of the Red Witch and the Scarlett Countess*. This legend concerns a terrified princess who tries to destroy a "tree of sexual fulfillment," in the process enraging her friend who then kills her. Clear parallels exist between this legend and what they have all been through. (The film's alternative title is simply *The Red Witch*.) That night Nora is ordered to endure the previous form of punishment herself, a punishment of eternal pleasure and eternal torment. This will drive her mad and prevent her from ever leaving the group. The tables have turned; the members of the group are not headed towards spiritual freedom and enlightenment, but are prisoners, inmates.... Or not?

In the end the main participants all seem to have been awarded the fates they deserve. Those who have been open-minded enough to benefit from Britt's fantasy-therapy have made themselves free, while those who only seek pleasure and self-gratification have merely enslaved themselves. Gunilla is not dead — the knife was a toy — and she is free to rejoin Janne, having been one of the wisest members of the group all along.

To some Sarno had created a deeply profound and symbolic tale that resonated with references to Oryphic, Dionysian and Hermetic mysteries while to others it was just weird-ass avant-garde sexploitation, by turns hilarious, bizarre and trippy. Sarno's psychological approach to sexuality, his use of literary references and the close-ups that informed his film language occasionally earned him comparisons to Bergman, comparisons he invariably and modestly shrugged off. A "poor man's Bergman" perhaps....

He used Lindberg again in *Swedish Wildcats*, also shot in 1972. In a bordello scene where rich clients bid for the sexual services of beautiful prostitutes costumed as exotic animals, Lindberg is glimpsed all too briefly as a snarling leopard.

That same year she began her participation in a series of Swedish-German co-productions which would include parts in such films as *The Swinging Co-eds*, *Love in 3-D* and *What School-girls Don't Tell*, this last one figuring as one of the legendary German "school-girl report" films. Entitled *School-girl Report Part Four; What Drives Parents to Despair* (in literal translation), its tag was changed to the more upbeat *Campus Swingers* for the Stateside market where "college" and "campus" were buzz words for unbridled sex and where a negative term like "despair" would never be allowed to creep into a movie title.

They Call Her One-Eye

In 1972 Lindberg starred as Madeleine in *They Call Her One-Eye*, which along with *Young Playthings* is the film she is today principally remembered for outside Sweden. These two movies were as different as could possibly be, although Lindberg brought to them the same sense of wide-eyed innocence.

In *They Call Her One-Eye* it is an innocence quickly shattered, as Madeleine is raped at around the age of seven by a scraggly hobo in the opening scene. It is an experience that leaves her permanently mute, but with the support of loving parents she recovers enough to function more or less normally in the physical sense and is able to help with chores around the farm.

But her sheltered existence leaves her unprepared to deal with the nasty likes of the pimp Tony who is played to the slimy hilt by Heinz Hopf. He gives her a lift one day in his pimp-mobile after she misses the bus, and he takes her home and drugs her into unconsciousness. Then he injects her with heroin to keep her enslaved in his rural brothel, stabbing out one of her eyes with a scalpel after she rips up the face of her first customer with her nails.

He has faked a letter to her parents who now think that their precious daughter has run away and hates them. In the meantime she submits to survive, servicing a range of violent and kinky customers. She engages in the sex but it's always a torment to be endured. When she finally makes a trip back to the old farm she is shocked to run into her parents' funeral procession; they have committed suicide out of grief. Now she snaps and begins plotting her revenge on Tony and his inner circle of sickos. She takes karate lessons and shooting practice on the side and saves enough money to buy a hot getaway car.

Finally she gets her revenge, blowing away the guilty as well as a number of innocent policemen. Thereafter she steals one of their patrol cars and races away to spread death and carnage on the highway, killing even more innocent people for no apparent reason. If there is a message it seems to be that revenge also destroys the avenger, even if she herself survives to ride off into the sunset.

Director Bo Arne Vibenius (credited as Alex Fridolinski), had started out by producing Saab commercials for an advertising agency and later worked on a pair of Bergman films that included *Persona*. Perhaps it was being at the beck and call of a perfectionist like Bergman that eventually drove him over the edge, or perhaps it was desperation over the failure of his debut film, *When Marie Met Fredrik*, a "family picture" shot in 1969 and scored with Beethoven. Whatever the reason, he went full throttle on the sex and violence in an effort to make "the most commercial film ever with absolutely no limits." As he defiantly enthused many years later, "I shot it exactly as intended.... Love it or hate it, I don't give a shit!"[20]

The end result was a disturbing cocktail of gore, porn and violence in the American grindhouse tradition but it still had the slow pace and contemplative style of an arthouse film. This added a certain bizarre dimension to the ghastliness as it veered from hallucinatory to genuinely erotic to repulsive and back again. It fetishizes the sex and violence with inventive scoring and arty photography while managing to create in spots a perversely compelling atmosphere.

But it lacked punch. It wanted to be an in-your-face 42nd Street movie but it was made in Sweden and it showed. The car chases, for example — hardly a staple device in Swedish cinema — are rather ridiculous, staged as they are with pipsqueak European automobiles. (It's just not the same when a *Volkswagen* goes crashing into a ditch.) Furthermore in America such a film would have been set in a grimy urban milieu but this is all quaint Swedish countryside, shoot-outs in windblown little fishing villages and whatnot. Even Tony's bordello seems to be set up in what appears to be a summer house. Perhaps lack of money forced Vibenius to shoot in rural settings, but the film is also very consciously constructed to resemble a western. It takes place in wide open spaces and starts and ends with lonely horizons, while the flowing high-plains drifter leather coat that a shotgun-toting Lindberg dons in the concluding scenes is also pure wild west. Likewise the slow-motion gore sequences clearly owe a debt to Peckinpah's *The Wild Bunch* which Vibenius not surprisingly claims as a favorite. And the last scene even features a pack mule. It exudes more the pastoral naturalism of Bergman and hardly jibes with the nastiness that transpires.

Save for Hopf's vile Tony, the film has no real acting and yet Lindberg's presence, if not performance, carries the picture. She threw herself completely into the role and is convincing as the frail and naive waif, if perhaps less so as the reconstituted Rambo.

A lot of strange things happened on the set, and rumors still circulate. As Daniel Dellamorte reports in his book *Svensk Sensationsfilm*, real ammunition was used in the shooting sequences, and Lindberg was asked to inject a salt solution during the drug-taking scenes. She was obliged to drive a cop car at top speed, sirens wailing, even though she had no license, and it is further reported that a real corpse was used during the sequence when her eye was punctured by a scalpel. All this led some to conclude that the director was mad as a hatter.

Hard-core pornographic frames that included female anal penetration were also spliced into the film, and although they could be and often were deleted from screening prints this was clearly the most controversial element. Lindberg's contract precluded any participation in the porn scenes but Vibenius persuaded her to okay the use of the inserted frames, and she has regretted that ever since. This has sparked debate among devotees of the film for years, some claiming the frames give the film an edge of appropriately squalid realism while others argue they are merely exploitive. *Deep Throat* was at the time a huge hit and there were those who predicted that explicit sexuality would soon be incorporated into all genres. Perhaps Vibenius thought so too. In any case he was ahead of his time: It would take almost another thirty years until someone picked up where he left off— that someone being the French director Virginie Despentes whose hard-core sex and revenge film *Rape Me* caused a stir in 2000. Yet perhaps even more transgressive than the hard-core pornography in *They Call Her One-Eye* are the numerous scenes of a semi-naked, one-eyed Lindberg fondling and loading up a syringe with heroin. Madeline has been abused and victimized in every sense.

Despite the slow pace the film's mere premise was harrowing enough to win it comparisons to brutal '70s American rape-revenge classics like *I Spit on Your Grave*, *Ms. 45* and *Last House on the Left* (the latter title thought by some to be a remake of Bergman's *The Virgin Spring*), and it received more attention abroad than virtually any other Swedish exploitation movie. Since then it has attracted a growing cult following and one of its biggest fans is Quentin Tarantino. He admits that *One-Eye* inspired Daryl Hannah's mean, eye patch-wearing Elle Driver character in *Kill Bill*.

In Sweden the censors were disgusted and banned *One-Eye* completely. "The only Swedish film ever banned in Sweden" boasted its publicity. It didn't open domestically until two years later, in 1974, and then sans 26 minutes of footage. It was a textbook case of what Swedish censors hated most: gratuitous sexual violence.

They Call Her One-Eye was, like *The Daughter*, also a clear example of a Scandinavian director's trying to cater to the U.S. market, but this was even too much for the Americans. When AIP released it in the U.S. they felt compelled to remove the hard-core frames and shortened the infamous eyeball gouging scene.

Vibenius wasn't finished; he directed the even more bizarre *Breaking Point* in 1975, this time under the pseudonym of Ron Silverman Jr. This futuristic "pornographic thriller" about a frustrated middle-aged man who works a boring office job was another curious concoction. When his family goes on vacation his life turns into a hallucinatory chaos of guns, sex and rape. *Breaking Point* was tasteless, violent, pornographic and some would certainly say misogynist—all meant no doubt to reflect the sickness endemic in society at large. It was also aimed at the export market and was also banned on Vibenius' home turf. And like *They Call Her One-Eye* it was in no way, shape or form particularly Swedish.

In 1973 Lindberg, like her Danish compatriot Birte Tove, traveled to the Far East to make movies, temporarily relocating to Japan where she did photo-shoots, made television appearances and performed dance acts. She did two films that year credited as Kurisuchina Rindobaagu. One was called *Sex and Fury* and stands as a classic of '70s martial arts exploitation. *The Porno Star Travels Around Japan* was the other and had a somewhat more easy-going pace.

Torgny Wickman enticed Lindberg to return to Sweden with an offer to act in his 1974 picture *Anita: Swedish Nymphet*. Here she plays a rebellious but troubled 16-year-old nymphomaniac who has sex with a variety of strange men, one of whom is in the process of hallucinating, before fashionably long-haired psychology student Erik, played by Stellan Skarsgård, "cures" her. This movie was a big hit in Germany, a classic "Schweden film." That year she also appeared in Mac Ahlberg's variation on the Fanny Hill theme, *Around the World with Fanny Hill*.

By now Lindberg had made films with Sarno, Wickman, Ahlberg and others. Some of the movies were triple-X rated, but she herself never participated in the hard-core action and became increasingly hesitant to act in such films as the years wore on. In one instance she left the set of a film in protest.

Confessions of a Danish Cover Girl

Back in Denmark old warrior Knud Leif Thomsen returned to something that resembled familiar form with his 1974 picture *Confessions of a Danish Cover Girl*. Since *The School for Suicide* he had drifted away from contemporary issues to make a number of films based on historical novels, but now he was back with a movie that took on modern topics like women's lib and the power of the media to distort issues of identity.

The central character is Vivi. Despite good looks that hint at something other than a working-class background she is forced to toil away in a bottle factory to make rent while her layabout boyfriend, played by Søren Strømberg, nurses dreams of rock stardom and spends his time jotting down song lyrics in their shabby apartment. They need money and he knows a photographer who pays cash to girls who pose in the nude. She finally relents and ends up as a centerfold in a men's magazine.

Life imitated art or rather vice versa in Thomsen's casting of Vivi. For this role he chose Lise-Lotte Norup who was fresh off her performance as Ingrid in *Adventure in Denmark* and still a certifiable pin-up queen. She was a real life centerfold who had lived all the ups and downs of the life and knew what it was like to be public property.

A bloke from the neighborhood finds her pictures and begins to make obscene phone calls and to stalk her. She flees to the west coast of Jutland to find peace but he follows her, jumping on the same bus at the last moment. On the way Vivi meets and is befriended by Harriet, a middle-aged man-hating woman who quotes Germaine Greer and hides a damaged psyche behind sun-glasses. They agree to teach the stalker a lesson.

Strømberg, who had come to life as the prophet of pornography in *Gift* eight years before, had now in Thomsen's scheme of things reached the final stage of devolution and become a degenerate sleaze living off his girlfriend (actually things hadn't changed much!). And the "new man" that that revolution had created was also on display in the guise of the stalker, a painfully dysfunctional introvert repressed to the point of psychosis, a pathetic loner who had no sense of self and was unable to relate to actual flesh-and-blood people.

But feminism was no answer. In Thomsen's view it was equally destructive, yet another philosophical trap. The stalker takes refuge in pornographic fantasies and is destroyed by them, while Harriet seeks solace in radical feminist dogma and is also destroyed. Both have lost their individuality and humanity and eventually they lose their minds. If the sexual liberationists were robots so too were their sworn enemies, the radical feminists.

Vivi emerges as the hero of sorts because she acts according to her feelings and not philosophies. She rejects the rote wisdoms of both the porn liberationists and the feminists, and in a final act of compassion she reaches out to make personal contact with her spiritually wounded pursuer and attempts to break through his wall of fantasy.

Issues that Thomsen addressed here such as victimization, loss of identity and the mindset of women who participate in commercial porn were not being dealt with anywhere else in the realm of commercial cinema, and the film was praised as bold and topical by a few. However, most reviewers dismissed it; one called it hysterical. Additionally a number of professional porn models stated in the press that it wasn't like that and that the psychology was all wrong. This was ammunition for critics who claimed that once again Thomsen had populated a film with characters who were not real people but rather the exaggerated constructs of a director with an axe to grind. These were all valid criticisms that could be argued, but again, as with *Gift*, perhaps reviewers should have judged it more as an allegory. The film's rather bleak and straightforward style persuaded critics that it was intended as realism, but that was never Thomsen's game.

Confessions of a Danish Cover Girl has striking similarities to *The Duel* and *Gift*, and the three films could be considered a kind of trilogy — a "trilogy of dissent," so to say. They all address Thomsen's main concern, namely that people who allow themselves to be programmed by philosophies are doomed. Despite their flaws as film art they provide in many ways a more revealing picture of the era than the films that idealized it, particularly those made for primarily commercial purposes.

Confessions ... suffered an ironic fate. Thomsen's producers had wanted a much more explicit picture than the one he delivered, and the following year it was re-released in a stronger version with additional actors performing in explicit new scenes. Here was yet another example of one of the era's most glaring ambiguities; a movie that attempted to debunk the sexual status quo being sold as something that simply reinforced it all, i.e., a porn film. Thomsen, Norup and Kirsten Rolffes who played Harriet disowned this version and had their names removed from the credits.

Danish society was now much more fiercely politicized as well as fragmented. Socialism, Communism, gay rights, women's lib, the Vietnam War, anti–Americanism, and the environment were all subjects that aroused heated debate, but there was one topic that was no longer politically charged: pornography. Danes had become so inured to porn that even films containing bestiality failed to cause much of a stir. Porn no longer constituted an attack on the establishment, and the next glad porn series, the so-called Astrology films, showed just how viewer-friendly, marketable and accepted explicit screen sex had become.

Danish Pastries

Danish Pastries was the first of the Astrology films. It opened in 1973, in the middle of summer — just as all the films of the series would so as to sell a maximum number of tickets to tourists. For once it didn't seem to be a drawback if the word Danish was connected to pastries, as long as they were naked pastries.

The film was directed by Finn Karlsson. Since *Stine and the Boys*, Karlsson had gone on to helm another relationship film, *Tomorrow My Love*, but he had not really lived up to expectations. His next job was working as an assistant to Ole Ege on *Bordello*. He helped with the script and co-directed but reportedly walked off the set, unhappy with the film's quality. And now a year later he had his own glad porn film in something of the same style, just as explicit and in spots just as silly but more coherent and professionally crafted. He now could claim the dubious distinction of being the only "serious" Danish director to make a hard-core pornographic feature film, even if the results were anything but serious.

Right after the inventive opening credits (a red psychedelic blob that quivers to the

Sexy naked apparitions appear out of the mist in *Danish Pastries*.

jangly theme song) the viewer is plunged straight into hard-core lesbian action perpetrated by two gals from a ladies' boarding school, supposedly located in a small Swiss village but with an unmistakable Danish look to it. The school is run by a mysterious astrological society and the girls are anything but ladies, throwing themselves at each other for lack of men folk. An upcoming astrological phenomenon called the Venus Passage will soon darken the skies over the village, alarming the elders of the board who fear it might send the girl's already over-active libidos into orbit. They have created a substance that dampens the sex drive, and they send a clean-cut sober young fellow named Armand on a mission to deliver the powder to the school. He also happens to be a virgin and also happens to be Ole Søltoft.

Arriving in town, he eventually bumps into nutty professor Archibald Bomwitz who is on a similar mission but armed instead with a powerful aphrodisiac. In the jumble they get their suitcases mixed up and Armand ends up dumping the aphrodisiac into the town's water supply. Generously imbibing of the liquid at meal time, the girls turn into hyperventilating hussies, throwing themselves at Søltoft and each other and then dashing in various states of undress to the town's bordello where 20 minutes of group sex follows. Søltoft has managed to remain aloof and fully clothed and now from his perch atop a cabinet observes the orgy in wide-eyed wonderment. Afterwards everyone parades down to the reservoir and dives in. Via the magic of underwater photography viewers are then treated to a nude, rude aquatic ballet scored by an extended version of "What the World Needs Now."

As with the *Bedside* series, many of the secondary "non-performing" parts were played by well known folk-comedy actors. (By this time porn chic was all the rage in America, and now even there so-called real actors were appearing in porn films in non-performing parts, so this was perhaps no longer so pioneering.)

Søltoft never sheds his clothes and in this film underplays his part marvelously, leaving the mugging and overacting to porn veteran Bent Warburg (as Bomwitz) and Sigrid Horne-Rasmussen (the prudish headmistress), both of whom are more than up to the task and steal far too much screen time from the real stars of the film, the female students. These girls cavort about the ancient passages of the school in loose-fitting purple robes that are easily shed at a moment's notice to facilitate a myriad of nude activities that include fighting, wrestling, sex of all types and just wandering aimlessly about.

This relatively large cast of mostly quite attractive women seems to be ever in motion, imbuing the film with a rousing female physicality. They climb over tables to get at each other; they tussle about on the floors and dash through the old hallways and streets in a sexual frenzy. All this gives the movie a vibrancy and erotic energy that scenes of actual fornication cannot equal. The festive tone and up-tempo pace of the film, accentuated by the rockish upbeat organ music, stand in sharp contrast to so many hard-core movies of the period which tended to be bleak and depressing affairs.

There was some brutality in the film, most notably a startling scene in which the girls drag a new student up onto a table and sadistically strip, bully and humiliate her. They manage to work themselves into a sexual lather and in the process she slips out a gap in the pile of writhing bodies to wander off to a new lesbian encounter. It is a prolonged scene that provides merciful respite from the plot and has an edge of realism to it that would prompt at least one critic to compare *Danish Pastries* (at its best) to the period erotic films of Walerian Borowczyk.

The film bears witness to a certain amount of technical finesse. The dream sequence in particular, which represents Bomwitz's subconscious reaction to his failure to obtain an erection, stands out as perhaps the most bizarre of its kind ever to appear in an erotic film. It opens with a surreal landscape of curvaceous female flesh and segues into scenes of a naked man who reaches out to catch beautiful nude women. They flit teasingly past him in a kind of psychedelic ballet while his limp member is shown in close-up, all this depicted with the aid of superimposition, rear-screen projection, tinting and experimental music. Finally erection is achieved, heralded by dramatic music and a close-up image. He now struggles in tattered clothing against the wind, stiff member and all, spinning slowly up and away into the air.

This is the showpiece of the whole film and perhaps the oddest single moment in the annals of Danish erotic cinema, and it is clearly intended not just to dazzle but to get to the Freudian root of the matter.

All in all, the spirit and energy provided by the girls and the jaw-dropping dream sequence go some way towards compensating for the idiotic plot and the foolish overacting of Warburg, who like most of the men folk in this picture was nothing to write home about. Søltoft, however, acquitted himself well.

The year 1973 would prove a busy one for Denmark's eternally boyish star. In addition to appearing in *Between the Sheets* and *Danish Pastries* he acted alongside England's faded bombshell, Diana Dors, in the Vernon Becker (Swedish-American) co-production *A Man with a Maid*. This was a 3-D film, shot in "Wondavision" and billed as "the clas-

This landscape of female flesh constitutes another dream sequence image from *Danish Pastries*.

sic underground Victorian novel, now a daring comedy." The picture didn't open in the U.S. until the spring of 1977, re-dubbed *The Groove Room*. It was later re-released there under a host of different titles such as *What the Butler Saw, Teenage Tickle Girls* and *Tickled Pink*, proving that a 3-D porn film is harder to kill than a vampire. Becker himself had produced some of the key Swedish sex films going back to *Inga and Greta*, but as a director was more of a novice, *Dagmar's Hot Pants* being his only previous credit.

There were more Astrological films to come, five more in fact, all directed by Werner Hedman and starring Søltoft. And although they contained hard-core porn, they were considered comedies first and porn second.

Some had fairly inventive plots. *In the Sign of Taurus* (1974) features a rich count who dies and leaves his fortune to the first child to be born out of wedlock — and in the sign of Taurus, encouraging the young folks of town to get naked and get to work. This film featured Suzanne Bjerrehuus, a hairdresser's daughter who would go on to become Miss Denmark (and subsequently a popular TV game show host and author of an influential book about surviving cancer). *In the Sign of the Twins* (1975) features two competing record company producers, each attempting to sign a contract with a Swedish songstress. The resultant intrigues involve kidnapping, general hilarity and hard-core sex.

The fourth installment of the series, *In the Sign of the Lion* (1976), was, like the previous film, set in the '30s. It centered on two older women who had worked in the castle of Count Johan at the turn of the century when anything went. They sit down together to write a memoir of the times but it turns out to be so risqué that they decide to publish it under the name of their nephew, a shy young man who is mystified by all the interest he suddenly arouses in young women.

These films were cast with the usual suspects, the by now familiar troupe of legit

In the Sign of Taurus: Ole Søltoft and Susanne Breuning get cozy.

A scene of psychedelic abandon from *In the Sign of Taurus*.

stars and bit players like Ole Søltoft, Otto Brandenburg, Søren Strømberg, Gertie Jung, Vivi Rau, Judy Gringer, Annie Birgit Garde, Louise Frevert and Gotha Andersen. The other actors and actresses who had performing roles in the sex scenes were usually only referred to by their first names in the credits, but they were also getting to be familiar to audiences and could count on steady work during this period. The *Bedside* and the Astrological films functioned as a kind of ongoing actors' workshop for people who otherwise would never have gotten their foot in the door of the film world. Their contributions definitely enlivened Danish cinema of the '70s, although others had had quite enough of them and the seemingly endless repetition of their work.

The last two films in the Astrological batch, *Agent 69 Jensen in the Sign of Scorpio* (1977) and *Agent 69 Jensen in the Sign of Sagittarius* (1978), were companion pieces that hinged on the zany antics of a spy called "69 Jensen" (Søltoft) who was on the hunt for a hidden microfilm. The story in both films was overshadowed by the madcap comic style but audiences didn't seem to mind as they sold more tickets than any of the other films in the series. Nonetheless times were changing and the end was near for this type of movie. As was the custom, they both opened in provincial small-town theaters where they could pack in the rubes — and in at least one drive-in theater — before coming to Copenhagen. This was truly a people's cinema.

Part Four

The Passing of an Era

The Danish glad porn films of the '70s are today held in low esteem by the academic film establishment, but in their own way they did achieve something: They advanced the notion of sex as a happy, carefree and upbeat affair — not such a small thing. Sex as something that wasn't deadly serious or cause for endless soul-searching. Bergman, roll over! But from all other perspectives they were simply business as usual and brought Danish cinema back to square one. The vilified folk-comedy that young movie-makers had tried to kill off back in the early '60s had simply been reinvented with porn added, while the various movements and rebellions proclaimed by the art film intelligentsia had all proved short lived. Cinema was after all a business.

But the times had also changed. Depicting sex in movies had once been a revolutionary pursuit, the *cause célèbre* of the radical set who hailed the "good pornography" and proclaimed open sexual expression a noble cause. They had waged war on the powers-that-be and had managed to rattle the older generation, but now the culture of explicit sexuality had become co-opted by commercial imperatives and depoliticized and trivialized. It had become just pornography, however happy-go-lucky it might be. As *In the Sign of Sagittarius* faded from screens, the era of Liberated Denmark came to an unceremonious close.

Porno films continued to be made in Sweden which had something that more closely resembled an autonomous adult film industry. Among those that Mac Ahlberg shot as the '70s wore on were two with Harry Reems, *Justine and Juliette* and *Bel Ami*. Joe Sarno, now shooting hard-core under a host of pseudonyms, made two in 1978; *Love's Island* and *Come Blow the Horn*. (Oddly the latter title is the Sarno film best known in Sweden today, thanks to a masturbation sequence that involves a special type of Swedish sausage.) Well into the '80s theatrically released porn films were still being made in Sweden, but Sinful Sweden as a somehow revolutionary concept had come to an end. If a single film can be named that marked its official passing it must be *Summer with Vanja* from 1980, the last proper summer film to get a release. It starred the attractive Finnish actress Oili Viirta and involved a typical summer romance, but with its hard-core trappings and decadent group-sex finale it was a long way indeed from the winsome yearning of *One Summer of Happiness*.

The long Swedish summer had lasted almost 30 years, but now the sun had finally set for good.

The mythology of an enlightened Scandinavia, based on countless films that spanned decades, would persist and persists to this day; but when it came to producing run-of-the-mill pornography, well, anybody could do that. By the mid–'70s even Catholic countries were producing hard-core films, and the new wonder women were American starlets like Marilyn Chambers and Linda Lovelace and not the hopelessly modest likes of Persson, Nyman, Tove, Nissen, Norup and Lindberg. *Deep Throat, Behind the Green Door* and *The Devil in Miss Jones* were now the trend-setting pictures that produced lines around the block. Even before this there had been talk that American-made porno was simply better. This startling admission adorned publicity for the Danish release of Phil Osco's 1970 film *Mona*: "Far better than what has previously been seen from Swedish and Danish producers. For the first time opponents of pornography have grounds to be worried. The USA is better at porno than we are." As the film's Danish distributor went on to elaborate: "This is hard, true-blue porno, and that is not what one would have expected from America. The film's strength is that the plot is not constantly interrupted by porn scenes. When porn scenes do occur (and they occur in plenitude) they are the logical result of what is happening in the story." Of course this was largely just hype to sell the movie, but *Mona* was indeed something new and heralded the beginnings of what would come to be called "erotic realism" by those who scorned the negative connotations of the term pornography.

Things were changing fast in the world of erotic cinema. The days when customs officials seized incoming prints and locked them up in steel mesh cages would soon come to an end, while the celebrated court cases that generated headlines and prompted important cultural figures like Norman Mailer to testify for the defense — imbuing the films with the cachet of social significance — also passed into history. Scandinavian sexuality was no longer being puzzled over in the pages of all the major magazines, and adventure seekers no longer had to book flights to Copenhagen to see movies banned everywhere else in the world. The puritanical legacy of the '50s had been shattered and even Hollywood was getting liberated. As for published pornography, the companies that produced it had by now morphed into faceless corporate entities. Swashbuckling renegades like the Theander Brothers, Berth Milton, Bent Næsby and Leo Madsen, who were willing to appear in connection with their product and philosophize about what they were doing, went on to other things or ceased to appear in public. In other words, now it was just business.

When the '70s drew to a close, Danish exploitation cinema came to an end, and this had implications for the country's image abroad. Rogue producers like Peer Guldbrandsen who made risky films with their own capital were out of the picture, and with Danish sexuality played out as a brand, foreign producers no longer swarmed the beaches, boutiques and model agencies looking for the latest Danish blonde to sign. All this helped put an end to the wave of co-productions that had changed the face of Danish cinema and for better or worse had shaped the country's identity on the movie screens of the world. No doubt to the relief of many, films like *The Daughter, The Sinful Dwarf* and *Swedish Fly Girls* were history.

As the '80s dawned funding for Danish films became almost totally contingent on state support, meaning that scripts had to be approved by the Danish Film Institute. Despite occasional dramas or youth films that were popular with a broad public, there was a trend towards granting support to smaller, more so-called artistic or experimental films. Most of these did poorly at the box office, confused audiences and garnered minimal play on foreign screens where New German Cinema was getting the lion's share of attention. Danish cinema once again receded into the shadows. Today the 1980s are considered something of a dark period, littered, as the dim view has it, with incomprehensible and inaccessible little films made by arrogant and self-absorbed directors to whom far too much public funding had been granted.

And yet one of these incomprehensible little films managed to get noticed. Titled *The Element of Crime*, it won the Bodil award and was even nominated for the prestigious Palme d'Or at the 1984 edition of Cannes. The arrogant and self-absorbed director who made it was of course a young Lars von Trier, and thus here in the deepest recesses of the early 80's darkness the seeds of the country's next film revival were planted. History was repeating itself. One can almost hear festival boss Gilles Jacob proclaim in a fit of enthusiasm: "Finally! A Danish film worth seeing outside Denmark!"

Much had changed. The collective global moviegoing audience was shrinking and von Trier's films were tailored for the art-house rather than the exploitation market. *Breaking the Waves*, for example, played at its peak in America on 26 screens while the Danish export hits of the '60s and '70s played on tens of thousands. But von Trier did represent a kind of continuation in that he was deeply influenced by some of these earlier films, and he too would explore erotic themes albeit in new and provocative ways.

A case in point was *The Idiots* from 1998. It had an erotic component that centered on seven seconds of intercourse footage, which caused significant commotion and showed that the conservative countries were still conservative. But things were loosening up even in these places. After much debate *The Idiots* was released uncut in the UK and in a landmark decision Norwegian censors also finally allowed it to screen in its entirety. (In March of 2006 pornographic films were finally permitted to be sold and screened in Norway without offending details censored out. The outlawing of pornography there had been the result of an unusual alliance between feminists and the Christian party who joined forces on this issue in the '70s after a fractious debate on EU membership had refigured the political landscape. Now, however, porn was legal — as long as it depicted "normal" sexual acts between adults that were not degrading to women or other human beings and did not contain scenes with children, corpses or animals.[1])

Perhaps even more daring than *The Idiots* was a Swedish film from 2004, *A Hole in My Heart*. Here director Lukas Moodysson portrays a severely dysfunctional family as they go about their life in a dreary project flat. The characters include a father who shoots porn movies in the living room and his teenage son who rarely leaves his room, where he sedates himself with dark throbbing industrial music. Moodysson's film was explicit enough to limit play to festivals in most countries, but it revealed among other things that Swedes had not lost their knack for dark social realism.

Other constants in the world of erotic cinema include censors that are still prone to pass a film if the director has presented the sex in a non-arousing manner. Michael Winterbottom managed it in 2004 with his film *9 Songs* which contains 35 minutes of genuine sex between actors Kieran O'Brian and Margo Stilley, but was passed by British censors because the sex was not arousing. Shades of *I Am Curious (Yellow)*. Winterbottom himself happily admitted that those who came expecting porn would be sorely disappointed. Another blow struck for erotic realism. And in the fall of 2006 the American outsider fable *Shortbus* managed to disarm critics by skillfully weaving its gay and straight sex into the narrative flow. In spite of its plentiful hard-core scenes critics were lauding it as a sweet and very funny comedy.

Danish writer Kim Skotte was one such critic. He had found *Shortbus* one of the most entertaining movies at Cannes and its absence from local screens prompted a rumination about the current state of sex cinema, Danish and otherwise.[2] In his own country he reckoned the film would get at best one-off festival play, and that seemed odd considering that sex in all its public manifestations was selling as never before. But perhaps not so odd:

> After all, that's advertising. In that context sex signifies the perfect consumer commodity. Sex appeal is directed at the pocketbook and is used to lure the consumer to everything from candy to booze ... while sex on film in the cinema has become synonymous with pornography. And when pornography itself is addressed, as in films such as Anders Morgenthaler's *Princess*[3] and Moodysson's *A Hole in My Heart*, it is presented as problematic. In other films sex is something frustrated people from New York talk about but get too little of.... We have traveled far from the time when characters in movies had a liberated, jubilant or just simply curious relationship to sex. Happiness, heartbreak, curiosity, euphoria ... these emotions frequently find their most basic expression in the sexual sphere, but physical sensuality plays an extremely modest role in contemporary film.

Commercial considerations had a lot to do with it, according to Skotte. The porn industry was booming as never before and porn was easily accessible, almost unavoidable. On the other side of the equation the commercial cinema market was dominated by expensive action pictures and family-friendly films tailored to appeal to the widest possible audience. Skotte went on:

> The film medium's desire and ability to engage such a vast audience is the greatest enemy of film art. In today's homogenized cinema market a sexual work of art such as Nagisa Oshima's *In the Realm of the Senses* would hardly get theatrical distribution in Denmark. In a way we're back to the pin-up. Sex as commercial stimulation is everywhere while sex as an expression of a liberated, physical zest for life is conspicuous by its absence everywhere except in the triple-X porn emporiums. Narrow-mindedness and pornography is not a pretty mix but that is where we have ended up in these neo-conservative times. *Shortbus* strikes a blow for sex for free people.

Hard-core pornography as an antidote to the hypocrisy of the culture of "tease" was a quaint idea indeed. The concept had been turned on its head and pornography was now the world's greatest consumer commodity. But for people who had experienced the '60s and '70s these ideas died hard. The veteran Swedish producer Inge Ivarson was one of these people and in 2002 he had given new life to the quaint idea that pornography could have educational value, releasing the fifth sequel to *The Language of Love — Language of Love 2000*.

Director Anders Lennberg filled in for Torgny Wickman while sex expert Maj-Briht Bergström-Walan from the original film was again on board to provide commentary. Ivarson took the opportunity to regale the press with some startling revelations about the original film. He claimed, for instance, that they never intended to show actual intercourse in the original film but that one of the actresses was deeply religious and refused to participate in something that was false.[4]

Two versions of this new film were made: a drama for theatrical distribution and a chapterized version for schools in which modern subjects such as AIDS, Viagra and so forth were examined. In the commercial version we get the story of the cool and crazy Stella Måne whose sex talk show becomes a huge hit, winning her rock star status. Everyone loves Stella, but deep inside she's lonely and unfulfilled and seeks solace in gay clubs. Will Stella find what she is looking for? asks the press release.

Did the 85-year-old Ivarson find what *he* was looking for? Namely, another hit late in life and career? No, not exactly, but no one disputed his contention that sex education and frank discussion are perhaps needed even more today than during the era of Sinful Sweden.

The Danish brand of open-mindedness remains unique, and as for that almost scandalous Danish inability to be scandalized, it survives to this day, particularly in the arts world and in the film milieu. The 1992 edition of the Danish Film Workshop festival, for example, featured none other than Ole Ege personally presenting his poetic ode to bestiality, *Bodil, a Summer Day in 1970*. It was drinks all around afterwards in the lounge of the Delta Bio theater as he basked in the renewed if somewhat more modest glow of celebrity, and this time without Simon Spies having sex on the floor. And in the late 90's the Copenhagen Film Museum presented a series of erotic classics that included all the most controversial titles, with Ege again on hand to present his film. (Imagine the outcry if a penny of taxpayer's money went to such ends in America.)

Even Lars von Trier's own studio, Zentropa, produced gay and straight hard-core pornographic films under the auspices of its daughter company Puzzy Power Inc., and nary an eyebrow was raised. Puzzy Power was founded in 1997 in the wake of Dogme95 and even came complete with its own satiric Dogme-like manifesto. With this Zentropa became the world's first mainstream film company with a department dedicated to the production of hard-core pornography. In this way Denmark is still "liberal" in sexual matters.

But when one digs a bit deeper and takes stock of how the issues play out today the picture becomes more complex. Danes *are* tolerant, absolutely; that is indisputable. But *why* are they tolerant? Because they are open-minded and enlightened and have a basic commitment to humanistic principals? Because they are "free"? Because they don't get angry about sexuality like the Americans? Because they don't care? Because they are blasé and indifferent? Because, perhaps, they tend to be followers too lazy to bother having fiercely held opinions that would put them at odds with the group concept that is central to their way of life? Or some combination of all of the above?

One thing that has definitely changed is the way Danish audiences identify with the film medium itself. In 1962 Danes were largely horrified to think that they were being represented by the characters in *Weekend*, but today it's hard to find anyone who isn't proud of the fame that Dogme95 has achieved in the wider world. By extension they are now being represented by the characters in films like *The Celebration* and *The Idiots*, not to mention *The Kingdom*, and few complain.

Those who do complain usually come from the right-leaning end of the political spectrum and are reflexively hostile to many of the current trends in Danish film production. DF (The Dansk Folkeparti), the far-right link in the current conservative coalition government that came to power in 2001 and was re-elected in 2005 and 2007, misses no opportunity via their cultural spokesperson, Louise Frevert, to criticize their sworn enemy. Lars von Trier. They accuse him of stuffing his films with anti–American propaganda and going over the heads of average Danes with his arcane choice of subject matter and obtuse style. But their agenda is broader than that. One suspects they would like to see the story of Liberated Denmark rewritten or better yet erased, and under the banner of defending Danish cultural values they've set out to right the wrongs committed by the "68'er generation." They even accuse an elderly but still active Klaus Rifbjerg of "terrorizing Danish cultural life" for decades, *Weekend* being one of his lesser sins.

The Mohammed cartoon crisis that erupted at the start of 2006 and resulted in the torching of Danish embassies across the Middle East inflamed and polarized the already heated debate on immigration.[5] It also shook up perceptions Danes had about who they were and what kind of country Denmark had become. Yet the subsequent debate over Danish values played out in some odd ways. Right-leaning parties used the controversy to profile themselves as absolutist defenders of free speech and all that is intrinsically Danish, and yet many of the values they champion, including the modern understanding of freedom of speech and freedom of expression, stem directly from the era of Liberated Denmark. For example, a Danish woman's freedom to go lightly clad on a hot summer day is considered an inalienable right, and the fact that a Muslim immigrant might disapprove or misread her signals is often thrown up as proof that Muslims cannot assimilate and seek to impose their own backwards values on Danish society. The whole immigration debate aside, this right to dress as one pleases, or to sunbathe topless in a public park on a sunny day if one chooses, is a direct outgrowth of a Leftist '60s-'70s consciousness.

There is no denying that the image most foreigners have of the country today was forged in the '60s. The positive if vaguely understood idea that Denmark is a tolerant and liberal place is a relic from this period. Some feared that this good reputation was obliterated in one week by the Mohammed cartoon affair, and those fears are not totally baseless as the international press was suddenly awash with reports about a place full of racism and close-minded thinking.

The storm seems to have abated without completely altering long-held stereotypes of Denmark, but it's a mixed picture. In a survey published in late 2006 Americans associated the country with three things: nudity, divorce and women's lib, all topics that could have been grist for the mill of endless witticisms 40 years ago on *Rowan and Martin's Laugh-In*. Europeans seem to be forming a somewhat more current and critical view — including many who live in Denmark itself. An editorial in *Politiken* on January 15, 2009, was representative of those who find the country's current rightward drift disturbing. Author Kamal Qureshi, a Dane of immigrant parentage, laid the blame for Denmark's tarnished reputation directly on the doorstep of DF. Qureshi decried the fact that the well-functioning, tolerant and (largely) non-discriminatory land he had known in his youth had become xenophobic and inward looking.

In Sweden the long held notion that Danes are good natured, open, relaxed and "cozy" has been replaced almost overnight by the perception that they are racist and intolerant. Swedes feel almost cheated, reports the head of Danish studies at Lund University, Hanne Sanders. "They wonder, 'what the hell has happened in that sweet little country next door!'" The immigrant issue today dominates Swedish perceptions of Denmark and at the same time allows Swedes to feel that they are the sole inheritors of the mantle of Scandinavian open-mindedness.

Movies have also played a part, or at least one movie, Thomas Vinterberg's *The Cel-*

Above and opposite: Katja Kean in two scenes from *Pink Prison*, a Zentropa Studios' Puzzy Power production from 1999 directed by Lisbeth Lynghøft.

ebration, which contains a scene with a racist sing-along. Although less than a scientific sampling, a group of Norwegian students did confide to this writer that they thought the scene did accurately depict Danish attitudes.

The new stereotype of Denmark as racist is surely just as superficial and potentially misleading as the old stereotypes that depicted police stopping traffic to let a family of ducks cross the road or teenagers having sex in a public telephone booth, but Sweden can indeed again lay claim to being the most liberal Scandinavian country if only by virtue of its ongoing commitment to a host of progressive causes, gay rights and sexual equality prominent among them. No other country is as active in engaging these issues as Sweden and no other country is as willing to combat purported injustices with legislative remedies.

Action takes many forms. In 2007 a "breast liberation" (Bara Bröst) group of young Swedish women shed tops in a public swimming pool in protest against the objectification of the female body. The movement quickly spread to other Swedish towns but the cause was only slowly taken up by their Danish and Norwegian sisters. And at the start of 2008 there was serious discussion in the Swedish government about banning "sexy" advertisements. Filmmakers have also produced documentaries that have turned the tide of debate, most notably *The Shocking Truth* from 2000 by Alexa Wolf. Purporting to show how pornography exploits and degrades women, the film set in motion a forceful discussion in that country that apparently put an end to the notion forwarded in the '70s that pornography could be fun, liberating and healthy, or at least harmless. Goodbye, Happy Hooker.

Marianne Eriksson, a member of the Swedish Left who at the time of writing also sits in the European Parliament, has been particularly outspoken on these issues. She saw her proposal for the criminalization of prostitution enacted the previous year, making it illegal in Sweden to solicit sexual services but not to provide them, thus putting the onus on the customer instead of the prostitute. "Get rid of the demand" is the theory, "prostitution is never voluntary" is the slogan. It was a bold move and clearly at odds with the policies of other European countries such as Germany and Holland which have legalized prostitution. "What differentiates us from The Netherlands and Germany," Eriksson would state, "is that we link this 'slave trade' with prostitution and pornography. Everyone in the EU is against human trafficking, of course, but we know that 90 percent of this commerce has to do with sexual exploitation — often out-and-out prostitution, but also other sex trades, like strip clubs and pornography."[6]

Some argue that the new law has only made it more dangerous for prostitutes who are now compelled to work in increasingly clandestine circumstances, and that it has spurred the growth of Swedish sex tourism abroad. In 2006 a Norwegian study cast doubts on the effectiveness of the Swedish legislation, and yet many consider it a success. Still, Eriksson has met opposition from her fellow countrymen in at least one area: the banning of pornography. "Swedes are very liberal when it comes to pornography," she admits, claiming that she doesn't want to ban it but only to start a serious debate on the subject.

The proactive Swedish solution that hinges on enacting this type of legislation has been slow to catch on in Denmark. A study taken in 2002 found that only 11 percent of Danes were receptive to this approach. Yet with advocates steadily promoting the idea in the media, that figure had risen to 22 percent by the end of 2006, with the percentage of Danes who opposed prostitution rising from 25 to 42 percent over the same period.[7] Instead of equating prostitution with sexual liberation as some did in the '60s and '70s, it was now linked in the public consciousness to (or) by the public to the global trafficking of women and their pitiable plight. When a public figure recently maintained that some prostitutes can like their work, he was quickly countered by a spokesman for the left-leaning SF party. "We just don't see prostitution as a part of the sexual revolution or as an expression of *frisind*."

It is hard to imagine the issue would have gained so much traction if it had remained solely a question of Danish women, but in any case the way the debate is framed has clearly shifted. In 1972 no less a figure than the Danish prime minister's wife playfully tarted herself up and performed in a mildly bawdy summer revue as a Nyhavn prostitute. That could never happen again. Prostitution is no longer fodder for comedy.

On the legislative front Denmark decriminalized (but did not legalize) prostitution in 1999 in an attempt to alleviate the pressure on already socially marginalized women. In May of 2008 Justice Minister Lene Espersen reiterated the government's intention not to criminalize the purchase of sex but instead to target the pimps and procurers. Debate over the issue continued to percolate throughout the summer as *Politiken* ran a series of muckraking articles on Copenhagen prostitution that tied it to international trafficking, and editorialized for something resembling the Swedish solution.

Others differed with the conclusions. A report that summer claimed that only a tiny fraction of prostitutes were trafficked, and one prominent critic, Danish sociology professor Henning Bech, believed the proposed cure to be misguided. "If there are social problems and drug problems connected with prostitution then those are the problems we should solve. But it's easier to demand new laws than to do something about the actual problems."

But at least among media figures there seemed to be an increasing willingness to turn to legislation, with some calling for widespread bans on pornography as well as prostitution and other perceived social ills. It's debatable if Danes can be persuaded to drop their traditional hesitance towards confronting these issues with legislation, but the fact that such ideas are gaining support indicates things may be changing.

Bech found these growing calls for some variation of the Swedish legislation alarming and blamed feminists. "Swedish feminism," wrote Bech, "has a tradition of moral criticism of sexual behavior, but in the early Danish feminist movement sexuality was not debated on moral grounds, aside from discussion about the exploitation of the female body in advertising."[8]

He sees this as an indication that Denmark is in the throes of a "new Puritanism" in which "sex is perceived as something dangerous and repressive and therefore must be made to seem a problem and to be forbidden." When sexual relations are seen through the prism of what could be called the absolutist Swedish approach to sexual equality, Bech has a point. In a buy-and-sell situation two parties are never equal, and hence prostitution can never be justified. Fair and enlightened enough perhaps, but this logic can also make sex itself problematic since two people are never equal; one always makes more money than the other, one is always older, one always has a better job, and so on. Hence their relationship in all its manifestations including the sexual is unequal and therefore potentially exploitive.

Bech asserts that this increasingly alarmist atmosphere around sexuality has led to, among other things, the pedophilia "witch hunts" which plagued Sweden in the 90s and to a lesser degree Denmark where, between 1995 and 2002, 132 cases resulted in only two convictions. He blames the strident and polarizing tone of the broader sexual debate in Denmark on the influence that Swedish, Norwegian and particularly Anglo-Saxon feminist literature has on the new generation of Danish feminists, and claims that this has led to extremist positions that are very "un–Danish."

What has always been traditionally very Danish, and still is, is the deeply ingrained belief that the state should not meddle in the private or moral affairs of its citizens. This belief, already touched on in these pages, transcends censorship issues that apply to film and literature. For example Denmark seems to be the only country that doesn't have laws against depictions of sexual violence (sado-masochism), and even bestiality remains technically legal.[9]

By the same token abortion is not a political topic in Denmark. There do of course exist opponents of abortion but it is not debated on any significant political level. The Christian People's Party, founded in 1970 largely on an anti-abortion, anti-pornography platform, dropped its anti-abortion plank altogether in 2007. Just as Danes don't like to pass laws that bear on personal, private or moral issues, they also don't like to be lectured on these subjects by their elected officials. Unlike their American counterparts, Danish politicians avoid engaging issues like teen promiscuity, for example. By the same token the Danish media doesn't pry into or make hay with politicians' sexual lives.

Odd as it may seen to an American observer, the Danish right, which otherwise loudly champions so-called Danish values, plays almost no part in today's moral or sexual debate. It's one camp on the left that agitates for the banning of prostitution and other voices at the same end of the political spectrum that call for its legalization. It was the left that created the concept of pornography as a liberating force, and now it is a faction of the same left that attacks the "pornification of the public space" as a major social ill.

This issue bears on increasingly sexualized commercial advertisements and the easy availability of porn, be it on magazine racks or on public TV (Denmark is the only country in the world that shows hard-core pornography on a non-coded TV channel[10]). The effect that all this might be having on the formation of sexual attitudes of teens is being actively debated. It's a rare example of sexual morality becoming a visible public issue, and it seems that for many the chief concern is for the children of immigrants from Muslim countries who have little understanding of Danish open-mindedness in its broader scope. This was never a topic in the '60s or '70s, but today it plugs directly into the wider debate about the emergence of a multi-ethnic society and the problematic aspects of immigration. It has caused some amount of soul searching as that curious creature called *frisind* is dissected and contemplated anew — its legacy and its value as a functioning dynamic in modern society.

After all these years, has conservative America ever managed to come to terms with the Scandinavian way of doing things? Apparently not. Sweden in particular has long been a target of hostility and remains so. *The Financial Times* of March 1, 2009, reported on the antipathy that Americans feel toward the concept of nationalization — and Sweden: "In the U.S., where the idea of being like Sweden is still held up as a bogeyman in national debate, the n-word implies socialism, which goes against many core American principles." Conservative Americans are still deeply suspicious of all the things they mistrusted about Sweden back in the '50s, and they have a few new complaints as well, like Sweden's unwavering commitment to gay rights.

Porn is still a part of the landscape today on Copenhagen's Istedgade Street.

This was put to the test in June of 2004 when Swedish priest Ake Green was convicted of a hate crimes offense and given a 30-day suspended sentence for sermonizing to his congregation on the small island of Öland that homosexuals were a "cancerous tumor on society." He additionally warned that the country risked a natural disaster because of its tolerance of homosexuality. In February of 2005 an appeals court threw out the case, ruling that it was not illegal to offer an interpretation of the Bible and urge others to follow it. In the latest twist, Sweden's chief prosecutor has stated that he felt Green's comments did amount to a hate crime and that he would seek a review.

This in turn prompted a "God hates Sweden" campaign on the Web, launched by an angry right-wing American extremist who felt that Green got a raw deal and that Sweden was going to Hell. However scattershot his aim — one can also visit his "God Hates Canada" and "God Hates America" files — his outburst stands as a lingering manifestation of the kind of anti–Swedish sentiment that still festers within the ranks of conservative America. "Super socialist Sweden" is still deeply suspect.[11] In this case the slings and arrows were unleashed by one man positioned far out on the lunatic fringe, but in the American heartland it's still the darkest '50s when it comes to trying to understand the Swedish way of life. One can imagine that if, for example, an uncut version of *One Summer of Happiness* had a revival run today in Idaho City or Birmingham, Alabama, there would be long picket lines and fiery Sunday sermons railing against what angry preachers might call "the land that decency forgot."

Denmark also continues to take lumps. Conservative American icon Bill O'Reilly, host of the popular Fox TV news show *The O'Reilly Factor* and author of several best-sellers that espouse right-wing viewpoints, appeared on the *Oprah Winfrey Show* in late 2006 to plug his new book about conservative values, *Cultural Warrior*. He used the opportunity to take some unexpected shots at Denmark: "Our troops fight for our country on the other side of globe, and we must fight for our values here at home. Would you want to live like they do in Denmark?" he asked rhetorically. "That's where profane and progressive forces are leading us. There anything goes: euthanasia, legalized drugs, unlimited access to abortion, etc., etc."[12]

The Danish prime minister, Anders Fogh Rasmussen, was Bush's closest alley in Iraq after Britain. He took heat for it, tagged by opponents as a lackey, a puppet, a dupe and worse — and O'Reilly's rant is the thanks he gets? One almost suspects that O'Reilly actually meant Sweden, given the propensity of some Americans to locate Denmark a bit too far to the east, or to confuse it with Holland. The Denmark O'Reilly conjured up is in fact a generic stereotype of Europe that could have fit a score of countries.

Norway, the only one of the three principal Scandinavian countries with a true Bible belt, seems to have escaped the wrath of conservative America, at least for the time being. It is misleading, however, to view the country as a monolithic entity and to label it conservative. Liberal and conservative forces, to use hopelessly diffuse terms, are at play in all three countries, and although their cinema was never particularly liberated there is a unique tradition of dissent in Norwegian literature that is highly respected in Sweden and Denmark. Writers such as Aksel Sandemose, Kjell Askildsen and the globetrotting bohemian Axel Jensen have, along with previously mentioned scribes such as Agnar Mykle and Jens Bjørneboe, caused controversy with their "immoral" texts. Norway is a more polarized society where the right still wields clout on moral issues, and where the cultural debate has always been and continues to be heated and fractious.

Appendix I

Jens Jørgen Thorsen: The Jesus Chronicles

"Any man who besmirches the Lord or soils His holy name, words or sacrament, shall have his tongue cut out while he is still alive and thereafter be decapitated, the head and tongue subsequently to be displayed upon a stage."
—The Danish blasphemy law as decreed in 1683

With uninhibited porn stars like Anne Viklund, Bodil Joensen and a host of uncredited others performing in films freed of all censorship, Danish movies of the early '70s broke almost all existing barriers and taboos. But for all the outrageousness that factored into the cinema of Liberated Denmark, the most controversial film was one that didn't show anything—because it was never made. It existed more as a threat, a promise, a provocation: a hard-core pornographic film that would depict the sex life of Jesus.

There have been many films about Jesus, from directors as diverse as Pasolini, Buñuel, Scorsese, Monty Python and of course Mel Gibson, and they have all generated controversy, but perhaps only in the early '70s and only in Denmark could a hard-core porn film about the son of God even be contemplated. This proposed film was the brainchild of one Jens Jørgen Thorsen, a natural-born provocateur whose threats to make this Jesus film rattled the world and shook the Danish government to its foundations.

Born in Copenhagen on February 2, 1932, Thorsen spent a large chunk of his adolescence in the shadow of fear and repression that hung over Nazi-occupied Denmark. There can be no doubt that his almost visceral hatred of authority figures sprang to a large degree from that experience. Yet he was also very much the product of a progressive set of attitudes and philosophies that came to fruition in postwar Denmark as the seeds of cultural radicalism, sown in the 1930s, flowered into new ideas about individualism, sexuality, art, family structures and so forth. This new way of thinking would lead to the liberal-social policies of the '60s and '70s and the formation of the social welfare state, not just in Denmark but throughout Scandinavia.

After high school Thorsen studied architecture and art history, became a painter and knocked about at various jobs. He worked as a bricklayer, wrote reviews for a daily paper, led a jazz band and put in time as a museum assistant. His knowledge of art history was thorough and in 1967 he wrote one of the definitive books on the subject, *Modernism in*

Danish Painting, but he soon grew disillusioned with the established art world and became one of its most indefatigable critics.

This critical bent led him to embrace Situationism in the early '60s. Drawing ideas from earlier art movements, Situationism was founded in 1957 by among others the artist Constand, the French theorist Guy Debord and the painter Asger Jorn. Jorn had earlier been a disciple of the German school of Bauhaus but was alarmed by its drift toward specialization and functionalism and put off by its embrace of the manufacture of designed objects. He soon launched his own movement, dubbed "Bauhaus of the Imagination."

In 1959 Asger Jorn's brother, Jørgen Nash, joined the international Situationist movement as well. Thirty-nine at the time, he also had a rebellious streak. During the war he had been involved in the Resistance and that got him thrown into Berlin's notorious Moabit prison.

The following year Jorn founded a Scandinavian headquarters for his Bauhaus of the Imagination, on a farm in Örkelljunga, Sweden. Dubbed Drakabygget, it became a play-pen, staging post, laboratory and safe house for rebellious artists of all types. Just about anybody was welcome.

In 1961 at the fifth International Situationist Congress in Göteborg, Sweden, Nash argued that "Situationists must also undertake practical activity in order to infiltrate the established art life." He aligned himself with a group of radical German artists known as SPUR whom other Situationists wanted to expel for their "factionalist activity based on a systematic misunderstanding of the Situationist thesis."[1] The discord grew. At the next annual congress in Paris Nash sided with SPUR and the whole lot of them were thrown out of the movement.

Nash then declared the foundation of The Second Situationist International, with Asger Jorn as a secret member, and the schism was complete. It was at this point that Jens Jørgen Thorsen came on board.

In 1962 Nash and Thorsen organized CO-RITUS, a group dedicated to creating outdoor "actions" which involved the participation of the public and included the screening of films. That same year Thorsen figured prominently in one of their first actions, which took place in Odense, at Galerie Westing, where SPUR work was being exhibited. To symbolize the persecution they felt SPUR was being subjected to, Thorsen, "the most Christ-like" of the bunch (he was actually short and rather "troll like") proceeded through the streets dressed in robes and carrying a heavy cross. The pope's legate in Munich, where SPUR had been hounded with particular zeal, demanded an apology. It never came.

SPUR spent time in Drakabygget. Thorsen made a movie with them, as did the noted Danish experimental filmmaker Albert Mertz who in 1961 had traveled to Munich to shoot *So ein Ding muss ich auch haben* with the group. The film pictured a dreary urban landscape as seen from the viewpoint of disenfranchised artists and sported a soundtrack of music played on toy instruments, this intended as a comment on the conformity and spiritual impoverishment that underpinned consumer society.

Drakabygget soon became the flesh and blood realization of that vaguely alluded-to "beatnik commune" that would intrigue and titillate viewers of *Lolita*. By the residents' own account it was now populated by "poets, farmers, butchers, writers, dentists, doctors, artists, art-historians, truck drivers, transvestites, nuclear physicists, journalists, exhibitionists, hairdressers, sociologists, nymphomaniacs and so forth."[2] It was a living, breathing refutation of the ivory tower concept of artists pursuing their visions in holy seclusion, cut off from the force and unpredictability of life itself. Their goal was to liberate the individual from subservience to authorities and institutions and to allow everyone to participate instead of consigning people to passive spectatorship. As Thorsen would state with characteristic lack of delicacy in 1963, "To turn a person into a spectator is to cut off his balls." Art, it was felt, should consist of situations rather than works, with the audience participating so that artist, work and spectator became one. This brand of Situationism was also an open revolt against the sanctimoniousness and elitism of art, and this was totally in line with Thorsen's own thinking. He was ready.

Film was considered an essential medium and a core group of commune dwellers, with Thorsen in the lead, took up the celluloid challenge. They wanted to create free, spontaneous, anti-academic films, "Situationist films," which according to Thorsen were part of a link in an open situation, the nature of the situation dependent upon the actions of the participants. In their actions and screenings several films were often projected at the same time. It was not the single film existing unto itself as a work (of art) that interested them as much as what the interplay between the films produced, and the atmosphere that resulted. Thorsen's own films were mostly constructed out of found footage, at least in the beginning.

Over the course of 1964 and 1965 the crew from Drakabygget organized five film festivals in Sweden and Denmark. The first one took place in their own camp. The focus was on short films and experimental work, and this was the first time that certain films by Chris Marker and other important artists were screened in Scandinavia. The authorities were unimpressed, however, and harassed them at every turn. It quickly became obvious that the kind of personal filmmaking they advocated could only be screened outside approved channels.

At one of their festivals in 1965 in Copenhagen they unveiled *Pornoshop*, a short film made by Thorsen, Novi Maruni and Niels Holt. It juxtaposed out-takes of commercial pornography available at the time with images that depicted sex in a more natural way. Innocent by today's standards, *Pornoshop* nonetheless created a furor in both Denmark and Sweden, and the film's screening at the Figaro Bio in Halmstad, Sweden, was raided by the police. Yet the filmmakers had been tipped off in advance and had swapped *Pornoshop* with a Donald Duck film, which is what the authorities confiscated.

The last festival had an anti-censorship theme and was to be held at the Atlantic Biograph, but the owners got cold feet. Thorsen & Co. were then compelled to re-organize as a film club, which was the only way unrated films could legally be shown, and move the screenings into a high school. As noted, the Danish press would dub 1965 "the year of porno," to some degree because of the attention this festival attracted.

Pornography was Thorsen's weapon of choice in his ongoing crusade to provoke the authorities and unsettle the bourgeoisie, and while his use of porn in the service of such idealistic ends seems hopelessly quaint today, it must be seen in the context of the times. In Denmark censorship was predominately seen as a way to control, not to protect. It was viewed as a means of repression and even, as the Wilhelm Freddie[3] case revealed, as a class issue. Consequently the fight for sexual freedom was considered a political as well as a personal struggle. In some circles free love was even deemed to be a socialist act, a rejection of jealousy, which was a capitalist emotion — treating people like personal property, owning another person. Yet Thorsen was never so doctrinaire. He was more of a happy anarchist. To him sex was a joyous thing, an affirmation of individuality and a declaration of freedom.

Several decades later Danish writer Bo Tao Michaëlis would reflect on Thorsen's use of pornography in his public provocations, pointing out that Thorsen's enthusiasm for and interest in it was far removed from the simple mechanics of intercourse that characterizes commercial pornography today. "Thorsen's pornographic universe was based on an interpretation of sex as a hedonistic revolt against Puritanism and a carefree, euphoric celebration of naturalness and affection. It was a liberation, a crossing of borders."[4] There existed at this point in the '60s no real hard-core pornographic industry, and of course no Internet. Pornography was not the omnipresent consumer commodity that it is today, the opiate of the consuming masses, so to speak.

Not all of Thorsen's short films concerned themselves with pornography, at least not of the sexual variety. *Do You Want Success?* was a Brylcreem hair gel TV commercial, or rather a lot of Brylcreem commercials. Thorsen had obtained duplicates and simply spliced them together, one after another. The endless repetition allows the viewer to turn a more analytical gaze on material that was only intended to be experienced in a short burst. The impression one gets from a sustained viewing, as the banality of it all becomes increasingly more grotesque and absurd, is, suffice it to say, not what the advertisers intended.

Perhaps more political if just as minimalist and conceptual was *Vietnam* from 1969. It consisted of but a single image: a dead Vietnamese with a crushed head. Various pieces of music are heard on the soundtrack, including "La Marseillaise" and the American national anthem.

By the mid– to late-'60s the Provo movement was something people connected with long-haired radicals from Holland, but Thorsen was his own creation, probably the most visible of all the holy fools in Denmark. At one point he painted a picture of Jesus on the wall of a train station — Jesus on the cross with an erection. And during his production of *Madama Butterfly* at Copenhagen's stately Royal Theater he threw flyers, flowers and stink bombs off the stage. Wherever Thorsen found his audience his aim was to prod them out of the lethargy of passive consumption, mental as well as physical.

In 1970 he directed *Quiet Days in Clichy* (see chapter 2). This film turned him into a true media star and he exploited his new celebrity status by issuing a host of beneficent proclamations, such as "We would have a better world if people would just fuck somewhat more frequently."

"What's next?" he was asked at some point. He wasn't sure but he said that his greatest desire was to make a pornographic film about Jesus.

The idea evolved:

> Of course we could, in connection with Catholicism — which when it comes down to it lives off pornography — aim our guns at the Pope, but I believe the best way to give the Pope a forceful kick in the ass is to turn up the heat on Jesus. He has always interested me, although the use of Jesus as an authority figure repels me. In the film when Jesus rises up out of the grave he'll ball a farmer girl. A nice blonde girl. That by itself signifies in my opinion what Jesus ought to stand for, instead of standing for the repression of life and eroticism.[5]

The tabloids picked up on his comments and began to fan the flames of a new scandal.

Danish Christian organizations were naturally appalled and closed ranks against

Thorsen. He spoke his mind any time someone shoved a microphone in his face. The provocateur was easily provoked. And while being exploited by the media was still a tenuous concept, this was in any event a case of mutual exploitation. Television considered him mostly off limits although he did appear in January of 1972 on the program *Focus on Jesus* to talk about his film, known variously as *The Sex Life of Jesus* and *The Many Faces of Jesus*.

It was all becoming such a sensation — why *not* make the film?

He applied for funding support from the Danish Film Institute in 1973 under the consultant arrangement which had just been created to give impetus to the production of more so-called artistic films. Via this procedure a filmmaker submitted his proposal directly to a consultant, a professional in some aspect of media, who would evaluate it and accept or reject it. In the beginning there were just two consultants, a journalist and a director.

Thorsen's Jesus film was the hottest of hot potatoes dumped immediately into their laps. The journalist said no, but then Thorsen resubmitted the script to the director, Gert Fredholm, who agreed to back it and secured 600,000 crowns of support funding. Fredholm promised that the film would be "blasphemous, pornographic, sadistic, obscene and poetic" and predicted a mighty controversy to follow.

Many Danes were shocked that Thorsen was getting state funding for this outrage. All sorts of rumors began to circulate about the film. At one point Thorsen was photographed with a sky-rocket between his legs, claiming that in his film Jesus would have a similarly gargantuan member. All hell broke loose. Petition drives were set in motion to stop him. Newspaper editors got sacks of angry letters and conservative politicians gave the fire and brimstone speeches of their careers. Five thousand young Christian demonstrators took to the streets in a mass protest. Many perceived the threat Thorsen posed as a serious danger to the whole political system.

Meanwhile the DFI held firm; this was a creative artistic decision and they would stand by it. Something called "the arm's length principle" stipulated that politicians should not meddle in cultural affairs, but this was bigger than all of them. The general public was, in any case, largely unaware of the existence of the DFI or the nuances of film funding and Thorsen bore the brunt of their wrath. Several political parties demanded that the film funding system be changed, but this was awkward since they had just voted it in.

Outside Denmark reaction was just as heated. After all, Thorsen just might do it. Denmark had recently abolished censorship and was being criticized for it around the world, the pope himself calling the country a "nest of sinfulness." Thorsen was seen as the worst case scenario come to life. He wasn't just any old hippie prankster; he had already made a very successful film that had caused controversy pretty much everywhere. Now look at what he was planning!

The German Catholic paper *Neue Bildpost* demanded that the Danish queen intercede in the affair (she didn't), while in America evangelist Billy Graham railed against Denmark as a modern Sodom and threatened to come over in person and talk some sense into Thorsen. The Dutch Parliament, an Argentine archbishop and various other state bodies and religious personages around the world protested. Denmark's reputation was taking a beating and even trade was falling off. Someone even threw a firebomb at the private residence of the Danish ambassador in Rome.

On August 20, 1973, the Vatican daily paper attacked the film project *and* the Danish government, and on the August 28 the pope himself slammed the movie as blasphemy and "a crime against the whole of the Christian religion" in his Sunday sermon. Thorsen responded by offering him a part in the film — as Judas.

Back home in Denmark many from Thorsen's camp on the left were taking a cooler approach, claiming they wanted to wait and see the finished film before judging. Others already understood perfectly what Thorsen was doing: he was creating a happening, not a film, and the audience was already a part of it. And as a happening it was a five-star masterpiece.

Danish critic Kaare Schmidt would later point out that Thorsen eventually managed to turn everyone against each other in ways that defied simple left/right dynamics, and that he succeeded in spotlighting the worst tendencies of the Danish social and cultural condition.

> Arts funding was revealed to be the means by which an entrenched cultural elite sucked money out of the pockets of average citizens, politicians were exposed as puppets and the civil servant class showed itself to be the real power at the controls, outside the bounds of democratic oversight. The populace was easily duped, Christians acted in an un–Christian manner ... those on the Right and Left were all just the same. All the prejudices that anyone could have were confirmed. The confidence that people had in their own judgment was undermined and innumerable egos took a beating.[6]

Thorsen couldn't have hoped for more than this.

Various schemes were cooked up to stop him and take his money away. Various political parties contemplated invoking a Danish law against blasphemy, which stipulated, "Those who publicly mock or deride or insult any religion or form of religious practice that is legally established in this country shall be punished with imprisonment of up to four months or, in extenuating circumstances, with a fine." There were also other laws against discrimination that could be invoked — but how could a film that didn't yet exist violate anything?

On November 27, 1974, the board rescinded Thorsen's grant when he couldn't give them a shooting schedule. He claimed it was for security reasons though it reportedly owed to the fact that France, where he planned to shoot the movie, had passed a law against allowing him to shoot as much as a single frame of film on their soil. His enemies were heartened by the decision to remove his funding but felt sadly cheated of final justice.

In the meantime a hard-core pornographic film about Jesus had actually been made and was now playing in Copenhagen. And virtually nobody noticed. *Jesus Is in the House* was the title and it was quite obviously attempting to hitch its wagon to Thorsen's star. As its publicity blurb read:

> Now comes the film that all of Denmark has talked about for months, the greatest Danish feature film ever produced.... Violence and sex fill the screen in the most uninhibited manner and the Roman orgies are beyond description. The wild and unrestrained nature of this film cannot be surpassed.
> The film is a vivid re-enactment of The New Testament as seen through Jesus' eyes. It is at times condemning and at times gruesome and bloody, but in spite of everything it is a clear and compelling hymn to love. It will be a painful confrontation for a lot of people. It's shocking — it's violent — but it's true."

Jens Jørgen Thorsen performs as Jesus on a street corner to earn money for his film after support was withdrawn (photograph courtesy Preben Niemeyer).

That *Jesus Is in the House* was a fiercely primitive piece of work was evident as soon as the crude hand-lettered opening credits hit the screen. The unheralded Finn Tavbe, a short fellow with long black hair, a pudgy face and a prominent proboscis, cut a less than commanding figure as Jesus. (He apparently never acted again — if acting is the word to use here.) His disciples were allegedly played by members of the radical theater troupe Solvognen (The Sun Chariot), who headquartered in Christiania, a squatted army base in the heart of Copenhagen; the rest were mostly non-actors and unknowns. Shooting took place in a lime pit, which passed as the Sinai Desert, and a stretch of Danish coast stood in for the Sea of Galilee.

In the film Jesus is surrounded by unrelenting sexual excess but never participates in the action himself, commanding a temptress who would seduce him to "Vanish, Satan." And so she does — poof!— in the movie's only use of special effects. The filmmakers claimed that unlike Thorsen's film, theirs wasn't blasphemous. As director Ib Fyrsting told a reporter, "I'm well aware that Thorsen puts great stock in depicting the sex life of Christ, but I've gone through the Bible many times with a fine tooth comb and I still can't find the slightest indication that Jesus went in for sex. Therefore in our film he doesn't either." At least Thorsen was getting people to read the Bible.

With his disciples gathered around him, Jesus dispenses holy wisdoms and dictates. He and the disciples roam the countryside, chancing upon sinful fornicators to whom they mete out brutal punishments. For having intercourse with a woman during her period a man is castrated and stabbed to death, and the woman is also killed. Rapists, adulterers, perverts of all types receive their due; some are stoned to death while one couple is burned alive in their dwelling. For some transgression a woman is staked to the ground and a lit candle is placed in her vagina. As it slowly burns down she screams and twists in pain. Growing bored with this the executioner smashes her head in with a shovel. (While the sex is explicit, the violence is fortunately less so.) It was claimed that all this was depicted in the Bible.[7] Yet some scenes appear simply gratuitous. At one point a woman is gang-raped in the woods, then later a passing priest throws himself upon her splayed and naked body, and after that a lesbian does the same before a nobleman upon a fine horse rescues her.

These scenarios of endless immorality and degradation call to mind de Sade's novel *Justine* and Pasolini's film *Salo*, while the stagy biblical sets evoke distant echoes of Fellini minus his craft and mastery of the medium. Very distant echoes. The static camerawork, the harshly lit interiors and the brain-dead acting deprive the film of any dramatic momentum and never permit the viewer to forget for a second that this is a lowly porn film. It becomes an almost imprisoning experience, and viewers searching for entertaining distractions, such as a moment of humor or genuine emotion, will search in vain. One is by turns numbed and bludgeoned. On the other hand it seems somehow appropriate that these appalling stories of sexual depravity, sadism and violence are being depicted in a squalid porn film. It could only have been made in Denmark and only in the mid-'70s.

The result is a curious mix. One is presented with an endless stream of Gospel citations peppered with the bestial over-amplified grunting and moaning of poorly dubbed pornography while a '70s Moog soundtrack drones in the background. The actors, shabbily draped in robes and sashes, appear to be taking it all seriously as the film lurches towards the concluding crucifixion scene.

Was it just a nasty piece of exploitation or a fearless subversive underground take

The much-wronged woman from *Jesus Is in the House*.

on the brutal founding precepts of Christianity in the spirit of Thorsen? It was a bit of both actually, a strange and disconcerting brew for those determined to see it through (which apparently included not a single film critic). Conceived out of a banal desire to exploit the Thorsen scandal, a true freak of cinema was born — a film so low and untouchable that nobody could even be bothered to throw together a protest.

With Thorsen now having no money to make his movie, things died down a bit. Probably despairing of ever getting the film made, he published the manuscript in book form. Yet in April of 1975 the case took a new turn when the DFI hired two new consultants, one of them being the Swedish filmmaker Stig Björkman, who announced that he intended to grant Thorsen 900,000 crowns. When the news became public, Thorsen's Jesus film scandal was resurrected.

This time it was the system rather than Thorsen that took most of the heat. Nothing could be done about him, but the government's cultural policies could be attacked and opponents seized on this issue. (It soon became fashionable for politicians to pound away at artists or institutions who received public funding for "dubious" projects, and in so doing they could grab the spotlight, promote a wider agenda and not least appear resolute. In this way the Thorsen affair gave birth to a kind of opportunistic political culture that is still very much alive today.)

In 1976, after much political wrangling and grandstanding, the district attorney declared that the film-to-be was a violation of Droit Moral, and the board, bowing to political pressure, rescinded the grant for the last time.

Even some of those who represented official cultural viewpoints waxed sentimental at the news that it was all over, among them Ib Monty, who paid tribute to Thorsen's spunk in the March 24, 1976, *Jyllands Posten*.

> Whether or not he's much of an artist in the traditional sense, he is absolutely top level as a stager of happenings. One man has taken on the whole cultural-political establishment here in this country. He has set in motion a cultural debate the likes of which has never been seen before, and one must hope he hasn't been driven to exhaustion.... The Jesus affair will undoubtedly figure as his masterpiece. It has already had greater impact than any film will ever have, and it has given us new and frightful insight into Danish political life.

But that was hardly the end of it all.

That same year, Thorsen took his crusade to Sweden where, with Stig Björkman's assistance, he applied for funding from the Swedish Film Institute. He managed to secure the sponsorship of a consultant, but Swedish television had the right to veto a film — and they did.

Thorsen's next plan was to shoot the picture in the UK, but here he ran into opposition that proved far nastier and more violent than what he had thus far encountered in Denmark or Sweden. Even the queen, in her capacity as head of the Church of England, spoke out against the project, "disgusting" being her adjective of choice. And the pope himself took yet another swipe at Thorsen. Finally he was denied permission to even enter the UK, without a whimper of protest from Denmark.

Next stop: Israel. Thorsen had declared that he would shoot the film there. Why not? That was the part of the world where the story was set and the defilement of the holy sites would rattle all of Christianity. Brilliant. This prompted more international protest but the issue was short-lived since pornography, as the Israeli government informed him, was illegal. And without porno, no Thorsen film. Or at least no Thorsen film controversy.

Other countries began preparing their excuses in advance.

The decision to rescind Thorsen's grant in 1976 had been made on very shaky legal grounds and a couple of years later he sued to get his money back. This court case would end up lasting 11 years, over the course of which figures from the Danish cultural world were called upon to give testimony in his defense. The court wasn't exactly choosy about who could testify, and one of those who did weigh in on Thorsen's behalf in 1981 was a virtually unknown student from the Danish film school, a skinny, recalcitrant kid named Lars von Trier. As noted, *Quiet Days in Clichy* had made a great impression on him and would, along with *Weekend* and *I Am Curious (Yellow)*, prove influential in forming the concept of Dogme95.

Finally, on October 10, 1989, the judge ruled that Thorsen's script had to be considered a "new and independent work" and thus it did not constitute a violation of Droit Moral under modern interpretation.

The ruling was a vindication of sorts for Thorsen although he never did get his grant back. Instead he applied for, and got, more funding under the new 50/50 arrangement which had been instituted that same year. Via this procedure the script was evaluated by a committee on more general criteria.

Now at long last he would make his Jesus film, although it would be based on a new script and would contain no pornography. Titled *The Return*, it opened theatrically in Denmark on March 13, 1992.

As a happening Thorsen's Jesus film had been top rate, but here and now, finally as a film, critics found it somewhat less so. Typical was Morten Piil's review:

> Thorsen's Jesus is but a new variant of the Henry Miller figure the director already portrayed in *Quiet Days in Clichy*—a relaxed lover-of-life, a champion of eroticism and an anarchist. Love is his weapon, and of course he feels solidarity with the plane hijackers in the film who were considered heroes in certain anarchist circles in the '70s. Just as predictable is the way the religious authorities oppose him, and in general he is kicked around and mocked. This Thorsen provocation, especially the erotic component, is in 1992 hopelessly past its sell-by date, and what remains is a clumsy, slow moving allegory full of old effects and shabby preachments.

Maren Pust filed for the Danish daily *Information*, March 13, 1992:

> This film has been in the works going all the way back to the beginning of the 1970s and the director Jens Jørgen Thorsen has been subjected to endless bureaucratic indecency that would amaze even Kafka.
>
> In *The Return* Jesus is sent down to earth to save it from apocalypse. He becomes enmeshed in a plane hijacking, falls in love, is sentenced to death and is liberated by the Church. In the end, disappointed by humanity, he flies up to our Lord with the girl he has fallen in love with.
>
> By now we have all heard so much about the Jesus film and how it would be really naughty with loads of sex, etc., but it must be said from the start that compared to the rumors it is exceedingly chaste. We see some corrupt priests send lustful glances in the direction of prostitutes and beatific young boys, and a couple of quite poetic scenes take place where Jesus and his lover throw themselves into gentle embraces.
>
> The film is a slapdash compilation of situations. Food is thrown, people fart ... charac-

A scene from Jens Jørgen Thorsen's *The Return*.

ters dance in clerical formality. It appears they had fun making the film, and that undoubtedly owes in part to the fact that they received carte blanche to goof around in the style of an amateur school play. It doesn't help that they have also attempted to make an action film out of the foolery: stunt man Martin Spang Olsen gets beaten around and falls downs the stairs ad nauseam, cars plow into each other and shots are fired wildly in all directions. It contributes nothing to the film and it is difficult to understand why they used such resources in this way.

There is one place in the film where the genuine "happening" atmosphere for which Thorsen is renowned shines through. Jesus has come to Denmark and eventually he pulls himself together and gets down to business. He talks to a crowd about how God exists in everything and the crowd is immediately lit by the holy fire, parading through the city streets in protest against the want and suffering abroad in the world. "Down with hunger," reads a sign. Police appear and proceed to attack the demonstrators, beating those who would oppose violence. And of course the peace-lovers fight back! In this brief flash the film calls its own bluff; it is obvious that all the slapstick effects were unnecessary when one little scene without any explosions or fireworks has managed to draw attention to the congenital absurdities of life.

The Return has a bit of a moth-eaten '60s comedy feel about it, on display in scenes such as the one in which the pope dances to a Tom Lehrer melody, "The Vatican Rag."

Thorsen had become a bit of an artifact. His vision of sex as an assault on bourgeoisie conformity was so very '60s and clearly out of synch with the early '90s when it was well known that (unprotected) sex could just as easily kill you as liberate you. Thorsen was very much a creature of his times, for better or worse, and the movie evinced that in every frame.

Thorsen survived the bad press. He knew what bad press was.

In 1998 the Danish Film Museum staged a retrospective called Super Love, an ode to all things late '60s revolutionary. Thorsen, now 66 and living in Sweden for some years, was naturally a part of the proceedings. As program notes promised, "Jens Jørgen Thorsen, the provocateur who never lost his fizz, will come and turn the Film House upside-down." And so he did, appearing in person with a clutch of spools on November 28.

Two years later, on November 15, 2000, he passed away.

Although he continued to the end to do colorful abstract paintings on large canvases, his lifestyle had grown more sedate in later years and he was much less in the public eye. But it wasn't like him not to try and get in the last word. And he did, after a fashion, as anyone can see when they visit his tombstone in Copenhagen's Assistens graveyard. There stands the simple phrase inscribed in the polished granite, "Freedom is not for sale."

Thorsen still casts a long shadow across Danish cultural life, and his memory was invoked by any number of writers when the Mohammed cartoon crisis broke in early 2006. His lampooning of the pope and other religious figures over the years, not to mentioned his wall painting of a sexually aroused Jesus, crystallized the whole freedom of speech issue decades ago. Ironically the Danish right, so passionate today in their defense of freedom of speech when it applies to the satirizing of Islam, was somewhat less so back when Thorsen was satirizing Christianity. As the Danish prime minister today defends that sacred democratic freedom in absolutist terms, Thorsen can only be chuckling in agreement from beyond the grave.

Sensitive Muslims, for their part, should be thankful that he isn't still around to give them a lesson in the liberating power of satire. He must also be credited for showing how religious so many people in Denmark really are. One of the main criticisms today is that fiercely secular Danes cannot understand the offense the cartoons caused to people of faith, but Thorsen was able, as seen, to light a fire under the people of faith and to bring them out *en masse*.

Below are credits for some of Thorsen's best-known films.

As Director

Quiet Days in Clichy, 1970 — Director & script: Jens Jørgen Thorsen — Producers: Klaus Pagh, Henrik Sandberg, Knud Thorbjørnsen, Anders Stefansen, Dirch Passer — Cinematography: Jesper Høm (b/w), Cinematography assistant: Teit Jørgensen — Music: Country Joe McDonald, Ben Webster, Young Flowers, Papa Blues Viking Jazz Band, Andy Sundstrøm — Actors: Paul Valjean (Joey), Bruce Johansen (Joey's voice), Wayne John Rodda (Carl), Louise White (Surrealistic girl), Ulla Lemvigh-Müller (Nys), Lisbet Lundquist (Jeanne), Avi Sagild (Mara), Susanne Krage (Christine)

The Return, 1992 — Director & script: Jens Jørgen Thorsen — Cinematography: Jesper Høm — Music: Jimmy Dawkins — Production: Jens Jørgen Thorsen, Superfilm — Actors: Marco di Stefano, Johnny Melville, Jed Curtis, Jean-Michel Dagory, Benny Hansen, Jacob Haugaard, John Hahn-Petersen, Paul Hagan

Dreams of Thirteen (U.S., 1974 release title)/ *Wet Dreams/Dreams of a Young Girl* (UK) — A compilation film in which 13 filmmakers contributed with works that bore on an erotic theme and were of approximately ten minutes each. The project was organized by Jim Haynes in the wake of his second "Wet Dream Film Festival" in Amsterdam in 1971 (see Appendix 3) and all the films were shot in Holland. Contributors: Heathcote Williams/Max Fischer/Nicholas Ray: "The Janitor"/Jens Jørgen Thorsen: "A Piece of Social Realism"/Lasse Braun, aka Falcon Stuart/Lee Kraft/Dušan Makavejev, aka Sam Rotterdam: "Politfuck"/Hans Kanters/Peter Gruelich/Geert Koolman/Oscar Gigard: "Dragirama"/Melvin Miracle/Niels Janette Walen (Longtime Haynes accomplice Jack Moore was slated to make a segment but apparently dropped out, or one of the above names is his pseudonym.)

AS ACTOR

Gold for the Tough Guys of the Prairie *(Guld Til Præriens Skrappe Drenge)*, 1971 — A Danish Western (!) wherein five tough hombres battle nasty villains, in the process getting help from an Indian girl, Shannahoo. This was a follow-up to *Tough Guys of the Prairie (Præriens Skrappe Drenge)* from 1970 where the heroes rode ponies instead of real horses. This time they got real horses, and a real Situationist in Jens Jørgen Thorsen who played the role of a cowboy. Both installments were closer to classic Danish folk-comedies than rough-hewn Westerns in the American sense and are affectionately known at home as "Danish potato westerns."

The Wolf at the Door *(Oviri)*, 1986 — A biographical film about the artist Paul Gauguin who is played by Donald Sutherland. Many Danish cultural personalities of the period acted in the film including Thorsen who played a drunk man in a ditch.

The Horsemen of Justice *(Retfærdighedens Rytter)*, 1989 — Experimental surrealistic version of a Christmas fairy tale. Thorsen played a man in a grilled-sausage wagon.

Appendix II

Ole Ege, the Gentleman Pornographer

"Without soul it's just hamburger."
— Ole Ege

(In 1996 Danish erotic pioneer Ole Ege, discussed earlier in this book primarily in connection with his film *Bordello*, sat down with another local cultural personality, Morten Lindberg [at one time known as the Danish Barry White and who today goes by the moniker of Master Fatman], to talk about his life and work. The biographical interview, published in the 1996 April/May edition of the now defunct arts tabloid, *Nat og Dag [Night and Day]*, paints a picture not only of Ege's participation in porn but serves to encapsulate almost the entire history of Denmark's racy past. We use this interview as a point of departure for our portrait of Mr. Ege, and it is also the source of all unattributed quotes.)

While the brash and the beautiful were busy grabbing headlines, no one in Denmark was more active in more phases of commercial porn production than the soft-spoken, self-effacing Ole Esper Ege. He started out snapping risqué still photos in the mid–'50s and went on to produce 8mm and 16mm short films of an increasingly explicit nature in the '60s before taking the final plunge into hard-core feature filmmaking in the early '70s, combining art, underground and exploitation in the process.

Ege was a man with persistence, some talent and the right idea at the right time. His story reads like the typical "small town boy makes it big," but in fact there was nothing typical about him and in the field of commercial pornography he was very much an anomaly.

To start with, he was always a loner and experimenter in a field where most of his competitors adhered to formula and convention. Although good at business, he never thought of himself as primarily a businessman and never considered his images to be product. In one of the most ruthlessly capitalistic and exploitive of industries he was apparently a man of conscience and in reflective moments known to describe himself as a very moral, very religious fellow.

Finally, he has remained visible and on record in an industry predicated upon anonymity. After his career in film production ended, he founded The Museum Erotica in Copenhagen and turned it into a local institution, that titilated untold numbers of tourists and aquainted a new generation of Danes with the facts of life. When not at work, he could often be found holding court for ad hoc groups of visitors and writers, tossing off bons mots about legends of yore like Bodil Joensen and Simon Spies and performing his duties as keeper of the flame of Copenhagen's flaming past.

His father was a police chief, 44 when he married Ege's mom, a good looking woman of 23. She gave birth to little Ole six years later, in 1934. Ege claims that both were virgins when they got married and that his father didn't know what a woman looked like without her clothes on. It was a very repressed time, he points out. Ege spent his childhood in Hobro, a small town in the middle of Jutland, the very definition of provincial.

His parents eventually divorced and Ole and his mom left town and traveled across the Kattegat Strait to Copenhagen where they found a modest two room flat. He continued his schooling, passed his exams and got a job as a trainee-clerk in an office. In 1954 he traveled to Canada to work in a gold mine.

But he was more interested in silver — silver nitrate that is, his traveling companion having taught him how to take photographs, develop the film and make prints. It was like being given the key to a secret world. When he returned to Copenhagen he was one eager amateur photographer. He was obsessed with photography and hatched plans to combine it with his other obsession — girls. Now he wanted to take pictures of girls, preferably with their clothes *off*.

He started hanging out at Copenhagen's legendary Dixi Bar. In the mid-'50s the joint was jumping. It had the longest bar in town and a jukebox stocked with swinging music from the States that you couldn't hear anywhere else. The Dixi was base camp for the "American Girls," Danish gals who were fascinated by all things American — cars, movie stars, rock 'n' roll, and not least the handsome GIs in uniform who would come up to Denmark from their bases in Germany to see the sights. Some of the best looking women in Copenhagen hung out at the Dixie. These women were not prostitutes. The servicemen would buy them drinks in exchange for conversation and perhaps a sight-seeing tour around town. Of course some got lucky, and no doubt all of them hoped they'd get lucky. But basically the girls just liked their style, their tempo, their brash American ways ... and the stuff they brought with them that you couldn't get in severely strapped postwar Denmark: chewing gum, nylons, Coca-Cola, cash to throw around and wild 45 records.

Ege didn't merit a glance from the finest of these dolled up "American Girls." He wasn't a GI in a smartly pressed uniform and he didn't possess Robert Mitchum moviestar looks. He was a slender, not particularly dashing Dane from Hobro who lived with his mom. But he was neatly dressed, he had charm, he had lines and he liked the same cool music. And he *could* speak fluent Danish, and he *had* been to Canada, at least. All that (and the promise of a modest amount of cash) was enough to talk a woman he met at the Dixie into coming over to his place and posing for some photos — in his room, with the door locked so his mom wouldn't wander in. He had the camera and the technology and could develop the film himself. He just needed what Hugh Hefner, Russ Meyer, Armando Bo and all the other great sexual pioneers needed at the start: a girl who would take her clothes off.

Ege claims that early on he realized one important thing about women: they like to be admired and feted. And maybe photographed. Lindberg speculates in the interview that Ege's makeover as a swinging photographer must have led to plenty of sex, but Ege demurs with evasive modesty. He says he got his share but denies he exploited his relationship with the models — a far cry from most makers of "dirty movies" who are eager to claim otherwise.

It was nothing too spectacular to begin with. His first subject wouldn't strip naked. There was some talk about a see-through nightgown.

There were other girls that Ege photographed in his room, dubbed Stork Studio, but he realized he had to do something more to get his business up and running and so he approached the newspaper *Politiken* about placing an ad. That was something that normally only officially certified photographers were allowed to do, undoubtedly to keep the likes of Ege out of the picture. The wrong fellow could ruin the good reputation of the whole profession. God forbid!

In any case he got his ad in. Some girls showed up.

His mom was a model at the art academy at Charlottenborg at that point, being paid 17 crowns per hour. He paid his models the same. "That's what they make at Charlottenborg," he told them, and that was fine — even though it was barely a pittance.

There was a party-like atmosphere in his room during these sessions, with Ege spinning the latest hot American records and pouring the vermouth. With some chat and some charm the photos got taken. One imagines a scene similar to Antonioni's *Blow Up*, Ege the poor man's David Hemmings. Nothing vulgar. He claims the pics were as innocent as could be (at least by today's standards).

He was taking tons of photos at this point, the kind of shots where you could see the girl's face and a glimpse of bosom. He put together a mail-order series but at that time Danish magazines would not accept advertisements that involved postal transactions, so he advertised in a Swedish magazine. That was fine since the magazine was also distributed in Denmark as well as Norway, and Ege got orders from all three countries. He was in business.

Not that it always went smoothly. The aforementioned Paragraph 234 of the Danish Criminal Code, a vague and to many hopelessly antiquated catch-all intended to regulate Danish morality, was now in the late '50s being aggressively enforced by the police as it suited them, making life hard for Ege in the process. Business was off and on.

In 1957 he got legitimate employment as the editor of a photography magazine produced by Lademann publishers. After hours he continued doing his own thing. His style was developing. He learned a second valuable lesson: it was one thing to take the pants off a woman and photograph her, and something else entirely to do it aesthetically.

Unfortunately his sexy photos stuck in the craw of the postal authorities and the tabloid *B.T.* blew the story wide open. Old man Lademann got a call from his elderly aunt who asked him what in God's name he'd gotten himself involved in. He had known nothing about Ege's other interests but let him keep his job in exchange for a promise to knock off with the other stuff, which he did ... for a while.

He had also been shooting a lot of 8mm film. His early work consisted of women yawning or stretching in wind-blown meadows or awkwardly soaping themselves down in tiny bathrooms hardly big enough for both of them to squeeze into. These were basically figure studies or home movies, but eventually he learned how to film women with some artistic grace and he began to shoot scenarios that included two women or a woman and a man, all containing full frontal nudity but without touching or evidence of arousal.

Ege's mother never approved of her son's occupation but she never threw him out. He moved out on his own accord, in 1964, and quit his editing job at about the same time. He now launched his own photography magazine called *Sofus*. He did all the work on it himself. It was a deeply serious undertaking and lasted ten issues, by which point he had had enough of deeply serious and threw himself back into the erotic genre.

But he had to walk a fine line, producing images that were as daring as possible without falling afoul of the law. He had already been dragged into court in 1957 and 1960 and compelled to spend vast sums on his defense, but he and his competitors, people like the flamboyant Leo Madsen and the Theander Brothers and Ole Ørsted of Venus Films, could make fortunes if they could navigate the choppy legal waters. These were uncertain but exciting times for a rogue photographer with a nose for business. It was a gambler's life and Ege did very well for himself, soon making enough to buy a villa in Gentofte in Copenhagen's exclusive "Whiskey Belt" and wheeling to work every morning in a white Mustang. And all this from pictures that were thoroughly soft-core.

By 1967 he had rolled the dice once too often. One day his offices were raided by the police and his entire inventory was confiscated. They had targeted the six biggest producers of Danish erotica, including Ege and Leo Madsen — though Madsen managed to slip through their net. He had been tipped on the raid in advance and cabbed all his goods over to Sweden in the dead of night. The subsequent court proceedings broke Ege. The villa, the white Mustang, the high-rent office space — gone.

But written censorship was abolished that same year and he realized the tide was turning in his favor. With his meager remaining assets he regrouped and founded Marmalade Films, now focusing on the production of 8mm movies. The problem with this was that unlike still photography he couldn't develop it himself, and since no one developed film in Denmark he had to send it to England, which was also highly problematic. He recalls getting lots of polite letters from Kodak-UK telling him they had confiscated his film because it contained indecent pictures.

Then he started sending the film to Stockholm. As noted earlier, Sweden, unlike the UK and Denmark, had not signed the Geneva Convention pact of 1923 which among other things obligated member countries to combat the production, sale and circulation of pornography. Ege soon became one of the biggest producers of 8mm erotic film in Denmark. This was partly because his films were in color, which was not so common at that time, and he had also begun to produce and sell 16mm shorts which were in great demand.

By now in late 1968, the soft-core market that he had helped to pioneer was history. The raids of 1967 had left a vacuum which had been filled with imported hard-core, mostly from Sweden but also from England where apparently hard-core could be made but not domestically distributed. Hard-core was now the only thing anybody would pay money for, so that's what Ege delivered. He also looked to foreign markets and placed ads in American magazines. He reaped a windfall of orders, but that was not without complications as the American postal authorities were at that point very attentive to packages coming from Denmark. They had their own censors and if they ruled that something was over the line they simply impounded it. For the American trade he wanted to avoid a company name with "film" or "photo" in it and so he threw them a curveball and named his mail-order operation "Danske Farve" (Danish Color). He knew they wouldn't understand that.

He was making good money again but having his doubts. He felt he was wasting his talent. There was no style or aesthetic attached to hard-core and he knew he could do better, but everything else was simply passé at this point. So he just decided that he would do "quality" hard-core.

Still, on a personal level, the exploitive aspects of the work came to trouble him more frequently.

Ege had his doubts in 1970 when the Japanese-American filmmaker and sculptor Shinkichi Tajiri approached him with the idea of making a documentary about the most outré Danish porno celebrity of the moment: Bodil Joensen, who had become familiar to consumers of porn as well as the tabloid trade for the sexual acts she performed with her animals. Although bestiality repulsed him, Ege was persuaded to participate and they secured Bodil's cooperation for a fee of 2000 crowns. The 20 minute, 16mm film they made was intended to be a respectful documentary, the antithesis of an exploitation film. Its international title, *Bodil, a Summer Day in 1970*, was low-key and tasteful enough, though in Denmark it got tagged with the less artful moniker of *The Boar Girl, Bodil (Ornepigen Bodil)*.

Ege shot scenes of Bodil in various situations, in her home surrounded by personal memorabilia and family photos and out in the fields engaged in her work. The film exudes a fascinating naturalism and in one sequence, where the naked farm girl tries to coax a stud into an unwilling mare, the viewer becomes gripped by the logistical challenges at hand and forgets what the film is really all about. But not for long, since scenes of Bodil's sexual dalliance with various animals are explicit and unflinching, cushioned only somewhat by Beethoven's Pastorale which they were forced to lay over the whole film when the sound on their tape recorder malfunctioned. If pornography is all about context then one might argue this isn't a pornographic movie at all, but just one of the most true and honest personal portraits ever filmed. Few were able to see it like that.

In his interview with Ege, Morten Lindberg refers to the film's beautiful pictures, the classical music and the scenes of a nude Bodil riding her horse through the landscape, all of which he likened to some

Just a country girl: Bodil Joensen interviewed on her farm.

kind of Nordic saga. It seemed clear to him that Ege had greater ambitions than to just make porno. But it also seemed obvious that things were going tragically wrong for Bodil, and Lindberg asks Ege whether he tried to persuade her to stop.

"No, I didn't," he replies, "but that was also probably the main reason why I left the business."

The film was completed in time for submission to the Wet Dreams Film Festival which was held in Amsterdam at the end of November 1970. It won the Grand Prix, something that Shinkichi Tajiri always regretted. As he wrote in 1972:

> Accepting the "Grand Prix" at the first Wet Dreams Film Festival was the worst mistake we made with our film, but we were too flattered by the response at the time to realize it. Today it is referred to as an "underground porno classic" and "porno" was precisely the label I was trying to avoid in making a tender documentary about a very special person.... (From the start) the porno leeches gathered around Bodil and ruthlessly exploited her as a sex curiosity. In the film I wanted to leisurely investigate and give human depth to a person who was being abused as a two-dimensional sex phenomenon, but lack of time and funds and the announcement of the upcoming Wet Dreams Film Festival pressed us to complete the film. We didn't think we could ever show it publicly and this seemed the ideal opportunity. Bodil has become, in spite of our efforts, porno's "superstar," but she remains more than a historical/political/revolutionary personality; she is a fragile and precious human being. PS: Contrary to rumors of suicide that reach me regularly every month or so — and must be indicative of a disturbed society that cannot comes to terms with her — Bodil lives!

Ege was also taken aback by the way Bodil was so thoroughly exploited. "That's why I call her 'pornography's Danish Jeanne d'Arc,'" he would often remark.

He was taken aback, but apparently not too taken aback since he included her in a scene in his next film the following year, the 54 minute featurette *Pornography — A Musical*. Billed as the first "porn musical," it consisted of 10 or 11 of Ege's short films and included explicit material as well as soft-core items that went as far back as 1964.

The musical component was provided primarily by American jazz legends Kenny Drews and Dexter Gordon who both lived for periods in Copenhagen in the '60s and '70s (as did another celebrated jazz musician, Ben Webster, who contributed music to *Quiet Days in Clichy*). A sequence of Gordon playing live in a Copenhagen club opens the movie on a dreamy note.

These segments are at their best when a romantic or playful home movie spirit shines through, and when this occurs it is almost exclusively in the earlier films. Ege's attempts to merge image and music into pure mood work best here in nostalgic set pieces like *Dream Girl*, where the camera pans over a lone beauty, and *Three Healthy Girls* in which three gals undress each other to up-tempo music and tussle about at a heated up pace.

The music is less effective and even distracting in the later hard-core sequences. Here wistful jazz juxtaposed with penetration close-ups and cum shots is simply absurd. (What Dexter Gordon thought about his music used in the service of such images is unknown.) *Pornography — A Musical* is a textbook example of the bind that Ege and other practitioners of quality porno found themselves in when market forces compelled them to cross the threshold from soft-core to hard-core. Why get Dexter Gordon to supply moody piano music when you can just get the actors, or anybody, to sit around a tape recorder and fake the moans and squeals? Explicit imagery virtually precludes any attempt at contextualization and atmosphere becomes superfluous; consumers of hard-core pornography are generally not out after classy atmosphere or an artistic experience. To his credit Ege occasionally attempts to set up the situations: boy meets girl and they walk through the streets to a room, rather than just commencing with the action from the opening bell. This calls to mind the old maxim that the best porn films start with the actors clothed. And by employing the short film format he deserves credit for keeping it simple and avoiding that device that is the curse of so many pornographic films — a plot. Still, he clearly has a much harder job creating atmosphere or fun in the explicit shorts, or, despite some inspired sequences, making them even unique at all. Hacks with Bolex cameras were grinding out similar stuff all over the world and one penetration close-up was pretty much the same as the next, no matter what the actors were wearing or what music was playing. It was a dead end for any filmmaker or photographer who aspired to express himself or create art, as Ege well knew.

We see some familiar faces here. Bent Rohweder who later performed in *Bordello* as the baker and in *Facts: Copenhagen Sex-Report* appears in *The American Girl* short, while a young Ilse Damsgaard of *24 Hours with Ilse* fame performs explicit sex in the short entitled simply *Ilse*. Finally, the unidentified, unfamiliar (and securely bound) female victim in *Spanking* deserves mention for her very bizarre facial expressions, captured in extreme close-up by Ege's fluid hand-held camera work.

In 1972 Ege made *Bordello*, described earlier. By that point he had met the love of his life, Ulla Bjergskov (later Ulla Ege Bjergskov), and he found that his immersion in the world of porno was disturbing his energies and affecting his personal life. That she was also in the film, not to mention pictured nude in a newspaper report on it, perhaps also complicated things. When filming began to interfere with his relationship with her, if only because he was so taken up with his work, he quit. Had he stayed in the business he probably would have been a multi-millionaire today.

Eventually his common-law marriage to Ulla dissolved. Looking for peace and quiet, he moved to the remote and bucolic island of Ærø and opened a nightclub.

For many years thereafter he lived a private life, but in 1992 he returned to the spotlight, publishing the book *Erotic Dreams (Erotiske Drømme)* and co-founding the aforementioned Museum Erotica together with business partner Kim Riisfeldt-Clausen.

The museum housed his impressive collection of erotic artifacts, photographs and publications that go back to the early 1900s. Much of what he himself produced between 1957 and 1972 was also exhibited in this historical setting, locked in display cases and appearing quaint, dated and harmlessly kitsch in some instances. It hardly does justice to the fact that his images were considered anything but harmless at the time, and that he personally knew and had feelings for many of the women pictured.

One wonders how a pioneering spirit like Ege would make his name today. Operating an adult website and spamming the multitudes with intrusive offers for cum-drenched cuties in a thousand positions? Hardly. That was never his game. The last glimmers of glamour have been extinguished, the soul has gone out of pornography, as difficult as it might be for some to comprehend that pornography can have soul ... and in the end there was no place for a gentleman pornographer except among the dusty glass cases in his own museum.

Postscript: The year 2008 brought bad luck when Riisfeldt-Clausen died after a fall at his home, and in March of 2009 economic problems forced the Museum Erotica to declare bankruptcy. Efforts to obtain support from the city fell on deaf ears and in June the process of selling off the contents began. Denmark's iron man of porn is still active and has a biography in the works, *Tabu— Fra Forbud Til Frigivelse (Taboo—From Prohibition to Liberation)*, but the shuttering of the museum marks the end of an era. No longer will startled tourists be handed promotional leaflets by the legions of good looking gals Ege employed to the task. No longer does he host wild parties on the premises or give personal guided tours. And no longer does he cruise the streets in his beloved 1972 Lincoln Continental emblazoned on the side with the museum's logo.

To the very end Ege retained a bit of the joie de vivre that motivated the founders of liberated Denmark. To these people sex was something to celebrate.

FILMS ABOUT OLE EGE

Ole Ege— The Naughty Boy (Den Grimme Dreng), 1996, 62 min. Directed by Torben Skjødt Jensen, produced by Steen Herdel & Co. and The Danish Film Workshop. A wealth of images and footage provide illustration for the many reminiscences and stories that Ole Ege tells with thoughtful engagement as he trolls back through his experiences in Danish erotica. Humorous tales and asides mix with more personal reflections to paint a full and intriguing portrait of this curious figure for whom the tag of "pornographer" is surely miscast.

More Sex Please (Tugt & Utugt), 2001. Produced by same production company as above. This film bears on wider erotic subject matter but Ege is interviewed and supplied the idea for the film.

Underneath the Skin (En Rem Af Huden), 2003, 24 min. Directed by Michael Noer, produced by The National Film School of Denmark and Julie Tarding. As promotional text describes it: "Ulla was one of his models but she vanished long ago. Ole is trapped by strange forces in the borderland between dream and reality, sensuality and pornography, love and destruction."

Appendix III

The Wet Dream Film Festival

The Wet Dream Film Festival was a major event in erotic cinema and many Danish films were screened over the course of the two editions that were held in 1970 and 1971. Oddly enough it took place not in Copenhagen but Amsterdam which was more widely considered to be the counter-culture capital of Europe.

The genesis of the festival can be traced back to one leisurely Sunday afternoon in 1969 when two former editors of the London underground paper *IT* met for a cup of tea. Coincidently they were both American expats, Bill Levy and Jim Haynes. Haynes in particular had been a creative force in the British underground for some time, having among other things co-founded The Arts Lab on Drury Lane which counted Christine Keeler, James Baldwin, Dick Gregory, Ronnie (R.D.) Laing and Mama Cass among its frequent visitors, and where a young David Bowie used to rehearse undisturbed. Prior to that Haynes had established a club called the UFO which boasted Pink Floyd and Soft Machine as house bands. *IT* had been going since 1966 but Haynes's involvement with the paper had by this point for all intents and purposes ceased.

Haynes and Levy bandied about the idea of starting up a paper about sexuality and sexual freedom. Al Goldstein's *Screw* had been founded in November of the previous year and was an obvious influence. Moreover both Haynes and Goldstein were of the same generation, born in 1933 and 1936 respectively, and drew from similar influences. Both were disciples of the unconditional honesty of Henry Miller and the uncompromising, disarming humor of Lenny Bruce. Yet Haynes and Levy wanted to do something different. *Screw* was characterized by its scathing irreverence and humor and they wanted to put the focus more on sexual liberation — and libertarianism — than humor.

They named their new paper *Suck* and then asked the playwright Heathcote Williams and a young Australian woman named Germaine Greer to join them on the editorial board. In 1970 Greer would gain worldwide fame with her book *The Female Eunuch*, but at this point she had only just swapped Shakespeare for sex as her main field of interest. She was writing for various underground papers, so she signed on to *Suck* as well.

They had their first meeting in the offices of *The Transatlantic Review* where Heathcote was an associate editor. He was at the time going out with Swinging London's iconic super model Jean Shrimpton, so she came along as well. (At some point during the meeting Heathcote and Shrimpton excused themselves and went into another room to make love.) Realizing that an explicit publication like *Suck* could never be headquartered in

London, they decided to publish it in Amsterdam where the noted Dutch Fluxus artist Willem de Ridder offered to oversee design and production.

As they predicted, the paper was cursed, railed against and banned in Britain. Scotland Yard even sent a couple of plainclothes officers over to Amsterdam to interrogate Haynes and de Ridder, while London's Compendium bookshop was raided for selling issues and Bill Levy was eventually barred from entering the UK altogether. On another occasion the police raided the Arts Lab. Ostensibly they were looking for drugs, but Haynes speculates that they were probably hoping to uncover issues of *Suck*. "In fact there were two copies of *Suck* in the building, which they did not find — they were under the pillow on my bed."[1] But the paper was safely ensconced in Amsterdam and there was nothing more the British authorities could do. *Suck*, promoted as "The First European Sex Paper," became an instant success.

It wasn't just a man's magazine intent on tease. In accord with its desire to "represent the entire pendulum of sexuality" there were many female contributors, and prominent among these was a journalist and "avant-garde feminist" from Denmark, Suzanne Brøgger. One of Brøgger's first appearances as a public figure in Denmark was back in 1967 when she had acted in the television satire *Kvindens uendelige frigørelse (Women's Endless Liberation)*, and she was to make waves again in 1973 with her first book, *Deliver Us from Love (Fri os fra kærligheden)*, which was an attack on patriarchal values and the conformity of the nuclear family. Among her contributions to *Suck* was a brutal account of being raped in Uzbekistan.

Suck did well from the outset but something was missing: a way to bring readers and writers of the paper together. Thus it was suggested they launch a film festival.

Haynes, with an assist from the Amsterdam Film Museum, took the lead in organizing it and his efforts paid off with people from all over the world attending. Jean Shrimpton jetted in from London to add an air of glamour while Al Goldstein arrived from New York to sit on the jury alongside luminaries such as Germaine Greer, Richard Neville and Michael Zwerin. People came from almost every continent and it was a huge success with shows selling out immediately. The jury awarded first prize to *Bodil, a Summer Day in 1970* by Ole Ege and Shinkichi Tajiri, and there were other notable moments, such as the screening of censored footage of Mick Jagger in bed from Donald Cammell's *Performance*. Jean Genet took the Blast from the Past prize for *Un chant d'amour*, and Christie Eriksson's *Snow White and the Seven Dwarfs* scooped up The Walt Disney Memorial Award. American sexploitation mogul Lou Sher was lurking around and picked up one of the festival's feature films, *Adultery for Fun and Profit*, for commercial distribution, while a documentary about the festival entitled *Naughty* was shot and prepped for a UK release.

After the success of the first festival there was pressure to do another one, and this second edition ended up taking place between October 20 and 25, 1971. There were more groundbreaking films and another jury chock full of underground luminaries. Among the returnees were Goldstein, Zwerin and Greer, while newcomers included Mama Cass (Elliot), William Burroughs, someone called Miss Angel and pro-porn feminist Betty Dodson among others. Haynes' good friend Jens Jørgen Thorsen was there to document the event and Lou Sher was back, offering two cash awards. One was the Golden Dildo Award, worth $1000 and to be given out at the jury's discretion, while $5000 was offered as a Sherpix Award to any film he thought had commercial potential in a U.S. theatrical release.

Sex was taking place everywhere and not just on the movie screen. As Haynes describes in his book:

> Willem de Ridder managed to find a large boat for us to hire. It was completely refurbished for the occasion with potted palms and water beds, a lot of food and an orchestra on board playing chamber music — all this was included in the price of the season ticket, which was absurdly cheap.... Four or five hundred people got on this boat and went sailing out to the North Sea for a four or five-hour boat trip. One room was a love room in which people were inside making love, and in another room people were listening to chamber music. It was an event that was not soon forgotten.[2]

As if that wasn't enough, the festival capped with a mega-orgy where over a hundred people shed their clothes and entwined their bodies.

People had sex and watched sex on film, but what exactly was it they were celebrating? Pornography? Haynes thought not. As he explained to *Variety* on the cusp of the second edition, "What most people don't understand about last year's Wet Dream Festival is that we are not concerned with pornographic aspects primarily, but with the libertarian concept. It is an attack on paternalism because it asks why people can't see any image they want."

Despite tentative plans to bring the whole thing to the U.S. there never was a third festival, and the *Suck* people ended up putting their time and effort into making a movie themselves. They had been talking about it for a long time — "a strong, positive, erotic movie," as Haynes put it.

Things seemed to fall into place when one day Haynes received a call from an Amsterdam advertising executive by the name of Max Fischer. He wanted to make a movie with Haynes and the *Suck* people and had managed to come up with $125,000 and the backing of a film company in Berlin. Levy and de Ridder were put off by Fischer and cool to his previous work and advised against it, but Haynes wanted to forge ahead. He took the lead and gathered together a group of filmmakers that included Jens Jørgen Thorsen,[3] Lasse Braun, Nicholas Ray and Dušan Makavejev and a bunch of relative unknowns and first-timers. Thirteen in all. Each piece would be about ten minutes long and connected by interviews and talk that bore on *Suck* and sexual freedom in general.

For Haynes the whole project turned out to be a negative experience:

> The sad thing about it is that all these filmmakers made their own little films: the film that Jens Jørgen Thorsen made [*A Piece of Social Realism*] was wonderful, the film that Heathcote Williams made was a delight: everyone made these great little films and Max [Fischer] ended up stringing them together with some fellow singing very strange songs in a graveyard in Amsterdam: and what these strange songs in a graveyard in Amsterdam had to do with sexual freedom or these little movies, I never understood.

It was a financial flop, as least as far as Haynes was concerned:

> The movie — usually under the title of *Wet Dreams*, which upset Bill and Willem — circulated all over Europe, Canada and America [where it was released in 1974 as *Dreams of Thirteen*].... In England the movie circulated under the name *Dreams of a Young Girl*. Once, walking in Brewer Street, I looked in the window of a porn shop and there it was on video cassette and I was too broke to go in and buy it."[4]

Appendix IV
The Players

What happened to the people who participated in this era? How did they deal with their fame? Where are they today? It's not possible to provide details on all those who played some part in the wider story, but via these profiles the strange, inspirational and sometimes tragic fates that befell some of the key figures are here revealed.

Ahlberg, Mac Like Stellan Skarsgård he was one of the few who was able to hone his craft in the world of Swedish sexploitation and then go on to bigger things internationally. After *Sex in Sweden* in 1977 he left his homeland, and after *Hoodlums*, a gangster picture filmed in Italy in 1979, he left directing. That same year he landed in the States where he lensed *Nocturna*, a horror comedy that starred Yvonne De Carlo, known to fans of 1960s television for her role as Lily Munster. And that's where he stayed, shooting exploitation and grindhouse-horror pictures like *Hell's Night*, *Parasite* and *Chained Heat*. He quickly gained a reputation as an ace cinematographer and became Stuart Gordon's cameraman-of-choice for more highly regarded horror films like *Re-Animator*, *From Beyond* and *Dolls* from the mid-'80s. He also went on to work with the likes of Wes Craven, John Landis and Renny Harlin.

By the mid-'90s the man who had once directed films with Harry Reems and had been considered Sweden's foremost smut peddler was shooting positively mainstream fare like *The Brady Bunch Movie* and *A Very Brady Sequel*. His stock-in-trade, however, was horror and exploitation and that's what he returned to, staying active into his '70s to team up once again with directors like Stuart Gordon (*King of the Ants*) and Charles Brand whose *Dr. Moreau's House of Pain* is at the time of writing his last credited film.

Andersen, Gotha Denmark's most unlikely porn film actor (albeit non-performing) went on after *Bordello* to appear in other sex movies such as *Between the Sheets* and *In the Sign of Sagittarius* before playing his last part as a judge in Lars von Trier's *The Element of Crime* (1984). Plagued by diabetes, Andersen died that same year at 63.

To those who were in grade school when Andersen was in his prime, he was a heart-warming character whose hammed up style of comedy was the source of countless belly-laughs, but to the younger generation he was a much more bizarre and, dare it be said, grotesque figure whose rubbery visage and unconscionable overacting was just plain goddamn weird. In the mid-90's a cult TV series, entitled simply *Gotha,* was dedicated to this more post-modern interpretation of his legacy.

But to most he is still best remembered as a comedian who loved to entertain children, rather than as a buffoon who acted the court jester in porn films.

Andersson, Harriet Andersson and Bergman became lovers on the set of *Summer with Monika*, each betraying their respective mates, a situation that Bergman used as grist for his dramatic mill in subsequent films such as the recent *Faithless*. Andersson was to make more films with Bergman in the coming years and the two are inseparably bound in the public consciousness, perhaps unfairly since Andersson also went on to work with many other outstanding directors including Jörn Donner, Sidney Lumet, Lars von Trier and Mai Zetterling (in the controversial *Loving Couples*) in a career that spanned seven decades and was to include over 100 film roles and 50 stage performances.

In 2005 Andersson again caused a sensation in Sweden when extensive conversations with the journalist Jan Lumholdt were published in book form. Much about her tempestuous relationship with Bergman had already been revealed in the director's own autobiography, *Laterna Magica*, but she supplied a wealth of new insights, stories and observations, all delivered in a refreshingly humorous, unsentimental and open-hearted fashion.

In the intervening years she lived a full life but also experienced her share of challenges and tragedies. She endured a physically abusive lover (who was also a famous actor), had a miscarriage in the fifth month of a pregnancy and lost a protracted and traumatic court case over custody of her daughter.

In the end she never completely managed to escape the shadow of Bergman. As the elderly Gloria in Lars von Trier's *Dogville,* she played alongside Lauren Bacall. "Tell me about Mr. B," inquired Bacall on the set. "Who seduced who?"

Arnfred, Morten After helping Ole Ege shoot *Bordello* in 1972 he went on to greater things: a pair of highly-praised dramas in the late '70s, *Me and Charly* and *Johnny Larsen.* They earned Arnfred accolades as one of Denmark's best directors with the latter film regarded by some as the best Danish movie of the whole decade. In the 80's he served as Lars von Trier's co-director on a number of pictures, including *The Kingdom* and *Breaking the Waves* where his ability to work with actors served the much more reticent von Trier well. He continued to make his own movies and today remains one of the most respected directors in the business.

Axel, Gabriel The most accomplished Danish director to contribute to the debate about

Gabriel Axel pages through a script.

sexual freedom in the '60s was hardly a young man at the time, but he is still going strong today. The freedom he had to make sex pictures and then to leave the subject entirely and make completely different types of films, including one that would win an Oscar, epitomizes what is best about the Danish film industry — or what *was* best. With virtually all directors today forced for financial reasons to submit scripts to the Danish Film Institute for approval, this kind of freedom to dabble in exploitation cinema or to make films that advocate a political position would seem to be a thing of the past.

Following his erotic period Axel made a couple more folk-comedies in 1975 and 1976, and then he moved to France where he lived from 1977 to 1987 and produced television. There he had more freedom to choose his projects, and today he is regarded somewhat more highly in France than in Denmark where he has had a more checkered relationship with the public.

In 1987 he directed his next Danish film, *Babette's Feast*, an adaptation of a Karen Blixen novel which turned out to be his big comeback. It won the Oscar in 1988 for best foreign film and along with Bille August's *Pelle the Conqueror*, which had taken that honor the year before, signaled the beginning of Denmark's return to the spotlight.

He followed up with a pair of less well received films: *Christian* in 1989 and *Royal Deceit*, a re-telling of Hamlet from 1994. He then apparently reached bottom, at least in terms of public reception, with an "experimental love story" entitled *Leïla* which contained no dialogue and was narrated in French. Despite major financial production support from the DFI, it opened in Copenhagen in 2001 in just a single secondary theater and sold a mere 841 tickets.

This didn't manage to lessen *his* enthusiasm for the movie. On April 7, 2003, on the occasion of his eighty-fifth birthday, *Politiken* published a tribute headed "The Young Man of Danish Film." Here it was recounted how Axel had recently introduced *Laila, the Pure* at a theater in Paris "with all the enthusiasm of a first-time director."

Few filmmakers in the U.S., or perhaps anywhere, could have survived all the ups and downs that Axel has. "You're only as good as your last film" was an adage he never paid any attention to, refusing to let the successes *or* the failures go to his head. Every time you start making a film, as he once put it, you begin from scratch.

The *Bedside* and *Zodiac* Series Films In 2005 and 2006 the *Bedside* and *Zodiac* series films were released on DVD and sold surprisingly well. When shown on TV they attracted large audiences, the top scorer being *Bedside Manner* which was shown in March of 2008. Danish critic Lars Gorzelak ascribes this to nostalgia but also to the way the films treated sex. "The films are uplifting because they describe sex as something that, in our innermost being, we know permeates everything we do. Generally speaking the message of the films is simple: sex is good and happy people are sexually liberated people." Gorzelak adds, "What attracts viewers to these films is the openness to sexual exploration, their erotic energy and the lack of realism evidenced in the 'folkcomedy-esque' spirit and visual language, proving that popular film forms and sexuality go hand-in-hand. We ought to do away with prudish dismissals and acknowledge these films. They are in no way laughable or something to be ashamed of. To the contrary, they are a phenomenon we have every reason to be proud of."

Dahlerup, Ulla The provocative young woman who in 1963 had all of Denmark discussing diaphragms continued to stir up debate, taking up the feminist banner in the early '70s. After a Mother's Day demonstration in 1970 she and 25 compatriots boarded a bus but refused to pay more than 80 percent of the fare because women were paid approximately 80 percent of what men were paid to do the same work. The police were called and the ladies were carried off the bus. A photo of an officer lugging away a smiling Ulla Dahlerup came to symbolize the whole era of radical feminist politics.

Dahlerup had a knack for political theater. At one point, disguised in a black wig, she let herself be smuggled over the border to call attention to the illegal trade in human beings. She wrote fiery polemics for various papers and magazines over the years. She penned a column for *E.B.* for a while but proved too inflammatory even for them.

A playwright, columnist, lecturer and ceaseless agitator through the '70s and '80s, she made what appeared to be a jolting turn to the right in the '90s when she began to vent fiercely anti-immigrant opinions. It was a startling transformation for a woman who had come to be considered a champion of all things progressive.

Frevert, Louise   Educated as a classical ballet dancer, she later became a choreographer, dramatist, author and politician. So reads her online biography. What it doesn't mention is job experience of a more libidinous bent that would seem dramatically at odds with her current ultra-conservative positions, namely, her participation in one of the *Bedside* and two of the *Zodiac* films. In what other country could a woman who acted in hard-core pornographic films, is a declared lesbian and at time of writing is a belly-dancer-for-hire become a spokesperson for the most conservative political party?

Certainly her political positions regarding film, which include attacks on von Trier's *Dogville* as leftist prattle and proposals that his funding be cut, seem anything but enlightened or progressive. This also casts doubt on the assumption that participation in a porn film was somehow proof of a liberal mindset. Perhaps what it really shows is that in Denmark sexuality is still considered a private matter.

Or semi-private, perhaps. In November of 2005 elections were held to determine who would be Copenhagen's next mayor and Frevert stood as DF's candidate. Shortly before election day a homemade poster was discovered on a wall that sported a picture of a young Ms. Frevert about to orally pleasure a male actor. "Louise Frevert goes all the way" read the tagline. The incident got wide coverage in the press but she initially shrugged it off, and apparently so did most voters. Election analysts predicted that if anything it would win the controversial 52-year-old sympathy with voters already at peace with her "varied past."[1]

After the election DF dumped her as their education spokesperson in the Copenhagen area (she remains their cultural spokesperson)—not because of the poster or her racy past but because she lost the election by a landslide and because of some earlier anti–Muslim statements found on her website. In comparison the suggestive 30-year-old picture was the least of her worries.

Now that she is divested of her powers as educational spokesperson, it remains to be seen what will become of her proposal to make folkdancing mandatory in Danish schools.

Grete, Anne   After following up *Without a Stitch* and *Bedside Manner* with the Swedish film *The Lustful Vicar* in 1970, Anne Grete also acted in a play that same year, wearing only a strategically placed smattering of daisies, white go-go boots and a long blonde wig. It was deemed a fiasco. That caused her to seriously rethink her career and she enrolled in acting school in an effort to land better parts. Yet that didn't dissuade her from appearing in more Swedish sex films, among them *Tomorrow My Love* and *Dagmar's Hot Pants, Inc.*, both from 1971.

A decade later she had matured into a successful stage actress and her marriage had produced two children. It was hard to connect her to the Anne Grete of old, not least because she simply let her hair remain its natural dark color, but the past caught up with her in 1982 when *Without a Stitch* was released on video.

"That film has really plagued me," she commented to the press.[2] "I thought I was going to participate in an honest and serious film about female orgasm dysfunction — and it turned out to be nothing but nonsense! ... The kids are another reason I'm not wild about the re-release."

Guldbrandsen, Peer   Not all of his movies were trashed by critics. He had a long and amazingly prolific career as a writer, producer and director and did receive occasional praise, most notably for *Retribution*, a 1955 crime melodrama that was set during the Occupation. But the majority of movies he pumped out during the '60s were simply dismissed and he in turn became much more hostile towards the whole of the country's film establishment, earning him the tag of Danish cinema's *enfant terrible*.

Guldbrandsen's studio, Novaris, went bankrupt in 1971, a year after he produced *The Daughter*. It was taken over by a consortium, of which he was a member, and stayed afloat until it was bought by Rialto Film in 1974. That spelled the end of his career in motion pictures. Over a period of 11 years he had produced 46 movies. That only one had received any public support is amazing in light of the fact that today almost every single commercial feature receives state funding. If all of Guldbrandsen's films had had to be appraised and approved by funding bureaucrats back then it is a safe bet that half of them would never have been made and '60s/'70s Danish cinema, and to some degree American sexploitation cinema, would have looked very different. As noted, there was funding available from 1964 on and he got almost none of it.

After leaving film production he returned to his first love, acting, and achieved some acclaim there. His last role was in 1980 and after that he faded from the picture; by the time he died in March of 1996 he was a largely forgotten figure. Yet he remained a rugged individualist to the last, a self-made man who defied the critics and did it his way. A man who stood strong because he stood alone. A man who took chances. And yet he was also a man forever haunted by the fact that he was involved in one of the most lopsided film deals in history — on the wrong side.

Hænning, Gitte Her nude appearance in Gabriel Axel's 1967 film *Hagbard and Signe* is enough to earn her a place of honor in this book but it was hardly her only claim to fame.

Her first breakthrough came in 1955 when the elfin eight-year-old and her dad Otto covered the song "Ich heirate Papi" ("I Want to Marry Daddy") which the German crooner Erich Langenfeld, a.k.a. Gerhard Froboess, had originally sung with his daughter, the child star Conny.

"Little Gitte," as she became known, achieved more visibility two years later when she and her father participated in a TV benefit show to raise donations for the victims of Russia's invasion of Hungary. By 1960 she had matured into something of a Danish Brigitte Bardot, her new look on display in the film *Ullabella* in which she played a schoolgirl who falls in love with her teacher. She was widely praised for her performance and critics lauded her ability to convey a newly awakened sexuality.

She had another song hit in 1961 with a cover of "You're 16," and her acting now took a backseat to her recording career. She developed a full-throated style in the mold of pop torch singers like Sandie Shaw and Petula Clark and began to score hits outside Denmark, particularly in Sweden and south of the border where in 1962 she debuted on German TV with her version of Brenda Lee's "I'm Sorry."

She was 16 herself by now and had grown up fast. She confided to a Danish reporter that she had seen a lot, "maybe too much" in her young life, and she despaired of the fact that she only had one girlfriend her own age. She mostly hung out with men — older men.

In 1963 she won a major song contest in Germany with "Ich will 'nen Cowboy als Mann" that went on to top the charts there, and the next year she was back in the #1 slot with "Vom Stadtpark die Lanternen" which she sang together with Rex Gildo.

She was in great demand now in Germany — touring, appearing on TV shows and releasing records — and she eventually moved there. She was, along with another Danish teen idol called Vivi Bak, the kind of Nordic gal that Germans loved to love. Bak (Bach to German fans) and Hænning even acted together in the 1966 movie *The Pipes* which was directed by Vojtéch Jasny, one of the key figures in the Czechoslovakian new wave. The film was about a pipe-smoking man's relationship with three different women, Bak, Hænning and Janne Brejchová (who was Milos Forman's first wife). It contained daring erotic scenes and is considered in some quarters to be the best film that Hænning and Bak ever made.

In 1973 Hænning made a comeback of sorts in Germany when she won the German Melody Grand Prix with the song "Junger Tag." But pop was not her only specialty: she also became accomplished as a cabaret singer and she had sung jazz standards going back to her teenage years. She has since returned to her native Denmark and it is as a jazz vocalist in the big band tradition that she is best known there. She celebrated her sixtieth birthday on June 28, 2006, and was paid fitting tribute in the Danish press.

Hegeler, Sten and Inge Sten turned 85 on April 27, 2008, and as of this writing continues to be active in the sexual and moral debate. He celebrated his birthday by publishing his twenty-seventh book and is engaged in discussions with a Chinese publishing house to have Hegelers' book *The ABZ's of Love* printed there. Some things never change: the Chinese want him to rewrite and soften some passages in the text and he doesn't want to. Inge went on to study medicine and became a doctor. The couple divorced in 1983 and she died suddenly of a heart attack in 1996.

Hellström, Margaretha The debutante actress who played Britt, the toymaker in *Young Playthings*, never made another film and left Sweden to do missionary work in Biafra.

Lindberg, Christina Like so many of her compatriots, Lindberg saw her acting career come to an end in the 80's when the roles dried up. She then became a kind of celebrity journalist, having earned a degree in the field back in 1976. She penned a "Dear Christina" sex advice column and later conducted a series of legendary interviews with Swedish celebrities while both parties lounged naked in a sauna.

At some point between 1990 and 1993 she was lured out of retirement to appear briefly in an independent gore film called *Sex, Lies and Video Violence* which featured cameos by other Swedish celebrities as well as Brandon Lee who happened to be in town. Post-production took some time, however, and it wasn't completed and released until 2000. Her performance here is actually a reprise of her role in *They Call Her One-Eye*, complete with eye patch and sawed-off shotgun.

This cameo notwithstanding, her days in sexploitation were far behind her and her last film — or video, rather — which she wrote, produced and directed in 1993 was an instructional guide on the gathering of edible mushrooms called *Christinas Svampskola*. It's rumored to have become an instant collector's item among her old fans. Lindberg had become a *mycologist*.

At time of writing she is the editor-in-chief of the official Swedish Aviator's Association magazine and makes occasional appearances at screenings of her old films. Apparently she still has a sense of irony about her film career as she at one point agreed to pose in the come-hither style of her pin-up days for an album cover — but now clad in full stewardess attire.

Norup, Lise-Lotte Ms. Norup was raised in a conservative home in a well-to-do suburban town where the neighbors apparently looked askew at her career in sex films (various nude appearances, roles in three *Bedside* films not to mention *Adventure in Denmark*, and others). A Danish actors' directory says it took her ten years to recover from being typed as a sexpot. She had to reinvent herself as a singer, a regular guest on TV quiz shows, and an actress in summer stage

Lise-Lotte Norup in *Curtains for Mrs. Knudsen*.

comedies before the good people were ready to forgive her. With all this and bit parts in various films, she was by the '80s deemed respectable again and ready to proceed further, participating in an early '90s soap series, more substantial appearances in features and the publication of at least three cook books.

Much has been said in this book about Danish open-mindedness and the freedom of actors to perform in sex films without being stigmatized, but judgments were certainly passed on some actors in broader society, and they passed judgments on themselves. The towns, villages and neighborhoods in Denmark can no doubt be just as small minded and prejudice-ridden as anywhere else, even if the society as a whole is more easy-going. Middle-class conventionalism certainly also thrives in the "sexual paradise" of Denmark.

Essy Persson "The next Garbo" never became the next Garbo, nor the next Harriet Andersson. But at least for a while she seemed to be living the dream existence of hip movie stardom — jetting around Europe resplendent in the latest mod fashions, flashing her famous smile as the paparazzi swarmed, flying to Rome to shoot a science fiction film one day then off to Paris or Barcelona the next. She hung out in exotic locales, met the coolest people, attended the hottest parties, fell in love and got tons of offers from Hollywood. Typical was the incident that occurred on one of her frequent flights between Sweden and the States. While she was in the process of boarding the plane the pilot spotted her name on the passenger list, and after she was seated he had to rush back and tell her he had seen her movie twenty times. She was the ultimate embodiment of the liberated Scandinavian female animal; men fell in love with her on the street, men pursued her on the set.

The shooting of the 1967 Italian-German-Spanish sci-fi co-production *Mission Stardust* offers a snapshot of the times. In this picture Essy was cast as the platinum blonde rocket ship commander, Thora, who strides about in an assortment of skin tight space suits. During the location shoot on the Canary Islands (which was supposed to pass for a moon landscape) shooting was suspended when parts for some kind of space rocket never arrived. The cast and crew were forced to kill time in a hotel for three weeks, time they spent trying to seduce each other. One day Essy answered a knock at her door. There stood a dashing Portuguese actor on the other side, sans clothing and ready for action, forcing her to retreat to the folds of the bed sheets and fend him off with some desperate rhetorical sleight-of-hand.

One of the producers of that film, an Italian, who was also smitten with her, showed more tact, though not much more. On location in Spain he took a room right next to hers and she had to wrestle a large piece of furniture in front of the door that connected the two rooms to keep him at bay. When she returned to Stockholm he plagued her with phone calls which she politely endured, until she grew tired or bored and handed the phone to her sister, who kept on: "Si, Salvatore, Si, Si...." At one point he flew to Stockholm, took a room in the city's top hotel and wooed her *parents*, inviting them to the fanciest restaurant where he asked their permission to marry Essy. She almost died of laughter. As for the suitcase filled with expensive ladies' garments and fine crafted leather goods that he gave her, she dumped it all off at a second-hand store.

But while Essy was barricading doors to hold off love-crazed suitors and undergoing the headache-inducing process of having her hair pulled back to make her look like an alien with stretched eyes, other actresses were beating her out for the more challenging roles that might have helped her escape from the sexploitation ghetto. *Therese and Isabelle*, shot the following year, purported to be such a role but wasn't, and she never did land that part that might have led to serious recognition of her talents. And so, after co-starring with Vincent Price in the British hor-

The face that launched a thousand sighs; Essy Persson in *I, a Woman*.

ror film *Cry of the Banshee* in 1970, she was through, moving back to Sweden and retiring as a movie star in 1971. Although she would continue to appear in Swedish television productions, her film career had lasted just five years.

Reports vary as to why. In his book *Cult Movie Stars* author Danny Peary writes, "Unfortunately, while Persson and the film [*Thérese and Isabelle*] eventually got good reviews, it wasn't until after the daily press ripped her apart for looking too old for the role." Peary implies that it was this harsh critical reception that drove Persson out of the film industry. She herself maintains that all the traveling wore her out and brought on recurring asthma attacks. Ultimately she simply lacked the desire or energy to go on, turning down both movie and stage offers for a career as an artist. The high-flying times were over.

In 1973 a reporter caught up with her to find her living a life that was anything but glamorous. She was now 31, a single mother living in a one-room flat in Stockholm with her infant son. At that point she was enrolled at the Royal Academy of Art in Stockholm, which was no small accomplishment since normally only 12 new students are admitted annually out of a pool of approximately 600 applicants. She felt herself now more than ever psychically violated by her involvement in *I, a Woman*, claiming the film had ruined her life and the shame of it all had driven her "underground." She was now more politically aware and concerned herself with social problems, particularly women's issues, no doubt spurred on by her own experiences.

She was, in fact, one of the first actresses of the era to bring lawsuits against producers who she felt had unduly exploited her. That occurred first in 1966 in connection with the Swedish film *Sadist*. She objected to the fact that racy publicity stills were used without her knowledge and that a nude stand-in was employed with the clear implication that it was her body viewers were seeing. That case got big coverage in the Swedish press. Some suspected it was just a publicity ploy and felt that her participation in *I, a Woman* deprived her of the moral right to complain about such things. Two years later she brought the same charges against the producers of that very film. The case was tried in a Stockholm court which found that the movie had violated her artistic reputation and Guldbrandsen's company was ordered to pay her 5,000 crowns in compensation and 11,000 in court costs.

As noted, she continued to do occasional TV work, and via reruns of *Shanty Town (Söderkåkar)*, a six-part TV series adapted in 1970 from a lowbrow stage show of the same name, she became familiar to a new generation of Swedish viewers through the '80s. And there was one more feature film, *Flourishing Times*, in 1980. An ambitious tragicomedy co-produced by the Swedish Film Institute, it starred the now 39-year-old and happily married Essy Persson Falenius as an unfaithful wife. She did have one scene in bed (with lots of sheets). She did the picture more as a favor to the producer, who was a personal friend, than as any kind of attempt at a comeback. By this point she had graduated from the Royal Academy of Art and had achieved some success as a painter. Her husband ran a lucrative travel business and they lived in a fashionable neighborhood on the outskirts of Stockholm.

After that the trail goes cold. She became once again a private person cloaked in all the anonymity that implies, and even the tabloids stopped prying into her affairs.

Could it be possible for the woman who had redefined how female sexuality was portrayed in the movies to simply drop out of sight? For decades? In America where seemingly every B-movie starlet is touring the convention circuit it could never happen, but in Scandinavia where privacy is more respected and B-cinema less so, and where old actors are perhaps less financially strapped, apparently yes. Aside from a short interview on a Swedish TV program in the mid-'90s nothing more was officially seen or heard from her until she kindly consented to an interview for this book on June 29, 2005.

At that point she was living in a weather-beaten cottage full of pet birds in the seaside town of Heestrand, on the west coast of Sweden, where she was considered something of a loner and eccentric by the local chattering classes. When asked what her favorite movie was she replied that none of them were her favorites.

On the occasion of her fiftieth birthday a local fan planted a sign by her house that proclaimed the little road it was on to be "Essy Persson Lane." This humble enough gesture caused an uproar with the local townsfolk. It seems like the little black and white movie she made four decades ago is anything but forgotten — or forgiven. She is still in fact considered a tarnished figure in the eyes of many Swedes of a certain generation. Strange, really. Who even remembers all the countless women who performed pornographic gymnastics in hundreds of Swedish hard-core films of the '70s? But they still remember Essy Persson, and a potent aura of scandal still clings to *I, a Woman*, this comparatively chaste little low-budget drama from 1965.

Such was the power of screen sexuality in a more innocent time.

Sarno, Joe As best he himself can recollect he made upwards of 200 feature films, and even during his Swedish period he cranked out movies in other countries including the U.S. Following his Scandinavian adventure he moved back to America on a more full-time basis. He continued making films, but the theatrical market for exploitation was disappearing and his career as a producer of cost-effective erotica was coming to a close. His last real film of this period was the 1984 picture *Dirty Blonde*.

After that he made ends meet as a script-doctor and did various types of free-lance work.

In 2004 the 85-year-old Sarno was lured out of retirement to produce another film called *Suburban Streets*, a.k.a. *Lust for Laura*. In this erotic drama a well-endowed redhead returns after many years to her home town only to send sexual shock waves through the community.

Sarno at time of writing is in demand on the revival circuit where he is occasionally honored with retrospectives like the one organized by the Turin Film Festival in 2006. His work is being reappraised today by a new generation of film scholars who take exploitation seriously. In 2004 he and his wife and longtime collaborator Peggy Steffans appeared with a now 54-year-old Marie Liljedahl in the documentary *Lost Innocence: the Story of Inga* to talk about old times.

Sjöman, Vilgot After the *I Am Curious* pictures he made a lot more films, but nothing gained him nearly as much attention. In 1977 he made the far more daring *Taboo* and nobody outside Sweden really noticed. The cast of homegrown all-stars included Viveca Lindfors, Stellan Skarsgård and perennial bad guy Heinz Hopf as a mean sadomasochist.

The film centers on Kristoffer, a controversial lawyer who specializes in the rights of sexual minorities, and Sarah, a young girl who falls in love with him. Their relationship leads Sara into a shadowy realm of deviant sexuality. She attends orgies and transvestite parties and encounters sadists, masochists and other sexual non-conformers. Kristoffer's idea to unite all the minorities into a common front is doomed as internal squabbling erupts and the project collapses. In the end he at least gets a book out of the whole thing—a book about how bankrupt the sexual revolution is.[3] In Sweden the film caused controversy but in a wholly negative sense for Sjöman; the critical community was united in its condemnation and it almost stopped his career in its tracks.

He was ever the outsider, attacking entrenched moral and political positions with films that also manage to express deeply personal viewpoints. As the years wore on he became an unrelenting critic of the "new Puritanism" in Sweden which followed in the wake of political and sexual liberation, and his outbursts alienated him from his comrades on the left who had also, to his great disappointment, rejected the *I Am Curious* films. After the whole amazing *I, Am Curious* experience he shunned the spotlight for many years. He turned down an interview request with this writer in 1994, elaborating in a note, "The trouble is that I'm less and less inclined to do that sort of thing. Maybe there is a peculiar reason for it: I have been 'exploiting' myself too heavily...."

He was forever typecast in the wider world as the rebellious director of *I Am Curious (Yellow)* and although his later films explore a broader range of topics, many of them remain undeservedly obscure outside Sweden. In 1995 he attempted a comeback with *Alfred*, a bio-pic about Alfred Nobel, but it failed to sell tickets and reviews were only lukewarm. After that he worked mostly as a writer. In 2005 he was again prominent in the news when he sued a TV station for violating his artistic integrity by broadcasting one of his films with commercial breaks. He won the lawsuit and the appeal.

Sjöman suffered a cerebral hemorrhage and passed away on April 9, 2006.

Strømberg, Søren The marathon man of Danish B-movies went on to participate in over 145 films,[4] an astonishing number in light of the country's annual average production of 20, but he was fated to live with the fact that he never got a part as good as his first one, that of the arrogant Per in *Gift*, and that he never went on to fulfill the promise he showed and become a great actor.

He stayed busy, perhaps too busy, acting in anything that came his way. No bit part was below him and the new wave of sex films provided steady if often less than challenging work. Parallel to his film career he also acted in live theater, everything from Shakespeare to a touring production of the same nude ballet Lotte Tarp starred in, but by then he was thoroughly typecast as a "porn actor," even though he never appeared in "performing" roles.

His rates fluctuated; he recalls once reading a couple of lines for a bottle of liquor, and yet by the end of the '70s he was a millionaire. And then his luck changed again.

The sex film boom ended and the parts dried up at about the same time that his personal life started to unravel. His first marriage (Grethe) had ended in divorce and his second (Lillian) was clouded by a paternity suit (which he always contested). He purchased and ran at various points a restaurant, a hotel and a pub. He was a stand-up guy beloved by his friends, but he also possessed a difficult temperament as his wives could attest. Maybe there really was a bit of Per in him.

The early '80s were not kind to him. His face became puffy from too much drink. On the occasion of his fortieth birthday E.B. ran the first of what would become a regular cycle of "Søren Strømberg is finished" articles, this one quoting him as saying that he was so apathetic that he couldn't even be bothered to commit suicide. At one point he was accused of stealing a single bottle of beer.

Now he was typecast in a new role, that of the washed up actor, and he played it well. As if to rub salt in his wounds, the paper invariably ran the old photo of him and a topless, ravishing Birte Tove from *Bedside Highway*. Here was a fellow who had performed with some of the hottest women of the era, in movies seen around the world, and now this. How low could a man fall? If one subscribed to the dim view, his film career paralleled his life. In his first role he played the prophet of this new amoral philosophy, and then in reality he reaped its harvest, becoming increasing more dissolute and artistically unfocused, living proof of what happens to people when they don't believe in anything.

He went through a couple more marriages. At the start of 1987 he said his farewells to Denmark in an article in *E.B.* He would travel to the Grand Canary Islands and then on to the United States and never come back. It was enough to bring a tear to one's eye, noted the reporter. In an echo of his old director Knud Leif Thomsen he claimed that all cultural life in Denmark was politically controlled, that its excessive socialism was suffocating him to death and that, on top of it, he was a victim of the Jante Law.[5]

By the end of 1988, after a couple of years of tramping around America, he was back, living in a borrowed flat with his fifth wife, Lenni, and hoping to get acting work again.

He began to throw himself into the bar life. He was no stranger to it and in earlier times had even embarked on several extended drunks with old friend Dirch Passer (who died in 1980 of a massive heart attack minutes before he was to have gone on stage in a clown costume). But now he was gone for days and waking up with paralyzing hangovers. Three years later Lenni was gone too. Strømberg married six times and after each divorce the ex-wife reportedly cleaned him out.

By the mid-'90s he was holed up in a tiny flat that contained little more than a TV and a couple of sticks of furniture. That's how *E.B.* found him in March of 1996, looking much older than his 52 years, not puffy and bloated but quite the opposite, thin and almost fragile ... just old. The tabloid had been shadowing him for many years like the angel of doom. He was their story, and now they took the opportunity to once again proclaim him finished. How finished could a man be? They ran all the photos from happier times: the broadly smiling lad with guitar in hand, and the newly married couple, kissing, both images from 1966. And there was the old photo of him and Tove ... and big smiles all around with Søltoft in 1974. And the most recent picture from 1993, toasting to his last wife, a Norwegian woman he met in a bar, who by now had also left him.

"When I die," he stated after divorcing her, "I want to go to the grave alone, without any grief-stricken mourners. I've always been best in one-man shows."

And so he did, dying of cancer at the age of 56 on May 14, 2001.

Tarp, Lotte Ms. Tarp was 16 when she appeared nude in *Crazy Paradise* and 17 when she acted in *Weekend*. Both of the films were released in 1962 and thus, in a flash, Tarp managed to typecast herself as Denmark's # 1 blonde bimbo long before the term had been coined. And if she had more to offer viewers than just a great body, her next major performance, in 1964 as the first of the semi-naked tabloid cover girls, failed to hint at it.

Victor Andreasen, at the time the editor of *E.B.*, the tabloid that pioneered published nudity in Denmark, got the idea after he saw a five-line wire report about a girl who had been arrested on a Chicago beach for sporting a topless bikini. He then instructed his secretary to find a beautiful, well-endowed fashion model, dress her in the same attire or lack thereof and snap some pictures down on Hornbæk beach. Said model turned out to be Lotte Tarp, and the next day a picture of her being admired in the sand by some soldier boys ran on the front page. Thus began the tradition of "page 9" girls in the paper. It's still going strong today, but at the time it was a shock to the system and among Andreasen's many critics were editors from papers in the provinces who accused him of corrupting youthful morals.

The next year Tarp did another nude scene in the Arne Mattsson–directed Swedish horror-thriller *I, the Body*. This tawdry psychological tale about an old man who torments everyone around him was a *tour de force* of sinister atmospherics and contained a number of perverse and sexually daring scenes that startled viewers.

The following year Tarp spent a week with Salvador Dalí at his house in northern Spain as his muse, model and playmate. "Do with me what you will," she told him.[6]

At that point Dalí was being bombarded by letters and phone calls from two American TV producers who wanted to do a special on him. He wasn't interested but they turned up at his door anyway. He decided to teach them a lesson and invited them to lunch the next day. When they arrived he was poised with knife and fork above Tarp who was laid out totally naked on his table save for a strategically placed flounder on her waist and a lobster between her breasts. The Americans were shocked.

Dalí feigned indignation: "You're late, I'm in the middle of lunch — go!"

Leave they did, but not before Dalí's secretary had made another appointment with them for dinner that night at a local hotel. At this appointment, Tarp appeared as Dalí's deaf-mute nurse. After the Americans had arrived and were seated Dalí made his grand entrance, moaning and gasping as he crawled across the floor to their table, apparently afflicted by some terrible illness. Whenever they tried to make conversation he groaned in pain, and every time food was brought in he sent it back to the kitchen. They became increasingly frustrated and tried to communicate with Tarp, but being deaf and mute she could only smile at them. Finally they gave up, left the restaurant and were never heard from again.

A photo of Tarp as main dish at Dalí's naked lunch became famous, and he also made four sketches of her during her stay.

In 1966 she played alongside Oliver Reed and Michael Crawford in the British crime comedy *The Jokers*. Tarp was known and appreciated by the British public as "the Danish Pastry" but was used here mostly for decorative purposes.

The following year she married theology-student-turned-aspiring-writer-director Henrik Stangerup. He was the first man to take her seriously, as she would recall, and it was in his films that she would reveal her true range. She played the somber wife of a minister in crisis in Stangerup's first picture, *Give God a Chance on Sunday*, one of the most keenly discussed films of 1970.

Her next film, *Dangerous Kisses* (1972), was about a doctor who falls in love with his psychiatric patient, Birthe, only to discover that her condition is more serious than he realized. Tarp was Stangerup's inspiration to make the film and he wrote the part of Birthe specifically for her. She in turn submitted a raw and passionate performance that was rewarded with a Bodil.

She had created these two highly regarded films (and a son) with him in the early '70s, but their relationship was a stormy one and they divorced in 1975.

Tarp continued to do live theater as well, in 1976 appearing in the production of *Vidunderlige Kælling*, a nude ballet. In 1980 the Swedish director Stig Björkman cast her as the lead in another psychological drama, *A Woman's Mind*, where she played a wife who considers leaving her husband and child to go off with an American she has met. It was another part written specifically for her and was fiercely experimental in nature, marked by a slow rhythm, long scenes and a hazy formlessness in which the past and present and fantasy and reality all merge in her mind.

As the '80s wore on the parts dried up for Tarp and for many of her compatriots in the acting profession who had also come of age during the era of Liberated Denmark. In the meantime she began to write her own plays and did TV work. She also performed in revy productions, which are satiric theatrical skits that function as a kind of modern day vaudeville and take aim at political or cultural figures in the news.

In September of 1990 she enrolled in the Danish film school's manuscript line. She successfully capped her studies there a couple of years later with the well received graduate project (TV) film called *Long Live Freedom*. In the coming years she would return to the school to teach and she also co-wrote episodes for a number of popular TV series.

In 1998 she broke through as a writer in a major way with the autobiographical *Det Sku' nødig Hedde Sig* (an almost untranslatable idiomatic expression roughly akin to "We wouldn't want people to say..."). The book boldly confronted a shameful taboo that haunted the postwar generation: the legacy of children parented by Danish women and German soldiers during the Occupation — of whom Tarp was one. Danish women who had engaged in such relationships were brutally stigmatized after the war. Scorned as "field mattresses," many had their heads forcibly shaved in a show of public humiliation. As for Tarp, toward the end of the war her father was transferred to the Eastern front, where he died in battle. She was left to an uncertain fate on the steps of an orphanage, later to be retrieved by an aunt and uncle. They brought her up in their home but never divulged that her beautiful "older sister" was really her mother and her "mother" was in fact her grandmother. It was a family plagued by dark secrets and an unspoken shame, and Lotte was packed off to a boarding school at the earliest opportunity. As one critic termed it, hers was the story of a survivor who persevered and triumphed over her own self-loathing and loneliness.

After that she threw herself into still more projects. In 2001 she wrote and staged a theater piece: *At the End of the Universe There's an All-night Store*. To the shock of family and friends she was admitted to hospital shortly after the opening and diagnosed with advanced lung and liver cancer. She fought it but to no avail, passing away on October 24, 2002.

Even in Denmark where there is something of a tradition for reinventing oneself, Lotte Tarp's various transformations were remarkable. She broke out of the blonde bimbo mold to become by turns a serious actress of stage and screen, a teacher, author, lecturer and playwright — an inspiring figure who never stopped challenging herself and who from all indications had much more to say.

Theander, Peter and Jens The Brothers Theander had their fortunes made with the abolition of censorship in Denmark in 1969 and never looked back. Quality conscious and armed with good business sense, they reinvested their profits into color presses and into commissioning and translating different story lines for their XXX-rated photo-plays. They not only survived in one of the most fiercely competitive fields, but prospered. Their commitment to publishing the most far-out and freakish images paid dividends in 1972 when they featured a black male model whose member was so long that he could tie it in a knot. Sales went through the roof. By 1987 they had, according to their own publicity, 100 employees and office and storage facilities the size of an entire football field. In recent years they've also been quick to exploit film reproduction technologies such as video, DVD and the Internet. They long ago stopped appearing in public in connection with their product, and the memory of the brash young rebels who were going to shatter all of society's sexual barriers is a distant one indeed.

Thomsen, Knud Leif The man who foretold the future with his film *Gift* in 1966 made one more movie after *Confessions of a Danish Cover Girl* and then quit the film profession altogether in 1977, declaring himself fed up with Denmark's cultural condition and its socialist tendencies and moving his family to France.

Through the '80s Poul Schlüter's conservative government ruled Denmark but that did little to mollify Thomsen, who stayed away. He claimed his homeland still suffered from "socialitis" and continued to assail his political opponents from afar with regular columns published in Danish papers. He passed away in October of 2003, having remained to the end a cantankerous moralist, a preacher and a modern day romantic.

Tove, Birte Born in 1945, the same year as Lotte Tarp, Tove took the same path to stardom. Tarp and Tove attended the same boarding school, where together they dreamed of becom-

Knud Leif Thomsen directs Sisse Reingaard in a scene from *Gift*.

ing movie stars, and both were "discovered" by photographers on Hornbæk Beach. Yet in contrast to the dramatic twists and turns that Tarp's life would take, Tove was consistently profiled as a dedicated homebody whose family came first.

After bowing out of the *Bedside* series and surviving her Hong Kong exploitation trilogy, Tove launched a singing career. It was apparently short-lived since already in 1980 she was announcing in the press that she was ready for a comeback, as either a singer or an actress. Not that she lacked for offers, but they were almost always of the unprintable variety.

Although she stayed busy in the early '80s organizing several seasons of well-received revy (satiric theatrical skits in a sort of vaudeville mode), she still hoped to revive her film career. "Does anyone need a washed up sex star?—If so just call," headlined the first of many "what ever happened to Birte Tove?" articles. At this point she was still getting singing gigs, mostly at nursing homes.

All through the '80s love-hungry fans continued to write her with various propositions of a personal nature, only to get back a Christmas card photo of Tove & family with "thanks but there's no room for more" scrawled on the back. In 1987 she reunited with a graying but still eerily boyish Ole Søltoft in a Christmas comedy special. (Søltoft was fated to never grow old, dying suddenly from a blood clot on May 9, 1999, at the relatively young age of 58.) At that point she was working shifts "on call" as a nurse at a nursing home.

In 1994 she hosted a TV show, but fans hoping for a taste of the old sassiness were quickly put straight. Being a nurse, she talked mostly about health issues, non-sexy stuff like Salmonella-free cooking, Parkinson's disease and dental hygiene. That same year she performed at an AIDS benefit.

Her fiftieth birthday in 1995 did not go unnoticed in the press. She had some wrinkles around her eyes but her flawless smile was still intact and she still looked good. She was at that time touring, performing songs and monologues with her daughter. They had a show at Tivoli but most of the gigs were at nursing homes. And she was still working night shifts. The year before she had actually gotten a part in Lars von Trier's *The Kingdom*—as a nurse, fittingly—and she also appeared in the second installment in 1997. She acquitted herself well although her parts were minor.

She had always fended off advances from drooling male fans by nodding toward her longtime steady and remarking that she was taken, but in 1995, after 25 years of marriage, that outwardly perfect relationship ended and they divorced. The fans remained, now sending their proposals by e-mail. "I'm old enough to be your grandmother," was her new line.

Back problems forced her out of the nursing profession in 1997 and today she lives in a modest three room flat north of Copenhagen, runs a flea market and wears used clothes.

It's all a far cry from her heyday in the early '70s when she was making a fortune, causing riots at publicity appearances and bumping into the likes of Bruce Lee and Jimi Hendrix at parties. Did she ever regret that fame was so fleeting? Yeah, actually, commenting now and again in the press that she wished she had taken proper acting lessons from the start and had become better known in America.

Wickman, Torgny The sex films he began producing in 1969 turned out to be a deal with the devil; they earned him an international breakthrough but also apparently the scorn of critics and people in the business who never forgave him. Before making the sex films he had enjoyed the freedom of being able to explore different subjects and genres, but after this point he was more-or-less imprisoned in the sexploitation ghetto, his work dismissed and ridiculed by the critics. His one subsequent attempt at a "serious" film, *The Decoy* (1971), was a failure despite the participation of many respected actors and technicians including Bergman's cinematographer Sven Nykvist. Critics called it boring and audiences shunned it. It was not an export success and even today is a relatively ignored work in the Wickman oeuvre—undeservedly.

His last feature film, the halfhearted porn comedy *Practice Makes Perfect* (1977), also flopped and Wickman returned to his roots as a maker of documentaries and short films. But he was now *persona non grata* in the Swedish film industry and was refused funding for most of his subsequent projects. Over the next 20 years he only managed to complete three documentaries, the last in 1994, yet remained a true cineaste to the end (often citing Elia Kazan as his idol) and refused to retire. According to friends and relatives he stayed busy into his eighties, producing by his own count about ten pages of synopsis and script work per day before peacefully passing away in 1997. Who knows how many worthy films he might have made had the powers-that-be in the Swedish film industry not turned against him? Looking back, one can say that while his films were often short on technical polish they exuded a sincerity and devotion lacking in many of the movies churned out during the era of Sinful Sweden.

Windeløv, Vibeke   The woman who served as Lars von Trier's trusted producer and close family friend on *Breaking the Waves* and other films has since left Zentropa but is still one of the most respected and high-profile business women in the Denmark. And yet a little known and not particularly well advertised fact is that she honed her skills in hard-core pornography, clocking in as production boss on the Astrological film *In the Sign of the Scorpion* in 1977.

Zetterling, Mai   After the scandalous *Night Games* Zetterling directed several more films in Sweden and one in Denmark called *Doctor Glas* (1968). Her Swedish film of the same year entitled *The Girls* was her most overtly feminist work although feminist themes could be found in almost all of her pictures. She never returned to her homeland on a permanent basis and became more of an international figure, living and working in various countries including the UK, the U.S. and France. Still, she remained to the end the quintessential strong willed Swedish woman who went on to explore feminist themes in her later directorial work in a bold and uncompromising manner. She was a figure not unlike Lotte Tarp: an energetic, indomitable and creatively active woman who survived a difficult upbringing — in her case poverty — to keep rediscovering and reinventing herself. Much of this story was told in her autobiography from 1984, *All Those Tomorrows*.

Like Lotte Tarp, her life was also brought to a close by cancer, in March of 1994 at the age of 68. She had remained active to the end. She performed in the 1993 Swedish film *Grandpa's Journey* alongside Max von Sydow, and was in London directing *The Woman Who Cleaned the World*, based on her own script, when she passed away.

Appendix V
English and Original Titles

This appendix lists English-language release titles followed by the titles under which they were released in their country of origin. An asterisk after a title indicates that an official English title does not exist or cannot be found and that the English version provided here is a literal translation of the original title. Films produced in English-speaking countries are not included here. A single entry (e.g. *Amour*) means that the foreign and English titles are the same, and when more than one English title is listed the first entry is usually the title that was used in America.

The Abyss (Afgrunden) 1910
Adventure in Denmark (Chun Man Dan Mai) 1973
Agent 69 Jensen in the Sign of Sagittarius/In the Sign of Sagittarius (I Skyttens Tegn) 1978
Agent 69 Jensen in the Sign of Scorpio/Emmanuelle in Denmark (I Skorpionens Tegn) 1977
Always Trouble (Altid Ballade) 1955
Amour 1970
Anita: Swedish Nymphet/Anita (Anita — Ur en Tonårsflickas Dagbok) 1974
Ann and Eve/Anybody's (Ann och Eve — de Erotiska) 1970
Around the World with Fanny Hill (Jorden Runt med Fanny Hill) 1974
Babette's Feast (Babettes Gæstebud) 1987
Bamboo House of Dolls (Nu Ji Zhong Ying:hk, Kvindefængslet I Bambushelvedet:dk) 1974
Be Dear to Me (Ingen Tid til Kærtegn) 1957
Bedside Head/Danish Bed and Board (Rektor på Sengekanten) 1972
Bedside Highway/Highway through the Bedroom (Motorvej på Sengekanten) 1972
Bedside Manner/Bedroom Mazurka (Mazurka på Sengekanten) 1970
Bedside Sailors (Sømænd på Sengekanten) 1976
Bel Ami 1976

The Beloved Family* (Den Kære Familie) 1962
Between the Sheets/Bedside Romance/Danish Pillow Talk (Romantik på Sengekantan) 1973
The Birthday Party (Liderlige Lisbeth) 1971
Blackjackets (Raggare!) 1959
Blonde in Bondage/Nothing but Blondes (Blondin i Fara) 1957
The Blue Balloon (Vilde Pornolyster) 1971
Bodil, a Summer Day in 1970 (En Sommerdag Med Ornepigen Bodil) 1970
Bordello/The Best Bit of Crumpet in Denmark (Bordellet — en Glædespiges Erindringer) 1972
Breaking Point 1975
Breaking the Waves 1996
Britta — The Artist's Model (Het Är Min Längtan) 1956
Campus Swingers (Schulmädchen — Report 4. Teil — Was Eltern Oft Verzweifeln Lässt) 1972
The Cats (Kattorna) 1965
The Celebration (Festen) 1998
Christian 1989
The Christine Keeler Story/The Christine Keeler Affair (Affæren Christine Keeler) 1963
City Street "Heroes" (Stenbroens "Helte") 1965
Come Blow the Horn! (Fäbodjäntan) 1978
Come to My Bedside (Der Må Være en Sengekant) 1975

Confessions of a Danish Cover Girl (Rapportpigen) 1974
Copenhagen Call-Girls (Villa Venneley/Call Girls Centralen — Villa Venneley) 1964
Crazy Paradise/Once Upon an Island (Det Tossede Paradis) 1962
Curtains for Mrs. Knudsen (Det Er Nat med Fru Knudsen) 1971
Cynthia's Sister (Overklassens Hemmelige Sexglæder) 1974
Daddy Darling 1968
Dagmar's Hot Pants, Inc./Dagmar & Co. (Dagmars Heta Trosor) 1971
Dangerous Kisses (Farlige Kys) 1972
Danish Blue/Man's Best Plaything (Det Kærlige Legetøj) 1968
Danish Dentist on the Job (Tandlæge på Sengekanten) 1971
Danish Escort Girls/Jumpin' at the Bedside (Hopla på Sengekanten) 1976
Danish Pastries (I Jomfruens Tegn) 1973
Day of Wrath/Day of Anger (Vredens Dag) 1943
Days of Sin and Nights of Nymphomania (Mellem Venner) 1963
Dear John (Käre John) 1964
The Decoy (Lockfågeln) 1971
Defiance (Trots) 1952
Delusion* (Blændværk) 1955
The Depraved/Exposed (Exponerad) 1971
Do You Believe in Swedish Sin?/Swedish Sin (Som Hon Bäddar Får Han Ligga) 1970
Doctor Glas (Doktor Glas) 1968
A Dog's Life (Mondo Cane) 1962
Dogville 2003
The Doll (Vaxdockan) 1962
Dorian Gray/The Evils of Dorian Gray/The Secret of Dorian Gray (Il Dio Chiamato Dorian) 1970
The Dress (Klänningen) 1964
The Duel (Duellen) 1962
The Element of Crime (Forbrydelsens Element) 1984
Eugenie ... The Story of Her Journey into Perversion/De Sade 70/Eugenie/Philosophy in the Boudoir (Die Jungfrau und die Peitsche) 1970
Facts: Copenhagen Sex-Report (Sådan er Porno) 1971
Faithless (Trolösa) 2000
Fear Has 1,000 Eyes (Skräcken Har 1000 Ögon) 1970/73
First Prize Irene (Il Primo Premio si Chiama Irene/Danimarca — l'incredibile realtà della nuova morale) 1969
Flourishing Times (Blomstrande Tider) 1980

For the Sake of Friendship* (...För Vänskaps Skull...) 1965
491 1964
Freedom to Love (Freiheit für die liebe/Frihed til at Elske) 1969
Gertrud 1964
The Girl and Pan* (Pigen og Pan) 1943
Girl Without a Name (Flicka Utan Namn) 1954
The Girls (Flickorna) 1968
Girls at Arms (Piger i Trøjen) 1975
Girls Without Rooms (Flamman) 1956
Give God a Chance on Sunday (Giv Gud en Chance om Søndagen) 1970
Golden Bananas (Liebesmarkt in Dänemark) 1970
Grandpa's Journey (Morfars Resa) 1993
The Green-eyed Elephant (Elefanter på Loftet) 1960
Grimm's Fairy Tales for Adults (Grimms Märchen von Lüsternen Pärchen) 1969
Guess Who's Sleeping with Us Tonight?/The Swingin' Pussycats (Rat' Mal, Wer Heut bei uns Schläft...?) 1969
Guilt/Guilt: Together with Gunilla/With Gunilla Monday Evening and Tuesday (Tillsammans med Gunilla Måndag Kväll och Tisdag) 1965
Hagbard and Signe/The Red Mantle (Den Røde Kappe) 1967
Harry and the Butler (Harry og Kammertjeneren) 1961
Heaven and Hell* (Himmel og Helvete — No, Vejen til Helvede — dk) 1969
Hit House 1965
A Hole in My Heart (Ett Hål i Mitt Hjärta) 2004
Hoodlums/Gangsters 1979
How to Behave in a Fourposter Bed/Danish Delights (Takt og Tone I Himmelsengen) 1972
Hunger (Sult) 1966
Hunting Edible Mushrooms with Christina* (Christinas Svampskola) 1993
I, a Lover (Jeg — en Elsker) 1966
I, a Nobleman/the reluctant sadist (jeg — en marki) 1967
I, a Woman (Jeg — en Kvinde) 1965
I, a Woman 2 (jeg — en kvinde 2) 1968
I, a Woman 3/daughter, the (3 slags kærlighed) 1970
I Am Curious (Blue)/(Jag Är Nyfiken — En Film i Blåt) 1968
I Am Curious (Yellow)/(Jag Är Nyfiken — En Film i Gult) 1967
I Love Blue (Jeg Elsker Blåt) 1968
I, the Body (Morianerna) 1965

I Want to Have That Thing Too* (So Ein Ding Muss Ich Auch Haben)
The Idiots (Idioterne) 1998
Illicit Interlude/Summer Interlude (Sommarlek) 1951
Inga/Inga: I, a Virgin/Inga: I Have Lust (Jag, en Oskuld) 1968
Inga and Greta/Inga Two/The Seduction of Inga (Någon att Älska) 1969
In the Realm of the Senses (Ai No Corrida — Japan, I Sansernes Vold — dk) 1976
In the Sign of the Gemini (I Tvillingernes Tegn) 1975
In the Sign of the Lion (I Løvens Tegn) 1976
In the Sign of the Taurus (I Tyrens tegn) 1974
Jan Goes to the Movies* (Jan Går til Filmen) 1954
Jesus Is in the House/The Bloody Cross (Jeg Så Jesus Dø) 1975
Johnny Larsen 1979
Journey to the Seventh Planet 1962
Juliette de Sade/Heterosexual (Juliette de Sade) 1969
Just Once More (Chans) 1962
Justine and Juliette (Justine och Juliette) 1975
The Key Hole* (Nøglehullet) 1974
The Kingdom (Riget) 1994, 1997
Ladies' Man (Damernes Ven) 1969
Laila, the Pure (Leïla) 2001
The Language of Love (Kärlekens Spräk) 1969
Life on the Hegn Farm* (Livet på Hegnsgaard) 1934
Live Show in Kopenhagen (?) 1973
Look Out, Little Man!* (Lille Mand, Pas På!) 1968
Love in the 3rd Position/Siv, Anne and Sven 1972
Love in 3D (Liebe in Drei Dimensionen) 1973
Love Mates/Do You Believe in Angels? (Änglar, Finns Dom?)
Love Me Darling (Med Kærlig Hilsen) 1971
Love's Island (Kärleksön) 1978
Loving Couples (Älskande Par) 1964
Lust for the Sun (*Around the World with Nothing On*, aka *Searching for Venus, Searching for Venus Around the World, A Trip Around the World*) 1958/1961/1963
The Lustful Vicar (Kyrkoherden) 1970
Maid in Sweden/The Milkmaid 1971
Malamondo (I Malamondo) 1964
A Man with a Maid/A Man in the Making/Victorian Fantasies/The Groove Room/Teenage Tickle Girls/What the Swedish Butler Saw (Champagne på Sengekanten, Champagnegaloppen) 1975

Me and Charly (Mig og Charly) 1978
The Mini-Skirt Gang 1975
Miss Julie (Fröken Julie) 1951
Mission Stardust/Operation Stardust/You Only Live Once (...4...3...2...1 Morte) 1967
More About the Language of Love/More from the Language of Love (Inge og Sten Spør) 1970
More Sex Please (Tugt & Utugt) 2001
Morianna/I, the Body (morianerna) 1965
My Life to Live/It's My Life (Vivre sa Vie: Filmen Douze Tableaux) 1962
My Sister, My Love (Syskonbädd 1782) 1966
My Uncle/My Uncle, Mr. Hulot (Mon Oncle) 1958
Never on Sunday (Pote tin Kyriaki) 1960
Night Games (Nattlek) 1966
Ole Ege — the Naughty Boy (Den Grimme Dreng) 1996
The Olsen Gang (Olsenbanden) 1968
One Among Many* (En Blandt Mange) 1961
One Summer of Happiness (Hon Dansade en Sommar) 1951
One Swedish Summer/As the Naked Wind from the Sea (Som Havets Nakna Vind) 1968
Oswalt Kolle: Your Husband, the Unknown Creature (Oswalt Kolle: Dein Mann, das Unbekannte Wesen) 1970
Pelle the Conqueror (Pelle Erobreren) 1987
People Meet and Sweet Music Fills the Heart/People Meet (Mennesker Mødes og Sød Musik Pstår i Hjertet) 1967
Persona 1966
The Pipes (Dýmky) 1966
Porn All Over the World* (Alverdens Porno) 1973
Porno — Made in Denmark 1972
The Porno Star Travels Around Japan/Journey to Japan (Poruno No Joô: Nippon Sex Ryokô) 1973
Pornography — A Musical (Pornografi) 1971
Pornography in Denmark (Pornografie in Dänemark — Zur Sache, Kätzchen) 1970
Pornoshop 1965
Practice Makes Perfect/Country Life (Ta Mej i Dalen) 1977
Princess 2006
Quiet Days in Clichy (Stille Dage i Clichy) 1970
Rape Me/Kiss Me (Baise-moi) 2000
Relations — The Love Story from Denmark/Tumult (Sonja — 16 år) 1969
Report from Stockholm's Sex Swamp* (Rapport från Stockholm's Sexträsk) 1973/74
Reptilicus 1961

Retribution* (Gengæld) 1955
The Return (Jesus Vender Tilbage) 1992
Rikki and the Men* (Rikki og Mændene) 1962
Royal Deceit/The Prince of Jutland (Amled, Prinsen af Jylland) 1994
Sadist (Träfracken) 1966
School for Suicide (Selvmordsskolen) 1964
The Seventh Seal (Det Sjunde Inseglet) 1957
Sex and Fury (Furyô Anego Den: Inoshika Ochô) 1973
Sex Galore (Sex en Gros) 1971
Sex in Sweden/Molly 1977
Sex, Lies & Video Violence* (Sex, Lögner & Videovåld) 2000
Sexy Girls of Denmark (Dan Ma Jiao Wa) 1973
Shanty Town* (Söderkåkar) 1970
The Silence (Tystnaden) 1963
Sin Alley (Bundfald) 1957
The Sinful Dwarf/The Abducted Bride/The Toy Box (Dværgen) 1974
Smile Emil (Smil Emil) 1969
Soft Shoulders, Sharp Curves (Die Auto-Nummer, Sex auf Rädern)1972
The Song of the Red Ruby (Den Røde Rubin) 1970
Sonja/Operation Lovebirds (Slå Først, Frede) 1965
Soya's 17 (Sytten) 1965
Stimulantia 1967
Stine and the Boys (Stine og Drengene) 1969
A Strange Romance (En Mærkelig Kærlighed) 1968
A Stranger Knocks (En Fremmed Banker På) 1959
Street Without End (Gade Uden Ende), 1963
Summer with Monika/Monika, the Story of a Bad Girl (Sommaren med Monika) 1953
Summer with Vanja* (Sommaren med Vanja) 1980
A Sunday in September (En Söndag i September) 1963
Sweden: Heaven or Hell? (Svenzia: Inferno e Paradiso) 1968
Swedish and Underage/Eva/Eva: Was Everything but Legal/Eva: Diary of a Half Virgin (Eva — Den Utstötta) 1969
Swedish Fly Girls/Christa (Frigjorte Christa) 1972 (produced 1970)
The Swedish Mistress (älskarinnan) 1962
Swedish Punks (Raggargänget) 1962
Swedish Sex Games/Let Us Play Sex/The Intruders 1974
Swedish Wedding Night/Wedding: Swedish Style (Bröllopsbesvär) 1964
Swedish Wildcats/A Man with a Maid/Every Afternoon 1972
The Sweet Life (La Dolce Vita) 1960
The Sweet Life of Majorca* (Mallorcas Søde Liv) 1965
The Swinging Co-eds/Sex at the Olympics (Mädchen, die Nach München Kommen) 1972
The Swinging Stewardesses/Sweet Sensations/Stewardesses Report (Die Stewardessen) 1971
Taboo (Tabu) 1977
Tenderness/Danish Love/Romantic Memoirs (Baksmälla) 1973
That's How They Do It!* (Sådan Gør de Det!) 1972
That's How They Do It—Again!* (Sådan Gør de Det — Også!) 1973
There Comes a Day* (Der Kom en Dag) 1955
They Call Her One-Eye/Hooker's Revenge/Thriller: A Cruel Picture (Thriller — En Grym Film) 1972–74
Three-Cornered Bed/Do You Want to Remain a Virgin Forever? (Willst du Ewig Jungfrau Bleiben?) 1969
Threesome (trekanter) 1972
Ticket to Paradise (Biljett till Paradiset) 1962
Time of Desire (Hästhandlarens Flickor) 1954
Tine 1964
To Ingrid, My Love, Lisa!/Yes!/Yes! (Count the Possibilities)/(Kvinnolek) 1968
To Love (Att Älska) 1964
Tomorrow My Love (i morgen, min elskede) 1971
Torment/Frenzy (Hets) 1944
24 Hours with Ilse (Et Døgn med Ilse) 1971
Two* (To) 1964
Two Times Two in the Fourposter (Halløj i Himmelsengen) 1965
Ullabella 1961
Unmarried Mothers (Ogift Fader Sökes) 1953
Veil of Lust/Veil of Blood/Vampire Ecstasy (Den Pornografiske Jungfrun) 1973
Venom/Gift (Gift) 1966
Vibration (Lejonsommar) 1968
The Vicious Breed (Farlig Frihet) 1954
The Virgin Spring (Jungfrukällan) 1960
Weekend 1962
What Are You Doing After the Orgy?/Dog Days (Rötmånad) 1970
What Schoolgirls Don't Tell/Secrets of Sweet Sixteen (Was Schulmädchen Verschweigen) 1973
When Marie Met Fredrik* (Hur Marie Träffade Fredrik) 1969
While the City Sleeps (Medan Staden Sover) 1949/50

Who Said "Scandalized"?* (Hvem Sagde Forarget?) 1968
Who's Doing What to Whom? (Hvem Skal Med Hvem?) 1971
Why? (Hvorfor Gør de Det?) 1971
Wild Strawberries (Smultronstället) 1957
Winter's Light/The Communicants (Nattvardsgästerna) 1963
Witchcraft Through the Ages/Witch, the Witches (Heksen, dk/Häxan, se)
Without a Stitch (Uden en Trævl) 1968
Without Kin (Frændeløs) 1970
A Woman's Mind* (Kvindesind) 1980
Women of the World (La Donna nel Mondo)— 1963
The Word (Ordet) 1955
A World of Strangers (Dilemma) 1962
Young Girls Disappear in Copenhagen* (Unge Piger forsvinder i København) 1951
Young Playthings/Intimate Playthings/The Red Witch 1972

Notes

A substantial amount of information was derived from the clippings file at the Danish Film Institute in Copenhagen. Many of the old newspaper clippings in that file lack page and section numbers, and authors are frequently not credited or credited only by initials or abbreviations. In the notes below each article has been identified as completely as possible. English translations of Danish headlines (and all other necessary translations in the book) are the author's.

Introduction

1. Phyllis Kronhausen and Eberhard Kronhausen, *The Sex People: Erotic Performers and Their Bold New Worlds* (New York: Playboy, 1975).

Part One

1. This nationalistic adoration of nature was taken to dark extremes by the Nazis, who considered their forests so sacred that they contemplated banning Jews from entering them.

2. Tapani Suominen, "Norden som fiktion," *Löntagaren,* September 3, 2001, http://www.lontagaren.fi/lt2001/lt0107/l010903-k1.html.

3. "Man smider" (One Drops One's [Underwear]), *Berlingske Aftenavis,* August 8, 1961.

4. Freddie's case hinged primarily on two works of art. One was a painting, *Fornojelsernes Legionærer* (The Defenders/Soldiers of Pleasure), which depicted, as a court official soberly put it, "a naked man who from behind leads his member into a naked woman's genitals." The other was a sculpture, the bust of a proper lady, resolute of gaze and of apparent high breeding. This work had been made by another artist and Freddie's contribution to this otherwise run-of-the-mill piece was a semi-aroused penis that ran from ear to cheek. These two works, among others, had been seized by the authorities back in 1937 during the scandal-plagued *Sex Surreal* exhibit for which Freddie was also sentenced to 20 days in prison.

In January of 1961 he wrote to the justice minister and requested that his works be returned. Times were different now; the dark ages of the '30s were ancient history and it was time for a reevaluation of the charges. Or so Freddie hoped. But the authorities were unwilling to reopen the case, and so he announced to the Danish media that he had begun to make copies of the confiscated works and that soon they would be on display in a Copenhagen gallery. He kept his word, and the copies were duly seized by the police.

In March of 1962 charges against Freddie were officially filed. Just as in 1937, the affair gave rise to a wider debate about the responsibilities inherent in artistic expression and the nature of "frisind." The debate turned pornography and censorship into fashionable political topics and gave the public an issue about which everybody could have a strong opinion. It didn't hurt that Freddie himself was a very colorful character. Moreover, court cases against erotic novels such as *The Song of the Red Ruby* and *Sexus* were also taking place at this time, and soon the trial against *Fanny Hill* would begin, creating even more buzz around the issue. At the more *déclassé* end of the spectrum periodic crackdowns were launched against smuttier newsstand fare such as tabloids and pulp paperbacks. Censorship was truly the issue of the day.

Freddie's case finally came to trial in September of 1962. The original artworks as well as the copies were transported to the courtroom under guard and put on display—*under sheets* so the public couldn't see them! The verdict was mixed: The painting was acquitted but not the bust, which was still ruled obscene.

Freddie immediately appealed, and the board of the city's art academy was asked to reevaluate the works—for the fourth time. Once again they contemplated the bust, that absurdist art prank that had already traveled many times to and fro in a guarded police van, with a sheet over its head like some hideous Medusa that could inspire mass perversion in all who gazed upon it. Finally in January of 1963 Freddie was acquitted of all charges and got back all his artworks, including the bust. All the works were driven to his studio in a police car.

The trials had jolted the whole system and altered the way that pornography would come to be regarded as a prosecutable offense and as a mode of artistic expression. With the enthusiastic collusion of the yellow press, "the Freddie Affair" had come to figure as the first media circus of the decade, and the lessons learned would not be lost on filmmakers soon to fight the same battle. But that was hardly the end of Wilhelm Freddie. He continued to throw wild parties and remained a rabble-rouser and a fierce advocate of freedom of expression until his death in 1995.

5. Jes Stein Pedersen, "Perversitetens mudderpøl" ("The Mud Puddle of Perversity"), *Politiken*, May 25, 2002.

6. *Sexual Behavior in the Human Male*, 1948; *Sexual Behavior in the Human Female*, 1953; *Kinsey and Women*, 1955.

7. Dogme95 is the back-to-basics film movement launched in 1995 by Lars von Trier and Thomas Vinterberg; it also came to include Søren Kragh-Jacobsen and Kristian Levring. They formulated a set of rules intended to force filmmakers back to a more primitive and, they hoped, honest style. Von Trier in particular was inspired by a number of earlier Danish films profiled in this book. For more information refer to Jack Stevenson, *Dogme Uncut* (Santa Monica CA: Santa Monica Press, 2003).

8. The folk-comedy genre was born in the '30s, and the films could include melodrama as well as humor. Folk comedies espoused traditional "down home" values and were usually set in a Danish neverland of sunny, rural landscapes. They were scored with the popular music of the day and populated with recurring types played by the same beloved actors over and over.

9. "Livlige discussion i Studenterforeningen" (Lively Discussion at the Student Union), *Århus Stiftstidende*, October 30, 1962.

10. [Credited to] Thop, "'Weekend' samtaleemne i Berlin" ("Weekend" Is the "Talk of the Town" in Berlin), *Ekstra Bladet (EB)*, June 26, 1963.

11. Ise Keller, Letter to the editor, *Vestkysten*, October 28, 1963.

12. Elmard Larsen, "'Weekend' skal repræsentere Danmark" ("Weekend" Represents Denmark), *Jyllands Posten*, November 8, 1963.

13. [Credited to] Mother to two girls in the U.S.A., "Flov affære" (Embarrassing Affair), *B.T.*, November 11, 1963.

14. [Credited to] Eric C., "Blæse være med respekten" (Never Mind Respect), *Kalundborg Folkeblad*, September 17, 1964.

15. Sven Rye, "Hollywood har lavet om på 'Weekend'" (Hollywood Has Remade "Weekend"), *Ekstra Bladet*, December 8, 1966.

16. Paul Newman's encounter with a convention of Swedish nudists in Hitchcock's *Torn Curtain* from 1966 is an excellent example of how the wider world saw the phenomenon—and Swedes—at that point in time.

17. "Det glædesløse liv" (The Bleak Life), *Ekstra Bladet*, June 25, 1963.

18. Ib Monty, "Nyt Skridt Frem for dansk Film" (New Step Forward for Danish Film), *Jyllands Posten*, July 4, 1963.

19. "Viser folk noget andet end det de regner med" (Show People Something Other Than What They Expect), *Århus Amtstidende*, July 2, 1963.

20. A humanistic and open-minded approach to life based on the philosophies of Nikolaj Grundtvig (1783–1872), whose concept of the "school for life" led to the establishment of the Danish folk high school system and to a general belief that people should continue to learn and broaden their horizons throughout the whole of their lives.

21. The (in)famous monster movie made by the American Sidney Pink. Erotic content is nil in the three films Pink made on his sojourn to Denmark in the early '60s (*The Green Eyed Elephant* and *Journey to the Seventh Planet* being the other two), which were savaged by Danish critics with little understanding of or sympathy for B-movie aesthetics.

22. Nils Thorsen, "Kedeligere striptease har man ikke set" (A More Boring Striptease You Have Never Seen), *Politiken*, March 27, 2005.

23. Nan Henningsen, "Jeg hader alle der gaar over gevind" (I Hate Anyone Who Overdoes It), *Information*, April 3, 1964.

24. Jørgen Leth, "Frontkæmpere" (Soldier on the Front Lines), *Politiken*, April 5, 1964.

25. Nan Henningsen, *Information*, April 3, 1964.

26. Ove Brusendorff and Poul Malmkjær, *Erotik i Filmen—Den Nøgne Bølge* (Erotica in Film: The Naked Wave) (Copenhagen: Thaning & Appels, 1965), p. 74.

27. Vilgot Sjöman, *I Was Curious: Diary of the Making of a Film* (New York: Grove, 1968), p. 3.

28. Kathrine Skretting, "Filmsex og Filmsensur: Sengekant-filmene i Skandinavia, 1970–1976" (Film Sex and Film Censorship: The *Bedside* Film Series in Scandinavia, 1970–1976), *Norsk Mediatidsskrift* **10** (2003), 75–95.

29. A film funding arrangement launched in 1964 to support productions that had literary or artistic merit but had difficulties competing with commercial films. It was similar to the Film Reform Agreement that had been enacted in Sweden in 1963 and reflected a growing awareness in Scandinavia that film was, or could be, art.

30. "Siv Holm angriber filmatiseringen af 'Jeg — en Kvinde'" (Siv Holm Attacks the Film Adaptation of *I, a Woman*), *Sjællands Tidende*, September 23, 1965.

31. [Credited to] P.G., "Liderlige æbleskiver" (Horny Donuts), *Aktuelt*, September 18, 1965.

32. Sven Borre, "Bag kulisserne" (Behind the Curtains), *Ekstra Bladet*, October 12, 1967.

33. Kenneth Turan and Stephen F. Zito, *Sinema: American Pornographic Films and the People Who Make Them* (New York: Praeger, 1974), p. 72.

34. "Dansk film i Tokio" (Danish Film in Tokyo), *Fyens Stiftstidende*, June 16, 1968.

35. Turan and Zito, p. 74.

36. *Ibid.*, p. 66.

37. Danny Peary, *Cult Movie Stars* (New York: Simon & Schuster, 1991), p. 430.

38. [Credited to] Gorm, "'Gift' blev frikendt i aftes" ("Gift" Found Not Guilty Last Night), *Aktuelt*, February 16, 1966.

39. "Pornografi en snigende gift" (Pornography an Insidious Poison), *Skanderborg Amts Avis*, April 9, 1966.

40. *Sight and Sound* **17**, no. 6 (June 2007), p. 23.

41. John Waters, e-mail to author, June 23, 2006.

Part Two

1. Vilgot Sjöman, *I Was Curious: Diary of the Making of a Film* (New York: Grove, 1968), p. 97.

2. Leonard Gross, "After Nudity, What, Indeed?" *Look*, April 29, 1969, p. 80.

3. "Martin Luther King actor mod sin vilje" (Martin Luther King an Actor Against His Will), *Århus Demokraten*, February 29, 1968.

4. Joe Bob Briggs, *Profoundly Erotic: Sexy Movies That Changed History* (New York: Universe, 2005), p. 226.

5. Knud Voeler, "Jeg — en provopige" (I, a Provo Girl), *Aktuelt*, December 12, 1967.

6. Hollis Alpert, "SR Goes to the Movies: On Being Curious Twice," *Saturday Review*, March 15, 1969.

7. Gross, "After Nudity."

8. J. Anker Nielsen, "Sex-revolution slår gnister i bornerte USA" (Sex Revolution Ignites Sparks in Prissy USA), *Politiken*, April 10, 1969.

9. Lotta Svedberg, "Ansikte mod ansikte: Lena Nyman" (Face to Face: Lena Nyman), *Chaplin*, no. 258 (Summer 1995), p. 40.

10. Bent Blüdnikow, "Lir uden lynlåse" (Tease Without Zipper), *Berlingske Tidende*, September 13, 2006.

11. A poll taken in 2006 (reported in the *Copenhagen Post*, 1–7 Dec. 2006, in article filed by Uzi Frank) revealed that the international public was just as likely to associate Swedish brands such as Ikea and Volvo with Denmark.

12. These were American exploitation sub-genres that surfaced in the '60s. These films tried, despite low budgets and censorship limitations, to be as mean, sick, nasty and depraved as possible. Films like *Shanty Tramp*, *The Defilers*, *Two Thousand Maniacs*, *Blood Feast* and *The Animal* attracted rowdy working-class audiences, and their lurid titles, blinking from the battered marquees of inner-city theatres, stood as proof to horrified suburbanites that the urban areas were in frightening decline. (The films of Poul Nyrup would definitely have qualified as "kinkies" and "roughies.")

13. A pseudo-documentary genre pioneered by the Italians in 1963 with *Mondo Cane*. The countless mondo films produced in the wake of this historic success were characterized by a sensationalist, travelogue approach and a love of ghoulish spectacle that gave them the kind of popular appeal that eluded most serious documentaries. The mondo genre is exploitation cinema in its purest form.

14. Mette Hjort and Ib Bondebjerg, *Instruktørens blik — en interviewbog om dansk film* (Danish Directors: Dialogues on a Contemporary National Cinema) (Copenhagen: Rosinante, 2000), p. 37.

15. [Credited to] jawa, "Det kære legetøj er solgt til USA for kæmpe-beløb" (Danish Blue Is Sold to the States for a Massive Sum), *Aktuelt*, August 25, 1968.

16. [Credited to] bk, "Film-nyt: Forsinket provokation" (Film News: Provocation Past Its Sell-by Date), *Vestkysten*, July 30, 1968.

17. [Credited to] tt., "Film og teater: Legetøj ... mon dog" (A Play-toy ... and Yet), *Randers Folkebladet*, July 30, 1968.

18. The term "Provo" indicates a sense of jubilant anti-authoritarianism. It refers to a formal movement that reached its apex in Holland in the '60s and '70s and was characterized by creative leftist anarchism channeled into "actions," "happenings" and pranks.

19. Edward De Grazia and Roger K. Newman, *Banned Films — Movies, Censors and the First Amendment* (New York: Bowker, 1982), p. 336.

20. "'Uden en trævl' laver ravage" ("Without a Stitch" Spreads Havoc), *Berlingske Aftenavis,* February 2, 1970.

21. Jørgen Larsen, "Forargelse over Danmark" (Indignation Rains Down on Denmark), *Berlingske Tidende,* February 2, 2006.

22. These interviews with Whitehouse and Langford are contained in the 2001 Danish documentary *Tugt & Utugt* (More Sex Please) by Torben Skjødt Jensen and Ghita Beckendorff.

23. Lizzie Bundgaard, "Ømhed er vigtigere end orgasme jagt" (Affection Is More Important Than the Hunt for Orgasm), *Ekstra Bladet,* April 19, 1969.

24. [Credited to] Bjørk, "7 børn så på forbudt film" (Seven Children Saw a Forbidden Film), *Aktuelt,* December 11, 1969.

25. "Lad os se den sex-film i skolerne" (Let Us See That Sex Film in the Schools), *Ekstra Bladet,* November 25, 1969.

26. Authored by school teachers Søren Hansen and Jesper Jensen and published in Denmark in 1969.

27. Hollis Alpert, "SR Goes to the Movies: Mine Eyes Have Seen the Glory," *Saturday Review,* May 16, 1970.

28. Kurt Poulsen, "Berømthed leder efter dansk pige: Jack O'Connell, USA-stjerne, i Danmark" (Famous Director Searches for a Danish Girl: Jack O'Connell, a Star from the USA, in Denmark), *Ekstra Bladet,* June 14, 1969.

29. "Filmmand: Nøgenhed er frihed og ikke spor sex" (Film Boss: Nudity Is About Freedom and Not at All About Sex), *B.T.,* July 12, 1969.

30. [Article heading unrecoverable], *Ekstra Bladet,* February 10, 1970.

31. Jens Jørgen Thorsen, "I seng med sveriges konge igen" (In Bed with Sweden's King Again), *Ekstra Bladet,* November 12, 1980.

32. [Credited to] Spect, "Det er ægte sex" (It Is Real Sex), *Politiken,* May 10, 1970.

33. A "genitals-only" penetration close-up performed by professional porn actors (usually), and simply spliced into a film to roughly conform with the action taking place.

34. Philip Lauritzen, [title unrecoverable], *Jyllands Posten,* May 16, 1970.

35. Claus Rdde, "Hvis er Hvems i pornofilm" (Whose Is Whose in Porno Film), *Aktuelt,* May 17, 1970.

36. Suzanne Giese, "Er han så revolutionær ham Thorsen" (Is He So Revolutionary, That Thorsen?), *Ekstra Bladet,* July 29, 1970.

37. "Miller forundret over forbud mod dansk film" (Miller Astonished About Ban on Danish Film), *Weekendavisen,* August 14, 1970.

38. "De dage, man bare lever" (The Days When You Just Lived), *NB,* January 16, 1970.

39. [Credited to] kk., "Danmark må købe 'Stilled dage i Clichy' tilbage, er ikke uartig nok til USA" (Denmark Must Buy "Quiet Days in Clichy" Back, It's Not Naughty Enough for the USA), *B.T.,* February 2, 1971. The author mailed Barney Rosset these passages and financial figures relating to his films. Rosset reportedly did read these texts but was not forthcoming with any corrections.

40. [Credited to] Lars, "Millionær med komplikationer" (Millionaire with Complications), *Aktuelt,* November 20, 1970.

41. "Stille Dage i Clichy Bryder Fransk sexmur" ("Quiet Days in Clichy" Breaks French Sex Barrier), *Ekstra Bladet,* February 26, 1971.

42. [Credited to] kais, "Morsom erotisk komedie i Kino" (Amusing Erotic Comedy in the Cinema), *Roskilde Tidende,* October 31, 1970.

43. "Svenskerne helt vilde med Ole Søltoft" (Swedes Completely Crazy About Ole Søltoft), *Ekstra Bladet,* February 8, 1971.

44. "Valgkamp med dansk porno" (Election Campaign with Danish Porno), *Jyllands Posten,* September 16, 1973.

Part Three

1. Paul Hammerich, *Opgang og nedtur* (Boom and Bust) (Copenhagen: Gyldendal, 1980), pp. 528–29.

2. Fabricated titles to nonexistent films.

3. Hammerich, *Opgang og nedtur,* p. 528.

4. [Credited to] Molle, "Det er dansk — Det er porno —" (It's Danish — It's Porn —), *Næstved Tidende,* April 21, 1971.

5. Morten Piil, *Danish Film from A to Z* (Copenhagen: Gyldendal, 2000), p. 228.

6. Henrik Iversen, "Dansk paradis i Cannes" (Danish Paradise in Cannes), *Berlingske Tidende,* May 16, 1971.

7. Nils Markvardsen, "Frigjort — på café med Birte Tove" (Liberated — a Meeting with Birte Tove at a Café), *eXtase,* no. 2 (November 2004), p. 6.

8. Sam Arkoff, *Flying Through Hollywood by the Seat of My Pants* (New York: Birch Lane, 1992), p. 195.

9. [Credited to] Pedro, "Om og om og om igen" (Do It Again and Again and Again), *Århus Demokraten,* January 30, 1971.

10. "Føler de er lokket ind i en pornofilm" (Felt They Were Lured into a Porn Film), *Aktuelt,* October 15, 1970.

11. Else Sander, "På kanten af virkeligheden" (On the Edge of Reality), *Ekstra Bladet,* April 15, 1974.

12. Phyllis Kronhausen and Eberhard Kron-

hausen, *The Sex People: Erotic Performers and Their Bold New Worlds* (New York: Playboy, 1975), p. 84.

13. [Credited to] blak, "Hvor den strutter" (How It Struts), *Århus Stiftstidende*, July 11, 1972.

14. Jens Rebensdorff, "Meget Vovet" (Very Risqué), *Berlingske Tidende*, July 10, 2005.

15. *Ibid*.

16. Neither achieved significant success in the States. Savage Rose, for their part, walked out on a contract with a major American record company because it stipulated they had to perform for the troops in Vietnam.

17. Per Olov Qvist and Peter von Bagh, *Guide to the Cinema of Sweden and Finland* (Westport CT: Greenwood, 2000), p. 111.

18. Jan Lumholdt, "I, Christina Lindberg," *Defekt*, no. 2 (1996), p. 16.

19. *Ibid*, p. 17.

20. Allan Bryce, "One Eyed Hacks!" *The Dark Side—The Magazine of the Macabre and Fantastic*, no. 95 (February/March 2002), p. 19.

Part Four

1. Bjørn Lindahl, "Norge tillader nu hardcore porno" (Hard-core Porn Now Permitted in Norway), *Politiken*, March 16, 2006.

2. Kim Skotte, "Sex: Kunsten på ordet" (Sex: Art in the Word), *Politiken*, December 27, 2006.

3. Released in the summer of 2006, *Princess* is an inventive mix of animation and live action tells the tragic tale of a young mother whose brief career as a porn star leads to her dissolution and death by overdose. Her brother, August, takes custody of his young, now motherless niece, who was left to be cared for in a bordello where she was the victim of abuse and violence. The outraged August now wages war on the porno industry in a movie full of sex, violence and at least one jolting castration scene.

4. Hanna Blanksvärd, "Sexfilmen som ska lära svenskarna att älska" (The Sex Film That Would Teach Swedes to Love), *Aftonbladet*, January 31, 2002.

5. In the fall of 2005 twelve cartoons depicting the prophet Mohammed were published in the conservative daily paper *Jyllands Posten*. Publication of the drawings remained largely a domestic issue until the start of 2006 when they came to the attention of an international public and created anger and ill will toward Denmark in Muslim countries, where in a handful of instances Danish embassies were set ablaze and economic boycotts were initiated.

6. www.sweden.se/templates/cs/commonpage_13325.aspx.

7. Sanne Maja Funch Christensen and Kim Faber, "Flere vil forbyde købesex" (More Will Forbid the Purchase of Sex), *Politiken*, December 27, 2006.

8. Tine Maria Winther, "Nypuritanisme er det værste vås" (New Puritanism Is the Worst Drivel), *Politiken*, January 14, 2006.

9. Thomas Krog and Margit Shabanzadeh, "Dyresex forbliver lovligt i Danmark" (Animal Sex Remains Legal in Denmark), *24 Timer*, November 29, 2006. Of European countries, only England actually has a law specifically prohibiting sex with animals. Controversy arose in Denmark in November of 2006 when an advisory board refused to recommend the passing of such a law. Holland has more recently passed legislation banning animal pornography.

10. Christian N. Eversbusch, "Porno-tv skader integration" (Porno-TV Damages Integration), *Politiken*, March 2, 2006.

11. This term has appeared in, among other places, the conservative American paper *The Liberty Banner*.

12. Anne Mette Lundtofte, "Bor Djævelen i Danmark?" (Does the Devil Live in Denmark?), *Politiken*, November 2, 2006.

Appendix I

1. *Situationists 1957–71 Drakabygget*, catalog text from the exhibition "Situationists 1957–71," which was mounted at Skånska Art Museum in Lund, Sweden, in 1971 by Elisabet Hagund and Kristina Garmer.

2. *Ibid*.

3. See chapter 1, note 4.

4. Bo Tao Michaëlis, "En provo er død" (A Provo Is Dead), *Politiken*, November 17, 2000.

5. Kaare Schmidt, "Thorsen og Kaos" (Thorsen and Chaos), *Kosmorama*, issue 199, 1992.

6. *Ibid*.

7. One might refer to *The X-Rated Bible*, a publication that for many years was being sold by the American Atheist Press.

Appendix III

1. Jim Haynes, *Thanks for Coming!* (London: Faber and Faber, 1984), p. 164.

2. Haynes, *Thanks for Coming!* p. 228.

3. Jim Haynes was visiting Henry Miller in Los Angeles when *Quiet Days in Clichy* came out, and Miller asked him to contact Thorsen when he got back to Europe and tell him that he greatly enjoyed the film. Haynes did so, and he and Thorsen became good friends. Haynes, *Thanks for Coming!* pp. 236–37.

Appendix IV

1. As the author was unable to obtain a viewing copy of *Taboo*, this description is largely dependent on the synopsis found in Daniel Dellamorte's *Svensk Sensationsfilm: en ocensurerad guide till den fördolda svenska film* (Sensational Swedish Films: An Uncensored Guide to Sweden's Secret Film History). Dellamorte detects a politico-religious message in *Taboo* which he claims gets mostly lost in all the sweaty confusion. He seems to perceive that Sjöman, despite his reputation as a serious filmmaker, has a secret love of sleaze. Dellamorte declares *Taboo* to be one of Sjöman's best films.

2. Lars Wikborg, "Frevert får stemmer på porno-plakat" (Porno Poster Wins Frevert Votes), *Urban,* November 15, 2005.

3. [Credited to] "Rud," "Orgasmen var ikke andet end gas" (The Orgasm Was Nothing but Hot Air), *Ekstra Bladet,* September 2, 1982.

4. Lars Aksel Jakobsen, "Mine dage med Dali" (My Days with Dali), *Aktuelt,* March 2, 1990.

5. Karsten Brønnum, "Et liv der gik i smadder" (A Life That Went to the Dogs), *Ekstra Bladet,* March 17, 1996.

6. The Jante Law consists of ten rules of behavior introduced in the 1933 novel *A Refugee Crosses His Tracks* by the Norwegian writer Aksel Sandemose, who lived in Denmark for a period. These rules, which include "Do not think you are special, do not think you are good at anything, do not think you are better than us," governed life in the mythical Danish town of Jante and can be boiled down to "Don't think you are anybody." The Jante Law is constantly invoked today in egalitarian Denmark whenever someone attempts something new or different or is considered too brash and must be "knocked back into place." (Or perhaps also when someone fails at something and must find an excuse.)

Bibliography

Arkoff, Sam. *Flying Through Hollywood by the Seat of My Pants*. New York: Birch Lane, 1992.

Bjørneboe, Jens. *Uden en trævl* (Without a Stitch). Copenhagen: Stig Vendelkærs, 1967.

Briggs, Joe Bob. *Profoundly Erotic: Sexy Movies That Changed History*. New York: Universe, 2005.

Brusendorff, Ove, and Poul Malmkjær. *Erotik i filmen: Den nøgne bølge* (Erotica in Film: The Naked Wave). Copenhagen: Thaning & Appels, 1965.

Bryce, Allan. "One Eyed Hacks!" *The Dark Side— The Magazine of the Macabre and Fantastic*, no. 95 (February/March 2002): 19–21.

De Grazia, Edward, and Roger K. Newman. *Banned Films*. New York: Bowker, 1982.

Dellamorte, Daniel. *Svensk Sensationsfilm: en ocensurerad guide till den fördolda svenska film* (Sensational Swedish Films: An Uncensored Guide to Sweden's Secret Film History). Published by author, place and date unknown.

Friedman, David F. *A Youth in Babylon: Confessions of a Trash-Film King*. Buffalo: Prometheus, 1990.

Hammerich, Paul. *Opgang og Nedtur* (Boom and Bust). Copenhagen: Gyldendal, 1980.

Hansen, Dino Raymond. *Subversive Film and Video*. Copenhagen: Danish Film Institute Workshop, 1992.

Haynes, Jim. *Thanks for Coming!* London: Faber and Faber, 1984.

Hegeler, Sten, and Inge Hegeler. *Kærlighedens ABZ* (The ABZ's of Love). Copenhagen: Chr. Erichsens, 1961.

Hjort, Mette, and Ib Bondebjerg. *Instruktørens blik — en interviewbog om dansk film* (Danish Directors: Dialogues on a Contemporary National Cinema). Copenhagen: Rosinante, 2000.

Holm, Siv. *Jeg — en Kvinde (I, a Woman)*. Copenhagen: Stig Vendelkærs, 1961.

Jeppesen, Peter, Ebbe Villadsen, and Ole Caspersen. *Danske Spillefilm 1968–1991* (Danish Feature Films 1968–1991). Esbjerg: Rosendahl, 1993.

Krarup, Helge, and Carl Nørrested. "Udviklingslinier I dansk eksperimentalfilm siden 1960" (Developing Trends in Danish Experimental Film Since 1960). *Kosmorama* 163 (March 1983): 28–34.

_____, and _____. *Eksperimental film i Denmark* (Experimental Film in Denmark). Copenhagen: Borgens, 1986.

Kronhausen, Phyllis, and Eberhard Kronhausen. *The Sex People: Erotic Performers and Their Bold New Worlds*. New York: Playboy, 1975.

Lumholdt, Jan. "Jag — Christina Lindberg" (I, Christina Lindberg). *Defect*, no. 2 (1996): 15–24.

Markvardsen, Nils. "Frigjort — på café with Birte Tove" (Liberated — a Meeting with Birte Tove at a Café). *eXtase*, no. 2 (Fall 2004): 4–13.

Morton, Jim. *Incredibly Strange Films*. San Francisco: Re/search, 1986.

Nørgaard, Erik. *Levende billeder i Danmark: Fra Den gamle Biograf til moderne tider* (Moving Pictures in Denmark — From the Old Cinema to Modern Times). Copenhagen: Lademann, 1971.

Nørrested, Carl. "Dansk film på sengekanten: Den danske pornofilms historie" (Danish Film on the Edge of the Bed: The Story of the Danish Porno Film). *Kosmorama* 195 (Spring 1991): 46–49.

Peary, Danny. *Cult Movie Stars*. New York: Simon & Schuster, 1991.

Piil, Morten. *Danske film from A til Z* (Danish Film from A to Z). Copenhagen: Gyldendal, 2000.

_____. *Danske Filmskuespillere: 525 portrætter* (Danish Film Actors: 525 Portraits). Copenhagen: Gyldendal, 2001.

Pink, Sidney. *So You Want to Make Movies: My Life as an Independent Film Producer*. Sarasota FL: Pineapple, 1989.

Qvist, Per Olov, and Peter von Bagh. *Guide to the Cinema of Sweden and Finland*. Westport CT: Greenwood, 2000.

Rosenmeier, Martine. *Det Erotiske Melodrama* (The

Erotic Melodrama). Copenhagen: Copenhagen University Press, 1992.

Rotsler, William. *Contemporary Erotic Cinema: A Guide to the Revolution in Movie Making.* New York: Ballantine, 1973.

Schepelern, Peter. *Filmleksikon* (Film Encyclopedia). Copenhagen: Munksgaard-Rosinante, 1995.

Schmidt, Kaare. "Thorsen og kaos" (Thorsen and Kaos). *Kosmorama* 199 (Spring 1992): 38–46.

Shipman, David. *Caught in the Act: Sex and Eroticism in the Movies.* London: Elm Tree/Hamish Hamilton, 1985.

Sjöman, Vilgot. *I Was Curious: Diary of the Making of a Film.* New York: Grove, 1968.

_____. *Oskuld förlorad* (Innocence Lost). Stockholm: Författarförlaget, 1988.

Stevenson, Jack. *Dogme Uncut.* Santa Monica, CA: Santa Monica Press, 2003.

_____. *Fleshpot: Cinema's Sexual Myth Makers and Taboo Breakers.* UK: Headpress, 2000.

Svedberg, Lotta. "Ansikte mot ansikte: Lena Nyman" (Face to Face: Lena Nyman). *Chaplin* 258, no. 3 (Summer 1995): 36–43.

Thorsen, Jens Jørgen. *Wilhelm Freddie: Brændende Blade* (Wilhelm Freddie: Burning Pages). Copenhagen: Privat Tryk, 1982.

Turan, Kenneth, and Stephen F. Zito. *Sinema: American Pornographic Films and the People Who Make Them.* New York: Praeger, 1974.

Vogel, Amos. *Film as a Subversive Art.* New York: Random House, 1974.

Index

Numbers in ***bold italics*** indicate pages with photographs.

ABBA (rock group) 206
Abramson, Hans 137, 138
The ABZ's of Love 24, 131, 262
Adler, Renate 81
Adultery for Fun and Profit 256
Adventure in Denmark 194, 195, 213, 263
Ahlberg, Mac 60, 61, 63, 65, 67, 85, 97, 100, 114, 146, 213, 220, 258
Alfred, Nobel 266
All Those Tomorrows 272
Allen, Johannes 137
Alpert, Hollis 92, 134
Always Trouble 37
The American Girl 253
American Girls (slang term) 42, 248
American International Pictures 170, 212
Amour 161, ***162***
Amsterdam Film Museum 256
Andersen, Finn ***51***
Andersen, Gotha 187, 189, 219, 258
Andersen, Hans 107
Andersen, Hans Christian 11, 128, 130, 141
Andersson, Benny 206
Andersson, Harriet ***12-15***, 16, ***17***, 20, 67, 87, 258, 264
Andersson, Solvig 136
Andreasen, Victor 268
Angel, Jørgen 182
The Animal 281
Animal Lover 156
Anne and Eve 206, 207
Antia: Swedish Nymphet 206, 213
Antonioni, Michelangelo 27, 28, 34, 65, 124, 136, 249
Arkoff, Sam 170
Arnfred, Morten 189, 259
Around the World with Fanny Hill 213

Around the World with Nothing On 56
The Arts Lab 255, 256
Askildsen, Kjell 232
Astrological film series 191, 215, 218, 219, 260, 261
Atlantic Biograf, CPH 235
Axel, Gabriel 37, 85, ***86***, ***87***, 103, 105, 106, 130, 146, 161, 162, 166, 187, 188, ***259***, 260, 262
Axen, Bent 30

Babb, Kroger 16, 20
Babette's Feast 260
Bacall, Lauren 259
Bad Barbara 199
Bagger, Rolf 109
Bak, Vivi 262
Balch, Anthony 81
Bamboo House of Dolls 196, ***197***
Bang, Claus 31
Bara Bröst 228
Bardot, Brigitte 32, 262
Bartholdy, Christian 116
Bauhaus of the Imagination 234
Baxter, Arnold 204
Baxter, Les 16
Be Dear to Me 177
The Beatles 56
Bech, Henning 229, 230
Becker, Vernon 217, 218
Beckett, Samuel 92
Bedside film series 191–193, 195, 198, 199, 206, 216, 219, 260, 261, 263, 271, 281
Bedside Head 191, 192
Bedside Highway 191, 192, 267
Bedside Manner 147, 157, ***158***, 159–161, 187, 260, 261
Bedside Sailors 199
Behind the Green Door 157, 221
Bel Ami 220
The Beloved Family ***70***
Bendtsen, Henning 86
Bentzon, Niels Viggo 79

Bergman, Ingmar 1, 7, 11, 12–14, 20, 21, 36, 39, 41, 50, 56, 57, 65, 78, 84, 82, 91, 100, 137, 207, 210–212, 220, 258, 259, 271
Bergström, Lasse 101
Bergström-Walan, Maj-Britt 132, 134, 223
The Berkeley Barb 155
Berlin Film Festival 8, 32, 106, 151
*Between the Sheets **xi***, 192, 217, 258
Bibbi Dances the Twist 54
Bille, Torben 199, ***200***, 201, 202, ***203***, 204
Biller, Anna v
The Birte Tove Report 198
The Birthday Party 169
Bjergskov, Ulla 253
Bjerrehuus, Suzanne 218
Björkman, Stig 242, 268
Bjorling, Gretchen 56
Bjørneboe, Jens 107–109, 232
The Blackboard Jungle 19
Blackjackets 19
Blixen, Karen 260
Blom, Tommy 206
Blonde in Bondage 19
Blood Feast 281
Blood of the Zombie 136
Blow-up 124, 136, 249
The Blue Balloon 168, 169
Bodil, a Summer Day in 1970 174, 224, 251, 256
The Bodil Award 22, 32, 45, 81, 87, 177, 222, 268
Bordello 187, 189, 190, ***191***, 204, 215, 247, 253, 258
Borowczyk, Walerian 216
Brandenburg, Otto 52, 219
Braun, Lasse 117, 186, 246, 257
Breaking Point 212
Breaking the Waves 222, 259, 272
Breckenridge, Myra 11
Brejchová, Janne 262

Breuning, Susanne **218**
Bristol cinema, CHP 19
Britta—The Artist's Model 19
Broberg, Lily **70**
Brøgger, Suzanne 256
Brown, Joe David 17–18
Browning, Tod 81
Bruce, Lenny 150, 255
Brüel, Birgit 32, 35, 104, 178
Brusendorff, Ove 56
Buchanan, Larry 102
Buckingham, Yvonne 49
Bundgaard, Lizzie 173
Buñuel, Luis 84, 233
Burroughs, William 81, 92, 256
Burton, Richard 35
Busck, Ole **139**

Cameo Moulin Theater, London 81
The Cameo theatre, NYC 154
Cammell, Donald 256
Camp Solbakken (Camp Sun Hill) 56
Campus Swingers 210
Canby, Vincent 156
Cannes film festival 32, 81, 82, 106, 148, 151, 152, 154, 162, 169, 180, 191, 208, 222, 223
Capital Pictures 36
Carlsen, Henning 43, 60, 81, 86
Carlton biograf, CPH 164, 167
Carry On film series 160
Casino 159
Cass, Mama 256
Cassavetes, John 44
Catcher in the Rye 115
The Cats 60
The Celebration 224, 225
Censorship in Denmark—A New Approach 154–157, 199
Centrum Theater, Oslo 19
Chambers, Marilyn 221
Champlin, Charles 97
Un Chant d'Amour 50, 91, 256
Chase, Brandon 136, 137
Che (stage play) 96
Chr. Erichsen's publishing company 24, 25
Chris, Erik 47, 48, 52, **54**
Christa (aka *Swedish Fly Girls*) 140–141, 160, 167, 169–171, 179, 208, 221
Christensen, Benjamin 32, 81
Christensen, Bent 28
Christian 260
Christian Democrats (Swedish) 59
The Christian People's Party 230
Christiania 240
The Christine Jorgensen Story **11**
The Christine Keeler Story 41, 49
Cinema 3, CPH 164
Cinema 57, NYC 93
Cinema-Video International 36
Cinemation (film company) 100
City Street "Heroes" **47**, 52, 53, **54**

Cleland, John 23
Club Green, CPH 181
Club Satisfaction, CPH 181
Club Venus, CPH 181, 182
Color Climax 117
Come Blow the Horn 220
Come to My Bedside 192, 193
The Coming Thing 199
Compendium bookshop, London 256
Confessions of a Danish Cover Girl 213, 214, 269
Conservative Student Association (Århus) 104
Constand 234
Constantin Film 32, 35
La Continentale cinema, London 33
Cook, Alton 20
Cooper, Alice 182, **183**
Copenhagen Call Girls 46, **48**, 50, **51**, 52
Copenhagen Film Museum 224
Copenhagen Night Film Festival 52
Copenhagen's Psychic Loves 165
CO-RITUS (actionist artist group) 234
Corman, Roger 38, 50, 73
Corona (Swedish film distribution company) 50
Country Joe McDonald 148
Crazy Paradise 37, **38**, 39, 68, 267
Cresse, Bob 102
Crilly, Spence 166
Crist, Judith 36
Crowther, Bosley 36
Cry of the Banshee 265
Cullhed, Sture 132
Cultural Warrior (book) 232
The Curious Female 97
Curtains for Mrs. Knudsen 195, **263**
Cynthia's Sister 204, **205**

Dagmar threater, CPH 150
Dagmar's Hot Pants 218, 261
Dahlerup, Ulla 45, 46, 260
Dalí, Salvador 268
Damsgaard, Ilse 177–180, 253
Dangerous Kisses 268
Danish and Blue 166
Danish Blue 103–**105**, 106, 114, 153, 161, 166, 172, 182, 204
Danish censorship abolished 116
Danish Dentist on the Job 186, 189
Danish Escort Girls 199
Danish Film Workshop Festival 224
The Danish Folkeparti 224
Danish Love 99
Danish Pastries **215**, **216**, 217
"The Danish Pastry" (slang term) 268
Danstrup, John 54–55
David Barling 36

Davis, Wray 36
Day of Wrath 82
Days of Sin and Nights of Nymphomania 46–48, **49**, 53
Dear John 57, 89
Debord, Guy 234
The Decoy 271
Deep Throat 157, 206, 212, 221
Defiance 12
The Defilers 281
de Grazia, Edward 92
de Jesus, Luis 204
Deliver Us from Love (book) 256
Dellamorte, Daniel 212, 284
Delta Biograf, CPH 224
Delusion 21
de Musset, Alfred 161
The Depraved 208
de Renzy, Alex 152, 154–157, 199
de Ridder, William 256, 257
de Sade, Marquis 85, 202, 207, 240
de Sica, Vittorio 37
Despentes, Virginie 212
Dessau, Bente **29**, 34, 35
The Devil in Miss Jones 221
Dirksen, Everett 96
Dirty Blonde 266
di Stefano, Marco **244**
Dixie Bar 248
Do It Yourself 167
Do You Believe in Swedish Sin? 159
Doctor Glas 272
Doctors from OH! Copenhagen 165
Dodson, Betty 256
Dogma95 30, 89, 90, 224, 243, 280
Dogville 259, 261
La Dolce Vita 18
The Doll 21
Donner, Jörn 57, 259
Dorian Gray 206
Dors, Diana 217
Douglas, Justice William O. 96
Drakabygget (commune) 234, 235
Dream Girl 252
Dreams of 13 (aka *Dreams of a Young Girl*) 246, 257
The Dress 88
Drews, Kenny 252
Dreyer, Carl Th. 1, 7, 26, 62, 82, 154
The Duel 26, **27**, 28, 56, 71, 214
Duhamel, Jacques 154
Dyer, Peter John 14

Easy Rider 95, 165
Edinburgh Film Festival 152, 208
Ege, Ole 2, 167, 174, 178, 187, 189–191, 215, 224, 247–253, 256
Eichelbaum, Stanley 34
Eisenhower, Pres. Dwight D. 18
Ekberg, Anita 18
Ekorre, Marie 199

Eksponent (student magazine) 45
The Element of Crime 222, 258
Emanuel, Aram 67
The Enemies of Porno 116
Eriksson, Christie 256
Eriksson, Marianne 228
Erotic Dreams 253
Erotica in Film: The Naked Wave 56
Espersen, Lene 229
Eugenie ... The Story of Her Journey into Perversion 207
Eva: Diary of a Half Virgin 136
Evensmo, Sigurd 115
Evergreen (cinema), NYC 93

Facts: Copenhagen Sex-Report 182, 184, **185**, **186**, 253
Faison, Ellen 145
Faithless 258
Falck, Gun 142, 145, 147
Falk, Lauritz 83
Fanny Hill (book) 23, 60, 74, 78, 115, 116, 279
Fanny Hill (movie) 97, 113
Faster, Pussycat! Kill! Kill! 67
Fear Has 1,000 Eyes 136
Fear of Flying 97
Fellini, Federico 65, 159, 207, 240
The Female Eunuch 255
Figaro Biograf, Sweden 235
Film as a Subversive Art 22
Film censorship abolished in Norway 222
The Film Fund (Danish) 60, 72, 104
The Film Reform Agreement (Swedish) 57, 281
First Prize Irene 128–130
Fischer, Max 246, 257
Flaming Creatures 96
Flemming, Kurt 73
Flesh 168
Flo & Eddie (rock group) 182
Flourishing Times 265
Fo, Dario 60
Focus on Jesus (TV program) 237
Fogelström, Per Anders 13
Fønss, Aage **105**
For the Sake of Friendship 137
The Forbidden 102
Forså, Marie 207
Four for the Morgue 136
The 400 Blows **17**
491 57, **58**, 88, 89
Franco, Jesus 207
Freaks 81
Freaks, Bloodsucking 202
Freddie, Wilhelm 23, 235, 279–280
Frederiksen, Inga 49
Fredholm, Gert 237
Free, White and 21 102
Freedom to Love 172, 173, 174
French New Wave 20, 26–28, 32, 114, 137

Frevert, Louise 219, 224, 261
Frieda 82
Friedman, David F. 16, 20
Froboess, Gerhard 262
Frost, Lee 102
Fyrsting, Ib 240

Gaël, Anna 67
Galerie Westing 234
Gamst, Joan **112**
Garbo, Greta 7, 32, 67, 264
Garde, Annie Birgit **188**, 219
Gasolin (rock group) 206
Genet, Jean 23, 50, 60, 91, 256
Geneva Convention Pact of 1923 250
Gerber, Paul 199
German school of Bauhaus 234
Gertrud 62, 154
Gibson, Mel 233
Giese, Suzanne 150
Gift (aka *Venom*) 71–**75**, 76–79, **80**, 81, 82, 103, 111, 116, 138, 139, 143, 213, 214, 266, 269, **270**
Gildo, Rex 262
The Girl and Pan 79
The Girl from Denmark 165
Girl in Trouble 136
Girl Without a Name 130
The Girls 272
Girls at Arms 198, 206
Girls Without Rooms 19
Give God a Chance on Sunday 268
Glargaard, Poul 136, 193, 194, 204
Globe Theater, NYC 35
God Hates Sweden 232
Godard, Jean-Luc 27, 43, 168
Gold for the Tough Guys of the Prairie 246
Golden Bananas 207
Golden Pheasant Club, CPH 176
Goldstein, Al 113, 114, 255, 256
Gordimer, Nadine 43
Gordon, Dexter 252
Gordon News Films 155
Görling, Lars 57, 59
Gorzelak, Lars 260
Gothenburg Film Festival 82
Graham, Billy 4, 237
Grand Guignol 204
Grandpa's Journey 272
Grede, Kjell 57
Green, Ake 232
The Green Berets 145
The Green Eyed Elephant 280
Greenwich Village Story 140
Greer, Germaine 190, 213, 255, 256
Grete, Anne 107–109, **110**, 111, **112**, 113, 159, 160, 221, 251
Grimm's Fairy Tales for Adults 206
Grindhouse cinema 146, 202
Gringer, Judy 74, 219
The Groove Room 218
Gross, Jerry 100
Gross, Leonard 94

Grove Press 91–93, 95–97, 105, 107, 153
Grundtvig, Nikolaj 45, 280
Guess Who's Sleeping with Us Tonight? 182
Guilt 59
Guldbrandsen, Peer 59–65, 67, 68, 85, 102, 104, 114, 136, 141, 142, 144–146, 202, 221, 261, 265
Gyldmark, Sven 68

Hænning, Gitte 86, **88**, 262
Hagbard and Signe 86, **88**, 103, 161, 262
Hagen, Paul **38**
Hakim, Gaston 16
Hale, Wanda 35, 39
Hamlet 260
Hammerich, Paul 116, 163
Hamsun, Knut 81
Hannah, Daryl 212
Harris, Jack 111, 112
Harry and the Butler 28, 59
Harvard Film Archives 91
Hawaii Biograf, CPH 164
Hawn, Goldie 171
Haynes, Jim 246, 255, 256, 257, 283
Häxan (aka *Witchcraft Through the Ages*) 32, 81
Heaven and Hell 118, **119**, **121**, **123**, 127, 130
Hedman, Werner 218
Hefner, Hugh 170, 172, 248
Hegeler, Inga 23–24, 76, 104, 131, 132, 135, 172, 262
Hegeler, Sten 23–24, 76, 104, 131, 132, 135, 172, 262
Hein, Wilhelm 187
Heinrich, Susanne **69**, 71
Hells Angels 142, 145
Hellström, Margaretha 209, 262
Helmuth, Frits **27**
Hendrix, Jimi 271
Henningsen, Poul Xi
Henriksson, Margaretha 132
Her and She and Him 67
Herndon, Roy L. 113
Hertoft, Preben 135
Hilbard, John 191
History of the Blue Movie 152
Hit House 52
Højlund, Asger 46
A Hole in My Heart 222, 223
Holm, Siv 25, 67, 68, 141, 142
Holm, Stig 68
Holm, Sverre 68
Holmsen, Egil 18
Holt, Niels 235
Høm, Jesper 148
Hopf, Heinz 208, 210, 212, 266
Horne-Rasmussen, Sigrid 216
The Horsemen of Justice 246
House of Pain and Pleasure 94
Hovmand, Annelise 177, 180
How, Mom? 23

How to Behave in a Fourposter Bed 191
Human Sexual Relations 25
Hunger 81, 86, 95
Huun, Sigrid *119*, *121*, *123*

I, a Girl (book) 139
I, a Lover 68
I, a Man 67
I, a Man (book) 68
I, a Nobleman 68, 85, **86**, **87**, 146
I, a Woman (book) **24**, **25**, 141
I, a Woman (movie) 59, **60**, 61, **62-65**, **66**-68, 71, 72, 96, 99, 100, 104, 113, 114, 141, 142, 157, **264**-266
I, a Woman 2 68, 114, 141, 204
I, a Woman 3 (aka *The Daughter*) 68, 102, **142-144**, **146**, 147, 165, 202, 204, 206, 212, 221, 261
I Am Curious (Blue) 89
I Am Curious (Yellow) 88-93, **94**, 95-97, 103, 105, 108, 113, 134, 136, 137, 139, 148, 150, 153, 222, 243, 266
I Am Curious Beaver 97
I Am Curious but Not Yellow 97
I Am Curious Gay 97
I Am Curious Tahiti 97
I Am Furious 97
I Am Not Curious but Yellow and Blue All Over 107
I, an Actress 67
I Changed My Sex 11
I Love Blue 115
I Spit on Your Grave 212
I, the Body 159, 268
I Was Curious: The Diary of the Making of a Film (book) 95, 105
The Idiots 30, 90, 222, 224
Ilse 253
The Immoral Mr. Teas 39, 68
In the Realm of the Senses 223
In the Sign of Sagittarius, Agent 69 Jensen 219, 220, 258, 272
In the Sign of Scorpio, Agent 69 Jensen 219
In the Sign of Taurus 218, **219**
In the Sign of the Lion (aka *I Tyrens Tegn*) 218
In the Sign of the Twins (aka *I Tvillingernes Tegn*) 218
Infred, Elinor 49
Inga 98, **99**, **100**, 206
Inga and Greta (aka *Inga 2*) 142, 206, 218
"Inga's Theme" (song) 206
International Situationist Congress 234
IT (underground newspaper) 255
Ivarson, Inge 159, 223, 224
Iversen, Henrik 169

Jacey Tatler Theater, London 81
Jacob, Gilles 222
Jacobsen, Ole 180, 181

Jacobsson, Ulla 8, **9**
Jagger, Mick 256
Jan Goes to the Movies 37
Jante Law 267, 284
Janus Films 16, 41, 59
Jasny, Vojtěch 262
Jedig, Leif 48, 54
Jensen, Axel 232
Jensen, Jesper **29**
Jessen, Ulla 193, 206
Jesus Is in the House 238, 240, **241**
Joensen, Bodil 156, 174–176, 233, 248, **251**, 252
The Jokers 268
The Jolly Boys 52, **53**
Jong, Erica 97
Joplin, Janis 148
Jørgensen, Christine 11, 12
Jørgensen, William, Jr. 11
Jorn, Asger 234
Journey to the Seventh Planet 280
Jules and Jim 114
Juliette de Sade 113
Jung, Gertie 137, 187, 204, 219
Just Once More 19
Justine (novel) 240
Justine and Juliette 220

Karlsson, Finn 139, 215
Kaye, Danny 11
Kazan, Elia 271
Kean, Katja **226**, **227**
Keeler, Christine 41, 255
Keller, Ise 33
Keller, Keith 62, 111
The Keyhole 199
Kill Bill 212
King, Martin Luther 91
The Kingdom 11, 38, 224, 259, 271
Kinsey, Alfred 24. 78
Kinsey and Women 75
Kjaer, Diana 97
Kjærulff-Schmidt, Palle 21, 28, 30, 137
Kondrup, Katinka 201
Koplev, Jette 204
Korch, Morten A. 23
Korzen, Benny 140, 179
Krag, Eiler 24, 25
Krage, Susanne 148, 149, **152**, 245
Kragh-Jacobsen, Søren 280
Kristensen, Helge 151
Kronhausen, Eberhard 5, 76, 105, 172–176, 178, 279
Kronhausen, Phyllis 5, 76, 105, 172–176, 178, 279
Krusenstjerna, Agnes von 82
Kruuse, Jens 30, 150
Kuchar, George 67
Kurosawa, Akira 20, 86

The Lady Birds 115
Lamartine 161
Lamb, John 154, 155
The Language of Love 130, **131**, **133**-136, 159, 172, 223
Language of Love 2000 223

Lanterna Film 139, 179
Larsen, Elmard 34
Larsen, Gunnar 154
Larsen, Helge 23
Lassen, Casten **99**, **100**
Lasso Round the Moon 157
Last House on the Left 212
The Last Tango in Paris 157
Laterna Magica (book) 259
Lawrence, D.H. 92
League of Nations Pact 131
Led Zeppelin (The New Yardbirds) 115
Leduc, Violette 67
Lee, Bruce 271
Lehrer, Tom 244
Leila (aka *Laila, the Pure*) 260
Lennberg, Anders 223
Lenz, Werner M. 182
"Letters from Copenhagen" (TV episode) 42
Levring, Kristian 280
Levy, Bill 255–257
Lewis, Herschell Gordon 53, 165
Life on the Hegn Farm 21
Liljedahl, Marie **100**, 101, 206, 207, 266
Lind, Mogens 30
Lindberg, Christina 207, 208, 210–213, 221, 262
Lindberg, Morten 247, 248, 251, 252
Lindfors, Viveca 266
Lindgren, Lars-Magnus 20, 57
Lindström, Jörgen **40**
The Little Red School Book 134
Live Show in Kopenhagen 186
Lolita 66, 234
London Film Festival 152
Long Live Freedom (TV) 269
Look Out, Little Man! 103
Lord Langford 118, 282
Lorna 50
Los Angeles Free Press 113
Lost Innocence: The Story of Inga 266
Louise, Helli 179
Love in the Third Position 98
Love in 3-D 210
Love Mates 20, 21, 57
Love Me Darling 186, 187, **188**, 189
The Love Merchant 98
Love Rebellion 98
Lovelace, Linda 221
Love's Island 220
Loving Couples 82, 259
Lundquist, Lisbet 140, 178, 179, 180, 245
Lust for Laura 266
Lust for the Sun 56
The Lustful Vicar 159, 261
Lynghøft, Lisbeth 226
Lyon, Sue 66

Madame Tussaud's Chamber of Sexual Horrors 117

Madsen, Gerda 204
Madsen, Leo 103, 104, 163, 221, 250
Mahrt, Preben *66*, 204
Maid in Sweden 207
Mailer, Norman 92, 96, 221
Makavejev, Dušan 90, 246, 257
Malamondo 102
Malmkjær, Poul 56
Malmros, Nils 114, 115
A Man with a Maid 217
Manfred Mann (rock group) 169
Manson, Charles 209
The Many Faces of Jesus 237
Mardi, Marianne **126**
Mardore, Michael 152
Marker, Chris 235
Marmalade Films 250
The Marriage 114
Maruni, Novi 235
Mason, James 66
Masters and Johnson 25
The Matadors (rock group) 79
Mattsson, Arne 7, 206, 207, 268
Meineche, Annelise 107, 157, 158
Mercur theatre, CPH 190
Merry Studio 191
Mertz, Albert 234
Metropol theatre, CPH 190, 191
Metzger, Radley 47, 64, 66, 67
Meyer, Russ 20, 39, 50, 68, 97, 98, 140, 192, 248
Michaëlis, Bo Tao 236
Midnight Cowboy 95
Miller, Henry 23, 73, 92, 147-**149**, 150-153, 157, 255, 283
Milton, Berth 131, 221
The Mini Skirt Gang 197, **198**
Miss Julie 11
Miss Lutzi 177
Mission Stardust 264
Modernism in Danish Painting 233
Mohammed cartoon crisis 225, 245, 283
Mona: The Virgin Nymph 221
Mondo Cane 281
Mondo Teeno 102
Monika, the Story of a Bad Girl 16
Monty, Ib 43, 168, 174, 179, 242
Moody, Dr. Howard 92
Moodysson, Lukas 222
Moore, Jack 246
More About the Language of Love **135**
More Sex Please 254
Morgenthaler, Anders 223
Moseholm, Erik 30
Mossin, Ib **110**
Movie Club, CPH 174, 181
MPAA Ratings system 135
Ms. 45 212
The Museum Erotica 247, 253
My Life to Live 43
My Sister, My Love 88
"My Situation" (song) 79

My Uncle 68
Mykle, Agnar 23, 157, 158, 232

Næsby, Bent 167, 168, 182, 221
Naked Fog 98
Nana (novel) 67
Nash, Jørgen 234
National Catholic Office for Motion Pictures 86
Nellemose, Karin 21
Never on Sunday 21
Neville, Richard 256
New German Cinema 222
New Wave (Danish) 37, 137
Newman, Paul 280
Nicklin, Cy 180
Nicolaisen, Preben 47
Nielsen, Gerhard 73
Nielsen, K. Axel 116
Nielsen, Sunny **44**
Night Games 82, **83**, 272
Nilsen, Lillebjørn **119**, **123**
9 Songs 222
Nixon, Richard 96, 180
Noël, Magali 159
Nørby, Ghita **38**, 71, 162, 180
Nordgren, Erik 16
Nordisk Film Studios 26, 123
Norlin, Sven 50
Nørrested, Carl 39, 68, 168
Norup, Lise-Lotte 195, 196, 213, 214, 221, **263**
Norwegian Censorship Law of 1969 115
Novaris Studio 60, 61, 68, 136, 261
Now (novel) 137
Nygade theatre 1-2, CPH 164
Nykvist, Sven 271
Nyman, Lena **58**, 88, 89, 93, **94**, 96, 148, 221
Nyrup, Poul 46-54, 81, 202, 281

O'Brian, Kieran 222
O'Connell, Jack 67, 140, 169, 170
Ole Ege—The Naughty Boy 254
Olsen, Lisbeth 168, 204
The Olsen Gang film series 204
Onassis, Aristotle 93
Onassis, Jackie 93
One Among Many 22, 23
One Summer of Happiness 7-**9**, **10**, 11-14, 16, 21, 206, 220, 232
One Swedish Summer 98, 114
O'Reilly, Bill 232
Oscarsson, Per 81
Ørsted, Ole 167, 250
Osco, Phil 221
Oshima, Nagisa 223

Pagh, Klaus 147
Palads Theater, CHP 62
Palladium Studios 68, 107, 108, 158, 191
Palme, Olof 91
Paragraph 234 (of Danish criminal code) 103, 106, 116, 249

Paramount Studios 148
Pasolini, Pier Paolo 233, 240
Passer, Dirch 37, 68, 150, 159, 162, 191, 267
Peary, Danny 265
Peckinpah, Sam 211
Peeping Tom 79
Pelle the Conqueror 260
Penthouse Magazine 67, 199, 208
People Meet and Sweet Music Fills the Heart 87
The People of Värmland 8
Performance 256
The Perfumed Garden of the Shaykh Nefwazi 23
Persona 211
Persson, Essy **60**, 61, **62-66**, 67, 68, 114, 141, 142, 221, **264**-266
Petersen, Karen Birgit **48**, **51**
Petersen, Tommy 79
Petré, Gio 21, 60, 114, 141, 142, 206
A Piece of Social Realism 246, 257
Piil, Morten 243
Pink, Sidney 280
Pink Prison **226**, **227**
The Pipes 262
Plånborg, Conny 160
Platan Foto 54
Playboy magazine 82, 97, 141, 170, 207
Points of Rebellion 96
Polanski, Roman 180
Porn All Over the World 167
The Porn Star Travels Around Japan 213
Porno—Made in Denmark 187
Pornography—A Musical 167, 252
Pornography and the Law 172
Pornoshop 235
Portnoy's Complaint 95
Powell, Michael 79
Practice Makes Perfect 271
Price, Vincent 264
Princess 223, 283
Private Club, CPH 177, 179, 181
Private Magazine 131
The Problem Girl (TV show) 49
Production Code, the 16, 22
Profumo, Dennis 41
Provo (term) 281
Psychomontage 172
Puggaard-Müller, Bjørn 137, **138**, 187
Pust, Maren 243
Puzzy Power Inc. 224, 226, 227
Python, Monty 233

Quiet Days in Clichy 147-**149**, 150-**152**, 153, 154, 159, 160, 178, 236, 243, 252, 283
Qureshi, Kamal 225

Radio Mercur 46
Ragazzi, Renzo 128
Raggare films 19, 52

Rape Me 212
Rasmussen, Anders Fogh 232
Rasmussen, Sigrid 102
Rau, Vivi 193, 198, 199, 219
Ray, Nicholas 246, 257
Rayns, Tony 81
Rdde, Claus 149
The Red Witch 210
Reed, Joel 202
Reed, Rex 94
Reems, Harry 220, 258
Reeperbahn 108
A Refugee Crosses His Tracks 284
Reinecker, Herbert 68
Reingaard, Sisse 79, **80**, **139**, 140, **270**
Reitzel, Hans 23
Relations—The Love Story from Denmark 136, 137, **138**
Report from Stockholm's Sex Swamp 186
Reptilicus 46
Retribution 261
The Return 243, **244**
Revolution 140
Rialto Film Company 261
Richards, Cliff 134
Ride Hard, Ride Wild 165
Rifbjerg, Klaus 3, 28, 30, 137, 225
Riisfeldt-Clausen, Kim 253
Rikki and the Men 41
Rock Around the Clock 19
Rodda, Wayne John **152**, 245
Rohweder, Bent 253
Rolffes, Kirsten 214
Ronnie's Club, UK 115
Rosset, Barney 92, 93, 107, 153, 282
Rotsler, William 94
Royal Academy of Art (Stockholm) 265
Royal Deceit 260
The Ruling Class 180
Rye, Sven 36
Ryg, Jørgen 55, 68

Saario, Ismo **126**
Sadist 265
The Saga of the Red Witch and the Scarlett Countess 210
Saga Studios 46, 115
Saga Theater, CPH 145
The Saga War 145
Salo 240
Salomonsen, Vic 75
Sandberg, Anders 191
Sandemose, Aksel 232, 284
Sanders, Hanne 225
San Francisco Film Festival 34, 83
Sarno, Joe 67, 98, 99, 101, 206, 208–210, 213, 220, 266
Savage Rose (rock group) 206, 283
SBA Agency 148, 153
Scattini, Luigi 101
Schade, Jens August 87

Schlüter, Poul 269
Schmidt, Kaare 238
Schollin, Christina 20, 57, 89
Schønbergske publishing house 23
School for Suicide **55**, 56, 213
School Girl 199
Schou, Effie 176, 186
Scorsese, Martin 159, 233
Scott, Tom **144**, 145
The Screening Room 155
Screw (underground paper) 113, 114, 255
Scum of the Earth 67
Selby, Hubert 92
Sellers, Peter 66
The Sensualist 67
Sensuela 124, **126**, 127
Seventeen Magazine 71
The Seventh Seal 78
Sex and Fury 213
Sex Circus 166
Sex Galore 167, 174
Sex in Copenhagen 181
Sex in Sweden 258
Sex, Lies and Video Violence 263
The Sex Life of Jesus 237
The Sex People: Erotic Performers and Their Bold New Worlds 175, 176, 279
SEX-69 117, 155
Sex Surreal (exhibit) 279
Sexual Freedom in Denmark 154, 156
The Sexually Responsive Woman 172
Sexus 23, 152, 279
Sexy Girls of Denmark 193–195, 206
Shadows 44
"Shakin' the Battle Hymn" (song) 52
Shanty Town (TV series) 265
Shanty Tramp 281
The Sharks (rock group) 52
Shaw Brothers 193, 196, 197
Sher, Lou 256
Shipman, David 16
The Shocking Truth 228
Shortbus 222, 223
Shrimpton, Jean 255, 256
The Silence 39, **40**, 45, 92, 100
Sin Alley 21
"Sin and Sweden" (article) 17, 18
Sin in the Suburbs 98
The Sinful Dwarf 199, **200–203**, 204, 221
Sinners a la Carte 98
Situationist films 235
Sjöberg, Alf 11
Sjöman, Vilgot 57, 58, 88, 89, 91–97, 148, 153, 266, 284
Skarsgård, Stellan 206, 213, 258, 266
Skin, Skin 81
Skoglund, Eric 91, 132
Skotte, Kim 223

Smidt, Karine **48**
Smile Emil 139
Smiles of a Summer Night 20
Smith, Jack 96
The Smut Peddler 67
Snow White and the Seven Dwarves 167, 256
So You Want Success? 236
Soft Shoulders, Sharp Curves 187
Sofus (magazine) 250
Søltoft, Ole 68–**70**, 71, **158**–160, 186, 191, 192, 194, 199, 216–**218**, 219, 267, 271
The Song of the Red Ruby (book) 23, 157, 279
The Song of the Red Ruby (film) 158, 159, 178
Sonja 67
Sornum, Børge 147
Soya, Carl Erik 68, 186, 192
Soya's 17 68, **69**, **70**, 71, 107, 158, 159, 160
Spafford, Robert 41
Spanking 253
Sparrow, Anne 201
Spies, Simon 190, 192, 204, 224, 248
Sprogø (island) 175
Sprogøe, Ove 37, 162
SPUR (German artist group) 234
Stangerup, Henrik 268
Stark Studio 249
Steckler, Ray Dennis 53
Steeger, Ingrid 171
Steele, Tommy 52
Steffans, Peggy 98, 266
Stegelmann, Jakob 52
Stegger, Karl 192
Steinthal, Herbert 43, 91, 92
Stilley, Margo 222
Stimulantia 137
Stine and the Boys **139**, 215
A Strange Romance 114
A Stranger Knocks 22, 23, 82, 113, 157
Straw Dogs 95
Street Without End 35, 41–43, **44–46**
Strindberg, Göran 8
Strømberg, Søren **75**, 79–**80**, 111, 143, 167, 187, 191, 192, 213, 219, 266–267
Studio 1–2, CPH 164
Studio Publicis theatre, Paris 32
Suburban Pagans 94
Suck (underground paper) 190, 255–257
Summer and Love 13
Summer Interlude 12
Summer with Monika **12**, 14–17, 20, 258
Summer with Vanja 220
The Sun Chariot (Danish performance group) 240
A Sunday in September 57
Sundh, Inger 136, 142, 145, **146**, 206

Sundquist, Folke **9**
Super Love 245
Svensk Film Industri 16
Svensk Journal Film 130
Sweden: Heaven or Hell? 101, 102, 128, 130
Swedish and Underage 136, 139, 142, 159
Swedish massage (slang term) 181, 182
The Swedish Mistress 57
Swedish Pentecostal movement 59
Swedish Punks 19
Swedish Sex Games 206
Swedish Wildcats 98, 210
The Sweet Life of Majorca 54
The Swinging Co-eds 210
The Swinging Stewardesses 171

Taboo 206, 266, 284
Taboo—From Prohibition to Liberation (book) 254
Tages (rock group) 206
Tajiri, Shinkichi 251, 252, 256
Tarantino, Quentin 212
Tarp, Lotte 28, 31, 35, 86, 148, 267–269, 271, 272
Taschner, Gurli 104, 105
Tati, Jacques 20, 68
Tavbe, Finn 240
Taxi Driver 135
Taylor, Elizabeth 35, 197
Teenage Mother 101
Teenage Tickle Girls 218
Tenderness 99
Thaning and Appel publishers 60
That's How They Do It! 167
That's How They Do It—Again! 167
Theander, Jens 117, 118, 182, 221, 250, 269
Theander, Peter 117, 118, 182, 221, 250, 269
There Comes a Day 37
Therese and Isabelle 67, 264, 265
Thestrup, Knud 116
They Call Her One-Eye 210–213, 263
The Thief's Journal 23
Thomsen, Agnethe 63, 67, 114, 141
Thomsen, Christian Braad 77
Thomsen, Knud Leif xi, 26, 55, 71–74, 76–78, 81, 93, 105, 106, 109, 116, 138, 213, 214, 267, 269, **270**
Thorsen, Jens Jørgen 2, 76, 147–**149**, 151–153, 157, 233–**239**, 240–246, 256, 257, 283
The Three-Cornered Bed 206
Three Healthy Girls 252
Threesome 136, 137
Thunberg, Anne Marie 90
Tickled Pink 218
Time of Desire 18

To Ingrid My Love, Lisa 98
To Love 57
Tofte, Per **121**
Tømming, Bent 168, 169, 199, 204
Tomorrow My Love 215, 261
Torment 11, 82
Torn Curtain 280
Tough Guys of the Prairie 246
Tove, Birte **xi**, 140, **158**, 160, 169, 170, 187, **188**, 193–**197**, **198**, 208, 213, 221, 267, 269, 271
Trans Lux Theater, NY 35
The Transatlantic Review 255
Troell, Jan 50, 57
Trolle, Børge 73, 74
Tropic of Cancer 148
Tropic of Capricorn 23
Truffaut, François 17, 114
Tulio, Teuvo 124, 125, 127
Turan, Kenneth 94, 155, 156
Turin Film Festival 266
24 Hours with Ilse **177**, 178, 179, **180**, 181, 253
Two 137
Two Thousand Maniacs 281
Two Times Two in the Four Poster 68, 70
Tynan, Kenneth 172

UFO (London underground club) 255
Ullabella 262
Ulvaeus, Björn 206
Umiliani, Piero 102
Underneath the Skin 254
Unmarried Mothers 16

Valenti, Jack 113
Valjean, Paul 148, 151, **152**, 245
"The Vatican Rag" (song) 244
Veil of Lust 98
Vemmer, Mogens 41–45
Vendelkær, Stig 25, 60, 104, 107
Venice Film Festival 11, 83
Vennerød, Øyvind 120, 123, 124, 130
Venus Films 167, 250
Vest, Nils 167, 168
V.I. Films 136
Viallet, Pierre 68
Vibenius, Bo Arne 211–213
The Vicious Breed 19
Vidunderlige Kælling (nude ballet) 268
Viirta, Oili 220
Viklund, Anne 233
Villaume, Astrid **80**
Vinterberg, Thomas 225, 280
V.I.P. Distribution 111
The Virgin Spring 20, 212
Voeler, Knud 91
Vogel, Amos 22, 107
Volman, Mike **183**
von Sydow, Max 272
von Trier, Lars 1, 11, 30, 38, 89, 90, 222, 224, 243, 258, 259, 261, 271
Voss, Thorkild 104

Waiting for Godot 30
The War Game 82
Warburg, Bent 216, 217
Warhol, Andy 67, 168
Watermelon Man 102
Waters, John 83, 99
The Way to Hell 123, 124
Webster, Ben 245, 252
The Weedons 52
Weekend 27–**29**, 30, **31–34**, 37, 41, 43, 45, 50, 78, 81, 86, 89, 104, 129, 137, 139, 145, 178, 224, 225, 243, 267, 280
Weekend Sex 103
West Side Story 22, 52
Wet Dream Film Festival 12, 246, 252, 255–257
What Are You Doing After the Orgy? 207
What School-girls Don't Tell 210
What the Butler Saw 218
When Marie Met Fredrik 211
White, Louise 149, 245
White Coaters (slang term) 135, 159
White Ecstasy 145
Whitehouse, Mary 118, 282
Who Said Scandalized! 103
Who's Doing What to Whom? 167
Why? 173–**175**, 176, 181, 185
Wickman, Torgny 130–132, 135, 159, 213, 223, 271
Wide-Open Copenhagen '70 156, 157
Widerberg, Bo 57
Widow, Oleg **88**
Wild Angels 50, 73
The Wild Bunch 211
Wild Strawberries 21
Williams, Anne Sheldon 201
Williams, Heathcote 246, 255, 257
Windeløv, Vibeke 272
Winston, Archer 82
Winterbottom, Michael 222
Wiskari, Werner 41
Without a Stitch 107–**110**, 111, **112**, 113, 114, 136, 137, 147, 157, 158, 176, 261
Without Kin 147
Wolf, Alexa 228
Wolf at the Door 246
Wolter, Erling 182
The Woman Who Cleaned the World 272
A Woman's Mind 268
Women of the World 102
Women's Endless Liberation (TV satire) 256
Wood, Ed 11, 53, 126, 127
Woodstock (festival) 148
Woodstock (movie) 150

The Word 26
A World of Strangers 43

The Year of Porno 77, 235
Yi Lui, James 195
Young Girls Disappear in Copenhagen 51

Young Playthings 208–210, 262
Your Husband, the Unknown Creature 182
A Youth in Babylon 16

Zentropa Studios 224, 226, 272
Zero Population Growth 193

Zetterling, Mai 11, 82–84, 259, 272
Zito, Stephen 94, 155, 156
Zola, Emile 67
Zwerin, Michael 256